Infidelity

THE FAMILY THERAPY AND COUNSELING SERIES

Consulting Editor
Jon Carlson, PsyD, EdD

Infidelity

A Practitioner's Guide to
Working with Couples in Crisis

Edited by

Paul R. Peluso

Routledge
Taylor & Francis Group
New York   London

Routledge
Taylor & Francis Group
270 Madison Avenue
New York, NY 10016

Routledge
Taylor & Francis Group
2 Park Square
Milton Park, Abingdon
Oxon OX14 4RN

© 2007 by Taylor & Francis Group, LLC
Routledge is an imprint of Taylor & Francis Group, an Informa business

Printed in the United States of America on acid-free paper
10 9 8 7 6 5 4 3 2 1

International Standard Book Number-13: 978-0-415-95390-0 (Hardcover)

Library of Congress Cataloging-in-Publication Data

Infidelity : a practitioner's guide to working with couples in crisis / [compiled by] Paul R. Peluso.
    p. cm. -- (The family therapy and counseling series)
    ISBN 0-415-95390-1 (hardcover)
    1. Adultery. 2. Married people--Sexual behavior. 3. Marriage--Psychological aspects. I. Peluso, Paul R.

HQ806.I54 2006
616.89'1562--dc22
        2006039147

Visit the Taylor & Francis Web site at
http://www.taylorandfrancis.com

and the Routledge Web site at
http://www.routledge.com

*This book is lovingly dedicated to my wife, Jennifer P. Peluso,
and to my parents, Sam and Roseann Peluso. They have
each taught me valuable lessons in fidelity.*

Contents

PART II

THE TREATMENT OF INFIDELITY IN COUPLES THERAPY

PART III

THE IMPACT OF INFIDELITY ON COUPLES AND FAMILIES FROM DIFFERENT SOCIAL, CULTURAL, GENERATIONAL, AND SEXUAL PERSPECTIVES

Part IV

Professional Reflections and Conclusion

About the Editor

Paul R. Peluso is currently an Assistant Professor and Program Coordinator of the Mental Health Counseling program at Florida Atlantic University. He is licensed as a marriage and family therapist, as well as a mental health counselor in Florida, and an Approved Supervisor from the American Association of Marriage and Family Therapy. He serves on the editorial board of several peer-reviewed journals, including the *Family Journal* and the *Journal of Individual Psychology*. Dr. Peluso is also currently the associate editor for quantitative research for the *Journal of Counseling and Development*. He is the co-author of the book *Couples Therapy: Integrating Theory and Technique*. In addition, he is the co-author of two upcoming books on non-linear thinking and counseling, and techniques of counseling. His research interests include family and couples development, parenting, and attachment theory.

Contributors

David C. Atkins is Assistant Professor of Clinical Psychology in the School of Psychology at Fuller Theological Seminary. He received his doctorate in clinical psychology from the University of Washington, where he studied with Drs. Neil Jacobson and John Gottman among others. Dr. Atkins has authored or co-authored a variety of articles, predominantly focused on couples, couple therapy, and infidelity. His work on infidelity has examined both national trends in infidelity and couple therapy outcomes with infidelity. He is a long-time collaborator with Dr. Andrew Christensen in studying Traditional and Integrative Behavioral Couple therapies. Currently, they have a research grant from the National Institutes of Mental Health to use mathematical modeling techniques in studying couple therapy process. In addition, Dr. Atkins provides statistical consultation to researchers across a variety of disciplines and fields, though primarily on couples-oriented research.

Donald H. Baucom, Ph.D., is Professor of Psychology at the University of North Carolina. He has conducted the largest couple-based intervention treatment study to date, funded in part by the National Institutes for Health, evaluating the efficacy of a couple-based intervention for breast cancer. His six books about couples include his widely used text co-authored with Norman Epstein entitled, *Enhanced Cognitive-Behavioral Therapy for Couples: A Contextual Approach* (American Psychological Association). Through his approximately 150 publications, he has helped to shape the field's understanding of the role of cognitions in intimate relationships. He lives in Chapel Hill and is ranked as one of the top marital therapists and researchers in the United States.

Katie Berman, M.Ed., is currently pursuing an Ed.S. in Marriage and Family Therapy at Florida Atlantic University. She also holds a degree from the University of Florida. Her interests include working with couples and families in crisis, children and adolescents who are affected by their parents' infidelities, and individuals and couples with sexual dysfunctions. She is past president of Chi Sigma Iota Counseling Honors Society, and has co-authored articles in the areas of play therapy, acculturation, and children and poverty.

Emily M. Brown, LCSW, is the Director of the Key Bridge Therapy and Mediation Center in Arlington, Virginia. She is a Licensed Clinical Social Worker, a Marriage and Family Therapist, and a divorce mediator, and works with couples, individuals, and families at the Center. Her work focuses on relationship issues, resolving "old baggage," and personal growth. She has a special interest in group therapy addressing issues of loss and betrayal. She also presents workshops for therapists on working with the issues of infidelity, marriage, and divorce. She has written extensively on affairs and divorce, including "Patterns of Infidelity and their Treatment," and *Affairs: A Guide to Working Through the Repercussions of Infidelity*.

Beverly Burch, Ph.D., is in private practice in Berkeley and is a clinical consultant with The Sanville Institute in Berkeley. She has published two books on psychodynamic theory, *On Intimate Terms* (1992) and *Other Women* (1997), exploring issues of gender and sexuality. Her first book of poetry, *Sweet to Burn*, won the Gival Poetry Prize and a Lambda Literary Award.

Alastair P. C. Davies received his B.Sc. in Applied Science from the University of Wolverhampton, England, in 1987 and his M.A. from Florida Atlantic University in 2005. He is a Ph.D. candidate in evolutionary psychology at Florida Atlantic University. His research interests include mate poaching, infidelity, and the origin of sex differences.

Stephen T. Fife, Ph.D., is an Assistant Professor in the Department of Marriage and Family Therapy (MFT) at University of Nevada, Las Vegas. His research interests include the process of change in marital therapy, conceptualization and treatment of interpersonal conflict, forgiveness, and the role of theory in the clinical work and training of MFT practitioners. He has presented his research at local, national, and international conferences. He also maintains a clinical practice in Las Vegas, Nevada.

Nancy Gambescia, Ph.D., maintains an active private practice specializing in relationship and sex therapy. In addition, she teaches and supervises psychotherapists in the assessment and treatment of sexual dysfunctions and couples therapy. She has 30 years of clinical and teaching experience in working with couples. Dr. Gambescia is an approved supervisor and clinical member of the American Association of Marriage and Family Therapy, Society for Sex Therapy and Research, and a certified sexologist and diplomate of the American Board of Sexology. Dr. Gambescia has co-authored three books: *Erectile Dysfunction, Hypoactive Sexual Desire,* and *Treating Infidelity* (Norton) and several chapters in textbooks that focus on relationship and sexual issues. She completed her clinical training at the Council for Relationships (formerly Marriage Council of Philadelphia) and her doctorate at the University of Pennsylvania (1983).

Aaron T. Goetz received his B.A. in psychology from the University of Texas at Austin in 2002 and his M.A. from Florida Atlantic University in 2005. He is a Ph.D. candidate in evolutionary psychology at Florida Atlantic University. His research interests include men's anti-cuckoldry tactics and sexual coercion in intimate relationships.

Kristina C. Gordon, Ph.D., is Associate Professor of clinical psychology at the University of Tennessee. She also is Vice-President for Science for the American Psychological Association's Division 43: Family Psychology and is chair of their task force on empirically validated couple and family therapies. She has authored numerous articles and book chapters on forgiveness, couple therapy, and dyadic processes. She is co-author (with Douglas Snyder and Donald Baucom) of *Getting Past the Affair: A Program to Help You Cope, Heal, and Move On* (Guilford Press) and a companion treatment manual for clinicians. Dr. Gordon conducts research on forgiveness and family processes and maintains a small private practice.

Joanne Hall is currently enrolled in the M.A. in Pastoral Studies (Counseling) program at St. Paul University, Ottawa, Ontario. Her clinical and research interests are in the areas of couple relationship processes, infidelity, and resolution. In 2006, she received an Ontario Graduate Scholarship for research on forgiveness in the context of committed couple relationships. In particular, Ms. Hall is exploring how forgiveness functions in the process of healing in couple relationships that have experienced infidelity.

Richard C. Henriksen, Jr., Ph.D., is currently an Associate Professor in the Sam Houston State University, Department of Educational Leadership and Counseling, a Licensed Professional Counselor, an Approved Clinical Supervisor, and a National Certified Counselor. His counseling experience has been in multicultural issues, substance abuse, multiple heritage issues, community mental health, and acute mental illness. He has also been a consultant to school counselors and has provided counseling services to students in elementary and secondary schools. He has authored a theory involving "Multiple Heritage Identity Development" and has authored book chapters, journal articles, and professional association articles in the areas of diversity and human rights.

Susan M. Johnson, Ed.D, is one of the originators and the main proponent of Emotionally Focused Couples Therapy (EFT). She is Professor of Clinical Psychology at The University of Ottawa, Director of the Ottawa Couple and Family Institute and the Center for Emotionally Focused Therapy. She received her doctorate in Counseling Psychology from the University of British Columbia in 1984. She is a registered psychologist in the province of Ontario, Canada, and a member of the editorial board of the *Journal of Marital and Family Therapy,* the *Journal of Couple and Relationship Therapy* and the *Journal of Family Psychology.* She is a Research Professor in the Marital & Family Therapy Program at Alliant University in San Diego.

Deborah E. Kessel is a doctoral student in the School of Psychology at Fuller Theological Seminary. She received her M.A. in clinical psychology at Fuller and her B.A. in psychology at St. Olaf College in Northfield, Minnesota. Her research focuses on the influence of religiousness on sexual infidelity in marital relationships. In addition, she is working on a review of adolescent sexuality, with a special interest in the intersection of abstinence education, religious teachings, and sexual behavior of adolescents. She currently resides in Pasadena, California.

Kathleen J. Kilborne is a 2006 graduate of the psychology program at Furman University in Greenville, South Carolina.

Heather B. MacIntosh, Ph.D., obtained her doctorate from the University of Ottawa in Clinical Psychology where she studied the use of EFT with childhood sexual abuse survivors and their partners and same sex marriage. She is currently on faculty at St. Paul University, Ottawa, Ontario, in the Counselling program and maintains a private practice with children, couples, and individuals dealing with the impact of trauma in their lives and relationships. Her primary research and clinical interests involve developing applied interventions for working systemically with adult trauma survivors and their infants, children, and partners and with traumatized children and their parents, helping rebuild safe attachment in these most intimate and important relationships.

Jessica H. Moon is a doctoral candidate in the School of Psychology at Fuller Seminary. She received her M.A. in psychology at Fuller and her B.A. in psychology at the University of California, Los Angeles. Currently she has a variety of research interests ranging from infidelity to neuropsychology. She has focused on communication patterns of couples and the effects of secret infidelity on marital relationships. In addition, she is investigating the correlation between dopamine agonist medication and compulsive behaviors in patients with Parkinson's disease. She resides in Pasadena, California.

Augustus Napier, Ph.D., received his doctorate in clinical psychology from University of North Carolina Chapel Hill in 1968, and did clinical training at the University of Wisconsin-Madison where he apprenticed under and worked with Carl Whitaker. He founded and directed The Family Workshop, a treatment and training center in Atlanta. He is the co-author of *The Family Crucible* (with Whitaker), the co-author of *The Fragile Bond* (with his wife and professional partner, Margaret). Most recently, he co-edited (with Bill Nichols, Mary Anne Pace-Nichols and Dorothy Becvar) *The Handbook of Family Development and Intervention*. He is in retirement from practice and lives in the mountains of North Carolina where he is working on a memoir, and on a book of poems and photographs.

Frank Pittman, M.D., is a psychiatrist as well as a family therapist and author of several books including *Private Lies: Infidelity and the Betrayal of Intimacy* (1989) and *Man Enough: Fathers, Sons and the Search for Masculinity* (1993). He has over 45 years of experience working with couples and families in crisis, and currently resides and practices in Atlanta, Georgia.

Paul R. Rasmussen, Ph.D., is Professor of Psychology at Furman University in Greenville, South Carolina. He is a licensed clinical psychologist, speaker, and author. He is the author of *Personality Guided Cognitive Behavioral Therapy* (2005) and is on the editorial broad and a co-editor of the clinical strategies column for the *Journal of Individual Psychology*. In addition to his teaching, he maintains a part-time clinical practice where he sees adolescents, adults, couples, and families.

Todd K. Shackelford, Ph.D., received his Ph.D. in psychology from the University of Texas at Austin in 1997. He is an associate professor of psychology at Florida Atlantic University, and chair of the Evolutionary Psychology Area. His current research interests include conflict between the sexes, particularly with regard to sexual behavior.

Michael Shernoff is a Manhattan psychotherapist in private practice, and is on faculty at Columbia University School of Social Work. For seven years he was the online mental health expert for TheBody.com, the largest HIV/AIDS web site in the world. In the 1980s he coauthored the pioneering AIDS prevention workshop Eroticizing Safer Sex. He has written extensively on mental health issues of gay men and HIV/AIDS, and is a frequent lecturer and presenter at conferences worldwide. He is the author of *Without Condoms* (Routledge 2006).

Douglas K. Snyder, Ph.D., is Professor and Director of Clinical Psychology Training at Texas A&M University. He has been recognized nationally for his research on marital assessment and for his outcome research on marital therapy, receiving the American Association for Marriage and Family Therapy's 1991 award for Outstanding Research Contribution and the American Psychological Association's 2005 award for Distinguished Contributions to Family Psychology. He is coeditor of texts on *Treating Difficult Couples* (Guilford Press) and *Emotion Regulation in Couples and Families* (American Psychological Association). He has served as Associate Editor for the *Journal of*

Consulting and Clinical Psychology and the *Journal of Family Psychology*, and maintains a small private practice.

Catherine Ford Sori, Ph.D., is an Associate Professor in the Marriage and Family Counseling Program in the Division of Psychology and Counseling at Governors State University in University Park, IL; and Associate Faculty at the Chicago Center for Family Health. Dr. Sori has written numerous journal articles and book chapters on children in family therapy, illness, bereavement, and couples therapy. Her books include *Engaging Children in Family Therapy: Creative Approaches to Integrating Theory and Research in Clinical Practice* (Routledge, 2006), *The Therapist's Notebook for Children and Adolescents: Homework, Handouts and Activities for Use in Psychotherapy* (co-authored with Lorna Hecker, Ph.D. & Associates; Haworth, 2003); and Volume I and II of *The Therapist's Notebook for Integrating Spirituality in Counseling: Homework, Handouts, and Activities for Use in Psychotherapy* (co-edited with Karen Helmeke, Ph.D., M. Div.; Haworth, 2006). She recently co-edited (with Lorna Hecker, Ph.D.) *The Therapist's Notebook II: Homework, Handouts, and Activities for Use in Psychotherapy* (Haworth Press, in press), and is currently working on *The Therapist's Notebook III.* Dr. Sori is a licensed marriage and family therapist and an AAMFT Approved Supervisor.

Rona Subotnik, LMFT, is in private practice in Palm Desert, California. She is co-author of *Surviving Infidelity: Making Decisions, Recovering From the Pain, 3rd Edition,* and *Infidelity on the Internet: Virtual Relationships and Real Betrayal.* Her latest book, *Will He Really Leave Her for Me?* deals with the husband's lover to help her understand herself and the affair as it effects her and the married couple. Her web site: http://www.surviveinfidelity.com.

Gerald R. Weeks, Ph.D., is Professor and Chair of the Department of Counseling at University of Nevada at Las Vegas and in private practice. He is an Approved-Supervisor, and Clinical Member of the American Association of Marriage and Family Therapy, and is board-certified by the American Board of Professional Psychology and the American Board of Sexology. He has published 17 professional textbooks in the fields of sex, marital, and family therapy. Among his publications are *Couples in Treatment, Paradoxical Psychotherapy* (available in 6 languages), *Erectile Dysfunction, Treating Hypoactive Sexual Desire, Treating Infidelity,* and *The Handbook of Family Therapy.* Dr. Weeks has presented throughout the U.S. and Europe.

Series Editor's Foreword

Eighty percent of married men cheat in America. The rest cheat in Europe.

Jackie Mason

A woman talks to one man, looks at a second, and thinks of a third.

Bhartrihari, ca 65

"I THINK I CAN DO BETTER, SHOULD I SETTLE FOR SECOND BEST?"
The real question is, can YOU be a different partner? Most of the time we believe that we're wonderful and all we need to do is find a better partner. The truth is we need to BE a better partner. So what I would suggest is that you do all of the things you would do with "Mr. Wonderful" with "Mr. Mediocre", and see if it makes a difference.

Everybody seems to be looking for a better deal in America. Corporate values are impacting all aspects of life. Nowhere is this more apparent than in the world of relationships. Infidelity affects most couples. Today the problem seems magnified as the breaking of commitments and agreements has spread to the business and sports worlds.

I can still remember how I felt when as a teenager I went to the movies with some friends only to see my girlfriend come into the theater with another guy. She had told me she was going out of town with her parents. I never considered that she might be lying. I am sure that each of us carries such a memory of betrayal (and we are probably the bad person in someone else's memories as well!).

Infidelity means the breaking of trust. This occurs when one or both partners are not honoring the agreement to be faithful. Infidelity occurs at many levels whenever the terms of "exclusive" relationships are violated. Infidelity can occur in many different forms from the one night stand to ongoing philandering to a full-blown emotional and sexual affair.

Learning how to get past the affair and cope, to heal and move on, is a big part of most family therapists' practices. Therapy helps the couple get over the discovery and betrayal; understand how it occurred; take mutual responsibility for each person's role; and decide whether to stay together.

How does one effectively help a couple to move beyond the damage and live a fulfilling life whether together or apart? Paul Peluso and his collaborators have done an amazing job. The reader will develop a solid understanding of infidelity, including how people are impacted as a result of their culture, social class, generation, and sexual orientation. Several seasoned approaches to the treatment of infidelity in couple's therapy are also provided. My favorite parts of the book are the final chapters that feature the work of Frank Pittman and Gus Napier. Drs. Napier and Pittman are perhaps the savviest clinicians of this generation. Their insights alone are worth the price of this book.

Jon Carlson, PsyD, EdD
Series Editor

Preface

Infidelity. To put it simply, it was one of the most confusing challenges to confront whenever I saw a couple. So many elements to it were unpredictable and confusing. For example, what would the reactions and attitudes of the couple be? How would the "offended" partner react when she or he found out? Would the "offending" partner be remorseful and end the affair, or be defensive and blame the other person? Some couples would come in and all they wanted to talk about was the affair (to the exclusion of everything else in the relationship), while other couples would talk about anything *but* the affair. Another important—though unpredictable—element was the vast range of intense emotions that are often expressed (i.e., rage, despair, betrayal, bitterness, sorrow, and pain), which would threaten any therapeutic progress. Lastly, there was also the ever-elusive goal of *resolution*. At what point does the affair get "put behind" the couple? Many couples would seem to be progressing well, and then all of a sudden lapse back into an earlier pattern of anger, attacking, and defensiveness (seemingly) without cause or a trigger. All of this frequently left me scrambling for what to do. Often the strategy that I employed early in my career was the "fly by the seat of the pants" approach, cleverly disguised as "meeting the clients where they were at." However, what this really meant was that I was struggling to catch up with them.

After doing this enough times (and not particularly enjoying it), I found myself looking for a model of treatment that might help me work with couples dealing with infidelity. This was easier said than done! Would the *trauma model* fit? Primarily, this is where the therapist walks the clients through the experience, desensitizes the emotions, and reintegrates the aberrant experience into the narrative of the relationship. This often helped with "flashbacks" and other intense emotions. However, this didn't always fit with some couples. Another model that is often applied to understand the processes of dealing with infidelity is the *grief model*. In this model, the spouses (especially the aggrieved party) have to say "goodbye" to the old relationship (or at least their expectations of it) and work through the stages of grief made famous by Kubler-Ross (1977). This tended to make sense to me because there was an aspect of mourning that seemed to occur, and there was definitely the flood of emotions (shock, denial, anger, bargaining, etc.). The eventual goal is to be able to move forward from the "death" into a new relationship—which may be literal if the relationship ends in a breakup or divorce. Again, however, there were many times when a couple did not view the infidelity in this way, and the grief model did not fit.

In addition to the specific paradigms of treatment outlined above, I also considered applying particular theories of counseling that may prove to be useful in working with infidelity. In particular, the post-modern approaches seemed to have a lot of potential for being useful. For example, there is the narrative approach where the therapist encourages the couple to "externalize" the problem (in this case, the infidelity) as an entity for them to bond together and struggle against, rather than blame one another. This, of course, may be hard to swallow for some partners, since it avoids blame (especially when one partner is bent on getting revenge) and can seem to avoid important underlying dynamics that led to the infidelity. Another "post-modern" theory is the solution-focused approach. In this type of therapy, the therapist resists using the language of problems and encourages the couple to look for the solutions contained within the presenting concern. One way that this is done is to look at what the couple has done in the past for specific examples or experiences or the relationship that was functional and healthy. Then the therapist guides the couple to find a way to do that again in the present. This has the advantage of bypassing a lot of destructive affect and "re-hashing," but again may leave the "offended" partner feeling that his or her experience of pain has not been validated. So again, I found that no one theoretical approach seemed to fit all of the complexities that are presented when a couple has to confront an infidelity in the relationship.

At the end of it all, I began to feel somewhat discouraged, and believed that I was lacking something in my training that made me less of a couples therapist at best, or incompetent at worst. However, in discussing this with several of my colleagues, I felt relieved when I discovered that many of them also felt ill-equipped to handle the complex issues that couples present when there is an infidelity. In fact, they confirmed for me that there is very little formal training in handling this issue for most couples and family therapists. I was further bolstered when I read Whisman, Dixon, and Johnson's (1997) research that, although infidelity is the most often cited reason that couples come for counseling, it is the subject that couples counselors feel least prepared to handle. When I looked for any material that was available, I found a considerable number of books written for the lay person to figure out if their partner was cheating, or how to determine whether the relationship could be salvaged. However, very little of it was helpful for clinicians in working through the complex issues that these couples presented with when coming for treatment. What *was* available for clinicians was few and far between (happily, most of these authors have agreed to contribute a chapter to this text!).

Though this makes infidelity all the more daunting of a challenge to face as a therapist, on the other hand, nothing engages you more fully as a couples therapist as the issues presented with infidelity. This is probably for several reasons, including the raw emotions that are often present, the level of motivation for therapy that the couple has (at least at that moment), or the fact that the truth comes to the surface very quickly with many of these couples. Of course, this is not the case with *all* couples, but there is a lot of momentum that comes with the disclosure of an infidelity for a majority of couples. The question is how to best use this momentum. As a therapist, you begin to understand that the couples are ready to make radical changes (or at least entertain the possibility of making radical changes) in order to salvage the relationship. At the same time, there is a delicate balance that has to be struck between overly blaming the offending partner and holding them accountable for their behavior. Also a balance has to be maintained between demanding too much change of the partners (and scaring one or both members of the couple away) and not challenging the couple to examine the dynamics of the relationship that lead to the crisis. In the end, you realize that this is the ultimate in couples counseling, and that only the most skilled practitioners can successfully achieve this.

So when I was asked to contribute a volume to this series on Couples and Family Therapy, I reflected on these experiences and thought, "what would I most like to have had when treating these complex cases?" I thought about the lack of training for clinicians on this topic. I also considered the lack of a source for students or clinicians to go to as a professional reference tool where they could find the best information from clinicians and researchers on infidelity. Until now, there has not been a single source that has incorporated multiple perspectives on treating couples, and on the selected topics that are relevant to the practice of couples and family therapists. That is what this volume will strive to accomplish. Speaking for all of the chapter authors (to whom I am infinitely grateful for all of their hard work to make this text a reality), it is my hope that this goal has been achieved.

Paul R. Peluso
Boca Raton, FL
September, 2006

Acknowledgments

An edited text of this scope and magnitude could not be accomplished without the support of many people. First, I wish to acknowledge (and thank) Jon Carlson for his help in the early conception of this text, and for his continuing faith in my ability to make a substantial contribution to this family therapy series. I am indebted to him for it.

I also want to thank all of my co-authors on this project. Many of them gave me wonderful feedback and encouragement during this entire process. It was no surprise to me that I would obtain the level of professionalism that I would get from the best authors on the topic of infidelity. It was a surprise that so many of these distinguished individuals said "yes" and agreed to contribute to this endeavor! It's ultimate worth and value to the profession are due solely to them and their efforts.

I also want to thank the staff at Routledge who helped me through the design and editing of this book. Most especially I want to thank Dana Bliss for all of his guidance and humor. He made this project an absolute joy to work on.

Lastly, I must reserve my sincerest thanks to my assistant (and chapter co-author), Katie Berman. She was a tireless reviewer, effective interviewer, and overall sounding board on all aspects of this project. I am indebted to her for all of her efforts.

CHAPTER 1

Infidelity

Introduction and Overview

PAUL R. PELUSO

"I feel as if I am caught in an undertow and I'm being swept out to sea. I can't seem to swim back to dry land, and I am getting pulled under the water." With these words, a client described the feelings that she was having upon learning that her husband of over 20 years was cheating on her. This is a fitting metaphor for the experience of many couples when they enter into therapy following an affair or infidelity. Couples struggle to keep some form of connection to one another despite powerful emotional forces arrayed against them. However, they get swept away and pulled under by the emotions of betrayal as they seek to reach an understanding about how to be a couple after one (or both) have violated the relationship. This violation may be physical or emotional in nature, and the agreement between the partners may be unspoken, explicitly agreed to, or codified in a ritual of marriage. Questions about the meaning of the infidelity for each person, and the uncertainty about their commitment to one another, often propel these couples into therapy for help. The reality is that when couples come to therapy, they are looking for a way to keep their heads above water and not allow their relationship to become sucked down and drowned in the undertow of the affair.

It is a fact, however, that the help that these couples want is difficult to get. According to many couples therapists, infidelity is a topic that they feel least able to handle, even though it is the most often cited reason that couples come for counseling (Whisman, Dixon, & Johnson, 1997). In order for a practitioner to be able to begin to be prepared to understand the intricacies of a topic such as infidelity, it is important to understand some of the basic dynamics of the topic, such as the prevalence of infidelity, issues related to treatment, and the effectiveness of couples therapy with infidelity. This chapter will focus on the available statistics on the prevalence of infidelity in couples, and then provide an overview of the chapters of this book that will address the treatment issues and effectiveness of couples therapy in helping clients dealing with infidelity, with the goal of helping practitioners help couples get the help they need.

PREVALENCE STATISTICS

Just how pervasive is this problem of infidelity? This question is up for much debate in the literature. Some of the best estimates put the number somewhere between 20% and 40% of all couples have engaged in an infidelity (Blow & Hartnett, 2005; Glass & Wright, 1992; Lusterman, 1998). According to Glass and Wright (1992), approximately 25% of all couples entering couples therapy report infidelity as the presenting concern, and an additional 30% eventually reveal infidelity in the relationship. Yet, according to Widerman (1994, as cited in Blow & Hartnett, 2005), utilizing the General Social Survey in 1994 (n = 884 men and 1,288 women), only 78% of men and 88% of women said that they had never engaged in an affair. According to Blow and Hartnett (2005), this finding seems pretty stable across several studies, but only when (a) the focus is on sexual intercourse, (b) the subjects are heterosexual couples, and (c) the sample is large and is nationally representative.

Another indication of the prevalence of infidelity is the attitudes of people toward it. Again, in larger samples of heterosexual couples, people tend to disapprove of infidelity. However, this finding is somewhat weakened when factors such as culture, sexuality, behavior (i.e., type of infidelity), and past engagement in infidelity are taken into consideration (Blow & Hartnett, 2005). In addition, Treas (2002) found that, when measured in large cohorts, negative attitudes toward infidelity seem to change over time, and that younger generations seem to have a more tolerant attitude toward infidelity than older generations. Not surprisingly, Glass and Wright (1992) found that those who committed adultery also had a more permissive attitude toward infidelity. Approximately 90% of men and women who were unhappy in their marriage felt that there were conditions where an affair could be justified. This seems to indicate that there is a divergence of opinions on the question of infidelity, particularly in certain communities or subgroups of the population. For many of these subgroups, however, the attitudes on nonmonogamy are based on the idea that it is (a) a function of biological needs, (b) not destructive to the primary relationship, or (c) both. This seems to indicate that the "definition" of infidelity, as well as the meaning that is ascribed to the act of infidelity, are serious mitigating factors for couples. There are important dynamics for couples therapists to take into account when working with these couples.

Gender Differences

A common belief is that there are vast gender differences in who commits infidelities in committed relationships. There is some evidence that supports this assertion. Glass and Wright (1992) found in their survey that 44% of husbands had at least one extramarital experience, whereas only 25% of wives reported having an extramarital experience. In another representative sample, Atkins (2003) found that gender was a significant moderator in the rates of prevalence of infidelity. Specifically, men who had participated in affairs showed increased substance use, were older, and were more sexually dissatisfied in their marriages when compared to women who had engaged in infidelity (Atkins, 2003). Buunk and Dijkstra (2004) reported that men tend to engage in affairs in order to address sexual disappointment more than women do. However, they also noted a trend, that the lack of sexual fulfillment between genders as a cause for infidelity appears to be diminishing.

Another common factor that often mediates the occurrence of infidelity is satisfaction with the primary relationship. So what is the relationship of affairs and relationship dissatisfaction, and does it differ between the sexes? In one study, men and women who engaged in an affair had different levels of dissatisfaction in their marriage. Almost two thirds of women were unhappy in their marriage before the affair, while only 30% of men were dissatisfied in their marriage (Glass & Wright, 1992). According to Atkins (2003), individuals who participated in affairs showed greater marital instability, dishonesty, arguments about trust, narcissism, and less time spent with their spouse. Previti and Amato (2004), in a longitudinal study of married couples, found that instability in the relationship (what they term as "divorce proneness") was a significant predictor of later infidelity, and that infidelity was inversely correlated with marital happiness after the affair. In other words, there is a reciprocal effect between bad relationships and infidelity. Bad relationships increase the likelihood of infidelity, which, in turn, has a negative effect on marriages. It is clear that the evidence, though sketchy from a research perspective, does point to several couple factors that are important to address when attempting to understand and work with couples dealing with infidelity. Chief among these are trust and satisfaction. The good news is that couples therapists can be effective in these areas, but not without understanding the emotional, mental, and physical complexity of infidelity.

CHAPTER SUMMARIES

Given the complexity of this issue on the clinical, research, and theoretical levels, as well as its centrality in couples therapy, the chapters in this text have been assembled to provide the reader with an overview and understanding of virtually all aspects of the topic of infidelity. This text is organized into four main sections. The first section provides an overview of topics related to the understanding of infidelity, and includes the following chapters:

In Chapter 2: *Sex in Intimate Relationships: Variations and Challenges,* by Paul R. Rassmussen and Kathleen J. Kilbore, the authors provide a context for the issues of sex and intimacy in couples relationships. The chapter provides a definition for many of the various sexual expressions that are reflected in the book (e.g., nonmonogamy). In addition, they explore the ways that sexual expression can be used to unite and divide couples, and how this relates to the topic of infidelity.

In Chapter 3: *An Evolutionary Psychological Perspective on Infidelity,* by Alastair P. C. Davies, Todd K. Shackelford, and Aaron T. Goetz, the authors discuss infidelity from the perspective of evolutionary psychology. They look at the phenomenon of "mate poaching" and what the biological explanation for the occurrence of infidelity might be. They present research that sheds some light on the dynamics that contribute to infidelity, as well as the attitudes that shape infidelity-related behaviors such as jealousy.

The second section addresses the topic of the treatment of infidelity in couples therapy. It includes chapters on the following topics:

In Chapter 4: *Research on Couple Therapy for Infidelity: What Do We Know About Helping Couples When There Has Been an Affair?* Deborah E. Kessel, Jessica H. Moon, and David C. Atkins outline the research that has been conducted, to date, on the treatment of infidelity and provide a summary of clinical guidelines based on the existing research on infidelity. In addition, they identify several areas of future research to be considered.

In Chapter 5: *The Intersystems Approach to Treating Infidelity,* by Stephen T. Fife, Gerald R. Weeks, and Nancy Gambescia, the authors detail their comprehensive model for treating the many aspects of infidelity. Regardless of how the infidelity is presented, the intersystems approach provides a flexible "roadmap" for therapists to use. Their exhaustive assessment and treatment mapping guidelines present therapists with the information to make the best treatment choices for the couple.

In Chapter 6: *Treating Infidelity: An Integrative Approach to Resolving Trauma and Promoting Forgiveness,* by Douglas K. Snyder, Donald H. Baucom, and Kristina C. Gordon, the authors detail their research-based model of forgiveness following the disclosure of an affair. Their work integrates an insight-oriented approach with cognitive-behavioral couples treatment to provide therapists with a method for addressing this issue in treatment.

In Chapter 7: *Forgive and Forget: A Comparison of Emotionally Focused and Cognitive Behavioral Models of Forgiveness and Intervention in the Context of Couple Infidelity,* by Heather B. MacIntosh, Joanne Hall, and Susan M. Johnson, the authors discuss how Emotion Focused Therapy (EFT) uniquely addresses an important level of pain and healing when dealing with infidelity:

the attachment level. They outline the elements of the "Attachment Injury Resolution Model" and relevant research findings to address how it may be superior to other approaches.

In Chapter 8: *The Affair as a Catalyst for Change,* Emily M. Brown presents a classification of affairs based on the emotional condition of the couple prior to the affair. She details the many ways that affairs can help a couple uncover underlying issues that have gone unaddressed, which contribute to the affair. She also presents practical methods for couples therapists helping couples to recover from the infidelity.

The third section looks at infidelity and its impact on couples from different social, cultural, generational, and sexual perspectives. This section includes the following chapters:

In Chapter 9: *Cyber-Infidelity,* Rona Subotnik discusses a new and pernicious method for being unfaithful: the Internet. She presents an in-depth model for understanding the unique aspects of the cyber-affair, as well as how to work with couples.

In Chapter 10: *Infidelity: A Multicultural Perspective,* by Richard C. Henriksen, Jr., the author provides readers with an overview of how culture adds a whole new dimension to the acceptance and treatment of infidelity in couples. The chapter looks at several cultural subgroups and their conceptualizations of infidelity. In addition, practical treatment considerations are offered for practitioners from different cultural backgrounds.

In Chapter 11: *Male Couples and Monogamy: Clinical and Cultural Issues,* author Michael Shernoff challenges couples and family therapists to examine many of the heterosexual stereotypes related to infidelity and introduces alternative understandings about the nature of *nonmonogamy* in male couple relationships. In addition, he presents suggestions for working with couples on many of the accompanying issues that surround nonmonogamy.

In Chapter 12: *Lesbian Couples: The Infidelities of Women, Sexual and Otherwise,* Beverly Burch discusses many of the unique aspects of working with lesbian couples, including issues that arise from the interconnectedness among ex-partners and present lovers. She presents several in-depth case studies to draw out how each couple must decide on what the nature and level of commitment is, and how to negotiate the emotional needs surrounding nonmonogamy.

In Chapter 13: *"An Affair to Remember": Infidelity and Its Impact on Children,* Catherine Ford Sori discusses the lasting impact that affairs have on children of all ages in the family. She details the challenges of working with children when an infidelity occurs, as well as practical treatment options for couples and family therapists to use for children at all developmental levels.

The final section includes reminiscences from two master therapists in the field who have each contributed much to the field of couples therapy. The chapters in this section are as follows:

In Chapter 14: *Reflections of a Master,* by Frank Pittman, Katie Berman, and Paul R. Peluso, Frank Pittman presents his reflections about the moral aspects of infidelity, and the current state of couples counseling. He offers his unique insight and classic wit in answering tough questions on the subject, and providing guidance to beginning (and seasoned) therapists alike in dealing with infidelity.

In Chapter 15, simply titled *Reflections on the Affair: An Experiential Perspective,* Augustus Napier offers his perspective and reminiscences of over three decades on the treatment of couples and infidelity from the Symbolic-Experiential Family Therapy approach. In it, he echoes many of the dominant themes of the text, while simultaneously—and often poetically—constructing a fresh narrative. He reminds all practitioners that there is a boldness that is needed in the practice of couples therapy—especially when there is infidelity—that is often lost to many modern practitioners.

In Chapter 16: *Summarizing* Infidelity: *Lessons Learned Along the Way,* by Paul R. Peluso, the author outlines two basic fallacies that most beginning therapists operate under when working with couples dealing with infidelity. Utilizing two case studies, he details how these fallacies lead to unsuccessful therapeutic outcomes, and demonstrates how information presented in the other chapters of this book could be utilized in order to avoid these common problems.

CONCLUSION

One final note about the contents of many of these chapters: The reader may note that there are some overlaps in the citations, as well as in some of the information that is presented. The reason for this is simple: There isn't that much in the literature that has been written on the subject relative to other treatment issues (e.g., substance abuse). This volume represents perhaps the best synthesis, to date, of the various treatment approaches, treatment issues, and scholarly work that has been done in the area of infidelity and couples therapy.

REFERENCES

Atkins, D. C. (2003). *Infidelity and marital therapy: Initial findings from a randomized clinical trial.* Unpublished doctoral dissertation, University of Washington, Seattle.

Blow, A. & Hartnett , K. (2005). Infidelity in committed relationships II: A substantive review. *Journal of Marital and Family Therapy, 31*(2), 217–234.

Buunk, B. P., & Dijkstra, P. (2004). Men, women and infidelity: Sex differences in extradyadic sex and jealousy. In G. Allan, J. Duncombe, K. Harrison, & D. Marsden (Eds.), *The state of affairs: Explorations in infidelity and commitment* (pp. 103–120). Mahwah, NJ: Erlbaum.

Glass, S., & Wright, T. L. (1992). Justifications for extramarital involvement: The association between attitudes, behaviors, and gender. *Journal of Sex Research, 29*(3), 361–387.

Lusterman, D. D. (1998). *Infidelity: A survival guide*. Oakland, CA: New Harbinger.

Previti, D., & Amato, P. R. (2004). Is infidelity a cause or a consequence of poor marital quality? *Journal of Social and Personal Relationships, 21*(2), 217–230.

Treas, J. (2002). How cohorts, education, and ideology shaped a new sexual revolution on American attitudes towards nonmarital sex, 1972–1998. *Sociological Perspectives, 45*(3), 267–283.

Whisman, M. A., Dixon, A. E., & Johnson, B. (1997). Therapists' perspectives of couple problems and treatment issues in couple therapy. *Journal of Family Psychology, 11,* 361–366.

PART I

Understanding Infidelity

CHAPTER 2

Sex in Intimate Relationships
Variations and Challenges

PAUL R. RASMUSSEN AND KATHLEEN J. KILBORNE

INTRODUCTION

Sexual infidelity occurs when the sexual and/or intimacy needs of one or both members of a couple are not being satisfied in that relationship and when the constraints against infidelity are either weak or nonexistent. The urge for sexual relationships outside of the committed relationship, with a novel partner, is clearly not the exception (Rouse, 2002). While it may be true that a majority of adults do not act on those urges by pursuing an adulterous affair, the fact remains that monogamy may not be the natural inclination as those inclinations relate to our sexual urges; nonetheless, there are clear advantages of monogamy that do not relate directly to sexuality. In this chapter, we discuss some of the factors that contribute to sexual infidelities and some of the alternative forms of commitment that have emerged as a way of dealing with the forces that compel sexual betrayal. The position taken in this chapter is one of neutrality and the objective is simply to delineate those factors contributing to sexual frustrations in committed relationships and alternatives that many in our society pursue.

We begin by discussing sex and intimacy and distinguishing between these two functions in order to describe the tension that often emerges when the two are thought of as equivalent. To be sure, we often assume that if a couple is being intimate, they are engaging in sexual relations; likewise, we might assume that if someone is in a sexual relationship, they are intimate. However, is this really the case? Does one, by default or necessity, involve the other? The answers here are clearly "no." While we often use the two terms interchangeably, sex can and does occur in the absence of intimacy, and intimacy is not always associated with sexual activity. The fact is that the two represent different, albeit often harmonizing acts and emotions. The difference between sexual activity and emotional intimacy contributes in meaningful ways to the optimizing and sometimes, unfortunately, to the destruction of relationships. Without question, the task of balancing these two human experiences in a relationship contributes to a pinnacle of enjoyment and to the depths of emotional pain that can result from the betrayal associated with infidelity.

SEX VERSUS INTIMACY

The term "sex" best describes the act of physical, erotic contact that typically includes progression toward, if not completion of, orgasm. Sex does not require intimacy. "Intimacy" is a term that denotes a degree of emotional connection. In an intimate relationship people share personal thoughts, express private feelings, and act in one another's welfare. Intimacy involves feelings of love and closeness with another (see Mashek & Aron, 2004), while sex does not depend on love or any form of emotional connection or dependency. The connection between these terms lies in the fact that when sex and intimacy occur together, those involved are more romantic and *make love* with and to one another and typically enjoy a more enriching and fulfilling relationship (see Brehm, Perlman, Miller, & Campbell, 2002). In loving, intimate relationships, it is through the physical act of sex that the couple expresses feelings of passion, investment, and commitment to one another. To be sure, people can form intimate relationships that do not include sex and sex can, and often does, occur in the absence of intimacy.

The Traditional Orientation

In American society, the most common attitude toward sex and intimacy is that the two should occur together. Whether or not this includes the formal act of marriage or merely a commitment depends very often on the religious attitudes and practices of the couple. For those holding a more conservative and often religious commitment, intimacy develops prior to any engagement in sexual activity and in the most conservative orientations, only after marriage. Recent estimates, however, suggest that this traditional orientation to sex and intimacy is not as common as it once was. For instance, the proportion of Americans reporting that premarital sex is "not wrong" went from 24%

in 1969 to 47% in 1978, 51.5% in 1972, and 61.8% in 1982 (see Harding & Jencks, 2003; Thornton & Young-DeMarco, 2001). Since 1982, however, there has not been a significant increase in those reporting a more open attitude toward premarital sex; nonetheless, the largest proportion of our population views premarital sex as acceptable.

Recent efforts by various religious organizations have attempted to modify these trends, particularly as they relate to sexual activity among teens (e.g., virginity contracts), and given the lack of significant increase in attitudes toward premarital sex since 1982, perhaps they have been effective. However, the lack of change in attitudes since 1982 is not necessarily reflected in actual behavior. For instance, while the attitudes toward premarital sex may not have changed, the involvement in premarital sex has continued to increase. Recent estimates suggest that as many as 80% of couples engage in sex prior to marriage (see Rouse, 2002). However, these data are somewhat obscured by the changing attitudes concerning what exactly constitutes sex.

When Is Sex "Just Sex"?

While there has been some debate in recent years concerning what exactly constitutes sex, generally, we can consider sex to be whatever the person involved thinks it is. Thus, for some people sex may only involve intercourse where the male's penis enters the female's vagina, and any deviation from this either is not sex or is a sexual perversion. For others, any act that includes the touching of genitalia is sex, and at the very extreme, the mere thought of a carnal act may constitute sex. However it might be defined, sex may or may not involve intimacy.

Even in intimate relationships, sex is occasionally pursued specifically for the purpose of sexual gratification, including a drive for orgasm, and less as a show of intimacy. For instance, many couples engage in sexual activity that is more sexually aggressive than is the sex that characterizes lovemaking. In romantic encounters, the language is more nurturing, love affirming, and gentle; in purely sexual acts, the language is often more graphically sexual and the atmosphere more sexually charged. Indeed, many couples will go to great lengths to create a sexually heated environment. For instance, some couples will use fantasy or scripted or semiscripted scenarios (e.g., a simulated bar pickup), watch erotica or pornography, or practice prolonged flirtatiousness in order to build the sexual tension. Because people enjoy and often thrive on the sexual tension that may be created in such instances, many nightclubs gain their popularity through the ability to generate high sexual energy, and patrons frequent these establishments in order to bask in that sexual ambience.

Further, in the absence of emotional intimacy, many couples may continue to engage in sexual relations. In intimate encounters, each partner invests in the pleasure of his or her partner and in the demonstration of feelings of closeness. However, when intimacy has left the relationship altogether, the sexual energy felt is more self-serving, where each partner essentially uses the other as a source of his or her own sexual gratification. In these contexts, the enthusiasm for the act might be no greater for one's partner than for another; and it may not be uncommon to find that either or both partners desire, perhaps only through fantasy, sexual activity with another. Because the relationship commitment constrains sexual expression outside of the relationship, these urges can become a tremendous source of relationship strain and conflict.

The line where intimacy enters a sexual encounter or a sexually focused relationship is not distinct. At one end of the continuum, the task of sex is orgasm, and this can be accomplished with or without a partner and with and without intimacy. At one extreme, the person may express no investment in the pleasure, or even presence, of the other person. Such a situation may be present in various masturbatory acts and images, or perhaps, when watching pornography, engaging in sexual acts characterized by a focus on objects of fetish, or via quick sexual encounters with a partner (i.e., the *quickie*). At the opposite end, sex is an expression of love and devotion, and each partner invests as much in the pleasure of his or her lover as in personal satisfaction. Indeed, at this extreme, their sexual pleasure may be optimally synchronized because of the commitment to pleasing each other. Between these two extremes are acts of sexual engagements coupled with variable degrees of emotional closeness.

Attitudes Toward Sex and Intimacy

When both members of a couple share similar attitudes toward sex and intimacy, there is typically less conflict within the relationship. However, shared attitudes can vary greatly from one couple to another. Simpson and Gangestad (1991) have looked at the attitudes toward sex in committed relationships and have suggested that some couples tend toward a more restricted view of sexuality, while others possess a less restricted or even nonrestricted attitude concerning sex. These researchers use the term "sociosexual orientation" to describe these differences.

With a restricted attitude, an individual or couple holds that relationships should be monogamous, that sexual encounters outside of the relationship are not acceptable, and that sex and love are part of the commitment agreement (e.g., marriage). These individuals believe that sex requires love and should never take place without it. Individuals and couples scoring high on the restricted side of this continuum are more conventional and conservative regarding sexual attitudes and behaviors.

On the other hand, those characterized by nonrestricted sociosexual orientation are more likely to see sex and love as two very different concepts. These individuals often have a more open relationship and typically believe that sexual relations outside of the primary relationship are, to a varying degree, acceptable. In fact, many such individuals argue that their open sexual relationship enhances the sex and intimacy of the committed relationship (see Bergstrand & Williams, 2000). It is possible that while those on the unrestricted end of the continuum know how to combine sex and intimacy, they are also able to separate the two without losing the essence of their commitment. Further, research by O'Neill and O'Neill (1972) suggests that while open relationships bring novel concerns into play (e.g., emotional and logistical), those individuals who maintain nonrestricted attitudes toward sex and intimacy and who work to maintain their committed relationship report being happier than those in restricted relationships and are less likely to divorce (Bergstrand & Williams, 2000). However, before we conclude that open relationships are superior or preferable to closed relationships, it is important to consider further some of the pitfalls of open relationships. Individuals engaged in open relationships must contend with the reactions of others, which might be a difficult task in a restricted culture. As well, they must address feelings of jealousy and possessiveness, and work around the logistical challenges of a more complicated life than those in closed relationships (see Rouse, 2002). Further, struggles may exist relating to the violation of previously conceived notions of morality and fidelity, and certainly, the risk of acquiring a sexually transmitted disease is higher.

For some within the nonrestricted group, the line between sex and emotional intimacy is upheld; while sex outside of the primary relationship is acceptable, emotional intimacies should remain sacred to their commitment. Individuals who engage in *swinging* (see below) or other forms of open relationships most often fit this description. However, for others with a nonrestricted sociosexual attitude, it is acceptable to maintain outside relationships that include both sexual and emotional intimacies; the practices of polygamy and polyamory describe this nonrestricted view (see Anapol, 1997). Somewhere between the extremes, we might place the affairs that occur in restricted *monogamous* relationships.

Which attitude is best depends, of course, on the individuals and the nature of the relationship. To be sure, when the attitudes between the relational partners toward sex and intimacy are discrepant, conflicts are more common. Conflicts that occur typically emerge from the basic differences that occur between men and women. Men, generally, are more inclined to hold the attitude of sex for sex's sake, while women generally invest more in intimacy (see Glass & Wright, 1997). However, this may hold most true when men are involved in extramarital affairs, thereby providing a convenient rationalization for their behavior. That men are now and have for generations been more harshly judgmental of women who engage in premarital or extramarital sexual relationships reveals a long-standing double standard regarding men's attitudes toward sex as *just sex*. Sex is *just sex* when they are involved in extramarital affairs, but when a wife strays, the violation is something greater than merely sex for the sake of sex.

In some relationships, it is not uncommon for the partners to share related but different complaints about the relationship. For instance, women may complain about a lack of communication, underscoring the lack of intimacy they feel in the relationship; their male partner, however, may be more likely to complain about the lack of sexual activity (Glass & Wright, 1997). There are clearly exceptions to these perspectives, but these remain the most common complaints.

When one member of the relationship couple holds a more restricted attitude, relationship problems are almost inevitable, particularly if the partner with the nonrestricted attitude chooses to act on his or her convictions, in spite of his or her partner's lack of support for open sexual exploration. In such situations, which are common, it is far more typical to see the partner with the nonrestricted attitude pursue extramarital affairs rather than actually pursuing an open relationship. Again, it is more likely to be the male that pursues the extramarital affair, but far from exclusively the male (see Laumann, Gagnon, Michael, & Michaels, 1994). The importance of shared attitudes toward sex and intimacy relates deeply to the ability to commit to the success of the relationship in the long term. Two independent people, each with their own interests, who are committed to each other through their shared beliefs about what will make their relationship a success, are the most likely to achieve that success. The following sections describe the various types of attitudes, practices, and commitments that may lead to the achievement of this goal, whatever the mode of relationship may be.

MONOGAMY AND NONMONOGAMY

The picture portrayed by traditional cultural standards of the *perfect relationship* is often not true for many people. Frequently, the extraordinary contentment found at the outset of relationships deteriorates; perhaps the couple no longer feels the partnership meets their needs, and they may question their reasons for adhering to their previous commitment. Unhappy couples interact with each other unenthusiastically, engage in negative communication, and tend to think of each other in disapproving terms. Relationship stress is also associated with family, career, and health strain (Clements, Cordova, & Markman, 1997; Forthofer, Markman, & Cox, 1996). Clearly, in choosing to enter a long-term relationship, the partners must be prepared for the stresses and changes that are inevitable as two individuals work toward the common goal of relationship commitment and satisfaction.

Several factors positively predict lasting relationship satisfaction. First, sexual satisfaction and engaging in positive interaction are strongly correlated with marital stability and satisfaction (Lindahl, Malik, & Bradbury, 1997). In addition, Halford and Markman (1997) suggest that one of the most important features of long-term satisfaction is the ability to adapt to life circumstances that inevitably vary over time. Furthermore, they define precisely what clinicians consider a "healthy long-term couple relationship" in this way:

A developing set of interactions between partners, which promotes the individual well-being of each partner and their offspring, assists each partner to adapt to life stresses, engenders a conjoint sense of emotional and sexual intimacy between the partners, and which promotes the long-term sustainment of the relationship within the cultural context in which the partners live. (Halford & Markman, 1997, p4)

This definition raises a particular question: Is it necessary for the couple to remain monogamous to achieve long-term satisfaction? If not, the distinction between nonmonogamy and infidelity must be immediately stated; infidelity is associated with blatant dishonesty and betrayal (Glass & Wright, 1997) whereas nonmonogamy, if it is to be a viable option, must be negotiated within the couple (Jamieson, 2004). There are compelling reasons to choose monogamy, many of which are made salient by the overwhelming bias toward monogamy in Western culture (Barker, 2005). On the other hand, there are convincing alternatives demonstrated by those who select nonmonogamous lifestyles, although regrettably for these couples, attention to these preferences is missing entirely from most source materials related to relationship maintenance and enhancement. This lack of research consideration demonstrates a need for concern and understanding of the reality of **negotiated nonmonogamy**. An attempt is presented here by assessing some general aspects of monogamy versus nonmonogamy as they relate to sex and intimacy.

What causes people to choose monogamous relationships? Several factors make many people feel very good about monogamy. One of the most prominent features is sexual satisfaction, a reason that makes logical sense when we consider the intense physical attraction that often draws couples together at the beginning of a new relationship. It is not surprising that a normal characteristic of happy long-term couples is a sex life satisfying in its quality, frequency, and consistency (Spence, 1997). In addition, choosing to be monogamous with the partner is associated with a sense of deeper intimacy within the relationship, because partners are loyal to their agreement not to share themselves sexually with anyone else. Furthermore, intimacy and sexual desire are found to be positively correlated; the opportunity for deeper intimacy experienced in a monogamous relationship is also likely to be experienced with healthy levels of sexual desire (Spence, 1997). Overall, it is likely that the nature of long-term relationships will compel the couple to maintain the original degree of sexual satisfaction to as great an extent as possible; it seems that this undertaking is enhanced by the commitment to deep intimacy made by the monogamous couple. The importance of this commitment cannot be underestimated, as demonstrated already by the high correlation between sexual satisfaction and stability in long-term relationships (Lindahl et al., 1997).

In assessing the value of monogamy, an overall picture emerges that suggests that the announcement of monogamous devotion is a gesture of commitment to a partner about whom one cares deeply. Jamieson (2004) summarizes this view with the statement that "sexual fidelity is symbolic of trust and that sexual exclusivity is symbolic of 'specialness' in couple relationships." In our culture, there is an unequivocal norm of sexual exclusivity, especially within marriage. As expected, a strong negative correlation exists between a commitment to monogamy and the likelihood of extramarital sex (Wiederman & Allgeier, 1996). However, nearly everyone recognizes that on a biological level, sexual desires for many others over a lifetime is natural (Barash & Lipton, 2001); choosing monogamy, then, involves the willingness to overcome those urges in order to stay in the relationship.

Monogamy is, of course, the most popular form of committed relationship in our society, especially among heterosexuals, but common too among gay and lesbian couples (Rouse, 2002). However, why is it then that monogamy simply does not work for everybody? Why are so many monogamous couples in crisis, especially in the areas of sex and intimacy? In monogamous relationships, the challenge of maintaining sexual interest is often difficult and in many couples this challenge compromises the emotional intimacy of the relationship. Certainly, some couples are comfortable letting the sexual energies dissipate with time and age and come to focus more attention on the intimate and companionate aspect of love as the romantic urges decline (see Sternberg, 1986). This is perhaps more common among those maintaining traditional male and female stereotypes and advocating restricted sociosexual attitudes. It is also common among those invested in traditional religious communities where sex is seen as solely for the purpose of procreation, or as an act to be performed within very particular parameters.

In many monogamous relationships, the sexual energies, if not attended to, create conflicts that damage the intimacy and companionship of the relationship. As a result, many individuals end up as serially monogamous—moving from one relationship to another, exiting one relationship when the sexual energies are gone or the emotional intimacy lost. These factors help to explain the increase in divorce rates in our Western cultures. When the sexual and intimate energies in a marriage end, it is not uncommon or unreasonable for the partners to begin to consider alternatives to the relationship. One apparent alternative is to abandon that relationship in hopes of finding one that better fulfills personal needs. However, before one leaves, it is not uncommon for one or both parties to pursue a sexual or intimate relationship with another person. In some cases, this may introduce the couple to the idea of an open relationship, or to another form of nonmonogamy. More often, it leads to extramarital affairs and often to marital crisis.

For men, an extramarital affair often serves as a substitute for the sexual gratification missing in the primary relationship. As long as he is able to maintain secrecy, it may not be an active threat to the primary relationship. Women, too, are pursuing this option more often than before (Rouse, 2002) and in many cases, like for men, it is the desire to engage in purely sexual activities that motivates the affair. However, for women, the goal is more typically a replacement for the intimacy and validation that has been lost in the primary relationship (see Rouse, 2002).

Nonmonogamy

What causes people to choose nonmonogamous relationships? The same salient values discussed in the context of monogamy can also be applied to the analysis of nonmonogamy. The first factor is sexual satisfaction. Is it possible that the agreement of both partners to seek outside sexual interactions could increase sexual satisfaction within their relationship and lead to a greater overall sense of contentment? There are several pieces of evidence available to address this question. Whitehurst (1983) asserts that the probability for most people to achieve the long-term satisfaction expected from marriage is low, and that this leads many to explore *substitute satisfactions*; these substitutes may range from viewing pornography (alone and/or together) to active involvement with others. Additionally, participants in Jamieson's (2004) study had a general attitude that they were unable to stop cheating within the confines of monogamy, but then moved into nonmonogamy because they recognized it as a truthful, natural path for maintaining multiple relationships. Taken together, this research seems to suggest that dissatisfaction in the long-term couple is inevitable and that negotiating the terms of open nonmonogamy is more desirable than infidelity. Furthermore, Barash and Lipton (2001) illustrate the fact that sexual satisfaction with primary partners is often revived when they experience each other in a new way. Specifically, passionate love may be rekindled by going outside the primary relationship (Barash & Lipton, 2001). Previously, it was stated that the commitment to intimacy in monogamous couples is of utmost importance to sexual satisfaction, due to its association with long-term quality and stability of relationships. This assertion applies here as well: If exercising the freedom to choose among a variety of sexual experiences fosters deeper intimacy within the couple, then yes, nonmonogamy can be a way to produce long-term satisfaction between two partners.

In assessing the value of nonmonogamy, an overall picture, nearly identical to that of monogamy, emerges that suggests that the announcement of nonmonogamous devotion is like a gift to a partner about whom one cares deeply. Barker (2005) summarized this view with the statement that "[nonmonogamy] might be a better way of relating than monogamy, or that it might be more realistic, in that many people are attracted to more than one person" (p. 85). Nonmonogamy, then, might be a valid lifestyle that some might consider as a means of maintaining sexual and emotional satisfaction. Nonmonogamous individuals proclaim vigorously that sexual desires for more than one person over a lifetime are normal and natural, but choosing nonmonogamy as a lifestyle is essentially stating the willingness to allow the other the pursuit of the most appealing and healthy relationship (Barash & Lipton, 2001). Indeed, this suggests an inherent threat to the relationship created by the circumstance of nonmonogamy; yet no research exists that suggests that this threat is any greater or less than the threat created by the lack of sexual fulfillment and infidelity in a monogamous relationship.

Types of Nonmonogamous Relationships

Open relationships are those in which couples maintain an intimate investment in the relationship and share the tasks associated with being a couple or family, yet are nonrestrictive in sociosexual attitudes and nonmonogamous in practice. Do nonmonogamous, open relationships solve the problems associated with monogamy? Those who endorse open relationships seem to think so. Because they acknowledge the sexual pressures that often emerge in monogamy that frequently lead to temptations, frustrations, and adultery, they pursue open relationships as a means of protecting against the threat and pain associated with extramarital affairs (Rouse, 2002; Whitehurst, 1983). At the same time, the partners acknowledge the desire for a stable, committed relationship. While there are a number of varieties of nonmonogamy, recent estimates suggest that as many as 4% of monogamous couples had at some time been involved in an open relationship (Rouse, 2002). While the *traditional*, if such a term can be used, open relationship is one in which both partners permit the other to pursue relationships outside of the primary relationship, there are various ways of negotiating the terms of nonmonogamy. Two of these types of nonmonogamous relationships, swinging and polyamory, are discussed here.

Swinging

One form of open relationship is one in which the partners participate, often together, in sexual relationships with other people. Known as "swinging," or "the lifestyle," this open, nonrestrictive style of relationship has been around for some time and appears to be increasingly popular (Heinlein & Heinlein, 2004). Swinging is a term used to describe what has been referred to in the past as mate or wife swapping. While this activity typically involves couples—gay and straight—singles are occasionally included in the sexual activities. In this nonrestricted sexual practice, couples enter into relations with others specifically for the purpose of sex. Often these relationships are emotionally superficial (names may not even be shared), while in other cases, the couples may become close and intimate friends. Nonetheless, those engaged in the lifestyle are primarily interested in pursuing noncommittal, sexual relationships free of the burden of emotional entanglements. Couples engaged in this lifestyle also report the benefit of not having to worry about extramarital affairs, nor contend with the frustrations associated with an inhibited sex life. In a report by the North American Swing Club Association (NASCA), it was suggested that 15% of all couples had incorporated swinging in their marriage (McGinley, 1995). This number shows an increase over the last two decades (Rouse, 2002). No doubt, this increase reflects the advantages of pursuing the lifestyle with the availability of the Internet. Before the Internet, lifestylers were obligated to subscribe to swingers' magazines, which often had to be delivered to a secure location in a plain brown wrapper, or search the "seeking" sections of alternative culture circulars. Today, lifestylers are able to pursue contacts through the relative security of their home computer. Some might argue that this lifestyle is swarming with sexual liberals and deviants who are not part of the mainstream of society. However, in a recent report (Bergstrand & Williams, 2000) it was demonstrated that those involved in the swinging lifestyle are very mainstream and have backgrounds that are no more suggestive of deviancy than any others. In the Bergstrand and Williams survey, most swingers identified themselves as professionals, many physicians, attorneys, upper-level managers, engineers, teachers, and other common professionals. As many identified themselves as politically conservative as did politically liberal, and they were "slightly more likely than the general population to say they are members of a religious organization" (p. 5). Statistics also showed that swingers report higher levels of happiness and marital satisfaction than traditional monogamous couples in the general population. In addition, 62% of the respondents who identified themselves as swingers reported that swinging had improved their marriage, while only 1.7% said that swinging had made them "less happy." While these data might suggest the advantages of the lifestyle, it is important to note the potential bias in these data. Although the data appear to suggest some safety and benefit in swinging, it is imperative to understand that the data come from people actively involved in the lifestyle, who maintain unrestricted views of sexuality, and do not reflect the feelings and attitudes of those who tried the lifestyle and had a bad experience.

Polyamory

Another type of open relationship, polyamory, is a newer development than swinging and, like swinging, appears to be increasing in popularity (Anapol, 1997). Polyamory describes the nonrestricted sexual practice in which members of a couple permit not only sexual relationships with others but also the freedom to foster emotional intimacies, independent of sex. Those involved in polyamory allow their partners to pursue loving, intimate, sexual relationships outside of the primary relationship. Indeed, in polyamorous relationships, there may not be a primary relationship, as participants in this practice may not view any one partner as a primary partner. However, more typically, as reported by Anapol, one relationship remains primary.

Polyamory is unlike polygamy primarily because there is rarely a religious overtone to polyamory, although many who practice polyamory describe themselves as very spiritually oriented (Anapol, 1997). Another difference is that practitioners of polyamory do not typically marry those with whom they form intimate relationships. Further, polyamores are rarely limited to males with multiple wives. Polyamorous couples may be straight, gay, lesbian, bisexual, or some combination of sexual orientations. For instance, it may be common for a woman and man in a traditional relationship to have other lovers who are gay, straight, or bisexual. Like swingers, polyamores have found the Internet to be a convenient and useful resource for finding others who maintain similar socio-sexual attitudes, and many poylamores may start off as swingers.

The central, most visible differences between monogamous and nonmonogamous relationships are now evident, but what should be apparent through these descriptions are the numerous similarities between healthy monogamous and nonmonogamous couples. While implications beyond the issues of sex and intimacy were not discussed in detail here, there are many other aspects of a couple's relationship that will determine the success of an increasing degree of openness, such as family needs, spiritual beliefs, and past experiences with extramarital exploits. It is clear, however, that both types of relationships are dependent on satisfaction of many of the same sexual, emotional, and committal factors. With the ever-increasing visibility and apparent acceptance of nonmonogamy in our society, it remains to be seen how nonmonogamous couples' attempts at reconciling the difficulties with monogamy succeed. As of yet, little research exists on *negotiated nonmonogamy*. A single study comparing levels of satisfaction in monogamous and nonmonogamous homosexual male couples showed no significant difference in relationship quality and function (LaSala, 2004). Though issues for homosexual males might be very different from those of heterosexual individuals, it seems entirely possible that similar findings would result by examining heterosexual nonmonogamous relationships.

While there are alternatives to the traditional, monogamous relationship, most couples prefer to avoid the challenges of an open relationship. Unfortunately, the decree of commitment recited in a marriage ceremony and the honest and loyal intentions of those in a new relationship may not be enough to counter the changes that occur in a relationship and that impact each partner's sense of intimate and sexual contentment. In sections below we discuss, albeit briefly, obstacles to a sexually and intimately satisfying relationship, all of which can contribute to the potential for conflict and infidelity. Several factors beyond simply sexual urges and a desire for novelty contribute to infidelity and to the choice to pursue nonmonogamy. In following sections some of the factors contributing to the gap between sex and intimacy in committed relationships are discussed, along with recommendations for overcoming those gaps.

OBSTACLES TO THE UNION OF SEX AND INTIMACY

Surely, the excitement of falling in love is one of the most visible dramas in human culture, but at the same time, the awareness that relationships do not always live up to expectations can cause much suffering. For this reason, committed couples must consciously work to maintain the stability of the relationship in ways that will continue to meet individual needs. Ideally, preserving this balance will produce the enduring satisfaction couples so strongly desire at the beginning of their union.

TALKING OPENLY ABOUT SEX

Talking about sex is an important component of intimacy in a committed relationship. However, given the cultural constraints related to sexual activity, it is common for partners to differ in their beliefs of sexuality and intimacy. Because religions often denounce premarital sex and frequently suppress discussion of sexual involvements and activity, young adults whose sexual knowledge is limited to their religious teachings not only may come into relationships unprepared to accommodate or negotiate specific sexual desires expressed by their partners, but also may be unable to accept and express their own sexual urges. In some situations, because one was discouraged from open communications with parents about sex, there may be greater hesitancy in discussing sexual matters with a sexual and intimate partner. To the extent that the partners share those inhibitions, the barriers to open discussions are even greater and the challenge of overcoming them will be that much more significant. For couples or individuals hesitant about open communication about sex, it is useful to begin by getting more comfortable with the topic. This can be achieved through the reading of informative publications about sexuality and considering erotic films or stories. For those tentative about sex, it is probably better to avoid pornography as this may exacerbate their hesitancy. Once both the partners are more comfortable thinking about sex, they are likely to become more comfortable talking to one another about sex. In these talks, the partners can read a common article or book, or watch a gentle erotic film and talk about the idea and images that intrigued or excited them, or that were distressing. These efforts will help the couple to break down the barriers to open discussion about sex. In other cases, problems in intimacy develop because of problems related to sexual satisfaction. It is not uncommon for a couple to be quite content with their relationship as it relates to common career and family aspirations, mutual hobbies, and general compatibility between personalities. However, differences in attitudes toward sexual intimacy can be enough to create considerable relationship distress, and this distress can then begin to erode the quality of the relationship felt in the other areas. In order to cut through unspoken assumptions that may exist between the couple, each partner must commit to finding the facts about what his or her partner desires, rather than trying to read their minds. They may have been together for a long time, but neither partner should take for granted that they know what the other person is thinking or feeling. If open and honest communication is not prioritized, misinterpretations and misunderstandings may throw the couple's best efforts off course.

LIFE PRIORITIES AND CHANGING DEMANDS

Maintaining a close and intimate relationship is an undertaking that many enter into with naïve assumptions. Many young couples assume that the love and intimacy and the sexual energies that define the relationship will continue, without effort, throughout their lives together. It is this hasty assumption that frequently intensifies the frustrations and other difficulties that inevitably emerge in a relationship.

While a relationship is developing and the couple is enjoying the exuberance and novelty of a new intimacy, there is much to discuss and discover. The shared ambitions and interests, coupled with the physical attraction felt by each person, help to create the passion that leads to sexual intimacy and often to the desire to pursue those common goals and interest in a committed relationship. Whereas those who are in love focus in on their similarities and think their differences are unimportant, couples in crisis focus on all the ways they are different. As a relationship evolves, there is less and less new to discover about one another, and attractiveness wanes as a natural outcome of increasing familiarity. However, if a couple wants to sustain the intimacy in a relationship, it is wise to focus on the positive aspects of the relationship and to work to increase compatibility and compromise. It is best to let the differences, as much as possible, complement the union and be an opportunity to further each other's interests and activities, and this will help to increase overall compatibility.

It is very easy in a new relationship to see the benefits one receives, such as validation, partnership, and sexual fulfillment, and the power of those benefits easily outweighs the cost to being in the relationship. For instance, in a new relationship that is starting to take on greater passion and intimacy, close friends are often neglected, career ambitions become less important, hobbies are abandoned, and familial ties are taken for granted. The loss of any benefit provided by these activities is perceived, if noticed at all, as a small price to pay for what is gained by way of the new relationship. Unfortunately, as the relationship matures, the assessment of benefit may slowly shift, and often the cost of being in that relationship becomes more obvious at both a cognitive and emotional level. It is with this insidious shift that neglected friends, jobs, hobbies, and extended family reemerge as important components to one's fulfillment. The process of reincorporating these valuable aspects into each partner's life may increase the probability of intimacy problems. One reason why these problems develop is that while each partner may continue to value the relationship, other friends, activities, and goals become a threat to the existing relationship, because from the outset the partners abandoned these essential elements of who they are to be with each other. Now that the novelty of their union has worn off, where does that leave them as individuals? Because each person has his or her own ambitions and desires, and because in a committed relationship one's ability to pursue ambitions depends in large part on the cooperation of the partner, it is not uncommon for one or both individuals to develop concerns about how the other might react to his or her newly acknowledged desires. One or both people may begin to feel constrained by the conflicting aspirations of his or her partner and hugely insecure about the strength of their commitment. In such cases, it is imperative that open communication continues so that trust and love are not degraded by these uncertainties.

The ability to wholly benefit and enjoy our relationships with other people does not come without work and dedication. If the couple is committed to the real task of being in love, they allow each other to continue to experience all the parts of themselves, which were often the things that their partner fell in love with at the beginning. The devotion of time, honesty, and open communication to each other as individuals enables them to revel in the pleasures and comforts of intimacy. Similarly, the continued commitment to closeness and sexual relations requires this open, fully honest communication so that they may experience fully these human joys.

Another challenge that surfaces is the fact that changing life priorities inevitably present themselves as a function of evolving life circumstances. For younger couples, the relationship may have developed during the relatively carefree period of college or soon thereafter. While young adulthood has its unique challenges, this is a time in life when young people often have more free time and less financial obligations. On the horizon for young lovers is an increase in financial obligation that becomes unremitting and that frequently grows at a faster rate than income. Thus, career concerns often come to dominate life for many younger adults. Furthermore, the task of child rearing can erode the intimacy that a couple thought would sustain them throughout their lives together. As these life priorities mount, the need for members of a couple to provide support and validation increases, yet the time and energy each has to provide that support and validation decreases. As relationships develop, other priorities can intrude on time together and on the ability to nurture the relationship. To the extent that we commit ourselves to more than what can be done in our daily lives, the more we will face consequences in other areas of our lives. Subsequently, couples must find the time to be together, as much as possible, and when together, put other things aside and focus on the relationship. To rekindle the love and intimacy that defined the early phases of the relationship, it is useful to return to those activities that were pursued and enjoyed when the couple was still getting to know one another. When life becomes more complicated, the task of nurturing the relationship may not be one of the first priorities to which a couple tends if their energies are depleted. However, ignoring the commitment contributes to the deterioration of intimacy over time, and this may overshadow the moments of joy the couple might intermittently experience. Further, couples may resist taking the time to nurture and maintain the relationship because of guilt associated with leaving their children with a babysitter, for instance. These parents can remind themselves that they are doing their children a great service by modeling the choices and behaviors necessary to maintaining a committed relationship. Their children will benefit from these choices immediately by way of happier, more content parents, and over the long term by learning the importance of keeping a relationship vibrant.

RESENTMENTS

The challenges of child care, full-time or part-time employment, changes in friendships, and so forth, all have an impact on the extent to which each partner feels sexual or romantic. While some women may find sexual activity a welcome diversion from the routine and stresses of life, many other women come to see sex as simply another thing they have to do, or come to view their partner as one more individual placing demands on her limited time and energies. The young father and husband may view sexual activity as a desirable diversion to the challenges of work and family; however, if his partner does not welcome his sexual advances, this perceived rejection could contribute to an intensification of stress and resentment. During this period of young parenthood, more than just sexual activity is compromised; the stresses encountered by each parent eat away at the intimacy each feels toward the other. As the intimacy wanes, resentments that may further compromise the integrity of the relationship begin to intensify. Without a solid sense of commitment to the family and relationship as a whole, at this point each partner may begin to consider alternatives to the marital union. In such circumstances, the likelihood of infidelities, separation, and divorce increases.

Consistent, mutual support takes thoughtful planning but goes a long way toward preventing the buildup of resentment. As parents, the couple must commit to being a team, which means sharing responsibility for the family and decisions relating to the home and children. Checking in and making decisions together about things large and small, being willing to compromise, and consideration of the other person in day-to-day activities rarely lead to negative consequences. When decisions are made where one partner assumes the feelings or opinions of the other, negative consequences are common. Because of the availability of cell phones and the associated ready access we have to our partners today, decisions rarely need to be made unilaterally. Checking in with a partner as one makes decisions that affect both sends the message that he or she respects and values the partner's feelings. When one feels valued and respected, one is far more likely to feel an intimacy that strengthens the commitment.

Smart couples know that a consistent, fully satisfying sex life does not just happen. Like everything else, it takes time and planning. With all the demands adults face, it is easy to let the activities related to maintaining intimacy go, leading to resentment of the other's desire for sex when it occurs. If a couple is not protective of their time together, life demands will intrude leading to the deterioration of intimacy and neglect of sexual activities. Spontaneous sex can be fun. However, as life demands increase, when unencumbered moments occur, the first thought is more likely to be rest, rather than the exertion necessary for sex. The likelihood that both members of the couple will find the time and energy to take advantage of a stolen moment is low. It is necessary, then, to create time for sex and for intimacy. An evening once a week or twice a month that is committed to a night out together, alone, will do a great deal to enhance the intimacy of a relationship. In addition, taking one or two nights a week when both go to bed together—at the same time—and taking the opportunity to foster sexual intimacy will help to keep the relationship alive.

A third way to prevent resentment is to recognize that even in the closest marriage, everyone needs time alone. Therefore, each partner must allow the other time to take a needed break from the challenges of fostering a relationship. When one requests to have some time alone, or to spend time with friends, the other need not take it personally; in a healthy relationship, such time away is not a threat, while in a troubled relationship it may be. They can help make it easier for each other to take that time by picking up part of their partner's load while they are away. While men might be more inclined to take this time, and women more hesitant to take time away from family commitments, it is important to the relationship that both partners take that time. Nonetheless, each should be careful not to let their independent activities interfere with their home and family responsibilities and attention to the welfare of the relationship.

Overall, when each person feels individually supported, both in their role in the family and in their own interests, the likelihood that one will harbor resentment about sex and intimacy is much lower. However, mutual support may not come naturally, and this may be a task for the couple to resolve. Helping each other meet daily needs makes time for sexual intimacy all the more possible.

CONCLUSION

Sex and intimacy are critical aspects of a successful relationship. Unfortunately, despite the certainties of many young and in-love couples, these two critical factors do not necessarily occur together. That they do not is one of the factors contributing to the occurrence of sexual frustration, loss of emotional intimacy, engagement in extramarital sexual and intimate relationships, and eventual relationship separations and terminations. Some authors have made the argument that humans are not inherently wired for monogamous relationships and that the natural sexual urges cannot be contained in a simple relationship. Despite this, many couples have been able to maintain long-term, satisfying relationships free of sexual and emotional affairs; however, many others have struggled with these common human feelings and those urges and frustration associated with sexual fulfillment have contributed to a great deal of emotional pain among those in committed relationships. In response to the urge for sexual fulfillment, some couples have chosen to pursue nonmonogamous relationships. While occurring in a variety of forms, open relationships have been pursued as a means of providing sexual fulfillment and as a means of countering those energies that lead to infidelity. Although the research considering the success of such relationships is lacking, those few reports addressing open relationships have suggested that this alternative relationship style has been successfully pursued by many who have sought such experiences. However, it is understood that the data considered reflect the attitudes of those who are currently having success in these alternative styles. Future reports will undoubtedly reveal more about the implications of nonmonogamous relationships.

Whether or not a couple adopts a monogamous or nonmonogamous relationship, a couple's success does not often occur in the absence of attention to those factors that challenge committed relationships. The novelty of new, passionate relationships often obscures attention to the challenges that most couples will face. However, for those couples who are willing to talk about the nature of their sexual and emotional intimacies and who commit to overcoming the challenges they face, sex and intimacy can come together in a long-term and fulfilling way.

REFERENCES

Anapol, D. M. (1997). *Polyamory: The new love without limits.* San Raphael, CA: Inti-Net Resource Center.

Barash, D. P., & Lipton, J. E. (2001). *The myth of monogamy: Fidelity and infidelity in animals and people.* New York: W. H. Freeman.

Barker, M. (2005). This is my partner, and this is my . . . partner's partner: Constructing a polyamorous identity in a monogamous world. *Journal of Constructivist Psychology, 18*(1), 75–88.

Bergstrand, C., & Williams, J. B. (2000). Today's alternative marriage styles: The case of swingers. *Electronic Journal of Human Sexuality, 3(10).*

Brehm, S. S., Perlman, D., Miller, R. S., & Campbell, S. M. (2002). *Intimate relationships.* New York: McGraw-Hill.

Clements, M. L., Cordova, A. D., & Markman, H. J. (1997). The erosion of marital satisfaction over time and how to prevent it. In R. J. Sternberg & M. Hojjat (Eds.), *Satisfaction in close relationships* (pp. 335–355). New York: Guilford Press.

Forthofer, M. S., Markman, H. J., & Cox, M. (1996). Associations between marital distress and work loss in a national sample. *Journal of Marriage & the Family, 58*(3), 597–605.

Glass, S. P., & Wright, T. L. (1997). Reconstructing marriages after the trauma of infidelity. In W. K. Halford & H. J. Markman (Eds.), *Clinical handbook of marriage and couples intervention* (pp. 471–507). New York: John Wiley.

Halford, W. K., & Markman, H. J. (Eds.). (1997). *Clinical handbook of marriage and couples intervention.* New York: John Wiley.

Harding, D. J., & Jencks, C. (2003). Changing attitudes towards premarital sex: Cohort, period, and aging effects. *Public Opinion Quarterly, 67,* 211–226.

Heinlein, K. A., & Heinlein, R. M. (2004). *The sex and love handbook.* Do Things Records & Publishing.

Jamieson, L. (2004). Intimacy, negotiated nonmonogamy, and the limits of the couple. In J. Duncombe, K. Harrison, G. Allan, & D. Marsden (Eds.), *The state of affairs: Explorations in infidelity and commitment* (pp. 35–57). Mahwah, NJ: Erlbaum.

LaSala, M. C. (2004). Extradyadic sex and gay male couples: Comparing monogamous and nonmonogamous relationships. *Families in Society, 85*(3), 405–412.

Laumann, E. O., Gagnon, J. H., Michael, R. T., & Michaels, S. (1994). *The social organization of sexuality: Sexual practices in the United States.* Chicago: University of Chicago Press.

Lindahl, K. M., Malik, N. M., & Bradbury, T. N. (1997). The developmental course of couples' relationships. In W. K. Halford & H. J. Markman (Eds.), *Clinical handbook of marriage and couples intervention* (pp. 203–223). New York: John Wiley.

Mashek, D. J., & Aron, A. P. (2004). *Handbook of closeness and intimacy.* Mahwah, NJ: Erlbaum.

McGinley, R. (1995). History of swinging. Steve & Sharon's Internet Lifestyle Club. http://www.stwd.com/ss/info/history.html

O'Neill, N., & O'Neill, G. (1972). *Open marriage: A new lifestyle for couples.* New York: M. Evans.

Rouse, L. (2002). *Marital and sexual lifestyles in the United States: Attitudes, behaviors and relationships in social context.* Binghamton, NY: Hawthorne Press.

Simpson, J. A., & Gangestad, S. W. (1991). Individual differences in sociosexuality: Evidence for convergent and discriminant validity. *Journal of Personality and Social Psychology, 60*(6), 870–883.

Spence, H. (1997). Sex and relationships. In W. K. Halford & H. J. Markman (Eds.), *Clinical handbook of marriage and couples intervention* (pp. 73–101). New York: John Wiley.

Sternberg, R. J. (1986). *A triangular theory of love: Intimacy, passion, commitment.* New York: Basic Books.

Thornton, A., & Young-DeMarco, L. (2001). Four decades of trends in attitudes toward family issues in the United States: The 1960s through the 1990s. *Journal of Marriage & the Family, 63*(4), 1009–1037.

Whitehurst, R. (1983). Sexual behavior in and out of marriage. *Marriage & Family Review, 6*(3–4), 115–124.

Wiederman, M. W., & Allgeier, E. R. (1996). Expectations and attributions regarding extramarital sex among young married individuals. *Journal of Psychology & Human Sexuality, 8*(3), 21–35.

CHAPTER 3

An Evolutionary Psychological Perspective on Infidelity

ALASTAIR P. C. DAVIES, TODD K. SHACKELFORD,
AND AARON T. GOETZ

INTRODUCTION: THE EVOLUTIONARY PSYCHOLOGICAL PERSPECTIVE

Evolutionary psychologists attempt to make sense of current human thought, emotion, and behavior by careful consideration of human evolutionary history. Over this period of time, humans faced many adaptive problems that needed to be solved to survive and reproduce. Generation after generation, over millions of years, natural selection gradually shaped the human brain, favoring circuitry that was good at solving these adaptive problems of our ancestors. The study of psychological adaptations (or evolved psychological mechanisms) is central to evolutionary psychology.

An evolved psychological mechanism is an information-processing module that was selected throughout a species' evolutionary history because it reliably produced behavior that solved a particular adaptive problem (Tooby & Cosmides, 1992). Evolved psychological mechanisms are understood in terms of their specific input, decision rules, and output (Buss, 1995). Each psychological mechanism evolved to take in a narrow range of information—

information specific to a particular adaptive problem. The information (or input) that the organism receives signals the adaptive problem that is being confronted. The input, either internal or external, is then transformed into output (i.e., behavior, physiological activity, or input relayed to another psychological mechanism) via a decision rule—an "if . . . then" procedure. An example of the input, decision rules, and output of a psychological mechanism is appropriate.

Fruit can either be ripe or unripe. Because ripe fruit is more nutritious (i.e., calorically dense) than immature fruit, humans have evolved a preference for ripe fruit. The decision rule regarding the selection of fruit might proceed as follows: "If the fruit tastes sweet, then eat it." If all fruit was maximally saturated with sugar all of the time, then that particular decision rule would not exist. The output associated with this mechanism might be to eat the ripe fruit or to discard the unripe fruit. This example illustrates the fact that psychological mechanisms can operate without any conscious awareness or formal learning, and that we are often blind to their underlying logic. Do you enjoy calorically dense fruit because it provides nutrition needed to carry out activities related to survival and reproduction? Or do you simply enjoy sweet fruit?

Some psychologists seem to be hostile to the idea of applying evolutionary theories to human behavior. One cause of this unwarranted hostility is the misconception that evolutionary analyses are incompatible with (or less important than) nonevolutionary (e.g., sociological or cultural) analyses. Such critics fail to recognize that evolutionary and nonevolutionary approaches operate at different levels of analysis (Tinbergen, 1963). Evolutionary scientists are typically interested in causation at the ultimate (or distal) level. An ultimate explanation refers to the evolved function of a trait, behavior, or mechanism. This is in contrast to proximate explanations. Although, of course, the mechanisms by which proximate causes are effected have, themselves, evolved, proximate explanations refer to the immediate, nonevolutionary causes of a trait, behavior, or mechanism (e.g., the genetic or cellular causes). In our example of the input, decision rules, and output of a psychological mechanism associated with ripe fruit, one could correctly note that humans prefer ripe fruit because it is perceived to be sweet (proximate cause) and because it provides needed calories to perform duties related to survival and reproduction (ultimate cause). Although the explanations are fundamentally different, they are compatible and equally important.

The level of physical aggression or violence in society offers an additional example of a phenomenon where there exists a misconceived perception that there exists a conflict between evolutionary and nonevolutionary explanations. Nonevolutionary accounts argue that levels of violence are increased by depictions of it in the media causing individuals to imitate what they see. Thus, more media depictions of physical aggression lead to more imitations and thus more violence in society. While evolutionary psychologists do not disagree with this nonevolutionary account, they aver that such an account fails to explain *why* greater levels of media violence lead to imitation and, thus, to greater levels of actual violence. This can only be answered, argue evolutionary psychologists, by considering the adaptive value of violence.

Consequently, evolutionary psychologists contend that aggression evolved as a means for attaining reproductive goals, such as securing resources or mates. If individuals who are not prepared to use violence preemptively or in response to violence committed by other individuals are in an environment where there exists a significant proportion of individuals who readily use violence, the former individuals will be at a reproductive disadvantage. Evolutionary psychologists posit, therefore, that individuals have evolved a psychological mechanism that makes them sensitive to the level of violence in their environment, causing them to be relatively more ready to commit violence when they perceive there to be relatively high levels of violence around them. As a result, media depictions of violence activate this psychological mechanism in the individuals viewing them, causing the individuals to be more ready to commit violence themselves, even when levels of violence in their actual environment are relatively low (Daly & Wilson, 1988).

This example regarding violence illustrates that while nonevolutionary and evolutionary accounts of phenomena are frequently not incompatible, an evolutionary perspective is likely to provide a more complete understanding of the psychological processes underlying human behavior. Notwithstanding this, it is possible, and not uncommon, to have competing explanations at the same level of analysis (e.g., competing evolutionary psychological hypotheses); such debate is a healthy feature of science.

The modern application of evolutionary principles to the study of human psychology and behavior has opened up numerous new areas of research concerning infidelity. In the rest of this chapter, we discuss two of these areas. First we outline how romantic jealousy is hypothesized to have evolved to facilitate individuals in reducing the likelihood that their partners commit an infidelity and discuss why there are expected to have evolved sex differences in jealousy. We then discuss mate poaching, in which people are aware that the individuals with whom they are attempting to have sexual relations are currently in nominally exclusive relationships with others. Specifically, we outline findings regarding the frequency of poaching, and why people choose to poach or avoid engaging in it.

THE EVOLUTION OF ROMANTIC JEALOUSY

Individuals who commit an infidelity are attempting to increase their own reproductive success at the expense of that of their partners. Evolutionary psychological meta-theory, therefore, predicts that infidelity will have produced evolutionary selection pressures for individuals to evolve adaptations by which to reduce the likelihood of their partners committing an infidelity.

Romantic jealousy is hypothesized to be such an adaptation. Thus, in response to a partner's suspected or actual infidelity, individuals' psychological mechanism for jealousy is expected to be activated, causing them to be motivated to enact behaviors that either restrict their mate's interactions with individuals of the opposite sex or avoid the reproductive costs they might suffer as a result of an infidelity.

Due to a sex difference in parental investment, however, there is expected to be a sex difference in romantic jealousy. Among humans, women's obligatory parental investment is far greater than that of men. Once impregnated, women must gestate the child for 9 months and in the environment of evolutionary adaptedness, or EEA (the period during which modern humans were evolving), were obliged to lactate for several years after giving birth (Howell, 1979). In contrast, the physiological investment, namely, a single ejaculate, that men must make to produce a viable child is relatively tiny.

The relatively great obligatory physiological parental investment of women, in comparison to men, means that a woman's primary reproductive concern is expected to be ensuring that her child reaches reproductive age, so that she avoids wasting this investment. Accordingly, women are expected to be especially desirous to secure a long-term mate who is both able and willing to invest economically in the raising of her children. Perhaps the greatest threat to the reproductive success of a woman, therefore, is her physiological investment in a child going to waste if the child dies as a result of her long-term mate's withdrawal of his economic investment and his redirecting of it toward another woman. This leads to the expectation that, as a high level of emotional commitment from a mate is a reliable indicator of a willingness to continually provide resources, women will have evolved a psychology that causes them to prefer as long-term mates men who indicate that they are emotionally committed to them and so who are unlikely to be emotionally unfaithful.

In contrast, perhaps the greatest threat to the reproductive success of a man is being cuckolded, or unknowingly directing his economic investment toward children to whom he is not genetically related because they are the result of his long-term mate being impregnated by another man. Men run the risk of being cuckolded for, as women are internally fertilized, they can never be entirely sure that the child to whom their long-term mate gives birth is their own. A cuckolded man not only directly furthers the reproductive success of his same-sex rivals, but also has fewer resources to invest in children to whom he is genetically related and with which to attract both long-term and short-term mates. This leads to the expectation that men will have evolved a psychology that causes them to prefer as long-term mates women who indicate that they will not be sexually unfaithful to them.

Since men and women differ in whether romantic or sexual infidelity poses the greater threat to their respective reproductive successes, it is expected that there will be divergent sexual selection pressures across the sexes regarding the evolution of psychological traits to prevent romantic infidelity. As a mate's sexual infidelity poses the greater threat to the reproductive success of a man, men are expected to have evolved a psychology that makes them especially motivated to prevent their partners from being sexually unfaithful. Accordingly, men are hypothesized to be especially likely to experience sexual jealousy, such that they become especially distressed by signs, or actual instances, of their long-term mate being sexually unfaithful to them. In contrast, as a mate's emotional infidelity poses the greater threat to the reproductive success of a woman, women are expected to have evolved a psychology that makes them especially motivated to prevent their partners from being emotionally unfaithful. Thus, women are hypothesized to be especially likely to experience emotional jealousy, in which they feel especially distressed by signs, or actual instances, of their long-term partner forming an emotional attachment to another woman.

This hypothesized sex difference in romantic jealousy has received empirical support from numerous studies. Thus, Buss, Larsen, Westen, and Semmelroth (1992) found that among a sample of American college students, 83% of women but only 40% of men reported that they would find a long-term partner becoming emotionally involved with someone else more distressing than the individual having sexual intercourse with someone else. In contrast, 60% of men but only 17% of women reported that they would find a partner's sexual infidelity more upsetting. These self-report findings were paralleled in measures of both physiological arousal and brow muscle contraction. Thus, when asked to imagine the two types of infidelities, greater responses in terms of pulse rate, skin conductance, and frowning were reliably displayed by men to the scenario involving a sexual infidelity, and by women to the scenario involving an emotional infidelity. These sex differences in the level of distress felt in response to a sexual and an emotional infidelity have found empirical support from numerous other studies, across a broad range of cultures (e.g., Buss et al., 1999; Buunk, Angleitner, Obaid, & Buss, 1996; Sagarin, Becker, Guadagno, Nicastle, & Millevoi, 2003). One way by which a man can reduce his risk of incurring the reproductive costs associated with being cuckolded due to his partner's sexual infidelity is to reduce the likelihood of his partner's lover fertilizing her egg. This can be achieved by placing his sperm in competition to fertilize the egg with that of his partner's lover (Birkhead & Parker, 1997). Accordingly, it is expected that men will have evolved a psychology that motivates them to create sperm competition for this purpose. In accordance with this, Shackelford, LeBlanc, Weekes-Shackelford, Bleske-Rechek, Euler, and Hoier (2002) found that the greater the likelihood that a man's partner had been sexually unfaithful, as indicated by the amount of time that the couple had spent apart, then the more attractive he found her and the more eager he was to copulate with her. The fact that this finding was independent of the amount of time since the couple's last copulation indicates that men have a psychology that motivates them to place their sperm in competition with that of a possible lover of their partner, as soon as possible after the partner's suspected sexual infidelity.

For people to experience romantic jealousy, they have, of course, to believe that there exist individuals who are seeking to have romantic relations with their partners. Some of these individuals who attempt to have romantic relations with individuals who are already in nominally exclusive relationships may be unaware of the targeted individuals' current relationship status. Other individuals, however, are likely to be aware that the people whom they are pursuing are already in romantic relationships. In the rest of this chapter, we discuss findings regarding these latter individuals, or mate poachers.

HUMAN MATE POACHING

Just as it takes two to tango, it takes two to commit a sexual infidelity: the cheater and his or her lover. Nevertheless, although research investigating the psychology of individuals in exclusive relationships who cheat on their partners has been ongoing for several decades (for a review see Thompson, 1983), it was not until 1988 that even the idea of conducting research into the psychology of those individuals with whom cheaters commit a sexual infidelity was first suggested in a published work. This was made by Buss (1988) in an article investigating mate retention tactics (i.e., the ways that individuals attempt to prevent their partners from being unfaithful), in which he stated, "Several further research directions are indicated. The occurrence of mate retention tactics implies the presence of poachers" (p. 315). Over a decade would pass, however, before the first studies investigating the psychology of these *poachers*, who solicit individuals in exclusive romantic relationships to commit a sexual infidelity with them, were published. These studies were carried out in 2001 by Schmitt and Buss (2001). Schmitt and Buss formally defined mate poaching as "behavior intended to attract someone who is already in a romantic relationship" (p. 894). In addition, they provided the label *poached* to those "taken away from their established relationships" (p. 895), and the label *poachees* to "those whose partners are taken away from them" (p. 895).

Schmitt and Buss (2001) used the principles of evolutionary psychology to offer the following delineation as to how the psychology of mate poaching may have evolved. At any one time during the evolution of human psychology, there likely will have been individuals who had mates and individuals who did not have mates. It follows that individuals who had *only* psychological mechanisms that motivated desire for and successful mating with unmated individuals may have been at a relative reproductive disadvantage. This is because they would have been out-competed in the arena of reproduction by any men and women who, in addition, possessed psychological mechanisms that motivated the desire to mate with already-mated individuals (under certain conditions) and the behavioral output that enabled successful mating with them. Accordingly, the latter individuals possessing both types of mechanisms would have been selected for, whereas the former individuals would have been selected against.

In the following we discuss some of the findings of Schmitt and Buss (2001), as well as those of other studies that have extended the understanding of mate poaching. First we outline findings regarding the frequency of poaching. We then discuss findings regarding factors that either motivate people to poach or deter them from doing so.

THE FREQUENCY OF MATE POACHING

One of the goals of Schmitt and Buss (2001) was to determine the frequency of mate poaching. Results from a sample of American undergraduates, with an average age of 20 years and a standard deviation of 2.5 years, indicated that poaching is a prevalent phenomenon. For instance, 64% of men and 49% of women reported having, at some time, attempted to poach someone as a short-term mate; 83% of men and 81% of women reported that, at some time, someone had attempted to poach them as a long-term mate; and 43% of men and 49% of women reported that, at some time, someone had successfully poached them as a long-term mate. Similar results were found among a sample of mature individuals, who ranged from 30 to 65 years, and had an average age of 41 years and a standard deviation of 8.7 years. For instance, 60% of men and 38% of women reported having, at some time, attempted to poach someone as a short-term mate; 93% of men and 82% of women reported that, at some time, someone had attempted to poach them as a long-term mate; and 53% of men and 41% of women reported that, at some time, someone had successfully poached a partner of theirs as a long-term mate.

Employing the same formal definition of poaching as used by Schmitt and Buss (2001), Schmitt et al. (2004) generalized the findings of Schmitt and Buss regarding the frequency of poaching to non-college-based individuals outside of the United States. Thus, in a cross-cultural investigation consisting of community-based, as well as college-based, individuals from 53 nations spanning five continents, Schmitt et al. found levels of poaching that broadly paralleled those found by Schmitt and Buss. For instance, Schmitt et al. found that, in North American samples from Canada, Mexico, and the United States, 62% of men and 40% of women reported having, at some time, attempted to poach someone as a short-term mate and 63% of men and 52% of women reported having, at some time, attempted to poach someone as a long-term mate. In addition, 70% of men and 38% of women in samples from South America (including Argentina, Bolivia, Brazil, Chile, and Peru) reported having, at some time, attempted to poach someone as a short-term mate and 63% of men and 29% of women in samples from Africa (including Botswana, Ethiopia, and Zimbabwe) reported having, at some time, attempted to poach someone as a long-term mate.

Davies, Shackelford, and Hass (2006a) investigated whether significant percentages of individuals would still report having experience with poaching if they were presented with a survey whose devising was informed by a definition of poaching that more clearly demarcated poaching from general romantic attraction (i.e., the attracting of unattached individuals) than that which informed the devising of the surveys presented to participants in the two earlier studies. Thus, unlike the earlier definition, that formulated by Davies et al. made it explicit that to be considered a poacher, the pursuing individual must be aware that the targeted individual is already in a romantic relationship and that this relationship must be considered by all parties (poacher, poached, and poachee) to be exclusive or monogamous, such that any sexual relations outside of this relationship are viewed as violating it. The definition formulated by Davies et al. was, "Mate poaching occurs when an individual has, or attempts to have, sexual relations with a person that the former individual knows is already in an exclusive relationship with someone else" (p. 9).

As expected, out of a possible 10 comparisons (five categories across two temporal contexts of poaching), nine of the percentages of men in Davies et al. (2006a) who reported some experience with poaching were lower than the corresponding percentages in Schmitt and Buss (2001) ($p < .05$ by the binomial sign test). Four of these differences were significant ($z > 1.96$). For instance, 70% of men in Davies et al., as compared to 95% of men in Schmitt and Buss, reported that, at some time, someone had attempted to poach them as a short-term mate; 19% of men in Davies et al., as compared to 43% of men in Schmitt and Buss, reported that, at some time, someone had successfully poached them as a long-term mate. Further, seven of the 10 percentages of women in Davies et al. were lower than the corresponding percentages in Schmitt and Buss. Three of these differences were significant ($z > 1.96$). For instance, 27% of women in Davies et al., as compared to 63% of women in Schmitt and Buss, reported having, at some time, attempted to poach someone as a long-term mate and 64% of women in Davies et al., as compared to 79% of women in Schmitt and Buss, reported that, at some time, someone had attempted to poach their partner as a long-term mate.

In addition, each of the six percentages for men in Davies et al. (2006a) was lower than the corresponding percentages in Schmitt et al. (2004) ($p < .05$ by the binomial sign test). Four of these differences were significant ($z > 1.96$). For instance, 50% of men in Davies et al., as compared to 63% of men in Schmitt et al., reported having, at some time, attempted to poach someone as a long-term mate, and 19% of men in Davies et al., as compared to 52% of men in Schmitt et al., reported that, at some time, someone had successfully poached them as a long-term mate. Five of the six percentages for women in Davies et al. were lower than the corresponding percentages in Schmitt et al. Two of these differences were significant ($z > 1.96$). 27% of women in Davies et al., as compared to 52% of women in Schmitt et al., reported having, at some time, attempted to poach someone as a long-term mate; and 19% of women in Davies et al., as compared to 48% of women in Schmitt et al., reported that, at some time, someone had successfully poached them as a long-term mate.

These comparisons indicated that, as expected by Davies et al. (2006a), the stricter definition of poaching caused fewer general romantic attractions to be reported as poaches. Davies et al. stated, "We conclude that the percentages of participants in the current study who reported some experience with poaching may be more representative of the actual percentages of people who have experienced poaching" (p. 13). Nevertheless, the percentages of participants in Davies et al. who reported having some experience with poaching were sizable for all categories of poaching and across all temporal contexts.

Schmitt and Buss (2001), Schmitt et al. (2004), and Davies et al. (2006a) are all limited by their reliance on self-reports to secure data (Grimm & Church, 1999). Establishing the veridicality of the estimates provided by these studies would, as Schmitt and Buss (2001) noted, "be an extraordinarily difficult task, given that mate poaching is often conducted clandestinely, rendering observational studies all but impossible to conduct" (p. 912). Nevertheless, although imperfect, self-report may be the best way to secure estimates of the frequency of poaching experiences from large numbers of individuals. Further, as in the aforementioned studies, the collection of data through surveys in which participants are assured of the complete anonymity of their responses may better facilitate individuals in providing veridical accounts than might face-to-face interviews with counselors.

In sum, the findings of Schmitt and Buss (2001), Schmitt et al. (2004), and, in particular, Davies et al. (2006a) indicate that a significant proportion of individuals *actively* set out to steal other people's mates and that many of these individuals are successful in this endeavor. Thus, while counselors are well aware of the prevalence of infidelity, these three studies provide them with robust evidence that infidelity is frequently engaged in deliberately, not incidentally. In the following section, we consider a recent study whose findings may provide counselors with novel insights into the circumstances in which individuals are likely to engage in or avoid poaching.

When Do People Poach?
The Hierarchy of Mating Strategies Hypothesis

Although the aforementioned studies indicated that poaching is a highly prevalent method by which to secure mates, it also appears that many people never engage in poaching. Davies, Shackelford, and Hass (2006b) attempted to determine if there were any factors peculiar to poaching that either motivated individuals to poach or deterred them from doing so. Specifically, they asked participants to rate the extent to which benefits associated with poaching would motivate them personally to attempt to attract an attached individual instead of an unattached individual, and the extent to which costs associated with poaching would motivate them personally to attempt to attract an unattached individual instead of an attached individual. The benefits and costs considered in the study are listed in Table 3.1.

Table 3.1 Mean Ratings of Benefits and Costs

	Sex of Rater	
	Men	Women
	M (SD)	M (SD)
Benefit (Poaching Context)		
Freedom from the need to fully commit oneself to the poached	2.8 (2.5)	2.4 (2.3)
Person has been pre-approved by someone else (short-term)	2.9 (2.7)	2.3 (2.5)
Person has been pre-approved by someone else (long-term)	2.6 (2.5)	2.2 (2.6)
Person has been pre-approved by someone else (exclusive)	2.8 (2.6)	2.6 (2.9)
Excitement of an illicit affair	2.9 (2.8)	2.4 (2.5)
Challenge of trying to attract someone away from their partner (short-term)	3.6 (3.0)	2.3 (2.7)
Challenge of trying to attract someone away from their partner (long-term)	2.7 (2.7)	2.0 (2.4)
Challenge of trying to attract someone away from their partner (exclusive)	2.1 (2.4)	2.1 (2.6)
Gaining revenge on someone who has wronged you (short-term)	3.9 (3.0)	3.4 (3.0)
Gaining revenge on someone who has wronged you (long-term)	2.9 (2.8)	2.7 (2.7)
Gaining revenge on someone who has wronged you (exclusive)	2.3 (2.5)	2.5 (2.9)
Ego is boosted (short-term)	4.4 (3.1)	3.2 (2.9)
Ego is boosted (long-term)	4.2 (3.1)	3.5 (3.1)
Ego is boosted (exclusive)	4.0 (3.1)	3.8 (3.4)
Less likely to have to help raise or financially support the child	2.4 (2.6)	N/A (N/A)
Cost (Poaching Context)		
More bother and effort and less likely to be successful (short-term)	5.3 (2.9)	5.1 (2.9)
More bother and effort and less likely to be successful (long-term)	5.3 (2.9)	5.3 (2.8)
More bother and effort and less likely to be successful (exclusive)	5.6 (3.0)	5.7 (2.9)
Danger of being physically harmed (short-term)	3.9 (3.1)	4.8 (3.2)
Danger of being physically harmed (long-term)	4.0 (3.1)	5.0 (3.3)
Danger of being physically harmed (exclusive)	4.1 (3.2)	5.5 (3.0)

Table 3.1   Mean Ratings of Benefits and Costs

	Sex of Rater	
	Men	Women
	M (SD)	M (SD)
Stress of concealment and deception (short-term)	5.1 (3.0)	5.4 (2.9)
Stress of concealment and deception (long-term)	5.3 (3.0)	5.6 (3.0)
Stress of concealment and deception (exclusive)	5.9 (8.0)	5.8 (3.0)
Feelings of guilt and ethical concerns (short-term)	5.8 (2.8)	6.0 (2.8)
Feelings of guilt and ethical concerns (long-term)	5.9 (2.7)	6.0 (2.9)
Feelings of guilt and ethical concerns (exclusive)	6.1 (2.9)	6.6 (2.7)
Suffer shame and gain a bad reputation (short-term)	4.8 (2.9)	6.1 (2.9)
Suffer shame and gain a bad reputation (long-term)	4.8 (3.0)	6.3 (2.8)
Suffer shame and gain a bad reputation (exclusive)	5.0 (3.1)	6.5 (2.7)
Greater risk of raising baby on your own	N/A (N/A)	6.3 (3.0)
Sexually unfaithful to previous partner (exclusive)	6.0 (2.8)	5.8 (3.1)
Emotionally unfaithful to previous partner (exclusive)	4.8 (2.7)	4.5 (2.8)

Note. M = mean, SD = standard deviation, N/A = not applicable. See text for additional
  information.

In addition, Davies et al. (2006b) framed each question such that participants were equally attracted to the attached and the unattached potential mates.
This was done in order to control all variables extraneous to the relationship
status of the targeted individuals and the particular benefit or cost of poaching
considered in a particular question. The aim of this methodology was to ensure
that participants' ratings of each benefit and cost would be based solely on
whether the targeted individuals were attached or unattached. As such, Davies
et al. expected to gain insight into the influence that each benefit and cost associated with poaching would be likely to have on the decision-making process
of individuals contemplating whether or not to poach.

Further, it was hoped that phrasing the questions such that participants
were "equally attracted" to the potential mates, as opposed to stating that the
potential mates were "equally attractive," might better allow each participant
to apply his or her own criteria of attractiveness, including not only physical attractiveness but also such attributes as ambition, social status, wealth,
health, kindness, and generosity. It was argued that this was important
because several studies have found there to be sex differences and temporal
context effects in preferences along attributes of mates (e.g., Buss, 1989; Buss
& Schmitt, 1993).

To gain insight into motivations that are specific to poaching, Davies et
al. (2006b) mostly considered only benefits and costs that are exclusive to
poaching—that is, those that do not pertain to general romantic attraction or

attracting unattached individuals. Davies et al. also considered both a benefit and a cost that may also apply to general romantic attraction but which are especially likely to be encountered in the context of poaching. This benefit was, "Less likely to have to help raise or financially support the child." A question considering this benefit was presented to male participants only, as, argued Davies et al., it does not seem reasonable that poaching, in comparison to attracting an unattached individual, would provide women with a greater opportunity to avoid economically investing in any children thus produced. Accordingly, asking female participants to rate this benefit would be unlikely to provide insight that would be specific to poaching. Davies et al. used the following evolutionary reasoning to account for the sex-specific nature of the question regarding this benefit.

First, throughout the evolutionary history of humans, men could never have been certain that any child was their own. Second, due to their relatively small physiological investment in producing viable offspring, men could have increased their reproductive success in proportion to the number of mates that they would have been able to attain, and, displaying resources would have been important in facilitating attaining such mates (Buss, 1989; Buss & Dedden, 1990; Schmitt & Buss, 1996). Accordingly, men are expected to have an evolved psychology that motivates them to welcome opportunities that might enable them to avoid depleting their own resources through having other men unknowingly invest in their offspring—especially likely when poaching, as a poached woman already has a long-term partner. An awareness of modern DNA testing for paternity is unlikely to influence this motivation, for, as such testing did not exist during the period when humans were evolving, it could not have produced evolutionary selection pressures. Accordingly, as with other evolutionary-novel phenomena, DNA testing is not a stimulus that human psychology is expected to have evolved to be sensitive to during the process of motivating behavior.

The latter cost was, "Greater risk of raising baby on your own." A question considering this cost was presented to female participants only, for Davies et al. (2006b) contended that it does not seem reasonable that poaching a woman, as opposed to attracting an unattached woman, would increase this risk for a man. Accordingly, asking male participants to rate this benefit would be unlikely to provide insight that would be specific to poaching. Davies et al. (2006b) used the following evolutionary reasoning to account for the sex-specific nature of the question regarding this cost. Women's relatively great physiological investment to producing viable offspring is expected to have caused them to evolve a psychology that motivates them to be especially wary of mating with men who may not economically invest in their children (Buss & Schmitt, 1993; Buunk et al., 1996)—especially likely when poaching, as a poached man already has a long-term partner.

The foregoing aspects of Davies et al.'s (2006b) study are illustrated in *Question 1* from the survey presented to participants:

Suppose that there are two individuals to whom you are equally sexually attracted, and you know that one of them is in an exclusive relationship and the other is single. Would the suggested benefit "freedom from the need to fully commit yourself to the poached" motivate *you personally* to attempt to attract the *attached* individual, instead of attempting to attract the *unattached* individual? (italics in original)

As mating strategies have been shown to be sensitive to temporal context or relationship length for which the poacher pursues the poached (Barash & Lipton, 2001; Buss & Schmitt, 1993; Schmitt & Buss, 1996), where appropriate, Davies et al. (2006b) investigated participants' ratings of benefits and costs across three temporal contexts of poaching. These were poachings for a short-term sexual partner or affair, a long-term sexual partner or affair, and a new exclusive relationship, in which the poached permanently abandons his or her initial relationship.

METHODS

Participants in Davies et al. (2006b) were 215 undergraduates at a public university in the southeastern United States (125 men, M age = 19.9 years, SD = 3.2; 90 women, M = 19.8, SD = 4.2). Participants completed a survey that asked them to rate the likelihood that several benefits and costs exclusive to poaching would, respectively, motivate them to poach or deter them from poaching. Participants provided ratings on a 10-point scale, with 0 = *Definitely No*, 4 = *Probably No*, 5 = *Probably Yes*, and 9 = *Definitely Yes*. A rating of "5" or greater for a benefit was interpreted as indicating that the benefit would motivate the participant to attempt to attract the attached individual instead of the unattached individual (i.e., the benefit would motivate the participant to poach). A rating of "5" or greater for a cost was interpreted as indicating that the cost would motivate the participant to attempt to attract the unattached individual instead of the attached individual (i.e., the cost would deter the participant from poaching).

RESULTS

We first consider the mean ratings provided by men and women in Davies et al. (2006b) for the benefits and costs of poaching. Next, we present additional findings regarding sex differences relating to ratings of benefits and costs. Table 3.1 presents mean ratings and standard deviations by sex for all benefits and costs. The results of all statistical tests were evaluated at p = .05 (two-tailed).

Mean Ratings for Benefits and Costs Specific to Poaching

Both men and women gave all benefits associated with poaching a mean rating of less than 5.0, indicating that none of the benefits would motivate them to poach. The mean ratings provided by both men and women for the majority of the benefits were between 2.0 and 3.0. In contrast, the mean ratings given by both men and women for the majority (13 of 19) of the costs associated with poaching were above 5.0, indicating that these costs would deter them from poaching. Men gave a mean rating below 5.0 for five of the costs. Women gave a mean rating below 5.0 for three of the costs.

These results suggest that both sexes perceive the costs exclusively associated with poaching as outweighing the benefits exclusively associated with poaching. Davies et al. (2006b), therefore, argued that, ceteris paribus, when given the choice, both men and women will reliably choose to mate with unattached, as opposed to attached, individuals. As such, the results indicate that people will avoid poaching if there is a sufficiently attractive unattached individual available or attainable. In other words, for men and women to be motivated to poach, argued Davies et al., either any available attached individual must be perceived as being more attractive than any available unattached individual or there must be no unattached individual attainable.

These findings led Davies et al. (2006b) to suggest that, in some instances, poaching may be similar as a mating strategy (although not as morally reprehensible) to rape as depicted by Thornhill and Thornhill (1983) in their *mate deprivation hypothesis*. This hypothesis holds that rape is an evolved conditional mating strategy of men, engaged in when mates cannot be secured through nonaggressive strategies. Davies et al., therefore, argued that, in some instances, poaching may be an evolved conditional strategy by which individuals who are unable to secure unattached mates of acceptable attractiveness can avoid being left out of the mating game, without resorting to rape, in the case of men, or to aggressive seduction, in the case of women. This led Davies et al. to hypothesize that men and women may pursue a hierarchy of conditional mating strategies. First, they try to attract an unattached individual of sufficient attractiveness. If none of acceptable attractiveness is available or attainable, some men and women may then try to poach a sufficiently attractive attached individual. If none is available, some men and women may then resort to coercive mating strategies.

Davies et al. (2006b) stated that this *hierarchy of mating strategies hypothesis* is in accordance with the relative degree of opprobrium associated with these mating strategies. Thus, due to the fact that the costs incurred in terms of social standing increase as one moves down this hierarchy from attracting unattached individuals, through poaching, to coercion, individuals may do so only when the immediately higher strategy appears to be closed to them.

For several benefits and costs associated with poaching, Davies et al. (2006b) found sex differences. We outline these in the section that follows.

Sex Differences in Ratings for Benefits and Costs

Davies et al. (2006b) found several sex differences regarding participants' perceptions of benefits and costs exclusively associated with poaching. In discussing these sex differences, Davies et al. illustrated how evolutionary psychological reasoning can be used to account for human motivations.

Women rated the "danger of being physically harmed by the partner of the poached" a greater disincentive to poaching than did men, across all three temporal contexts: for a short-term sexual partner [t (212) = -2.14, $p < .05$]; for a long-term sexual partner [t (212) = -2.17, $p < .05$]; for a new monogamous relationship [t (212) = -3.05, $p < .05$]. Throughout human evolutionary history, physical violence has been a central feature of intra-male competition for mates, and is the primary reason why men have evolved to, typically, have a greater body mass than women (Geary, 1998). Any men who displayed a fear of being physically harmed in intra-male competition would have given their same-sex rivals a psychological advantage in such contests and, consequently, are likely to have had a relatively low reproductive success. Accordingly, men are expected to have evolved a psychology that causes them to be less likely to experience fear in response to threats of violence or more likely to self-deceive or to bluff about their fear. Hence, the lower ratings given by men.

Men gave a higher rating than women for the benefit, "challenge of trying to attract someone away from their partner," as a short-term sexual partner [t (213) = 3.33, $p < .05$] and for a long-term sexual affair [t (213) = 2.00, $p < .05$]. Men also gave a higher rating than women for the benefit of gaining an "ego boost" from successfully poaching someone as a short-term sexual partner [t (213) = 2.74, $p < .05$]. These findings might have been predicted through the following evolutionary reasoning.

Women's obligatory parental investment is far greater than that of men. Whereas men must solely contribute a single ejaculate, once impregnated, women must gestate the child for 9 months and, throughout much of human evolutionary history were obliged to lactate for several years after giving birth (Howell, 1979). During this period of gestation and lactation, evolving women would have remained infertile. In addition, in comparison to that of men, women's fertility exhibits greater variability over the lifespan, falling at a relatively fast rate from their mid- to late twenties until ending after menopause. This means that at any particular time during human evolution, the pool of fertile women will have been significantly smaller than the pool of fertile men. This will have been exacerbated by the fact that evolving humans, like humans today, were effectively polygynous (Alexander, Hoodland, Howard, Noonan, & Sherman, 1979), resulting in some men monopolizing sexual access to more than one woman. Consequently, a relatively large number of fertile men will have been competing for sexual access to a relatively small number of fertile women. In addition, the relatively small physiological constraint on the reproductive success of men means that once a man has impregnated one woman, he can, in theory, quickly move on to impregnate another. Thus, the incremental increase in reproductive success relative to same-sex rivals gained from each additional mate secured is far greater for men than it is for women.

The foregoing means that, in comparison to women, men are subject to a relatively greater intensity of intrasexual competition for mates. It follows that, relative to women, men may have evolved a psychology that motivates them to be more willing to undertake the challenges and risks associated with attracting mates for nonexclusive relationships (i.e., for short-term sex or long-term sexual affairs) and to gain more of a thrill from doing so (Wilson & Daly, 1985). The reproductive benefits that men, in comparison to women, can secure from having multiple mates also may account for the finding that men gave a higher rating than women for the benefit of gaining an "ego boost" from successfully poaching someone as a short-term sexual partner.

Women gave a higher rating than men for the cost, "suffer shame and gain a bad reputation" if one becomes known to have poached someone, across all temporal contexts: for a short-term sexual partner [t (209) = -3.22, p < .05]; for a long-term sexual affair [t (208) = -3.49, p < .05]; for a monogamous long-term relationship [t (207) = -3.64, p < .05]. Evolutionary psychological meta-theory predicts that, due to paternity uncertainty, men will have an evolved psychology that motivates them to avoid long-term commitments with women who have a reputation for being sexually promiscuous (Buss, 1989). Accordingly, it might be predicted that women will have, in turn, evolved a psychology that motivates them to avoid gaining such a reputation. This may account for the relatively high rating given by women to the cost associated with gaining a reputation for poaching individuals for relationships other than those that are both long-term and monogamous. This argument does not, however, account for why women wish to avoid a reputation for having poached someone for a monogamous, long-term relationship. Future research might query individuals about their views on forming an exclusive long-term relationship with someone who has a reputation for being a poacher. If men indicate that they would be unwilling to form a long-term relationship with women who have a reputation for poaching individuals for such a relationship, this would be consistent with women's unwillingness to gain a reputation for doing so.

Davies et al. (2006b) found it interesting that the only significant sex differences identified in their study were that men reported that certain benefits would be more likely to motivate them to poach and that women reported that certain costs would be more likely to deter them from poaching. They stated that, although it is important to keep in mind that men gave all of the benefits a rating of less than 5.0—indicating that none of the benefits would be likely to motivate them to poach—these sex differences suggest that, in comparison to women, for men to be motivated to poach, the attached individual need not be so much more attractive than the unattached individual. This led Davies et al. to predict that men may be more ready than women to move down the aforementioned hierarchy of mating strategies from general romantic attraction to poaching. This prediction is supported by findings that, across numerous world regions, men report engaging in more poaching attempts than do women (Davies et al., 2006a; Schmitt et al., 2004; Schmitt & Buss, 2001).

Davies et al. (2006b) discussed several aspects in which their study might be limited. In the next section, we consider these limitations and outline how Davies et al. suggested that they might be addressed in future research.

Limitations and Future Directions

As none of the benefits but most of the costs exclusively associated with poaching received a rating above 5.0, Davies et al. (2006b) concluded that their results indicate that men and women will choose to poach only when the attached individual is sufficiently more attractive than the unattached individual. They suggested that it might be argued, however, that they simply failed to identify any of the benefits exclusively associated with poaching that would motivate individuals to poach. Davies et al. believed this to be unlikely. This is due to the fact that they presented participants with all benefits exclusively associated with poaching that they identified from a review of the poaching literature, as well as additional potential benefits that they derived from evolutionary psychological principles. It, therefore, seemed reasonable to assume, argued Davies et al., that if there were benefits exclusive to poaching that *do* motivate individuals to poach, *at least one* of the benefits presented to participants in their study would have been among them.

As with any study that employs a self-report methodology, there is always the possibility that participants' responses may be influenced by social desirability concerns. Thus, participants may have failed to give any of the benefits a rating greater than 5.0 due to social norms that frown upon the stealing of the romantic partners of others. Davies et al. (2006b) contended that these concerns were somewhat mitigated by the fact that participants were assured both verbally and in written form of the anonymity of their responses. Self-presentation concerns may, however, still have made some participants reluctant to report that any of the benefits would motivate them to poach. Nevertheless, around 50% of men and 30% of women in their sample reported having attempted to poach someone at some time (Davies et al., 2006a). Thus, argued Davies et al., as it does not seem reasonable that self-presentation concerns would have prevented participants from admitting that any of the benefits would motivate them to poach, while failing to prevent them from admitting to actually having attempted to poach, it appears unlikely that such concerns greatly influenced participants' ratings of benefits. Davies et al. stated that it seemed reasonable, therefore, to accept the finding that none of the benefits considered in the study were substantial enough to motivate any of the participants to poach when the available attached and unattached individuals are perceived as being equally attractive.

Davies et al. (2006b) suggested that their finding that for men and women to be motivated to poach, any available attached individual must be perceived as being more attractive than any available unattached individual, indicates that an issue that should be investigated in future research is *how much* more attractive than an unattached individual must an attached individual be if someone is to be motivated to poach. Further, given the aforementioned hypothesis that men may be more ready to move from attracting unattached individuals to poaching, there would be value in such research investigating sex differences in any such attractiveness disparity.

Another limitation suggested by Davies et al. (2006b) is that participants were asked to rate each benefit in sequential order and before they had been presented with any of the costs. As ratings are likely to be relative, not absolute, the ratings given by participants may, thus, have been influenced by order effects and the fact that participants were unable to consider all of the benefits and costs before providing ratings. Further, we speculate that actual potential poachers might weigh up all benefits and all costs against each other simultaneously. In reality, therefore, the decision-making process undergone by individuals contemplating a mate poach may be more complicated than that suggested by the question format used in the present study, in which each benefit and cost was isolated from all others. Davies et al. stated that future research into the motivations for and against poaching that addresses these limitations might secure ratings that better reflect the influence that particular benefits and costs have on poaching decisions.

An additional potential limitation considered by Davies et al. (2006b) is that it was assumed in constructing the survey that the benefits and costs of poaching are independent. This assumption may not be correct. For instance, the costs, "risk of being physically harmed" and "stress of concealment and deception" may be related to the benefits, "challenge of trying to attract someone away from their partner" and "excitement of an illicit affair." Davies et al., therefore, suggested that there is likely to be value in considering such reciprocal relationships in future studies.

Davies et al. (2006b) suggested several variables not considered in their study that would be worthwhile considering in future research. These include whether the potential poacher is attached or unattached, whether he or she has dependent children, and whether the potential poached has dependent children. Davies et al. stated that such factors might affect any cost-benefit analyses conducted by individuals when they are deciding whether to poach.

SUMMARY AND IMPLICATIONS FOR COUNSELORS

Evolutionary psychology posits that the mind consists of numerous domain-specific psychological mechanisms, each of which evolved because it motivated behavior that solved a particular adaptive problem. By doing so, these mechanisms increased the reproductive success of individuals possessing them relative to that of individuals who did not possess them. As a result the mechanisms spread to fixation, such that all humans evolved to possess them.

From an evolutionary psychological perspective, therefore, infidelity is not seen as a psychological or behavioral disorder. Rather, infidelity is viewed as a strategy motivated by the proper operation of an evolved psychological mechanism by which individuals attempt to increase their own reproductive success at the expense of that of their partners. Infidelity, therefore, is expected to have led to the evolution of an additional psychological mechanism that causes individuals to experience romantic jealousy in response to a suspected or actual infidelity of their partner. This is because romantic jealousy motivates individuals to enact behaviors that reduce the likelihood that their partners will commit a romantic infidelity or facilitate them in avoiding the reproductive costs associated with being the victim of an infidelity. Further, through a consideration of the sex difference in obligatory parental investment, evolutionary psychological reasoning has identified that men are more likely to experience greater distress in response to a partner's sexual infidelity, whereas women are more likely to experience greater distress in response to a partner's emotional infidelity.

An evolutionary perspective also suggests that, as at any particular time during humans' evolutionary history a significant proportion of individuals will have been mated, humans will have evolved a psychological mechanism for mate poaching. In accordance with this, research presented in this chapter indicates that a significant proportion of individuals are aware that the individuals with whom they are attempting to have sexual relations are currently in nominally exclusive relationships with others. Moreover, by facilitating the identification of benefits and costs specifically associated with poaching and accounting for sex differences in the importance placed on them, evolutionary reasoning has allowed researchers to gain a greater understanding of why people choose to poach or avoid doing so. In addition, such reasoning has enabled researchers to secure findings that suggest that poaching is pursued only if there are no unattached individuals of sufficient attractiveness available. This has led evolutionary psychologists to hypothesize that people may pursue a *hierarchy of mating strategies*, in which poaching may fall between general romantic attraction and coercive strategies.

As we are not clinicians ourselves, we hesitate to offer specific advice as to how to counsel individuals who commit or are victims of infidelities. We hope, however, that this chapter has illustrated the value of using evolutionary reasoning to provide insight into infidelity. Accordingly, we suggest that by considering the selection pressures that resulted in the evolution of human psychology, counselors may better understand the motivations that lead individuals to commit infidelities and the distress experienced by those who are cheated on.

REFERENCES

Alexander, R. D., Hoodland, J. L., Howard, R. D., Noonan, K. M., & Sherman, P. W. (1979). Sexual dimorphisms and breeding systems in pinnepeds, ungulates, primates, and humans. In N. A. Chagnon & W. Irons (Eds.), *Evolutionary biology and human social behavior* (pp. 402–435). North Scituate, MA: Duxbury Press.

Barash, D. P., & Lipton, J. E. (2001). *The myth of monogamy*. New York: Freeman.

Birkhead, T. R., & Parker, G. A. (1997). Sperm competition and mating systems. In J. R. Krebs & N. B. Davies (Eds.), *Behavioral ecology* (pp. 121–145). Oxford: Blackwell Science.

Buss, D. M. (1988). The evolution of human intrasexual competition: Tactics of mate attraction. *Journal of Personality & Social Psychology, 54,* 616–628.

Buss, D. M. (1989). Sex differences in human mate preferences: Evolutionary hypothesis tested in 37 cultures. *Behavioral and Brain Science, 12,* 1–49.

Buss, D. M. (1995). Evolutionary psychology: A new paradigm for psychological science. *Psychological Inquiry, 6,* 1–20.

Buss, D. M., & Dedden, L.A. (1990). Derogation of competitors. *Journal of Social & Personal Relationships, 7,* 395–422.

Buss, D. M., Larsen, R., Western, D. and Semmelroth, J. (1992). Sex differences in jealousy: Evolution, physiology and psychology. *Psychological Science* 3: 251–255.

Buss, D. M., & Schmitt, D. P. (1993). Sexual strategies theory: An evolutionary perspective on human mating. *Psychological Review, 100,* 204–232.

Buss, D. M., Shackelford, T. K., Kirkpatrick, L. A., Choe, J. C., Lim, H. K., Hasegawa, M., Hasegawa, T., & Bennett, K. (1999). Jealousy and the nature of beliefs about infidelity: Tests of competing hypotheses about sex differences in the United States, Korea and Japan. *Personal Relationships, 6,* 125–150.

Buunk, B. P., Angleitner, A., Obaid, V., & Buss, D. M. (1996). Sex differences in jealousy in evolutionary and cultural perspective: Tests from the Netherlands, Germany, and the United States. *Psychological Science, 7,* 359–363.

Daly, M., & Wilson, M. (1988). *Homicide*. New York: Aldine de Gruyter.

Davies, A. P. C., Shackelford, T. K., & Hass, R. G. (2006a). When a "poach" is not a poach: Re-defining human mate poaching and re-estimating its frequency. Manuscript under editorial review.

Davies, A. P. C., Shackelford, T. K., & Hass, R. G. (2006b). To poach or not to poach: When do people steal other people's mates? Manuscript under editorial review.

Geary, D. C. (1998). *Male, female: The evolution of human sex differences*. Washington, DC: American Psychological Association.

Grimm, S. D., & Church, A. T. (1999). A cross-cultural study of response bias in personality measures. Journal of Research in Personality, *33,* 415–441.

Howell, N. (1979). *Demography of the Dobe !Kung*. New York: Academic.

Sagarin, B. J., Becker, D. V., Guadagno, R. E., Nicastle, L. D., & Millevoi, A. (2003). Sex differences (and similarities) in jealousy: The moderating influence of infidelity experience and sexual orientation of the infidelity. *Evolution and Human Behavior, 24,* 17–23.

Schmitt, D. P., Alcalay, L., Allik, J., Angleitner, A., Ault, L., Austers, I., et al. (2004). Patterns and universals of mate poaching across 53 nations: The effects of sex, culture, and personality on romantically attracting another person's partner. *Journal of Personality and Social Psychology, 86,* 560–584.

Schmitt, D. P., & Buss, D. M. (1996). Strategic self-promotion and competitor derogation: Sex and context effects on perceived effectiveness of mate attraction tactics. *Journal of Personality and Social Psychology, 70,* 1185–1204.

Schmitt, D. P., & Buss, D. M. (2001). Human mate poaching: Tactics and temptations for infiltrating existing relationships. *Journal of Personality and Social Psychology, 86,* 560–584.

Shackelford, T. K., LeBlanc, G. J., Weekes-Shackelford, V. A., Bleske-Rechek, A. L., Euler, H. A., & Hoier, S. (2002). Psychological adaptation to human sperm competition. *Evolution and Human Behavior, 23,* 123–138.

Thompson, A. P. (1983). Extramarital sex: A review of the research literature. *Journal of Sex Research, 19,* 1–22.

Thornhill, R., & Thornhill, N. W. (1983). Human rape: An evolutionary analysis. *Ethology and Sociobiology, 4,* 137–173.

Tinbergen, N. (1963). On aims and methods of ethology. *Zeitschrift fur Tierpsychologie, 20,* 410–433.

Tooby, J., & Cosmides, L. (1992). The psychological foundations of culture. In J. H. Barkow, L. Cosmides, & J. Tooby (Eds.), *The adapted mind* (pp. 19–136). New York: Oxford University Press.

Wilson, M., & Daly, M. (1985). Competitiveness, risk-taking, and violence: The young male syndrome. *Ethology and Sociobiology, 6,* 59–73.

PART II

The Treatment of Infidelity in Couples Therapy

CHAPTER 4

Research on Couple Therapy for Infidelity

What Do We Know About Helping Couples When There Has Been an Affair?

DEBORAH E. KESSEL, JESSICA H. MOON, AND DAVID C. ATKINS

Wife: I can not believe this, just can not believe it. Do you have any idea—any idea—what you have done? To me, to our family? I mean, who are you? I don't even know you any more. You certainly aren't the man that I married; that man would never have cheated on me—slept with some other woman and lied to me for six months. [starting to cry] Say something damn it; don't you have anything to say?

Husband: [Silence; looks up at therapist]

Infidelity is often experienced as a betrayal, and few relationship events can be as devastating. Couples and therapists can feel lost in a wash of emotion when an affair is revealed, and both may wonder what resources are available to them to move forward, make sense of their experiences, and heal their pain. Unfortunately, few couple therapy treatments deal explicitly with

55

infidelity or do so in passing, even though a host of self-help books have been written on the subject and research shows that a significant percentage of couples seek therapy specifically to address the effects of infidelity (Doss, Simpson, & Christensen, 2004).

The good news is that two recent research studies examined the efficacy of couple therapy for infidelity, though each took a unique perspective. Gordon, Baucom, and Snyder (2004) developed and tested a forgiveness-based intervention for infidelity. Their research puts forth a model of recovery from infidelity and interventions that are tailored to this process. Atkins, Eldridge, Baucom, and Christensen (2005) examined the efficacy of two broad-based couple therapies to treat infidelity. These research studies provide two alternative perspectives for couple therapy and infidelity: Are infidelity-specific procedures and interventions needed when there has been an affair, or can these couples be treated within the context of traditional, broad-based therapeutic approaches?

Our chapter focuses heavily on these two studies, trying to distill the clinically relevant aspects of their findings. Prior to examining that work, we briefly review the efficacy of couple therapy in general to provide a benchmark against which to compare the outcomes of the infidelity research. Finally, we note several areas of future research and provide a summary of clinical guidelines based on the existing research on infidelity.

OVERVIEW OF COUPLE THERAPY APPROACHES

A wide variety of couple therapies have been developed and are practiced in the community (Gurman & Jacobson, 2002); however, only a few have been subjected to empirical scrutiny (Baucom, Shoham, Mueser, Daiuto, & Stickle, 1998; Snyder, Castellani, & Whisman, 2006). In fact, only three couple therapy approaches have been tested in more than one outcome study: Traditional Behavioral Couple Therapy[1] (TBCT; Jacobson & Margolin, 1979), Cognitive-Behavioral Couple Therapy (CBCT; Epstein & Baucom, 2002), and Emotion-Focused Therapy (EFT; Johnson, 2004).[2] Based on behavioral and social-learning theory, TBCT focuses on teaching couples behavioral skills to address their relationship problems, and CBCT builds upon this by targeting attributions and other types of cognition. Conversely, EFT was developed from an attachment theory perspective and focuses on helping partners communicate emotions to one another around insecure bonding issues. A fourth therapy that is relevant for the current focus on infidelity is Integrative Behavioral Couple Therapy (IBCT; Jacobson & Christensen, 1996). IBCT builds on the change strategies of TBCT but shifts the focus of therapy to acceptance rather than change. The emphasis in IBCT is on (a) helping partners to have compassion and empathy for one another and (b) helping partners to achieve emotional distance from their struggles so that they can discuss them without intense negative affect.

TBCT is, by far, the most commonly studied couple therapy. Over 30 controlled studies have empirically tested the efficacy of TBCT (Shadish & Baldwin, 2005). Moreover, using the criteria of Chambless and Ollendick (2001) for delineating empirically supported treatments (i.e., superiority to no treatment or placebo in two or more studies or equivalence to already established treatment; use of treatment manuals or equivalent, clear description of therapies; characteristics and limitations of samples specified; and effects demonstrated by two different investigators), only TBCT was noted as an "efficacious and specific treatment." However, since the Baucom et al. (1998) review, further research on EFT and IBCT strongly supports both approaches as efficacious. In particular, IBCT was recently tested in the largest clinical trial of couple therapy to date (Christensen et al., 2004).

Several meta-analyses support the distinctions made in qualitative reviews of the efficacy of couple therapy. Hahlweg and Markman (1988) conducted the first meta-analysis of couple therapy in which they examined 17 studies of TBCT. They found that TBCT produced reliable change compared to control groups, and most couples maintained their improvements over the year following therapy. Nonetheless, there is a significant minority of couples that received no benefit from TBCT. In the most comprehensive meta-analysis to date, Shadish and Baldwin (2003) updated earlier meta-analyses and reported an overall, mean effect size of 0.84 for couple therapy in general, which implies that couples receiving treatment would be better off at the end of therapy than 80% of couples who did not receive treatment. In addition, the authors noted that this effect size for couple therapy compares favorably with effects of individual treatment for mental health problems and with medical interventions for physical health problems. After accounting for differences in study methodology (e.g., reactivity of measurement), there was little support for differential effectiveness due to treatment approach.

For the current research, the most pertinent issue is to what extent these various therapies are able to help couples. Or, put another way, what is the success rate of couple therapy? The meta-analyses provide percentages of couples improved relative to control groups, yet even these statistics boil down to tests of mean differences via inferential statistics. However, as Jacobson, Follette, and Revenstorf (1984) noted, statistically significant change does not imply that a distressed couple would be considered nondistressed at the end of therapy; in a similar vein, improvement relative to a control group does not address whether couples are satisfied and healthy functioning at the end of treatment. Therefore, statistical significance based on group means does not directly address the success rate of couple therapy. To address the issue of how individuals (or couples) change in therapy, Jacobson and colleagues proposed a method of clinical significance (Jacobson & Truax, 1991). Clinical significance classifies individuals (or couples) at the end of therapy into one of four categories: deteriorated, unchanged, improved, or recovered (for a review of clinical significance, see McGlinchey, Zimmerman, & Atkins, 2006).

Although there are some variations between studies, clinical significance results for couple therapies are more similar than different across studies and therapies (reviewed in Baucom et al., 1998). Most studies have found that approximately two-thirds of couples improve during therapy and that between one-third and one-half of couples are considered recovered at the end of therapy. Fewer studies have reported data on couples following therapy, but the data that do exist show that a proportion of couples (perhaps as many as one-third) do not maintain the improvement that they experienced in therapy. In an extreme example of deterioration following couple therapy, one study found that 38% of couples who had received TBCT divorced within 4 years following therapy (Snyder, Wills, & Grady-Fletcher, 1991).

Considering the qualitative reviews, meta-analyses, and clinical significance of the couple therapy outcome literature, the results illustrate that those therapies that have been tested are effective with a significant number of couples. However, there is a sizable proportion of couples who receive no benefit from therapy and others who are not able to maintain their therapeutic gains over time. Given these results, it is interesting to consider how infidelity has shaped and impacted the process and outcome of couple therapy. For example, common sense dictates that issues such as infidelity might alter the likelihood that couples respond positively to treatment, yet precious little research has directly assessed couple therapy and infidelity. However, Bennun (1985) found that jealousy was a particularly intractable problem for TBCT, and couple therapists report infidelity as one of the most difficult problems to treat (Whisman, Dixon, & Johnson, 1997). Moreover, infidelity is associated with increased levels of clinical depression in the noninvolved spouse, further complicating therapy with couples in which there has been an affair (Cano & O'Leary, 2000). It may, in fact, be the case that research focused on infidelity and other difficult problems in couple therapy may provide critical information to improve the overall impact of couple therapy.

Finally, as the preceding review suggests, the couple therapy outcome literature has, to date, tended to ignore or treat only in passing the issue of infidelity. For instance, when infidelity has been mentioned in these reports, it has typically been included in a list of presenting problems for therapy. Portraying infidelity in this manner suggests that infidelity is similar to other couple problems, just another problem on the list of problems that couples bring to therapy.

TWO STUDIES FOCUSED ON COUPLE THERAPY FOR INFIDELITY

Now that we have examined the broader couple therapy literature, we turn to focus specifically on infidelity and the efficacy of couple therapy when there has been an affair. The two published studies of couple therapy for infidelity took notably different approaches. Gordon et al. (2004) diverged from the tradition of treating infidelity as just another couple problem and conceptualized infidelity as a relationship trauma. Their treatment focused specifically on forgiving the betrayal a partner may feel when infidelity occurs. Atkins et al. (2005) used a broader approach to study the treatment of infidelity within couple therapy, culling participants from a randomized clinical trial comparing TBCT and IBCT approaches (Christensen et al., 2004). In the following sections, we consider what types of couples were involved in the two studies, what types of interventions were used, how and to what extent the couples changed, and also how the studies offer complementary findings for clinical work with affair couples.

Gordon et al. (2004)

In their study on infidelity treatment, Gordon et al. (2004) solicited couples who were seeking help in dealing with the aftermath of an affair. While the couples presented with communication problems and lowered problem-solving skills, this treatment focused on helping the couple work through the forgiveness process of the affair. Of the six heterosexual couples that participated in the study, only one partner in each couple had been involved in an affair, and the affair ended less than one year prior to the study. Couples where an individual was engaged in an ongoing affair and where both partners were involved in multiple affairs were excluded from the study. Five of the six couples were married, while the other was cohabiting, and five of the six couples had been together between 2 and 4 years, while the sixth couple had been married for 12 years. In two-thirds of the couples, the husband had been involved in the affair.

As might be expected in couples who have experienced an affair, couples reported moderately to highly elevated scores on symptoms related to PTSD, depression, and global marital distress. This was especially true of the non-affair partner. Therapeutic themes included mistrust, lack of physical and emotional intimacy, and fear of confrontation and conflict; in addition, poor communication was a common theme in these relationships, not simply related to the affair. Dysfunctional couple relationship patterns were not the only issues presented in therapy by these couples. A majority of the couples were experiencing major external stressors (e.g., job transitions, relocations, pregnancies, and family of origin problems) before, during, and after the affair. Given this presentation of couples and their problems, therapists needed to manage a variety of clinical issues in addition to the affair, including individual psychopathology that was often related to the affair, poor couple functioning in general, and stressors both internal and external to the couple.

The treatment protocol included 24 to 30 sessions and incorporated behavioral and insight-oriented strategies. There were three primary phases to treatment: (a) dealing with the impact of the affair (e.g., exploring emotional and behavioral disruption, setting new boundaries, maintaining and improving physical health, writing a letter to the partner, and education about flashbacks), (b) exploring the context and finding meaning (e.g., developing a shared understanding of how the affair came about, moving away from blaming to understand the context), and (c) moving on (e.g., focusing on forgiveness, remaining fears and questions). For more detailed information on the treatment approach of Gordon et al. (2004), please see Chapter 6 (this volume). Analyses at the end of treatment and at six months following therapy showed that the noninvolved partner reported improvement in marital satisfaction, depression, and symptoms of PTSD; moreover, they endorsed greater levels of forgiveness for their partner and the affair. These effects were largely maintained at six months following therapy, and the effect size for marital satisfaction of 0.70 is roughly comparable to what has been found in the general couple therapy literature. The results for the involved partners were somewhat different. Participating partners' depression and PTSD symptoms improved during therapy, but there was little change in marital satisfaction. Finally, marital satisfaction at post-therapy and 6 months following therapy hovered right around the cutoff for relationship distress. Thus, couples improved notably in several areas but did not report thriving relationships by the end of treatment.

Atkins et al. (2005)

While the Gordon et al. (2004) study used an infidelity-specific approach to couple therapy, Atkins et al. (2005) took a broader contextual approach, looking at how infidelity and non-infidelity couples fared in TBCT and IBCT approaches. As such, couples were recruited into the research study simply for marital problems and were not recruited based on infidelity. To be admitted into the study, couples met criteria for relationship distress on the Dyadic Adjustment Scale (Spanier, 1976) and the Global Distress Scale of the Marital Satisfaction Inventory – Revised (Snyder, 1997). Of the 134 couples in the larger study, 19 reported affairs by at least one partner. Contrary to the Gordon et al. study, only 32% of the affairs were revealed prior to the beginning of therapy, whereas 42% of affairs were revealed at some point during therapy, and 26% were not revealed at all during therapy.[3] Roughly 50% of the partners who engaged in an affair were men.

Participating couples received up to 26 sessions of either TBCT or IBCT at no cost. Because the primary study was a randomized controlled trial of the two approaches, infidelity was handled clinically in a manner consistent with the interventions of the given therapy. For example, couples receiving TBCT were taught communication and problem-solving skills to discuss the affair and subsequent problems, while couples receiving IBCT worked through the emotional impact of the affair and acceptance of the factors that led up to the affair. Because affairs were revealed at different times during therapy, there was great variability in the amount of time in therapy spent on the affair (M = 37.9%, SD = 31.2%).

Regardless of the amount of time spent on treating the affair, results showed a generally favorable outcome. Participants' marital satisfaction was assessed at four separate points during therapy. Not surprisingly, couples in which there had been an affair were significantly more distressed than non-infidelity couples at the start of therapy, and the involved partner reported greater marital problems than the noninvolved partner, quite different from the findings of Gordon et al. (2004). Furthermore, when compared to the couples in which there was no affair and couples in which the affair was openly discussed, the five couples where an affair was kept secret during the course of treatment were even more distressed initially. Even though couples grappling with infidelity began treatment with greater marital distress, they improved at a greater rate than non-affair couples. When therapy finished, infidelity couples who had addressed the affair in therapy reported levels of marital satisfaction similar to that of those couples in which there had not been an affair. The one caveat to this finding is that the secret affairs couples were almost universally treatment failures and highly distressed at the end of treatment. Similar to the Gordon et al. study, the effect size of change in marital satisfaction ($d = 0.91$) is comparable to the wider couple therapy literature, but couples with infidelity ended therapy right around the cutoff for marital distress.

Comparing the Two Studies: Common Themes and Contrasting Findings

The primary findings of these two studies of couple therapy for infidelity are largely congruent: Couples in which there has been an affair received significant benefit during therapy; at the same time, infidelity couples at the end of treatment still reported significant relationship distress on average. It seems likely that many couples in both studies are at high risk for continued relationship difficulties following therapy. There were also some notable contrasts between the two studies. Participants in the Gordon et al. (2004) study reported elevated levels of depression and PTSD symptoms, which was not found in the Atkins et al. (2005) research. Marital satisfaction gains in the forgiveness-based treatment were limited to the noninvolved partner, with the partner who had participated in the affair reporting no improvement in relationship satisfaction; partners in the Atkins et al. study improved regardless of affair involvement.

How do we make sense of the differences? First, consider the participants. The Gordon et al. (2004) study specifically recruited couples with affairs, whereas the Atkins et al. (2005) study recruited broadly for couples with marital problems. The difference in recruitment had ramifications for the types of couples that enrolled in the studies. In the Atkins et al. study only one-third of affairs were known at the start of therapy; post hoc analyses of outcomes based on when the affair was revealed suggested that couples in which the affair was revealed *during* therapy had somewhat better outcomes (Atkins, 2003). One possible interpretation is that affairs that are revealed during therapy allow the therapist an opportunity to intervene immediately with the couple around the issue of infidelity. It could be that this initial work in containing intense emotions at the revelation of the affair helps these couples to quickly move toward processing the meaning of the affair. Those couples in which the affair was revealed prior to therapy may have been struggling with the affair on their own for some time and perhaps these pre-therapy struggles were detrimental to moving forward with therapy. Thus, the Gordon et al. couples may be most similar to the Atkins et al. couples in which the affair was revealed prior to therapy.

The sample differences may also have some bearing on the individual psychopathology findings. The couples in the Gordon et al. (2004) study knew about the affair for some time (i.e., up to a year) and presumably were not able to effectively deal with the affair on their own. Thus, the study's method of recruitment may have selected for couples who had been deeply affected by the infidelity and unable to move forward. Finally, the Gordon et al. treatment approach focused almost entirely on the affair and did not include components for general couple functioning. This difference with Atkins et al. (2005) may explain why involved partners in the Gordon et al. study did not report gains in marital satisfaction during treatment. One of the take-home messages from these two studies is that there are a variety of kinds of infidelity couples, and it may be that a single approach is not effective for all types. A hybrid approach that includes both infidelity-specific and general couple therapy strategies may provide the most realistic and flexible strategy. Future research will need to follow up on these ideas.

AREAS FOR FUTURE RESEARCH

The research literature on infidelity is growing; however, more outcome research must be done if we are to learn how to effectively help partners understand the cause of the affair and work through its aftermath. The following areas have the potential to make significant contributions to the research literature on infidelity and to the clinicians who work with couples who have experienced affairs.

Secret Affairs

Research shows that couple therapy is not as successful when an individual has kept an affair secret (Atkins et al., 2005). It is quite easy to imagine why this would be the case, as it may speak to a lack of commitment to the primary relationship, or distrust and lack of communication with the primary partner. Case study analyses of the secret affair couples in the Atkins et al. sample suggest that partners engaged in both a clandestine affair and marital therapy with their spouse are truly ambivalent about their two relationships. As others have noted, affair relationships have none of the constraints of committed relationships such as marriages; thus, the process of resolving this ambivalence may tip disproportionately toward choosing the affair partners. Furthermore, ongoing research of the secret affair couples points to negative behavioral markers in the partner who has been unfaithful; participating partners having secret affairs display increasing levels of contempt over the course of therapy (Moon et al., 2006).

Affective Experience of Noninvolved Partner

Finding out that your spouse had an affair can be a devastating experience for the noninvolved partner. The revelation of an affair ushers in a host of emotions including rage, sorrow, shock, and shame. Whisman and Wagers (2005) found that major depressive episodes and post-traumatic stress disorder are the most common diagnoses found in noninvolved partners, particularly women. In these cases, assessment of marital distress, suicidal ideation, and homicidal ideation should follow. However, there is still limited research that addresses treatment for depression and PTSD in conjunction with infidelity. What are appropriate ways for therapists to treat depression and/or PTSD in combination with infidelity? Should treatment involve the involved partner? How is the method of disclosure of the affair related to PTSD symptoms in the noninvolved partner? Beyond psychopathology, what are strategies to help partners regulate their emotions in the face of a significant relationship betrayal?

Same-Sex Couples

Less research has been conducted on the effects of infidelity among same-sex couples (see Blumstein & Schwartz, 1983, for an exception), and no research has been conducted on infidelity in same-sex couples. However, basic research that has compared same-sex couples to heterosexual couples has found similarities in relationship quality and satisfaction (Blasband & Peplau, 1985; Kurdek & Schmitt, 1986). IBCT for heterosexual couples had produced clinically significant improvement in chronically distressed couples (Christensen et al., 2004), and extensions to same-sex couples has produced similar effects (Martell & Land, 2002). Further research assessing whether clinical implications from current infidelity research of heterosexual couples can be generalized to same-sex couples remains to be done.[4]

Infidelity Education in Premarital Counseling

Stanley (2001) has argued that participation in premarital counseling programs such as the Prevention and Relationship Enhancement Program (PREP) can lower a couple's risk for subsequent marital distress or termination. Furthermore, Allen et al. (2005) showed that focusing on "contextual approach factors," those factors that are likely to occur in the process of a developing affair, has been particularly effective in preempting the affair. This is great news for premarital counselors, but few (if any) programs systematically address the potential for an affair, nor has there been any research done on the effectiveness of addressing this topic and the later occurrence of infidelity.

RESEARCH-BASED GUIDELINES FOR WORKING CLINICALLY WITH INFIDELITY

Our earlier review of the research on couple therapy for infidelity focused on the empirical findings. Although complete descriptions of the therapeutic protocols are beyond the scope of the present chapter, in this section we put forth some suggestions culled from the research literature for clinical work with couples in which there has been an affair.

Assessment

As the Atkins et al. (2005) study demonstrated, many affair couples may not present for therapy with infidelity. Thus, assessment can be critical and may help therapists to avoid the surprising revelation of an affair midway through therapy. Although many therapists know this, few routinely ask their clients about infidelity. Naturally, couples and therapists may feel uncomfortable talking about infidelity because it is such a personal topic, and if infidelity is not relevant for a couple, it may feel awkward even to have raised the issue. However, given that approximately 30%–40% of individuals will have an affair at some point in their life (see Atkins, Baucom, & Jacobson, 2001; Wiederman, 1997), affairs, either currently or in the past, will be relevant for many couples seeking therapy. Thus, it is recommended to routinely assess infidelity as therapists would assess other issues such as domestic violence or substance abuse (Whisman & Wagers, 2005). Working with a couple where there is an undisclosed affair is a recipe for frustration if not disaster.

Assessing for infidelity shares many similarities with assessing domestic violence (O'Leary, Vivian, & Malone, 1992). Many individuals may not have revealed their affair to their partner at the start of therapy, and two assessment strategies may assist in honest reporting of infidelity. First, individual assessments with each partner will promote open disclosure. Many couple therapists use individual sessions (or half-sessions) as part of their routine assessment practice, but these can be particularly helpful to promote full disclosure with sensitive issues such as infidelity. However, therapists must be sure to provide guidelines for confidentiality in these sessions (e.g., "I will assume that anything you tell here today will be okay to share with your spouse in our joint sessions unless you tell me otherwise."). If an ongoing affair not known by the partner is revealed to the therapist, there are two primary options for moving forward: (a) the client can reveal the affair to their partner and continue with couple therapy, or (b) the individual can discontinue couple therapy and work with the therapist about what to tell the partner (e.g., "Given the results of the assessment phase of treatment, I think individual therapy might be most appropriate at the present time."). As this simple discussion of assessment highlights, the ethical issues around infidelity can be very tricky (Snyder & Doss, 2005), and many possibilities need to be weighed (e.g., What ethical responsibilities does the couple therapist have to the noninvolved spouse if he or she learns of an undisclosed affair in which there was unprotected sex?). A second method that can assist assessment and truthful reporting of infidelity is to use self-report measures that not only inquire about infidelity but specify a range of specific behaviors. Instead of purely inquiring "Have you had an affair?" questions can ask, "What is the greatest level of physical involvement with someone other than your partner?" with response categories from none to sexual intercourse.

When working with same-sex couples, the therapist should keep in mind that nonmonogamy is often explicitly negotiated within same-sex relationships and may look quite different from nonmonogamy in heterosexual couples. Martell and Prince (2005) provide several recommendations for therapists working with same-sex couples. Assessment should include the couple's definition of infidelity since many different definitions and expectations of fidelity may exist. These expectations of fidelity are more widely varied among same-sex couples than heterosexual couples. Since nonmonogamy is more common in homosexual relationships, assessing the couple's agreement about sexual activity outside of the marriage will help the therapist's understanding of infidelity for the particular couple.

During assessment of infidelity or following its disclosure, therapists should be sensitive to clients' assumptions about affairs, and it can be helpful to consider whether clients endorse certain myths of infidelity. The following statements are commonly believed myths arranged by Pittman and Wagers (2005) that inhibit couples from freely talking about infidelity. By bringing these myths to the surface and providing education, couples may feel freer to discuss infidelity.

1. Everybody is unfaithful. Infidelity is normal, expectable behavior.
2. Affairs can revive a dull marriage.
3. An affair proves that the individual does not love their spouse, so divorce is the natural consequence.
4. The "affairee" is always sexier than the spouse.
5. The affair is the fault of the noninvolved partner and proof that he or she somehow made it necessary for the individuals to have an affair.
6. Keeping the affair a secret will keep from doing damage.
7. Divorce is inevitable after an affair.

Language should also be used carefully to ensure neutrality and avoid bias (Linquist & Negy, 2005). Although most single individuals endorse that they plan to marry and expect to marry only once, couples may have different expectations in marriage and different definitions of infidelity. For example, one couple may consider emotional infidelity as serious as sexual infidelity (Glass & Wright, 1992). However, another couple may view emotional infidelity as harmless as long as there is no physical involvement. Clarifying couple differences ensures that the therapist does not make any assumptions about the expectations in the marriage.

In addition, therapists should be sensitive to the specific language of infidelity and avoid pejorative terms such as "cheated" and "unfaithful" (Whisman & Wagers, 2005). Besides the fact that they can carry negative connotations that may or may not be shared by the couple, it limits disclosures to conventional definitions. Because some instances of infidelity may be merely sexual, such as a one night stand, couples may be more reluctant to label these instances as "affairs." Instead, using the word infidelity and following up with an assessment of instances that violate the couple's expectations of exclusivity is recommended (Whisman & Wagers, 2005).

Infidelity Treatment Checklist

Working with couples who have experienced infidelity can be difficult. This checklist reviews areas of assessment and clinical judgment that may be helpful to incorporate in your therapy plan when working with infidelity couples.

1. During the intake session, ask about any history of infidelity as routinely as other topics such as domestic violence. Be aware that some couples may not have revealed their affair to their spouse and may not feel comfortable talking about this subject candidly.
2. Avoid terms that have negative connotations or convey the personal values of the therapist such as "cheated" or "unfaithful." Some even argue that the word "affair" would fall in this category.
3. In the case where infidelity exists, a thorough assessment of posttraumatic stress disorder, suicidal ideation, homicidal ideation, or other forms of stress should be made. These symptoms should be addressed immediately.
4. Talking about personal infidelity can be embarrassing and shameful. As a clinician, demystify and normalize infidelity in the session by educating the couple about infidelity.
5. All couples have different expectations of marital fidelity. Assess the individual's view of infidelity.
6. When working with same-sex couples, it is important to find out about the couple's expectation of monogamy.

CONCLUSION

There has been an incredible disconnect between clinical reality and research focus when it comes to infidelity. Couple therapists have largely been on their own when working with couples where there has been an affair as researchers have largely avoided this important topic. Thankfully, recent work has begun to study how couple therapy may be helpful for infidelity, and the initial results are optimistic. However, many more questions remain about how couple therapy can effectively help couples with affairs, and we look forward to seeing how the field progresses and matures.

NOTES

1. Originally, TBCT was referred to as Behavioral Marital Therapy and later, Behavioral Couple Therapy when the field as a whole recognized that there are committed relationships beyond marriage. More recently, Christensen and colleagues have referred to it as Traditional Behavioral Couple Therapy to clearly delineate it from later developments such as Integrative Behavioral Couple Therapy.

2. Note that additional therapies have been examined, and at times revealed impressive findings. For example, Snyder, Wills, and Grady-Fletcher (1991) found that Insight-Oriented Couple Therapy (IOCT; Snyder & Wills, 1991) at 4-year follow-up had better outcomes than Behavioral Couple Therapy (BCT). However, only the therapies noted in the text have been examined in multiple outcome studies.

3. These five "secret" affair couples are an intriguing but small group. In two cases, the therapist learned of the affair during an individual assessment session; the affairs were ended, and the spouses did not want their partners to know they had occurred. The other three cases represented ongoing affairs in which neither the spouse nor the therapist knew about the affair during the treatment. The research team and/or therapist learned of the affair following treatment.

4. *Editor's note:* Please see Chapters 11 and 12 in this volume for more information on gay and lesbian couple treatment.

REFERENCES

Allen, E. S., Atkins, D. C., Baucom, D. H., Snyder, D. K., Gordon, K., & Glass, S. P. (2005). Intrapersonal, interpersonal, and contextual factors in engaging in and responding to extramarital involvement. *Clinical Psychology: Science and Practice, 12,* 101–130.

Atkins, D. C. (2003). *Infidelity and marital therapy: Initial findings from a randomized clinical trial.* Unpublished doctoral dissertation, University of Washington, Seattle.

Atkins, D. C., Baucom, D. H., & Jacobson, N. S. (2001). Understanding infidelity: Correlates in a national random sample. *Journal of Family Psychology, 15,* 735–749.

Atkins, D. C., Eldridge, K. A., Baucom, D. H., & Christensen, A. (2005). Infidelity and behavioral couple therapy: Optimism in the face of betrayal. *Journal of Consulting and Clinical Psychology, 73,* 144–150.

Baucom, D. H., Shoham, V., Mueser, K. T., Daiuto, A. D., & Stickle, T. R. (1998). Empirically supported couple and family interventions for marital distress and adult mental health problems. *Journal of Consulting and Clinical Psychology, 66,* 53-88.

Bennun, I. (1985). Prediction and responsiveness in behavioural marital therapy. *Behavioural Psychotherapy, 13,* 186–201.

Blasband, D., & Peplau, L. A. (1985). Sexual exclusivity versus openness in gay couples. *Archives of Sexual Behavior, 14,* 395–412.

Blumstein, P., & Schwartz, P. (1983). *American couples: Money, work, and sex.* New York: William Morrow.

Cano, A., & O'Leary, K. D. (2000). Infidelity and separations precipitate major depressive episodes and symptoms of nonspecific depression and anxiety. *Journal of Consulting and Clinical Psychology, 68,* 774–781.

Chambless, D. L., & Ollendick, T. H. (2001). Empirically supported psychological interventions: Controversies and evidence. *Annual Review of Psychology, 52,* 685–716.

Christensen, A., Atkins, D. C., Berns, S., Wheeler, J., Baucom, D. H., & Simpson, L. E. (2004). Traditional versus integrative behavioral couple therapy for significantly and chronically distressed married couples. *Journal of Consulting and Clinical Psychology, 72,* 176–191.

Doss, B. D., Simpson, L. E., & Christensen, A. (2004). Why do couples seek marital therapy? *Professional Psychology: Research and Practice, 35,* 608–614.

Epstein, N. B., & Baucom, D. H. (2002). *Enhanced cognitive-behavioral therapy for couples: A contextual approach.* Washington, DC: American Psychological Association Press.

Glass, S. P., & Wright, T. L. (1992). Justifications for extramarital relationships: The association between attitudes, behaviors, and gender. *Journal of Sex Research, 29,* 361–387.

Gordon, K., Baucom, D. H., & Snyder, D. K. (2004). An integrative intervention for promoting recovery from extramarital affairs. *Journal of Marital and Family Therapy, 30,* 213–231.

Gurman, A. S., & Jacobson, N. S. (2002). *Clinical handbook of couple therapy.* New York: Guilford Press.

Hahlweg, K., & Markman, H. J. (1988). Effectiveness of behavioral marital therapy: Empirical status of behavioral techniques in preventing and alleviating marital distress. *Journal of Consulting and Clinical Psychology, 56,* 440–447.

Jacobson, N. S., & Christensen, A. (1996). *Integrative couple therapy: Promoting acceptance and change.* New York: Norton.

Jacobson, N. S., Follette, W. C., & Revenstorf, D. (1984). Psychotherapy outcome research: Methods for reporting variability and evaluating clinical significance. *Behavior Therapy, 15,* 336–352.

Jacobson, N. S., & Margolin, G. (1979). *Marital therapy: Strategies based on social learning and behavior exchange principles.* New York: Brunner/Mazel.

Jacobson, N. S., & Truax, P. (1991). Clinical significance: A statistical approach to defining meaningful change in psychotherapy research. *Journal of Consulting and Clinical Psychology, 59,* 12–19.

Johnson, S. M. (2004). *The practice of emotionally focused couple therapy.* New York: Taylor & Francis.

Kurdek, L. A., & Schmitt, P. (1986). Relationship quality of partners in heterosexual married, heterosexual cohabitating, and gay and lesbian relationships. *Journal of Personality and Social Psychology, 51,* 711–720.

Linquist, L., & Negy, C. (2005). Maximizing the experiences of an extrarelational affair: An unconventional approach to a common social convention. *Journal of Clinical Psychology, 61,* 1421–1428.

Martell, C. R., & Land, T. E. (2002). Cognitive-behavioral therapy with gay and lesbian couples. In T. Patterson (Ed.), *Comprehensive handbook of psychotherapy: Vol. 2. Cognitive-behavioral approaches* (pp. 451–468). New York: Wiley.

Martell, C. R., & Prince, S. E. (2005). Treating infidelity in same-sex couples. *Journal of Clinical Psychology, 61,* 1429–1438.

McGlinchey, J. B., Zimmerman, M., & Atkins, D. C. (2006). *Clinical significance and remission: Bridging two parallel treatment outcome constructs*. Manuscript submitted for publication.

Moon, J. H., Atkins, D. C., Eldridge, K., Sevier, M., Jones, J. T., & Christensen, A. (2006, November). How Do Secret Affairs Change the Way a Couple Communicates? Poster presented at the annual meeting of the Association for Behavioral and Cognitive Therapies, Washington, DC.

O'Leary, K. D., Vivian, D., & Malone, J. (1992). Assessment of physical aggression against women in marriage: The need for multimodal assessment. *Behavioral Assessment, 14,* 5–14.

Pittman, F. S., & Wagers, T. P. (2005). Teaching fidelity. *Journal of Clincial Psychology, 61,* 1407–1419.

Shadish, W. R., & Baldwin, S. A. (2003). Meta-analysis of MFT interventions. *Journal of Marital and Family Therapy, 29,* 547–570.

Shadish, W. R., & Baldwin, S. A. (2005). Effects of Behavioral Marital Therapy: A meta-analysis of randomized controlled trials. *Journal of Consulting and Clinical Psychology, 73,* 6–14.

Snyder, D. K. (1997). *Marital Satisfaction Inventory – Revised (MSI-R) Manual*. Los Angeles: Western Psychological Services.

Snyder, D. K., Castellani, A. M., & Whisman, M. A. (2006). Current status and future directions in couple therapy. *Annual Review of Psychology, 57,* 317–344.

Snyder, D. K., & Doss, B. D. (2005). Treating infidelity: Clinical and ethical directions. *Journal of Clinical Psychology, 61,* 1453–1465.

Snyder, D. K., & Wills, R. M. (1991). Facilitating change in marital therapy and research. *Journal of Family Psychology, 4,* 426–435.

Snyder, D. K., Wills, R. M., & Grady-Fletcher, A. (1991). Long-term effectiveness of behavioral versus insight-oriented marital therapy: A 4-year follow-up study. *Journal of Consulting and Clinical Psychology, 59,* 138–141.

Spanier, G. B. (1976). Measuring dyadic adjustment: New scales for assessing the quality of marriage and similar dyads. *Journal of Marriage and the Family, 38,* 15–28.

Stanley, S. M. (2001). Making a case for premarital education. *Family Relations: Interdisciplinary Journal of Applied Family Studies, 50,* 272–280.

Whisman, M. A., Dixon, A. E., & Johnson, B. (1997). Therapists' perspectives of couple problems and treatment issues in couple therapy. *Journal of Family Psychology, 11,* 361–366.

Whisman, M. A., & Wagers, T. P. (2005). Assessing relationship betrayals. *Journal of Clinical Psychology, 61,* 1383–1391.

Wiederman, M. W. (1997). Extramarital sex: Prevalence and correlates in a national survey. *Journal of Sex Research, 34,* 167–174.

CHAPTER 5

The Intersystems Approach to Treating Infidelity

STEPHEN T. FIFE, GERALD R. WEEKS, AND NANCY GAMBESCIA

In any committed relationship, there is an explicit or implicit commitment regarding intimacy. The nature of each couple's commitment is unique; however, it typically includes both sexual and emotional loyalty to one's partner and regulates interactions both within and outside of the relationship. Infidelity is any form of betrayal to the implied or stated contract between partners regarding intimate exclusivity. With infidelity, emotional and/or sexual intimacy is diverted away from the committed relationship without the other partner's consent. A violation of the commitment impacts the relationship on many levels and often results in a loss of trust, confusion, and immense pain.

The discovery of infidelity is often the initiating event that brings couples to therapy (Glass & Wright, 1997).Therapists must be aware of the potential reactions of both partners and possible consequences for the relationship, and a thorough knowledge of what to expect can help a therapist guide couples through the tumultuous period following the initial discovery and through the process of healing. Couples are often aided when therapists provide a "map" to help them understand common emotional reactions, what they might experience following the revelation of infidelity, and the process of forgiveness and healing (Olson, Russell, Higgins-Kessler, & Miller, 2002).

They are more likely to engage in the various stages of treatment if they know what to expect and trust that therapy can help them heal.

Because of the tenuous conditions surrounding infidelity, therapists often approach cases of infidelity with uncertainty and apprehension. Infidelity is one of the most common presenting problems for couples seeking therapy. Yet, it is one of the most difficult to treat, and therapists often feel unprepared for this kind of work (Whisman, Dixon, & Johnson, 1997). Just as couples are assisted by a road map to healing, therapists may also find it helpful to have a map or guide to follow when treating difficult relationship issues such as infidelity. This chapter is intended to provide clinicians with a useful guide to refer to in their work with couples.

THE INTERSYSTEMS APPROACH TO TREATING INFIDELITY

The intersystems approach is a comprehensive, empirically based clinical model designed to help couples heal from the aftermath of infidelity (Weeks, Gambescia, & Jenkins, 2003). Based on empirical literature and the authors' extensive clinical experiences, the intersystems approach provides both a theoretical framework for conceptualizing couples' problems and guidelines for intervention and treatment. The intersystems approach is an effective means of treating infidelity, given its systemic orientation, sensitivity to context, and theoretical and technical integration of various therapy approaches and techniques (Weeks, 1994).

Treatment of infidelity requires a flexible approach that takes into account the needs of the relationship system, the concerns of the couple, the partners as individuals, and the role of the therapist. The intersystems approach is grounded in a systemic worldview, meaning that infidelity is conceptualized as a relationship issue, even if there is a clear offending partner. With infidelity, partners suffer together, and they must heal together to overcome the serious relational trauma and injury. Therefore, aspects of individual and couples therapy are combined within a systemic orientation, addressing both individual and relationship concerns.

The intersystems model consists of three interconnected aspects of assessment and treatment: the individual risk factors of each partner, the couple's relationship, and influences from the families of origin on the present relationship. The couple is made up of two individuals, who bring to the relationship their own beliefs, expectations, defense mechanisms, etc. Each couple is unique and has developed qualities and patterns in their relationship—communication patterns, conflict resolution styles, roles, rules, and so on. Each individual also brings to the relationship a context that includes experiences with their family of origin. The intersystems approach helps the therapist be aware of the various factors contributing to couples' problems and provides direction for intervention and healing. As there may be considerable overlap of individual, couple, and family of origin issues, therapy may focus on multiple, interrelated problems at the same time.

The intersystems approach incorporates a variety of theoretical constructs and therapeutic interventions and aims to accomplish the following during the course of treatment:

- Facilitate couples' and therapists' navigation of the emotional turmoil that surrounds the revelation of infidelity
- Facilitate assessment of important individual and relationship issues
- Facilitate the important work of forgiveness
- Facilitate the identification and working through of factors that contributed to infidelity
- Facilitate communication that brings deeper, more comprehensive intimacy

The intent of the approach is not to return the relationship to its pre-infidelity state, nor is it merely focused on problem resolution. Rather, it is growth oriented and aims to help couples optimize their relationship (Weeks & Hof, 1995). Therefore, therapy emphasizes individual and relationship strengths and possibilities, rather than focusing exclusively on weaknesses and deficiencies. Treatment of infidelity typically passes through various phases. For the purposes of instruction, the phases are presented sequentially. However, our experience suggests that there is considerable overlap between phases, and the intersystems approach helps facilitate flexibility for therapists, resulting in a unique journey to healing for each couple.

PHASE 1: POSTDISCLOSURE REACTIONS, CRISIS MANAGEMENT, AND ASSESSMENT

Reactions to the Discovery of Infidelity

Few events in a couple's relationship will create as much emotional turmoil as infidelity. Couples' reactions may depend on several factors, including pre-existing marital circumstances, how the infidelity was discovered, and the personality characteristics of the individuals involved. In many cases, the revelation of infidelity turns a couple's world upside down. The previous security, stability, and control once felt in the relationship are lost with the betrayal. Common initial reactions to the discovery of infidelity include shock, anger, and denial (Humphrey, 1987). These are often accompanied by grief, pessimism, and self-doubt as the meaning and significance of the relationship bond are questioned. Confusion abounds, with both partners wondering if the relationship is irreparably damaged (Rosenau, 1998). In some cases, emotional reactions may include symptoms similar to post-traumatic stress disorder, such as hypervigilance, obsessive ruminations, flashbacks, difficulty concentrating, anger, irritability, depression, anxiety, sleep disturbances, and eating disturbances. Even suicidal ideations and homicidal threats can occur during this unstable time. Regardless of the specifics of the betrayal, therapists must be prepared to deal with the intense emotional responses that often follow the revelation of infidelity and know how to navigate several important aspects of therapy.

Crisis Management

When the discovery of infidelity is the event bringing a couple to therapy, they typically enter therapy in crisis, with the relationship stability severely shaken and the continuation of the relationship in doubt. Consequently, therapy sessions can be emotionally charged and overwhelming, even for the most experienced therapist. The first step is to help the couple calm down and regain some sense of stability and order. Crisis management at the beginning of treatment involves addressing the couple's emotions, commitment, accountability, and trust.

Emotional Reactions The emotional reactions of the betrayed and unfaithful partner are often very different, and each may have difficulty understanding the experience of the other, thus limiting their ability to provide empathy and support. Therapists must be able to explain to couples that such strong emotional reactions are to be expected (Cano & O'Leary, 1997). It is helpful to encourage the couple to postpone any decisions about terminating the relationship while in the midst of the initial shock and emotional turmoil. Therapists should let the couple know that the feelings of shock, anger, and despair will diminish over time, and when emotions have calmed down, they will be able to talk more effectively about the future of the relationship.

Given the intense emotions surrounding infidelity, the therapist must be prepared to work with clients in a way that encourages engagement in the process of therapy. Clinicians must remain nonjudgmental and maintain a position of therapeutic neutrality and balance with clients by actively listening, being accepting, and moderating the expression of emotion. A significant portion of the first few sessions involves managing emotions by allowing clients to give voice to their experience, while facilitating empathy toward each other. We do this by coaching them to listen carefully and nondefensively for the purpose of understanding their partner's experience.

The therapist should create a safe environment in which clients can discuss aspects of the infidelity. Some time should be devoted to appropriate fact-finding by the betrayed partner. However, searching for excessive details is rarely helpful and may lead to exacerbated pain and rumination over details. If the betrayed partner falls into excessive fact-finding, we redirect the client to consider, "What am I feeling?" and "What do I need?" We then help clients to express their feelings and needs to their partner. The unfaithful partner is to listen and acknowledge the pain and damage that their behavior has brought to the relationship.

Although it may be less obvious, the therapist must also be sensitive to the feelings of the offending partners. Being judgmental or ignoring their feelings and experience will likely alienate them and limit their participation in therapy. Partners guilty of infidelity will likely be experiencing their own range of intense emotions. They may be fearful of the relationship ending. They may also be afraid of hurting their partner. One, perhaps unexpected, emotion may be that of relief. Typically, the unfaithful partner has violated his or her own moral code with the infidelity. It may be a relief to finally have to deal with this once it is out in the open (Spring, 1996). Additionally, some may feel their own sense of loss and grief over having to terminate the affair, given that an emotional attachment may have developed. There may also be feelings of guilt and self-loathing (Spanier & Margolis, 1983). However, in some instances, there may be an inexplicable lack of guilt, particularly if the affair serves as a wake-up call for the other spouse.

Commitment   Commitment is at the heart of treatment for infidelity. Many partners are unsure if the damage done to the relationship can be repaired. Healing from infidelity can be a long and arduous process, which requires commitment and patience. Therapists must assess for individual partners' level of commitment, both to the relationship and to therapy. It is not safe to assume that because they are attending, they are committed to staying in the relationship or to continuing with treatment. Given the intense pain and anger that may accompany the discovery of infidelity, the betrayed partner may have a difficult time maintaining commitment to the relationship. The intensity of emotions may interfere with making sound judgments, leading to a premature decision to end the relationship.

If one or both partners cannot make up their minds about commitment to the relationship, we encourage them to at least make a commitment to therapy, so that they can thoroughly evaluate the relationship and their own feelings before making a decision. The hope is that by committing to therapy, each will come to a rational decision whether to continue or end the relationship, which may provide some sense of closure. After securing their commitment to therapy, the clinician can inquire further about each partner's level of commitment to the relationship.

For many couples, individual partners' commitment to the relationship is unequal. In order for the possibility of healing to be realized, both partners must develop a full commitment to the relationship. Many couples undermine the process of healing because of an inability or unwillingness to give their full commitment. In the case of ongoing infidelity, the unfaithful partner must agree to end the outside relationship in order for conjoint session to proceed. Continuation of the outside relationship will impair the unfaithful partner's ability to clearly evaluate the primary relationship and will undermine the process and purpose of couples therapy. In cases when an attachment to the affair partner has developed, therapists may have to work with the unfaithful partner to deal with feelings about the affair partner, to understand their motivation for the infidelity, and to prevent relapse. When a deeper attachment has formed, grieving needs to take place so that the unfaithful partner can commit him- or herself more fully to the primary relationship. Such discussions work best in individual sessions, given that they would only add to the pain of the betrayed partner.

Accountability and Trust   Honesty and trust are at the heart of committed relationships. Infidelity is a betrayal of both—a partner has violated the trust inherent in the relationship, and he or she has lied about it. We explain to couples that rebuilding trust is a long process, which will only be achieved through accountability and honest communication. Accountability refers to accepting responsibility for one's actions, the pain one has inflicted on the other, and the damage done to the relationship. Accountability requires what we call "absolute honesty," including the development of a communication plan in which partners keep in touch regularly and inform each other of their schedules and plans. Communication in person or by phone may be especially important at those times of the day when the affair occurred. Spouses must do what they say they are going to do and be where they say they are going to be. Betrayed partners, having already experienced overwhelming pain and sorrow, do not want to be further hurt or deceived. They want and deserve assurance that the infidelity and deceit have ended. Failure to do so only perpetuates mistrust, hopelessness, and anger.

Assessment

Each couple presenting with infidelity is unique, and a careful assessment will help the clinician develop an appropriate treatment plan. Knowledge of various typologies of affairs and possible risk factors can be helpful during assessment and when formulating a plan for treatment. Possible risk factors include low levels of marital satisfaction, low self-esteem, a permissive attitude toward infidelity, type and length of involvement with the affair partner, justifications, social and cultural norms, courtship attitudes and behaviors, biological factors, and the relationship to the affair partner (e.g., co-worker) (Atwater, 1979; Glass & Wright, 1985; Hurlbert, 1992; Treas & Giesen, 2000). Gender is also an important variable, and men and women generally engage in infidelity for different reasons (Atwater, 1979; Glass & Wright, 1985; Humphrey, 1987). Each may also respond differently to the discovery of the betrayal.

Some important dimensions to assess for include

- The type of infidelity (whether emotional, sexual, Internet infidelity, etc.)
- The time frame or duration in which the infidelity occurred
- Frequency of communication and/or sexual contact

- Location of encounters
- Risk of discovery (varies along a continuum from completely secret to open affairs)
- Degree of collusion by the betrayed partner
- Level of deception
- History of past infidelity (may include previous affairs and/or sexual addiction)
- Gender of the affair partner
- Unilateral and bilateral infidelity (one partner or both partners having been unfaithful)
- Relationship of the affair partner to the spouse
- Perceived attractiveness of the affair partner
- Social and cultural context of the infidelity

Developing a Definition of Infidelity With the Couple

The experience of infidelity is unique to each individual and couple, and the clinician must investigate the meaning of the betrayal for each partner. Given that there are numerous ways to define infidelity, the therapist must be sure that participants (clients and therapist) are using terms in the same way or with the same meaning. Partners may disagree over the definition of infidelity—and thus disagree over whether it has occurred. For example, some may not consider emotional intimacy as a violation of the relationship commitment. Others may disagree about what physical behaviors constitute infidelity, believing that only intercourse constitutes infidelity, whereas others hold that behaviors such as kissing constitute a breach of trust and commitment to fidelity. One way to determine if a line of trust has been crossed is to identify the onset of deceptive behaviors and communication. Acts that were intended to hide or deceive are a good sign that a violation has occurred. The therapist must work to understand each couple's definition of infidelity and tailor treatment accordingly.

PHASE 2: SYSTEMIC CONSIDERATIONS

As couples begin to rebuild confidence and commitment, there are important individual and systemic issues to consider. This approach is intersystemic (Weeks, 1989, 1994), meaning that it attends to the individuals who make up the system, the couple's relationship, and family of origin influences. Both assessment and intervention are grounded in a systemic perspective in which the relationship is viewed as a union of two partners whose interactions are fundamentally reciprocal and interdependent.

Individual Risk Factors

Many individual risk factors can contribute to partners' susceptibility. Some are situational (such as a midlife crisis), and some are rooted more in the individual. Risk factors may include mental and emotional illness, such as depression or anxiety, which can affect one's participation in the primary relationship. Personality disorders can also increase individuals' and couples' vulnerability to infidelity. The therapist should also consider biological factors, such as illness and age-related conditions. Thus, a therapist must conduct a thorough assessment of each individual. A combination of individual, couple, and psychiatric treatment might be necessary.

Relational Issues and Risk Factors

Infidelity often occurs within the context of relationship problems. The therapist must evaluate couples' relationship roles and expectations, communication patterns, conflict resolution style, problem-solving strategies, relationship enhancement activities, and emotional and physical intimacy. Problems in any of these areas can increase couples' vulnerability to infidelity. For example, persistent conflict or unresolved disagreements can lead to emotional distance, which increases the chance of one or both partners looking outside the primary relationship for emotional closeness and responsiveness.

We have found that emotional distance is often created and maintained by couples' use of anger and conflict. Anger is often the overt expression of underlying emotions, such as hurt, grief, fear, loss, guilt, shame, and so on (Johnson, 2004). However, without the awareness of underlying emotions, some couples tend to persist in their interactions at the level of anger and conflict, rather than connecting at a deeper emotional level. Expressions of anger do not convey safety, nor do they invite partners to listen for understanding. Instead, they invite self-protective responses, defensiveness, and retaliation, thus maintaining or increasing emotional distance.

The intersystems approach offers guidelines for therapists to help facilitate an exploration of attitudes about anger and conflict and to facilitate couple interactions that enhance communication, understanding, and intimacy. These guidelines include

- Exploring feelings, beliefs, and underlying emotions
- Learning to recognize the systemic, reciprocal nature of conflict and anger
- Expressing emotions and experience without blame
- Listening and communicating understanding
- Taking responsibility for feelings and behaviors
- Learning to take time-outs when needed
- Maintaining an attitude of negotiation and compromise

Intergenerational Considerations

Infidelity may represent a legacy inherited from and learned in one's family of origin. It is important to assess for the relationship between family dynamics in the families of origin and the current relationship. The focused genogram

(DeMaria, Weeks, & Hof, 1999) may be a useful intervention for examining family functioning and heightening clients' awareness of familial influences. The therapist assesses for previous infidelity, family secrets, incest, parentification, triangulation, enmeshment, and other dysfunctional patterns of interaction that may influence one's vulnerability to infidelity. We also use the genogram to help examine partners' attitudes about anger, conflict, roles, intimacy, and so on.

Reframing

In a majority of the cases we have worked with, infidelity is related to relationship dissatisfaction or dysfunction. Although the unfaithful spouse is not justified in the betrayal—and the therapist must carefully articulate in a nonjudgmental way that infidelity and the associated dishonesty are unacceptable in a committed relationship—the affair can be viewed as a symptom of the relationship problems. From a systemic perspective, both parties have participated in the troubled relationship and share responsibility for the quality of the relationship.

We have found that a carefully formulated reframe can help both partners understand the relationship context and to see their own part in the condition of the relationship. Reframing is a commonly used intervention that helps couples see a problem in a new way or give different meaning to a predicament in a manner that allows them to move forward from their current state. For each situation, there are many different ways to reframe the problem. However, every systemic reframe should incorporate two elements. First, the reframe should put the couple on the same level and help them see the situation systemically, instead of the linear view couples often hold in which one partner is good/right and the other is bad/wrong. Couples are invited to see their relationship in circular terms, and a systemic reframe helps them begin to accept that both members share responsibility for their relationship. A systemic reframe brings to light the underlying relationship dynamics, rather than the overt symptoms. For example, one couple constantly argued about many different topics, none of which revealed their underlying fear of intimacy and vulnerability. This couple used conflict to keep them safely apart, rather than address their insecurities. A systemic reframe given to this couple helped them focus on the underlying relationship dynamic, rather than the topics of conflict. Second, the reframe highlights the good and the positive in the relationship. When couples enter therapy, they tend to emphasize the negative aspects of the relationship, even viewing the past as if it were all bad. However, they may be failing to recognize the good in the relationship and the positive aspects of their problems (meaning how the problems have helped, protected, or otherwise served them). An effective reframe can help the couple develop hope for a positive outcome.

Developing a helpful reframe begins with the therapeutic relationship, for it is something that is done *with* clients, not *to* them. A therapist must come to know the couple in order to develop a reframe that fits with them. If the reframe is too dissimilar with the couple and their experience, they will likely reject it. Five important questions can help a therapist construct a reframe:

- How does the couple frame their problem?
- How does the couple's frame help to create and/or perpetuate the problem?
- What new frame would help the couple change?
- Why do you think this new frame would help the couple change?
- What are the steps you will use to help invite a change of the couple's frame?

Following a reframe, the therapist should evaluate the effectiveness of the reframe and consider future reframes. A single reframe is not likely to result in comprehensive changes in a couple's interaction patterns, and a therapist may need to cycle through these steps several times. Reframing the infidelity in a systemic manner facilitates an understanding of the relationship between the couple's dynamics and the betrayal. Couples come to see their relationship and the infidelity in systemic terms, which allows them to approach healing in a different manner, reducing the damaging patterns of anger and blame. Reframes may also address, in addition to relationship patterns, individual and intergenerational risk factors.

PHASE 3: FACILITATING FORGIVENESS

Regardless of the circumstances surrounding infidelity, forgiveness is a central aspect of relationship healing. The intersystems approach provides support for the couple, while at the same time requiring both partners to be active participants in a forgiveness process that is also relationship enhancing. The process of rebuilding is typically fraught with emotional ups and downs, and we have found that a systemic approach to forgiveness instills clients with optimism and offers solutions to common impasses.

The intersystems approach emphasizes the relational nature of forgiveness. Therapists must understand that aspects of the forgiveness process (e.g., humility, apology, remorse, softening, accepting responsibility, and extending forgiveness) are recursive, meaning that they are interlinked systemic phenomena. The actions of one partner may invite or facilitate movement in the other (either toward or away from forgiveness and healing). Understanding forgiveness in this systemic way will help clinicians create opportunities in which the process of forgiveness is more likely to move forward (McCullough, 2000; Worthington, 1998).

Prior to broaching the issue of forgiveness, the therapist should assess for the following about the unfaithful partner. Did this partner (a) apologize to the betrayed partner, (b) acknowledge fully the extent of the infidelity, (c) demonstrate remorse, (d) exhibit a willingness to change behaviors, and (e) cooperate with efforts to build in relational safeguards to ensure behavior change? In addition, the therapist should determine if the betrayed partner is (a) willing to listen to the spouse who was unfaithful, (b) trying to understand the factors that influenced the infidelity, (c) able to acknowledge that some aspects of the marriage are still good and worth preserving, and (d) able to recognize other problems that may have contributed to the infidelity.

Given the intense pain and confusion often following the discovery of infidelity, clients (particularly the betrayed spouse) may find the notion of forgiveness difficult to contemplate. Although the course of forgiveness is likely to be unique for each couple, clients' mutual desire to recover the relationship often provides the strongest motivation for engaging in the process of forgiveness. Therapists must engage the couple in finding reasons to stay together and motivation to work out the relationship and forgive. This is accomplished by maximizing *unifying factors* that bring a couple together and promote forgiveness. These unifying factors are empathy, humility, relational commitment, and hope (McCullough, 2000; Worthington, 1998). While working to enhance these unifying factors, the therapist also works to minimize or neutralize those factors that inhibit forgiveness and keep couples apart, such as narcissism, shame, anger, and fear (Emmons, 2000; Worthington, 1998; Worthington & Wade, 1999). From our systemic perspective, the unifying factors are interconnected, and a change in one can influence a change in them all.

Often the betrayed partner and the unfaithful partner view forgiveness differently, given the circumstances bringing them to therapy. Unfaithful partners may hope for forgiveness more quickly than their partners are able to give; and betrayed partners may start out feeling that forgiveness is near impossible. However, shortchanging the forgiveness process is rarely helpful and often leaves the betrayed spouse feeling twice victimized. Real forgiveness requires significant emotional, cognitive, and behavioral changes by both the betrayed and the unfaithful partner (Coleman, 1998; Gordon, Baucom, & Snyder, 2000).

The work of forgiveness begins with understanding both partners' definition of forgiveness. The important process of forgiveness is often derailed from the start because of common misunderstandings and constraining beliefs about the meaning of forgiveness. Forgiveness is often confused (by both clients and therapists) with constructs such as acceptance, excusing, condoning, pardoning, forgetting, and reconciling (Butler, Dahlin, & Fife, 2002). Such notions further exaggerate the relationship imbalance that results from the betrayal. Forgiveness has also been eschewed by many therapists because of a narrow definition that associates it only with religion, rather than understanding it as an essential and broadly applicable relationship construct. These types of misunderstanding and confusion often hinder participants' willingness to incorporate forgiveness into the therapy process.

It is important that clients understand that forgiveness does not mean that one partner is pardoning or exonerating the other from responsibility for his or her actions. Nor does it mean that one is accepting, condoning, or excusing the acts committed. With forgiveness, clients are not asked to give up their moral view of appropriate behavior—what is viewed as right or wrong can remain even after forgiveness. Thus, forgiveness does not require one to place oneself in harm's way or tolerate unacceptable behavior. Partners can forgive and still protect themselves. Because many clients misconstrue the meaning of forgiveness, clinicians may need to gently challenge client beliefs about forgiveness that constrain the possibility of healing and change (Wright, Watson, & Bell, 1996).

Unifying Factors

As mentioned above, forgiveness is cultivated by focusing on several interconnected unifying factors: empathy, hope, humility, and commitment. The development of relational unity is very helpful in facilitating the forgiveness process and provides a context in which the unfaithful partner can offer a sincere apology. These unifying factors are cultivated through various interventions offered during the course of treatment.

Empathy Empathy is widely recognized as a necessary condition for forgiveness (Coyle & Enright, 1998; DiBlasio, 2000; Worthington, 1998). Following the uncovering of infidelity, individuals often become absorbed in their own emotions, which, if they persist too long, will further polarize the couple. Partners must be encouraged to develop empathy for one another. However, therapists must be judicious in how they go about this. For example, a betrayed spouse who is asked to empathize with their partner may resist, feeling that they are being asked to share equal responsibility for the betrayal (Coleman, 1998). Although we view infidelity and healing from a systemic perspective, we do not believe that any circumstances justify violating the exclusive relationship commitment—infidelity is always wrong.

Developing empathy is important for both individuals in the relationship. Beginning with the unfaithful partner, empathy can be nurtured by facilitating nondefensive, empathic listening. Reducing defensiveness early on in treatment is critical because it opens the door for acknowledging guilt, accepting responsibility for the betrayal, becoming engaged in treatment, and facilitating empathy for the betrayed partner. In many cases, the unfaithful spouse wants to move quickly past the affair to rebuilding the marriage. Consequently, they may be impatient when the betrayed partner experiences prolonged grief and anger and demands accountability. Impatient partners have difficulty providing support and empathy, wondering if the other will "ever get over it." In such cases, the therapist would do well to review the expected "road map" to recovery and remind them that it is common for the betrayed spouse to have periods of doubt and emotional suffering, even long after the discovery of the infidelity.

Betrayed partners, on the other hand, are likely to be very sensitive about the issue of blaming, and they may refuse to consider the notion of empathy if they feel that the therapist is implying that they share blame for the transgression. Because of this, we suggest using caution when asking the betrayed spouse to identify with the unfaithful spouse's situation. Instead, we may ask them to consider a time when they were attracted to another person. Most can understand that attraction is common, even if infidelity is not acceptable. This kind of exercise can lead to greater openness toward the experience of the offending partner.

Humility   Empathy alone is insufficient to bring about forgiveness. Equally important in the healing process is humility (Worthington, 1998). Through humility, unfaithful partners accept responsibility for their actions and the damage that they have done to their partner and the relationship. An unwillingness to accept responsibility represents a major obstacle to healing and forgiveness. An attitude of humility is fostered through the encouragement of small confessions for portions of the betrayal. Through small confessions, unfaithful partners acknowledge and accept responsibility for their actions, which paves the way for a genuine apology. For example, the therapist might prompt the unfaithful partner to acknowledge the acceptance and/or initiation of phone calls, lunch dates, or emotionally intimate conversations that occurred before the relationship became sexual.

Humility in betrayed partners, on the other hand, is somewhat different. Therapists should gently encourage them to see beyond their victimization to recognize the imperfectness of all human beings. For instance, we might suggest to them that all of us, at times, behave in ways that are contrary to our own sense of right and wrong. We ask them to reflect on a time when they felt weak, vulnerable, or fallible. Doing so not only can help them develop greater humility and accept responsibility for their own actions, it also fosters greater empathy for their partner.

Commitment and Hope   In order to heal from the terrible disruption caused by infidelity, the therapist must help couples increase their relationship commitment and hope for the future. This is important because commitment and hope have a powerful bearing on present behaviors and decisions. We believe that forgiveness of infidelity is an act of sacrifice in the service of the relationship and, thus, will be highly influenced by commitment. Relational commitment includes psychological attachment, long-term orientation, the intention to persist, and cognitive interdependence (a sense of we-ness) (Agnew, 2000; Agnew & Gephart, 2000; Agnew, Van Lange, Rusbult, & Langston, 1998; Rusbult, Arriaga, & Agnew, 2001). Therapists can effectively focus on any of these, as they are reciprocally related and positively influence each other. Even the *desire* to stay together, despite a lack of confidence, can provide a starting point. The greater the partners' commitment, the more willing they are to sacrifice self-interest for the good of the relationship (Van Lange, Agnew, Harinck, & Steemers, 1997).

In order to invite greater commitment, we ask couples to reflect on moments of closeness, past agreements, promises, shared dreams, memories, and other bonds that have contributed to their relationship. In the emotional turmoil surrounding infidelity and unhappy relationships, couples often forget moments of closeness and joy from the past and disregard their personal investment in the relationship. In some instances, couples "rewrite" the past as if it were completely negative. For commitment to grow, couples must be assisted to remember feelings of love, investments, and good times from the past. Even in the early stages of treatment when couples may feel the most hopeless, we often ask about how they met, what attracted them to each other, and how the relationship began.

In addition to commitment, hope is also an important aspect of the forgiveness process. Although empirical research on the relationship between forgiveness and hope is limited, our clinical experience suggests a strong connection between the two (Worthington & Wade, 1999). A couple's sense of hope for the future is often tied to shared relationship goals. Although the basic relationship goal of having a happy marriage may have been severely compromised, couples likely have other shared dreams and goals that tie them together (e.g., raising healthy children, enjoying retirement together). The therapist must help the couple explore their shared goals as a means of increasing hope and commitment. We also discuss with couples the goal of a happy marriage that has overcome infidelity and has emerged stronger than before. The vision of this new relationship often nurtures an increase in hope, which may be accompanied by increases in we-ness and a willingness to apologize and forgive. Where appropriate, we share stories of other successful couples.

Apology

The focus on unifying factors prepares the couple for genuine apologizing and forgiveness. Infidelity is not something that can be accepted or tolerated; it can only be forgiven. For the betrayed partner, forgiveness can feel risky and threatening. Thus, for most people, forgiveness takes a leap of faith requiring remarkable courage. Two essential factors must be in place in order for forgiveness to occur: (1) a high degree of relational commitment and (2) a genuine apology from the unfaithful partner (Couch, Jones, & Moore, 1999).

The purpose of the apology is to promote healing in the damaged relationship. To genuinely apologize, the unfaithful partner must make clear the following: a sincere acknowledgment of the offense, genuine remorse, a commitment to change, and a true apology (Couch et al., 1999; Fincham, 2000; Fitness, 2001; Flanagan, 1992; Gold & Weiner, 2000; Worthington, 1998). The offending partner expresses genuine sorrow, regret, or remorse as well as the intention to make reparation for the pain and damage caused. If appropriately timed and delivered, the apology will invite an increase in empathy from the betrayed spouse (Fincham, 2000; Fitness, 2001; Gold & Weiner,

2000; Worthington, 1998). Empathy arising from a sincere apology affects the betrayed partner favorably by mitigating anger, decreasing motivation toward retaliation, decreasing motivation to maintain distance from the unfaithful partner, and increasing motivation toward conciliatory behaviors (Darby & Schlenker, 1982; McCullough, Worthington, & Rachal, 1997).

Typically, for an apology to be effective, it must be proportionately related to the offense committed and to the importance of the relationship (Tavuchis, 1991). However, because the offense of infidelity is so substantial, unfaithful partners often struggle to apologize effectively. Likewise, betrayed partners regularly have difficulty accepting the apology, even if they want to reconcile the relationship. Helping clients navigate this process is one of the most important tasks of the therapist. Before initiating an apology, the therapist must assess whether the unfaithful partner has a clear understanding of the damage caused by the offense, empathic appreciation of the partner's pain, sincere sorrow for the betrayal, and a commitment to remain faithful (Fitness, 2001; Steiner, 2000). Prior discussion, preparation, and rehearsal can help the offending partner be more effective. When apologizing, clients should be sincere, specific, and straightforward; express remorse; and only discuss their (the offender) behavior (Mitchell, 1989). They should avoid vagueness, excuses, justifying, minimizing, coercion, pleading, defensiveness, and manipulation. In some cases, clients may believe they understand the process of forgiveness and have already offered multiple apologies, but with limited results. Therapists should normalize this and engage clients in an exploration of why the apologies did not work and what would make them more effective.

Couples often struggle to know when forgiveness has been completed. Rather than representing forgiveness as a one-time event, we help clients understand that it is a process made up of multiple choices requiring time and patience. Daily reminders of the betrayal can trigger the return of unhappy feelings, and betrayed spouses may become frustrated that despite the desire and the decision to forgive, feelings of anger and resentment persist. Such intrusions often leave both partners discouraged with feelings that forgiveness is unattainable. Therapists must frequently remind clients of the natural course of forgiveness, explaining that it takes place in small steps, and occasional setbacks are to be expected.

Ultimately, the outcome of true forgiveness is change at the core of the relationship. Forgiveness helps restore the couple to a sense of we-ness, which was lost when the boundaries of the committed relationship were violated. Many couples who were successful in forgiving report that their marriages are stronger following the work of healing than they were before the infidelity. Although the misconduct is not condoned, some couples come to see that the mutual work to overcome the terrible situation resulted in an improved relationship that is large enough to encompass both their deep love for each other and the terrible offense (Freedman, 2000).

Potential Barriers to Forgiveness

The unifying factors and therapeutic techniques described above will be sufficient to initiate the forgiveness process for many couples. However, certain obstacles can prevent the development of relational unity, interfere with forgiveness, and delay the resolution of infidelity. The most common barriers include narcissism, shame, accusatory suffering, anger, and fear in one or both partners (Emmons, 2000; Worthington, 1998; Worthington & Wade, 1999). These emotional barriers can hinder partners' ability to accept responsibility for their behavior and develop empathy, humility, and commitment, thus precluding genuine apology and forgiveness. When couples do not respond to the usual treatment for infidelity, therapists must be able to identify and help remove these obstacles.

PHASE 4: TREATING FACTORS THAT CONTRIBUTE TO INFIDELITY

Once relational unity is restored and forgiveness has been successfully completed, couples are prepared for the fourth phase of therapy. This phase of treatment helps couples develop an understanding of the factors surrounding the betrayal, address the risk factors that contributed to the betrayal, and solidify their relationship so that infidelity will not happen again. In order for a couple to be confident that it will not recur, they must be sure that the underlying relational problems and other contributing factors have been resolved.

Using the intersystems approach, factors that contributed to the infidelity can be organized around three areas of vulnerability: relational discord, individual issues, and intergenerational influences. Some of the most common vulnerabilities include

- The inability to develop intimacy in the relationship
- Problems with commitment
- A lack of passion in the relationship
- Ineffectiveness in resolving conflict and anger
- Sexual addiction
- Life cycle transitions
- Psychiatric illness
- Fears about intimacy, dependency, or trust
- A value system that gives priority to pleasure and excitement over loyalty and faithfulness

An Intimacy-Based Treatment Approach

Because infidelity is a violation of a couple's commitment to intimacy, our approach is intimacy based. A lack of relationship intimacy is one of the most common contributors to infidelity. Therapists should reframe infidelity as an intimacy-based problem so couples can assess their intimacy and take steps to solidify it for the future. Treating these intimacy-based problems will strengthen the relationship and reduce the chance of recurring infidelity.

Robert Sternberg's (1986) triangular theory of romantic love provides a clinically useful model of intimacy. Sternberg's theory combines three equally important aspects of love: commitment, passion, and intimacy. *Commitment* refers to the intellectual and emotional decision to be with another person in an exclusive relationship. Couples who are committed to their relationship and to the process of therapy usually experience a positive outcome. *Passion* is a motivational aspect that draws two people together. It encompasses a sense of romance, physical attraction, sex, and a desire to be with the other person. *Intimacy* includes characteristics such as feeling a sense of closeness or connection, being concerned for the welfare and happiness of the other person, being able to count on them in time of need, sharing oneself, being honest and open, and providing and receiving emotional support.

Conceptualizing love in this way helps the couple and therapist evaluate strengths and weaknesses in the relationship and set treatment goals for the future. Difficulty in any area can put a couple at risk for infidelity. Using Sternberg's triangle, couples may be able to connect some of the motivation for the infidelity to a lack of commitment, passion, and/or intimacy. These areas can be addressed by exploring the following questions in therapy:

- Do both partners desire all three components as described in the triangle?
- Does each partner want the same level of intensity for each of the three aspects?
- How much togetherness and individuation does each partner want in the relationship?
- What prevents the partners from being able to identify and/or express the three aspects openly and freely?
- Does each partner have a realistic perception of what love involves?
- Does each partner have a realistic perception of what he or she can actually offer?
- Does each partner have a realistic perception of what the other partner can actually offer?

In some cases, therapists may find that couples can talk very effectively about the aspects of love, but have a hard time translating this into behavior. Ideally, partners work together and make adjustments so that there is greater congruency and synchrony in their relationship.

Treating Commitment Problems

Partners' commitment to the marriage or primary relationship is of critical importance and must be assessed early on in treatment. The ideal situation is to have both parties equally committed. However, given the circumstances surrounding infidelity, one or both partners may be undecided or unequally committed, with one desiring to stay and the other wanting to leave. In such cases, the therapist must work to facilitate increased commitment to the relationship by both partners. Even if commitment is low, couples therapy can precede effectively.

Often the first step in helping a couple increase commitment is to facilitate a discussion of what commitment means to each of them, what did they learn about commitment from their families of origin, and what kinds of behaviors demonstrate commitment. Commitment can also be enhanced by asking couples to reflect on and speak about how their relationship began, what attracted them to each other, and what was positive about the relationship in the beginning. Therapists can ask couples to share what is currently positive in the relationship, and they should be encouraged to continue the current positive behaviors and to reinstate those things that they previously found enjoyable in the relationship.

An exercise called the "three A's" can help build optimism and commitment. This involves couples *affirming* the importance of the relationship and their positive feelings of love, care, concern, and closeness; expressing *appreciation* for the things they like about each other; and expressing nonsexual *affection*. Increases in all three areas are important, but therapists may find that couples can most easily express appreciation. We often give couples the assignment to give at least three expressions of appreciation a day to each other. As couples experience growth in these three areas, commitment is likely to grow as well.

The second area of commitment pertains to their commitment to therapy. Given the emotional turmoil accompanying the discovering of infidelity, couples may not be in a position to effectively evaluate the relationship and make a firm commitment to staying. In fact, the initial reaction of many partners is to end the relationship immediately. Therefore, pushing either person to make a decision about commitment to the relationship at the beginning of therapy may be premature. In situations where couples struggle initially to make a commitment to the relationship, we instead ask for their commitment to therapy, even if the outcome is separation rather than reconciliation. The therapist should outline the course that therapy is likely to take in order to help clients have a realistic view of the process, length, and possible outcomes of treatment. After a few sessions, couples will likely have a sense of whether they are moving toward rebuilding or separation.

One possible outcome of infidelity is separation, leading to the dissolution of the relationship. If the couple has fulfilled their commitment to therapy by participating in an honest and thorough examination of self and the relationship, coming to the conclusion that it cannot be continued, then this is an acceptable outcome. If couples cannot come to a decision to end the relationship, but find it too painful to be together on a daily basis, a planned separation may be appropriate. To be effective, such a separation will include specific parameters, assignments, and a time frame. One of the most important considerations is that of putting the children first and committing to refrain from speaking negatively about the other partner. Therapy then proceeds on an individual basis, with the purpose of helping the partners achieve greater clarity about their participation in the relationship, what factors may have contributed to the couple's vulnerability, and the impact of the infidelity on themselves and the relationship. Ultimately, conjoint sessions should resume in order to evaluate the separation and the direction the partners want to pursue. If the outcome is separation, the therapist must shift roles from marital counselor to divorce mediator, helping the couple end the relationship with the least amount of pain, examining how the couple reached that point, and discussing how to co-parent effectively.

Treating Problems With Passion

Some cases of infidelity occur when there is a large discrepancy in sexual desire between partners in the primary relationship. The partner with higher sexual desire may feel frustrated, resentful, rejected, and hopeless about things improving. Low sexual desire—or hypoactive sexual desire (HSD)—is a common clinical phenomenon that is experienced by 30% of women and 17% of men at some point in their adult lives (Frank, Anderson, & Rubinstein, 1978). In cases of infidelity, a person may lack sexual desire toward the primary partner, but may feel desire toward others. Two common relational problems associated with low sexual desire are feelings of loss (losing a sense of self or feeling a loss of control) and anger or resentment toward one's partner. The treatment of HSD, typically involving a combination of couples and sex therapy, is complicated even more when infidelity is part of the picture. Those who work with couples in which HSD is an issue should consult Weeks and Gambescia (2002).

Treating Problems With Underlying Fears of Intimacy

Underlying fears of intimacy are common in couples therapy (Weeks & Treat, 2001), and we believe that a large portion of relationship problems are connected in some way to these fears. Often, partners are unaware of their own apprehensions regarding intimacy. For example, many people express a desire for intimacy in their relationship, but behave in ways that undermine intimacy when too much closeness occurs. Therefore, it is important to address intimacy concerns thoroughly in order to reduce a couple's vulnerability to future betrayals.

Intimacy fears can take many forms, and it may be helpful to share these with couples so that they can identify their own areas of struggle and how they react when they feel threatened by too much closeness. One common manifestation of intimacy fear is anger and interpersonal conflict, which serves to keep others at a distance. A fear of losing control or being oppressed by one's partner is another expression of a fear of intimacy, and distance may be a means of regaining or maintaining some semblance of control. An underlying fear of becoming too emotionally dependent can lead one to create distance, perhaps through an affair. A fear of rejection or abandonment can also make one vulnerable to infidelity. In its extreme, such a fear may unknowingly motivate one to reject the other first (by having an affair), instead of risking being the one who is rejected. Finally, personal insecurities or fear of exposure is another factor that points to a fear of intimacy. Partners fear that if their spouse "really knew" them, they would consider them unlovable and reject them.

Several interventions can help couples work through fears of intimacy and prevent the recurrence of future infidelity. First, it is often helpful to normalize intimacy fears. Explain that a fear of intimacy is common, and many couples have overcome this hurdle. Having the couple engage in an in-depth conversation of what intimacy means to each of them can help them become more united as a couple. It is also helpful to have couples consider various aspects of intimacy (e.g., emotional intimacy, physical intimacy, recreational intimacy) so that they can evaluate their strengths and weaknesses as a couple and make plans to focus specifically on certain domains. Fears of intimacy are often interlocking and reciprocal. Likewise, small increases in closeness and connection are also reciprocal and generative. Therapists can facilitate in-session exercises and provide homework that help clients increase their intimacy as a couple.

Exploring Expectations

In addition to difficulties in the three aspects of Sternberg's triangle, unmet expectations are often associated with infidelity. Many couples have shared with us long-standing frustration over expectations that have consistently been unmet in their relationship. Relationship expectations can be about any number of subjects, such as roles, responsibilities, parenting, sex, finances, and so on. Everyone enters into relationships with a variety of expectations, many of which were developed from their families of origin. When certain expectations are not met, frustration may set in. Therapists may incorporate into the therapeutic conversation Sager's (1976) method of conceptualizing and exploring relationship expectations by asking couples to reflect on

- Expectations that the partner was clearly aware of and verbalized to the other partner
- Expectations that the partner was clearly aware of but did not verbalize to the other partner
- Expectations that the partner was/is not aware of and therefore could not be verbalized

Therapists can ask couples to take some time to consider what they want to give and receive from their partner and then discuss this with each other. When couples have a difficult time identifying their expectations, it may be useful to ask them how their partner has disappointed them. Therapists can help couples identify expectations, evaluate them as to whether they are helpful for the relationship, and discard unproductive ones.

PHASE 5: PROMOTING INTIMACY THROUGH COMMUNICATION

Forgiveness alone is not sufficient to heal a damaged relationship. As discussed above, certain interpersonal problems likely preceded the infidelity and need to be addressed as the relationship is rebuilt. One important area to target in therapy is that of communication. Effective communication is essential to developing and maintaining deeper levels of intimacy for couples, and communication problems often create distance and limit emotional closeness. Without a foundation of clear communication, couples are vulnerable to infidelity and may not have the ability to repair damage to the relationship from the betrayal. Although not exhaustive, the systemic techniques reviewed in this section can be applied to cases of infidelity as well as a wide variety of other relationship problems.

Part of developing effective communication is overcoming past negative interactions and the assumption that future interactions will be the same. A common occurrence in the treatment of infidelity is for partners to make negative assumptions or judgments about the other's intentions, even if these are not verified in their interactions. Communication is often disrupted by such faulty presumptions, and partners may feel wounded or take offense when none was intended. Therapists should help couples examine their communication patterns to identify negative assumptions and judgments about each other's intentions. We often challenge these by asking couples reflection questions such as, "If your partner's intentions were good in this instance, how would you likely respond?" Then we encourage them to take a leap of faith by behaving in ways that acknowledge that their partner is generally a person of good will. We find that most often partners' intentions are good, even if their delivery is poor or awkward.

Effective communication does not come easily for some couples, and they often want to give up after repeated difficulties. We remind them that misunderstandings are common and that good communication takes practice and patience. Teaching couples communication and problem-solving skills is a popular approach used with couples. However, couples' efforts to incorporate these skills are often derailed by underlying emotions, attitudes, and beliefs (Jacobson & Christensen, 1996). To help restore derailed communication, we suggest to couples that each verbal interaction has two parts: affect (i.e., the feelings of each partner) and content. When disagreements arise, partners should be taught to explore the affect or underlying feelings of each other before attempting to address the content or solve the problem. Teaching couples the rules of fair fighting can help them accomplish this (Weeks & Treat, 2001). With these rules, partners' feelings about the problem take priority over the problem itself. We encourage cognitive and emotional self-disclosure, which when accompanied by compassionate listening, facilitates greater intimacy. Following this, couples are coached through a process of proposing and negotiating a solution to the problem. Although difficult to implement at first, couples can learn to use these skills effectively with practice.

Couples can also be educated about the circular nature of communication. This notion is grounded in the idea that couples interact with each other in a reciprocal or interconnected manner. Helping couples come to understand this concept can be a powerful facilitator of change. To encourage awareness of circular processes, we ask couples to observe how their behaviors fit together, paying attention to how their own behavior connects with the behavior of their partner. We help them see that there are no beginnings and endings, but instead their interactions form a dynamic circle. Helping couples understand the circular nature of communication opens up possibilities for change that are unavailable when they are thinking in an individual, linear fashion.

In addition to helping couples increase their awareness of interaction patterns, some basic communication techniques can bring very positive results. The therapist can teach couples to use *"I" statements,* which requires a partner to speak for him- or herself in a direct and nonaccusatory way. This reduces the likelihood of defensiveness on the part of the listener. *Reflective listening* is another process that helps communication proceed more smoothly. The listener is asked to listen nondefensively and to reflect back the affect and content of the message. An attitude of sincerity and caring provides a foundation for the effective use of this communication skill. Finally, being able to set one's opinions aside in order to hear what another person is saying provides *validation* to the speaker. Validation does not mean agreement, but it involves listening to understand, without interjecting bias or making judgments.

Additional efforts to enhance communication include making couples aware of common barriers to intimate communication. Such things as mind reading (one partner claiming to know what the other person is thinking, feeling, or intending to say), personalizing (perceiving offense when none was intended), distraction (one partner changing the subject), and polarizing language ("all or none" language such as *always* or *never*) can interfere with constructive communication. Gottman (1994) also identified four styles of communication that can create distance and damage intimacy in relationships: criticism, contempt, defensiveness, and stonewalling. Therapists can educate couples on these and help them become aware when their communication begins to take on one or more of these styles.

CONCLUSION

The discovery of infidelity is a serious relationship crisis that shatters much of the stability and security that is assumed in committed relationships. Given the seriousness of the offense and intensity of emotional reactions by both partners, cases of infidelity are often the most difficult to treat for couples therapists. The concepts and interventions presented in the intersystems approach to treating infidelity offer therapists a useful framework to guide their work with couples. A summary of the treatment phases and the bulleted points is presented in Table 5.1.

Approaching treatment from a systemic perspective and viewing infidelity as an intimacy-based problem allows therapists to offer to couples helpful ways to evaluate their relationship, as well as effective interventions that facilitate the healing and rebuilding of relationships. Attending to the individual,

Table 5.1 Summary of Bulleted Points

Treatment goals of the intersystems approach to treating infidelity	• Facilitate couples' and therapists' navigation of the emotional turmoil that surrounds the revelation of infidelity • Facilitate assessment of important individual and relationship issues • Facilitate the important work of forgiveness • Facilitate the identification and working through of factors that contributed to infidelity • Facilitate communication that brings deeper, more comprehensive intimacy
Phases of treatment	• Phase 1: Postdisclosure Reactions, Crisis Management, and Assessment • Phase 2: Systemic Considerations • Phase 3: Facilitating Forgiveness • Phase 4: Treating Factors That Contribute to Infidelity • Phase 5: Promoting Intimacy Through Communication
Important areas of assessment	• The type of infidelity (whether emotional, sexual, Internet infidelity, etc.) • The time frame or duration in which the infidelity occurred • Frequency of communication and/or sexual contact • Location of encounters • Risk of discovery (varies along a continuum from completely secret to open affairs) • Degree of collusion by the betrayed partner • Level of deception • History of past infidelity (may include previous affairs and/or sexual addiction) • Gender of the affair partner • Unilateral and bilateral infidelity (one partner or both partners having been unfaithful) • Relationship of the affair partner to the spouse • Perceived attractiveness of the affair partner • Social and cultural context of the infidelity

(continued)

Table 5.1 Summary of Bulleted Points (continued)

Guidelines for couples to enhance communication, understanding, and intimacy	• Exploring feelings, beliefs, and underlying emotions • Learning to recognize the systemic, reciprocal nature of conflict and anger • Expressing emotions and experience without blame • Listening and communicating understanding • Taking responsibility for feelings and behaviors • Learning to take time outs when needed • Maintaining an attitude of negotiation and compromise
Five important questions to consider when constructing a reframe	• How does the couple frame their problem? • How does the couple's frame help to create and/or perpetuate the problem? • What new frame would help the couple change? • Why do you think this new frame would help the couple change? • What are the steps you will use to help invite a change in the couple's frame?
Common areas of individual and relationship vulnerability	• The inability to develop intimacy in the relationship • Problems with commitment • A lack of passion in the relationship • Ineffectiveness in resolving conflict and anger • Sexual addiction • Life cycle transitions • Psychiatric illness • Fears about intimacy, dependency, or trust • A value system that gives priority to pleasure and excitement over loyalty and faithfulness
Questions to help couples address commitment, passion, and intimacy in their relationship	• Do both partners desire all three components as described in Sternberg's triangle? • Does each partner want the same level of intensity for each of the three aspects? • How much togetherness and individuation does each partner want in the relationship? • What prevents the partners from being able to identify and/or express the three aspects openly and freely? • Does each partner have a realistic perception of what love involves? • Does each partner have a realistic perception of what he or she can actually offer? • Does each partner have a realistic perception of what the other partner can actually offer?

couple, and family of origin risk factors helps couples identify and address idiosyncratic vulnerabilities to infidelity and protect their relationship from further betrayals. Interventions designed to facilitate forgiveness and enhance communication and intimacy can help partners heal from infidelity and strengthen their bond with each other. Therapists must be flexible so they can tailor their work to the unique needs of each couple and increase the possibility of a successful outcome for therapy.

REFERENCES

Agnew, C. R. (2000). Cognitive interdependence and the experience of relationship loss. In J. H. Harvey & E. D. Miller (Eds.), *Loss and trauma: General close relationship perspectives* (pp. 385–398). Philadelphia: Brunner-Routledge.

Agnew, C. R., & Gephart, J. M. (2000). Testing the rules of commitment enhancement: Separating fact from fiction. *Representative Research in Social Psychology, 24,* 41–47.

Agnew, C. R., Van Lange, P., Rusbult, C. E., & Langston, C. A. (1998). Cognitive interdependence: Commitment and the mental representation of close relationships. *Journal of Personality and Social Psychology, 74,* 939–954.

Atwater, L. (1979). Getting involved: Women's transition to first extramarital sex. *Alternative Lifestyles, 2,* 33–68.

Butler, M. H., Dahlin, S. K., & Fife, S. T. (2002). "Languaging" factors affecting clients' acceptance of forgiveness intervention in marital therapy. *Journal of Marital and Family Therapys, 28,* 285–298.

Cano, A., & O'Leary, K. (1997). Romantic jealousy and affairs: Research and implications for couple therapy. *Journal of Sex and Marital Therapy, 23,* 249–275.

Coleman, P. (1998). The process of forgiveness in marriage and the family. In R. Enright & J. North (Eds.), *Exploring forgiveness* (pp. 75–95). Madison: University of Wisconsin Press.

Couch, L., Jones, W. H., & Moore, D. S. (1999). Buffering the effects of betrayal: The role of apology, forgiveness and commitment. In J. M. Adams & W. H. Jones (Eds.), *Handbook of interpersonal commitment and relationship stability* (pp. 451–469). New York: Kluwer Academic/Plenum.

Coyle, C. T., & Enright, R. D. (1998). Forgiveness education with adult learners. In C. M. Smith & T. Pourchot (Eds.), *Adult learning and development: Perspectives from educational psychology* (pp. 219–238). Mahwah, NJ: Erlbaum.

Darby, B. W., & Schlenker, B. R. (1982). Children's reactions to apologies. *Journal of Personality and Social Psychology, 43,* 742–753.

DeMaria, R., Weeks, G., & Hof, L. (1999). *Focused genograms: Intergenerational assessment of individuals, couples, and families.* Philadelphia: Brunner/Mazel.

DiBlasio, F. A. (2000). Decision-based forgiveness treatment in cases of marital infidelity. *Psychotherapy, 37,* 149–158.

Emmons, R. (2000). Personality and forgiveness. In M. McCullough, K. Pargament, & C. Thoresen (Eds.), *Forgiveness: Theory, research and practice* (pp. 156–179). New York: Guilford Press.

Fincham, F. D. (2000). The kiss of porcupines: From attributing responsibility to forgiving. *Personal Relationships, 7,* 1–23.

Fitness, J. (2001). Betrayal, rejection, revenge, and forgiveness: An interpersonal script approach. In M. R. Leary (Ed.), *Interpersonal rejection* (pp. 73–103). New York: Oxford University Press.

Flanagan, B. (1992). *Forgiving the unforgivable: Overcoming the bitter legacy of intimate wounds.* New York: Macmillan.

Frank, E., Anderson, C., & Rubinstein, D. (1978). Frequency of sexual dysfunction in "normal" couples. *New England Journal of Medicine, 299*, 111–115.

Freedman, S. R. (2000). Creating an expanded view: How therapists can help their clients forgive. *Journal of Family Psychotherapy, 11*, 87–92.

Glass, S., & Wright, T. (1985). Sex differences in type of extramarital involvement and marital dissatisfaction. *Sex Roles, 12*, 1101–1120.

Glass, S., & Wright, T. (1997). Reconstructing marriages after the trauma of infidelity. In W. K. Halford & H. J. Markman (Eds.), *Clinical handbook of marriage and couples interventions* (pp. 471–507). New York: Wiley.

Gold, G. J., & Weiner, B. (2000). Remorse, confession, group identity and expectancies about repeating a transgression. *Basic & Applied Social Psychology, 22*, 291–300.

Gordon, K. C., Baucom, D. H., & Snyder, D. K. (2000). The use of forgiveness in marital therapy. In M. McCullough, K. Pargament, & C. Thoresen (Eds.), *Forgiveness: Theory, research and practice* (pp. 203–228). New York: Guilford Press.

Gottman, J. (1994). *Why marriages succeed or fail*. New York: Simon & Schuster.

Humphrey, R. (1987). Treating extramarital sexual relationships in sex and couples therapy. In G. Weeks & L. Hof (Eds.), *Integrating sex and marital therapy: A clinical guide* (pp. 149–170). New York: Brunner/Mazel.

Hurlbert, D. (1992). Factors influencing a woman's decision to end an extramarital sexual relationship. *Journal of Sex and Marital Therapy, 18*, 104–113.

Jacobson, N., & Christensen, A. (1996). *Integrative couples therapy: Promoting acceptance and change*. New York: Norton.

Johnson, S. M. (2004). *Creating connection: The practice of emotionally focused therapy*. New York: Brunner/Routledge.

McCullough, M. E. (2000). Forgiveness as human strength: Theory, measurement, and links to well-being. *Journal of Social and Clinical Psychology, 19*, 43–55.

McCullough, M. E., Worthington, E. L., Jr., & Rachal, K. C. (1997). Interpersonal forgiving in close relationships. *Journal of Personality and Social Psychology, 73*, 321–336.

Mitchell, C. E. (1989). Effects of apology on marital and family relationships. *Family Therapy, 16*, 283–287.

Olson, M., Russell, C., Higgins-Kessler, M., & Miller, R. (2002). Emotional processes following disclosure of an extramarital affair. *Journal of Marital and Family Therapy, 28*, 423–434.

Rosenau, D. (1998). Extramarital affairs: Therapeutic understanding and clinical interventions. *Marriage & Family: A Christian Journal, 1*, 355–368.

Rusbult, C. E., Arriaga, X. B., & Agnew, C. R. (2001). Interdependence in close relationships. In G. J. O. Fletcher & M. S. Clark (Eds.), *Blackwell handbook of social psychology: Vol. 2. Interpersonal processes* (pp. 359–387). Oxford, UK: Blackwell.

Sager, C. (1976). *Marriage contracts and couples therapy: Hidden forces in intimate relationships*. New York: Brunner/Mazel.

Spanier, G., & Margolis, R. (1983). Marital separation and extramarital sexual behavior. *Journal of Sex Research, 19*, 23–48.

Spring, J. A. (1996). *After the affair: Healing the pain and rebuilding the trust when a partner has been unfaithful*. New York: Harper-Collins.

Steiner, C. (2000). Apology: The transactional analysis of fundamental exchange. *Transactional Analysis Journal, 30,* 145–149.

Sternberg, R. (1986). A triangular theory of love. *Psychological Review, 93*(2), 119–135.

Tavuchis, N. (1991). *Mea culpa: A sociology of apology and reconciliation.* Stanford, CA: Stanford University Press.

Treas, J., & Giesen, D. (2000). Sexual infidelity among married cohabiting Americans. *Journal of Marriage and the Family, 62,* 48–60.

Van Lange, P. A. M., Agnew, C. R., Harinck, F., & Steemers, G. E. M. (1997). From game to theory to real life: How social value orientation affects willingness to sacrifice in ongoing close relationships. *Journal of Personality and Social Psychology, 73,* 1330–1344.

Weeks, G. R. (Ed.). (1989). *Treating couples: The intersystem model of the Marriage Council of Philadelphia.* New York: Brunner/Mazel.

Weeks, G. R. (1994). The intersystem model: An integrated approach to treatment. In G. R. Weeks & L. Hof (Eds.), *The marital relationship therapy casebook: Theory and application of the intersystem model* (pp. 3–34). New York: Brunner/Mazel.

Weeks, G. R., & Gambescia, N. (2002). *Hypoactive sexual desire: Integrating sex and couple therapy.* New York: Norton.

Weeks, G. R., Gambescia, N., & Jenkins, R. E. (2003). *Treating infidelity: Therapeutic dilemmas and effective strategies.* New York: Norton.

Weeks, G. R., & Hof, L. (Eds.). (1995). *Integrative solutions: Treating common problems in couples therapy.* New York: Brunner/Mazel.

Weeks, G. R., & Treat, S. (2001). *Couples in treatment: Techniques and approaches for effective practice* (2nd ed.). Philadelphia: Brunner/Routledge.

Whisman, M., Dixon, A., & Johnson, B. (1997). Therapist's perspectives of couple problems and treatment issues in couple therapy. *Journal of Family Psychology, 11,* 361–366.

Worthington, E. L., Jr. (1998). An empathy-humility-commitment model of forgiveness applied within family dyads. *Journal of Family Therapy, 20,* 59–76.

Worthington, E. L., Jr., & Wade, N. (1999). The psychology of unforgiveness and forgiveness and implications for clinical practice. *Journal of Social and Clinical Psychology, 18,* 385–418.

Wright, L. M., Watson, W. L., & Bell, J. M. (1996). *Beliefs: The heart of healing in families and illness.* New York: Basic Books.

CHAPTER 6

Treating Infidelity

An Integrative Approach to Resolving Trauma and Promoting Forgiveness

DOUGLAS K. SNYDER, DONALD H. BAUCOM,
AND KRISTINA C. GORDON

"How could you do it?" Sophie exclaimed. "You told me it was over. Now you're emailing her again. Is this ever going to end?" Sophie had discovered Micah's affair with a partner in his office six months earlier after Micah had loaned her his cell phone and she'd listened to a message from Rachael recounting their rendezvous at her apartment the previous Saturday. Micah had told Sophie he'd been finishing a contract at the office. The revelation of Micah's affair had triggered a cascade of angry exchanges that left both spouses reeling. Sophie had insisted that Micah move out, but she settled for sleeping in separate rooms. Micah had been transferred to a different division at his firm after Sophie had complained to one of his supervisors about his relationship with Rachael, but his adjustment to new responsibilities hadn't gone well and he'd just received an unfavorable review. Sophie had sought advice from her mother, and now her entire family regarded Micah with distrust. Micah and Sophie had recently begun sleeping together but hadn't resumed lovemaking or even holding one another in bed. Their cold detachment during mealtime was evident to their children, who lately had seemed more difficult to manage.

Now, in their therapist's office, Sophie exploded in a mix of tears and anger reminiscent of her reaction when she first learned of Micah's affair. This time Micah responded with his own anger. "What do I have to do to get you to understand that life goes on? I'm no longer seeing Rachael. I had to schedule a time for us to finalize a contract we worked on together last fall. If I drop that I'll be in even more trouble at the office. Besides, what difference does it make? For the past six months you've done nothing but rake me over the coals and monitor my every move. I'm tired of your punishing me. I've apologized and tried to make it up to you. But I'm not going to live the rest of my life this way."

Their therapist felt equally frustrated. They'd been working together for nearly four months, and at this point the couple seemed stuck. Every step forward seemed followed by a step backward. Couple therapy had been successful in helping Sophie and Micah to reduce their most antagonistic exchanges, but it hadn't been able to promote recovery of a more intimate or trusting relationship. Sophie couldn't move beyond focusing on "why" Micah had his affair, and Micah had long since given up trying to provide an explanation that would put Sophie's questions to rest. Sophie was terrified by the prospect that Micah's affair with Rachael would resume or a different affair would take its place. Micah sometimes hinted at problems in the marriage that had predated his affair, but resisted discussing these in session. Efforts to explore what had happened produced limited impact. Sophie wasn't about to excuse Micah for his affair, no matter what explanations he offered. Micah's efforts to comply with Sophie's new restrictions on his activities wore thin after the first few months. He no longer viewed discussion of his affair as a mechanism for healing the past, but instead as a barrier to moving forward. Every intervention by their therapist to help Sophie "move on" or to engage Micah in discussions of his affair met with further resistance and polarization.

How had the couple therapy become stuck? Are some relationship injuries too traumatic to permit recovery? Could Sophie's and Micah's therapist have protected the couple from some of the collateral damage following revelation of Micah's affair? Could the therapist have been more effective in integrating discussion of how or why the affair occurred with a process for moving on?

Clinicians are frequently likely to encounter individuals coping with infidelity—whether in the context of couple therapy aimed at recovery from an extramarital affair, individual therapy with someone struggling with his or her own affair or responding to a partner's affair, or interventions with children contending with consequences of a parent's infidelity. Representative community surveys indicate a lifetime prevalence of sexual infidelity of approximately 21% among men and 11% among women (Laumann, Gagnon, Michael, & Michaels, 1994); lifetime prevalence rates among older cohorts are higher. Broadening infidelity to encompass emotional as well as sexual affairs increases these rates among men and women to 44% and 25%, respectively (Glass & Wright, 1997). Infidelity is the most frequently cited cause of divorce (Amato & Rogers, 1997), with approximately 40% of divorced individuals reporting at least one extramarital sexual contact during their marriage (Janus & Janus, 1993).

Surveys of couple therapists indicate that they regard extramarital affairs as among the most difficult conflicts to treat and that they often feel inadequately trained to conduct effective interventions targeting them (Whisman, Dixon, & Johnson, 1997). Individual therapists are no more likely (and, indeed, may be even less likely) to feel competent in treating clients struggling with their own or a partner's infidelity. Among a spectrum of potential deficits may be the lack of a conceptual framework for viewing infidelity from individual, couple, or family-system based perspectives—as well as strategies regarding individual, couple, or family interventions addressing the often conflicting goals of individuals affected by the extramarital affair.

In this chapter we describe an integrative approach to working with couples struggling to recover from an extramarital affair. This approach draws on the theoretical and empirical literature regarding traumatic response as well as interpersonal forgiveness. It incorporates empirically supported interventions from both cognitive-behavioral and insight-oriented approaches to treating couple distress. It evolves from over 60 years of our collective clinical experience in working with couples struggling with deep interpersonal injuries as well as our own empirical research on couple therapy generally and mechanisms of forgiveness specifically. The affair-specific intervention model described here is the *only* couple-based intervention—designed specifically to address both individual and relationship consequences of infidelity—to have been empirically examined and supported in clinical research.

We begin by describing common adverse impacts of an affair on a couple's relationship and partners' individual functioning and then provide an overview of the conceptual model underlying our integrative treatment approach. Following this overview, we provide detailed descriptions of specific strategies for helping couples through three distinct stages of recovery: (1) dealing with the initial impact, (2) developing a shared understanding of factors contributing to the affair, and (3) reaching an informed decision about how to move on—either together or separately. Within each stage we identify challenges to treatment and specific strategies for addressing these challenges. We conclude with initial findings from a preliminary study examining the effectiveness of this integrative approach to treating infidelity.

THE TRAUMATIC IMPACT OF INFIDELITY

Both clinical observations and empirical investigations affirm the devastating impact that revelation of an affair typically has on a couple. For persons recently learning of their partner's affair (whom we refer to as the "injured partner"), research documents a broad range of negative emotional and behavioral effects including partner violence, depression, suicidal ideation, acute anxiety, and symptoms similar to post-traumatic stress disorder. Injured partners describe vacillating feelings of rage, overwhelming powerlessness, victimization, and abandonment (Abrahms Spring, 1996; Atkins, Baucom, & Jacobson, 2001; Beach, Jouriles, & O'Leary, 1985; Brown, 1991; Cano & O'Leary, 2000; Gordon, Baucom, & Snyder, 2004; Lusterman, 1998; Pittman, 1989; Reibstein & Richards, 1993). Similar to reactions observed in post-traumatic stress disorder (e.g., Resick & Calhoun, 2001), they report violation of fundamental assumptions regarding their participating partner, themselves, and their relationship (e.g., that partners can be trusted, that the relationship is a safe place)—shattering core beliefs essential to emotional security. Injured partners struggle with loss of control over an unpredictable future—exclaiming, "I don't know you any more; you aren't the person I thought you were" or "How could you do this? I thought I could trust you."

Given this unpredictability and ruptured trust, the injured person typically can't move forward with the relationship, even if the affair has ended. As long as injured partners don't have a clear sense of why the affair occurred, they can't trust their partners not to hurt them again. In the absence of this understanding, the participating partners (the partners who engaged in an affair) are likely to be seen as hurtful or even malicious people whose very faces or voices may serve as stimuli for painful emotions such as anxiety, confusion, anger, depression, and shame.

Such adverse consequences aren't restricted to injured partners. Among participating partners similar reactions of depression, suicidality, and acute anxiety are also common effects—particularly when disclosure or discovery of infidelity results in marital separation or threats of divorce. Anecdotal and some empirical evidence suggests that, regardless of culmination in separation or divorce, couples responding to infidelity exhibit disproportionately high rates of severe conflict and verbal or physical aggression, compared to maritally distressed couples not reporting an affair (Gordon, Heyman, & Slep, 2006). When children are present, the negative impact of their parents' turmoil frequently spills over into adverse consequences for them as well—increasing the likelihood of depression or withdrawal, disrupted social functioning, impaired academic performance, and a variety of conduct-related difficulties.[1]

The consequences of infidelity can be traumatic for the entire family. Given this conceptualization of affairs as interpersonal trauma, the literature on both traumatic responses and interpersonal forgiveness can be helpful when considering how to conceptualize and organize an effective treatment.

Treatments that arise from trauma theories generally assist clients in focusing more clearly on the trauma, expose them to the memories of the trauma, and help them to reconstruct their basic schemas about how the world operates and regain a new sense of control over their outcomes (e.g., Janoff-Bulman, 1989; Resick & Calhoun, 2001). Interestingly, these themes are echoed in newly developed forgiveness-based interventions. Studies have indicated that forgiveness-based interventions aimed at helping an individual cognitively reframe the interpersonal betrayal and gain a greater understanding of why the trauma occurred are effective in increasing participants' levels of forgiveness and in improving their levels of both individual and dyadic psychological functioning (e.g., Freedman & Enright, 1996; Worthington, 2005).

Similar to trauma-based approaches, in most theories of forgiveness the primary focus of the process is on developing a changed understanding of why the betrayal occurred and reconstructing a new meaning for the event (e.g., Enright & the Human Development Study Group, 1991; Gordon & Baucom, 1998; Rowe et al., 1989). Despite some differences, most theories of forgiveness are fairly consistent in their definitions of the end state of forgiveness, indicating three common elements: (a) gaining a more balanced view of the offender and the event, (b) decreasing negative affect toward the offender, potentially along with increased compassion, and (c) giving up the right to punish the offender further.

To date, both the trauma and forgiveness literatures have primarily emphasized interventions targeting individuals, with some exceptions (e.g., DiBlasio, 2000; Hargrave, 1994). Left largely unaddressed are how best to conceptualize the recovery process and what specific interventions to pursue when dealing with interpersonal trauma from a couple perspective. To this end, our integrative approach to helping couples recover from infidelity incorporates the strengths of two empirically supported treatments for relationship distress: cognitive-behavioral couple therapy (CBCT) and insight-oriented couple therapy (IOCT). In the section that follows we summarize therapeutic strategies from each of these approaches and describe their respective roles in treating couples struggling with issues of infidelity.

PROMOTING BOTH SKILLS AND UNDERSTANDING ESSENTIAL TO RECOVERY

Cognitive-behavioral couple therapy (CBCT) builds on skills-based interventions of behavioral couple therapy targeting couple communication and behavior-exchange by directing partners' attention to explanations they construct for each other's behavior and to expectations and standards they hold for their own relationship and for relationships in general (Epstein & Baucom, 2002). The structured, directed strategies offered within cognitive-behavioral interventions provide focus and direction to couples at a time when they are particularly needed.

Before couples can explore the meaning of an affair for their relationship or reestablish trust and intimacy, they first need assistance in containing the emotional turmoil and destructive exchanges that often characterize initial responses to the disclosure or discovery of an affair. Partners frequently need assistance in communicating feelings in a constructive manner and reaching intermediate decisions about how to set boundaries regarding involvement with the outside affair person, how much information to share with children or extended family, and how to interact with each other. Moreover, in exploring factors that placed their relationship at risk for an affair, couples frequently need to improve their ability to negotiate basic changes in how they interact and manage daily challenges of their relationship. Cognitive-behavioral couple therapy is particularly well-suited to these therapeutic objectives. However, CBCT's general focus on the present and the future also leaves important gaps in dealing with such couples. Many couples report that they can't merely move forward and put the affair behind them; they need some way to process the trauma that has occurred and some way to make sense of the past.

Insight-oriented couple therapy (IOCT) offers therapeutic strategies designed specifically to help partners understand current relationship struggles from the perspective of partners' developmental histories. In IOCT, previous relationships, their affective components, and strategies for emotional gratification and anxiety containment are reconstructed with a focus on identifying for each partner consistencies in their interpersonal conflicts and coping styles across relationships (Snyder, 1999). Hence, insight-oriented strategies in couple therapy offer the potential of helping partners to gain a better understanding of both their own and each other's developmental histories, the role that their respective pasts have played throughout their marriage, and how individual and relationship dynamics influenced by their pasts may have served as potential risk factors contributing to the participating partner's extramarital affair.

These revelations of vulnerability can help the partners develop more empathy and compassion for each other. Furthermore, as this increased understanding and insight evolve, they are placed within a cognitive-behavioral framework of developing a well-balanced set of attributions resulting in a richer and more coherent narrative for the event, along with a focus on what changes are needed in the relationship for the future. Thus, our couple-based intervention for extramarital affairs integrates cognitive-behavioral with insight-oriented interventions to provide a treatment strategy that balances the past, present, and future with an increased emphasis on affect and developmental factors.

This integrative intervention helps couples struggling to recover from an affair to accomplish three major tasks: (1) cope with the initial impact of an affair, (2) develop a shared understanding of factors contributing to the affair and influencing recovery, and (3) reach and implement an informed decision about how to move on—either together or separately. The components and challenges of each stage of treatment are described in further detail below. Although this stage model is presented in a linear fashion, our experience is that some individuals demonstrate a mixture of symptoms from various stages at a given time and might return to earlier stages after progressing through a later stage (e.g., reexperiencing Stage 1 phenomena after a flashback later in the process). Thus, the clinician should use the following recommendations as guidelines for treatment that can be adapted flexibly to meet a given couple's needs.

STAGE 1: ADDRESSING THE IMPACT OF AN AFFAIR

Treatment Challenges and Strategies

Couples entering treatment following recent disclosure or discovery of an affair often exhibit intense negative emotions and pervasive disruption of both individual and relationship functioning that challenge even experienced couple therapists. One or both partners may report inability to complete the most basic daily tasks of caring for themselves or their children and may be unable to function effectively outside the home. Individuals outside the couple's relationship—including friends, extended family, or the outside affair person—may interact with either partner in a manner that prolongs or exacerbates emotional and behavioral turmoil rather than promoting stabilization or recovery. Questions of whether to continue living together, how to deal with the outside affair person, whom to tell of the affair and what to disclose, how to attend to daily tasks of meals or child care, or how to contain negative exchanges and prevent emotional or physical aggression—all need to be addressed early on to prevent additional damage from occurring to the partners or their relationship.

Effective intervention requires explicit, active interventions by the therapist to establish and maintain a therapeutic environment. Doing so requires accomplishing three tasks: (1) establishing an atmosphere of safety and trust; (2) demonstrating competence; and (3) preparing the couple for therapy by providing a conceptual model for treatment. Safety and trust result from limiting partners' aggressive exchanges within sessions in an empathic but firm way. The therapist needs to describe his or her experience in working with affairs and similar relationship trauma and provide a brief overview of the three-stage treatment model that conveys a clear vision of how recovery progresses and what's required of participants along the way. Allowing partners to describe how they've struggled thus far needs to be balanced by a structured process that limits domination by discussion of the affair details, intervenes in the crisis to help the couple determine how best to get through the coming weeks, and promotes a collaborative effort to understand more fully the context of what has happened in order to be able to reach more informed decisions down the road.

During Stage 1 it is important for therapists to avoid getting lost in the chaos of partners' own emotional turmoil; this requires slowing interactions, keeping discussions focused on the most urgent or immediate decisions, and containing negative exchanges during sessions. Establishing and maintaining a therapeutic alliance with both partners can be particularly challenging; for example, injured partners often find it difficult to tolerate therapists' empathic responses to participating partners' guilt, hurt, or loneliness. Therapists should refrain from either encouraging or supporting unrealistic commitments, which can set the couple up for further failure (e.g., never speaking again to an affair partner who works in the same office); they also should avoid trying to exert influence over persons not included in the sessions (e.g., the affair partner or extended family). Just as important as containing destructive negative exchanges is confronting some couples' "flight into health" as a way of avoiding distress in the short term; instead, the therapist should work to promote tolerance for examining the affair more intensely in order to promote more enduring resolution in the long term.

Assessment

The first stage of the treatment encompasses assessment and management of the affair's impact. Using common assessment strategies for couples (Epstein & Baucom, 2002; Snyder, Heyman, & Haynes, 2005), basic aspects of couple functioning relevant to all couples should be assessed (e.g., satisfaction, communication skills, and commitment level). Furthermore, a conjoint session focused on gathering information about the couple's relationship history should be conducted, with specific attention paid to events and experiences leading up to the affair. In addition, the therapist should gather information about what the injured partner knows about the affair, how the affair came to light, and how the couple is currently dealing with its impact, looking at both strengths and weaknesses in the couple's current functioning.

Individual assessment sessions, one for each partner, also may be beneficial. In addition to further information about the status of the affair and each person's current commitment to the primary couple relationship, the focus of such individual sessions is on obtaining an individual history for each partner, paying particular attention to aspects of his or her development that may have influenced actions surrounding the affair. Examples of these issues may be patterns in past relationships, beliefs about marriage, and parental history and attitudes toward marriages. These sessions also allow the therapist to explore hidden agendas (e.g., the participating partner's goal of leaving the marriage) and screen for any potentially problematic areas such as suicidality or violence. Therapists should be careful about setting boundaries of confidentiality for these sessions as they may be left holding secrets confided by one member of the couple that can be detrimental to the therapeutic alliance. This problem can be avoided by informing the partners that information raised in individual sessions may need to be addressed in the conjoint sessions, but that the therapist will always discuss how and when to do this with the individual first.

Therapeutic Components of Stage 1

After completing the assessment, the therapist should have a good under-standing of how the couple is functioning. The therapist should then provide the couple with (a) the therapist's initial conceptualization of what may have led up to the affair, (b) a summary of what problems the couple is currently facing in their relationship and why they're experiencing these problems, and (c) a treatment strategy. Then the couple should be given an explanation of the stages of the recovery process and the trauma-response conceptualization described in the preceding pages. In addition to assessment and feedback, the first stage of therapy has five basic components: (1) boundary setting, (2) self-care techniques, (3) time-out and "venting" techniques, (4) emotional expressiveness skills and discussion of the impact of the affair, and (5) coping with flashbacks.

Boundary Setting   When a couple feels out of control and in crisis, pro-viding healthy boundaries can help to create some sense of normalcy and predictability. Because their own relationship has become dysregulated, set-ting boundaries or limits on how the partners interact with each other can be helpful. Moreover, setting strong and clear boundaries on interactions with the outside, third person is vital.

First, the couple's own relationship must be targeted to create a sense of safety in the relationship and minimize further negative effects. A major problem confronting many couples dealing with the impact of an affair is that negative emotions engendered by the betrayal may flood into many aspects of their functioning. Hence, couples reeling from an affair often need immediate assistance in setting limits on their negative interactions. For some couples, this involves making agreements about when, how often, and what aspects of the affair they will discuss. For other couples, problem-solving strategies may be directed toward temporary solutions designed primarily for "dam-age control." For example, if a common cause of arguments is a wife's anxi-ety regarding her husband's whereabouts, then her husband may agree to be zealous in checking in with his wife until some trust or security has been reestablished.

Second, in order for the injured partner to feel safe enough to engage in the therapeutic process, it is important for the participating partner to set strong boundaries on interactions with the outside third party. This is most easily achieved if the participating partner agrees to end the relationship with the third person with no further contact. However, this absolute termination is sometimes difficult to create for a variety of reasons. Some participating partners are unwilling to terminate all interaction with the outside person when the affair is discovered; sometimes logistics make it impractical to have no interactions, at least immediately (e.g., when the participating partner and third person work together); and at times, the outside person continues to contact the participating partner, despite being told not to do so. Because rebuilding trust is a crucial part of the therapeutic process, the therapist encourages the participating partner to be honest in stating what boundaries he or she is willing to set with the outside person at present and how that will be carried out, along with agreements for how the injured partner will be informed of contact with the outside person. However, it is crucial that the couple eventually together set limits on interactions with the outside person, particularly if the outsider insists on intruding into their relationship. From our experience, it is clear that continued interactions with the outside partner can have the effect of retraumatizing the injured partner and eroding the progress that the couple is able to make.

Self-Care Techniques   Because the emotional and cognitive sequelae of affairs often involve feelings of anxiety, depression, or shame, another major target of Stage 1 involves helping both partners to take better care of themselves in order to have more emotional resources to use as they work through the aftermath of the affair. The current treatment offers basic self-care guidelines that encompass three areas: (a) physical care, including such aspects as eating well, sleep, decreased caffeine, and exercise; (b) social support, with careful attention paid to what's appropriate to disclose to others and what is not; and (c) spiritual support, such as meditation, prayer, and talking with spiritual counselors if consistent with the partner's belief system.

Time-Out and Venting Techniques   In light of the intense negative interactions between the partners at this stage in the process, most couples need strategies that allow them to disengage when the level of emotion becomes too high. "Time-out" strategies are introduced, and partners are instructed on how to recognize when one needs to be called and how to do so effectively. In addition, instead of using time-outs to fume and plan a counterattack, the partners are instructed in how to use the time-outs constructively—for example, to "vent" their tension through nonaggressive physical exercise, or to calm themselves through relaxation strategies.

Discussing the Impact of the Affair   A common need for an injured partner is to express to the participating partner how she or he has been hurt or angered by the affair. It is likely that this need serves both a punitive and a protective function. By its punitive qualities, this discussion serves as a way to communicate that what happened was wrong and to ensure that the participating partner also feels as much discomfort as possible as a result of his or her actions. Often these interactions between the partners are rancorous and complicated by feelings of anger and guilt on the part of the participating partner. Frequently, the participating partner also has feelings of bitterness about an earlier hurt or betrayal in the marriage, which interferes with his or her ability to sympathize with the injured partner's feelings of betrayal. As a result, the injured partner is not likely to feel heard and may increase demands or comments, precipitating a negative interaction cycle between the partners.

The current treatment seeks to interrupt this cycle through three means. First, the couple is taught to use appropriate emotional expressiveness skills for both speaker and listener to help the injured person be more effective in communicating feelings and the participating partner to be more effective in demonstrating that she or he is listening (Epstein & Baucom, 2002). Second, the couple is given a careful conceptualization of why this step is necessary. The participating partner must understand that his or her own perspective of the affair will most likely not be effectively understood by the injured partner unless the injured partner is first able to experience that the participating partner truly understands and is remorseful for the effect of his or her actions on the injured person and the relationship. Finally, the injured partner is encouraged to write a letter exploring his or her feelings and reactions to the affair, which is first given to the therapist. After feedback from the therapist, the letter is then revised and read to the participating partner. This process allows injured partners to explore their reactions in a calmer manner, and then enables them to take time to express their feelings in ways that are not attacking or abusive and are more likely to be heard by the participating partner.

Coping With "Flashbacks"   A final but critical component in Stage 1 is the explanation of "flashback" phenomena and the development of a plan for how to cope with them. Because the reaction to an affair strongly parallels a traumatic response, both partners may encounter reexperiencing phenomena. For example, a husband may discover an unexplained number on a telephone bill, which may then remind him of the unexplained telephone calls during the affair and trigger a flood of affect related to his wife's affair. If the wife is not aware of this sequence of events, her husband's emotions may appear inexplicable, which in turn may cause her to question the progress they may be making in recovering from the affair. In working with couples, we explain the concept of a flashback in this context and how to address such experiences. We often provide a handout with a set of guidelines for addressing flashbacks. Within these guidelines, couples are taught to differentiate between upsetting events that reflect current inappropriate behavior versus events that trigger feelings, images, and memories from the past.

In contrast to Sophie and Micah, the couple described at the beginning of this chapter, some couples navigate the initial chaos following an affair more successfully in containing negativity and reaching preliminary decisions to help them minimize further damage. Maggie and Scott were such a couple. Their therapist helped them to set limits on their heated arguments, structure boundaries on their daily interactions as well as their discussions of Maggie's affair, and identify appropriate sources of individual support.

The first two weeks following Maggie's affair were devastating. Scott insisted on a divorce and threatened to tell their friends and families everything that had happened. Maggie felt desperate and too alone to end conversations with her affair partner. The couple's arguments disrupted mealtimes, interfered with sleep, and carried over into their interactions around the children. Basic household tasks went unattended; bills went unpaid.

At the end of their first therapy session three weeks after Maggie's affair became known, she and Scott agreed to a truce. Scott agreed to sleep in the guest room, and they took turns arranging separate meals with the children until they could participate in family rituals without antagonism. At their therapist's direction, they agreed to restrict discussions of Maggie's affair to 30-minute periods after their children were in bed or on the weekend when their children were at friends' homes. Scott agreed to prepare a short list of his most urgent questions; Maggie agreed to answer these honestly or to state that she was not yet ready to discuss a given question. They both agreed to postpone questions of "why" the affair happened until they were able to manage their emotions more effectively and sustain more productive discussions.

Both partners agreed that disclosing Maggie's affair to their families could make their recovery more difficult down the road. Scott identified a trusted friend whom he could draw on for confidential support and who had previously been helpful during times of crisis. Maggie found strength from a spiritual counselor and, within a week, ended all contact with the outside affair partner. Both Scott and Maggie understood that, for now, little actual recovery was likely to occur. Instead, they pledged toward an initial goal of not making things worse and took specific steps to ensure this.

STAGE 2: EXAMINING CONTEXT

After addressing the initial impact of the affair in Stage 1, the second stage of treatment focuses on helping the couple explore and understand the context of the affair. This second stage typically comprises the heart of treatment and demands the greatest amount of time. Injured partners (and sometimes participating partners) cannot move forward until they have a more complete and thoughtful understanding of why the affair occurred. Partners' explanations for the affair help the couple decide whether they want to maintain their relationship, what needs to change, or if they should move forward by ending their relationship.

Mitch had nothing left to say to Courtney about his affair. It was a stupid mistake, and one he deeply regretted. It had occurred one weekend when Courtney had been visiting friends out of town. He had run into a former girlfriend at a ballgame, they had gone to a bar for drinks afterward, and somehow ended up back at her place. He had not talked with her since. Courtney got wind of it from a friend of hers who had seen Mitch leaving the bar and getting into the other woman's car. Their marriage had been a wreck ever since.

Courtney kept asking him why he did it, and Mitch did not have a clue how to answer. He had tried chalking it up to unexpected stirring of an old flame that had just as quickly extinguished. He alternately blamed himself, solicitation by his ex-girlfriend, having too much to drink, or just plain inexplicable bad judgment. It did not matter—no number of explanations satisfied Courtney. He had been clear that it did not reflect any unhappiness with Courtney or their marriage. In fact, he had always regarded himself as happily married to a wonderful woman. But expressing that to Courtney had not helped. "If you can cheat on me when nothing is wrong, why should I believe you won't cheat on me again?" she exclaimed. "How am I ever supposed to trust you again? What am I supposed to change?"

Mitch kept waiting for time to heal her wounds, but Courtney's despair just grew deeper. He wished she could just get over it. He apologized repeatedly until Courtney told him she was sick of his apologies. He tried to make it up to her by spending virtually all his free time with her and their kids. He suggested a family vacation, but he and she remained as distant during their trip as they had been at home. Every discussion ended up worse than the previous one, and eventually Mitch refused to discuss the affair any further.

By the time they sought couple therapy, they were barely interacting except around essential household and child-rearing tasks. Their therapist's efforts to elicit explanations from Mitch for his brief affair met with silence or repeated assertions of "I don't know—it happened—I feel awful about it—and I'll never do it again." Courtney insisted she needed to understand why Mitch had been unfaithful if she was ever to trust him again, but just as quickly added that she would never understand. "Your betraying me will never make sense. It was wrong—no matter what reasons you come up with." The couple seemed as entrenched as they were miserable, and their therapist felt powerless to get them unstuck.

Treatment Challenges and Strategies

Couples need a roadmap for recovering trust and intimacy. It is not enough to contain the initial impact and reduce partners' negative exchanges. Injured partners, in particular, need ways to restore emotional security and reduce their fear of further betrayals. Both partners often crave mechanisms for restoring trust—injured partners for regaining it, and participating partners for instilling it. Reestablishing security is an essential precursor to letting go, forgiving, or moving on emotionally—either together or apart. Following an affair, couples who fail to restore security either remain chronically distant and emotionally aloof, craft a fragile working alliance marked by episodic intrusions of mistrust or resentment, or eventually end their relationship in despair.

The overarching goal of therapeutic interventions in Stage 2 is to promote a shared comprehensive formulation of how the affair came about. For injured partners this formulation facilitates greater predictability regarding future fidelity and a more balanced and realistic view of their partner (either a softening of anger or confrontation of enduring negative qualities). For participating partners an expanded explanatory framework promotes more accurate appraisals of responsibility for decisions culminating in the affair. For both partners, a comprehensive and accurate understanding of factors contributing to the affair prepares them for necessary individual and relationship changes aimed at reducing these influences.

Several challenges can undermine interventions during Stage 2 if not handled well by the therapist. First, it is important to emphasize to partners that "reasons" for the affair do not constitute "excuses." That is, participating partners are always held responsible for their choices to have the affair while delineating the context within which they made that decision (Allen et al., 2005). Second, when exploring aspects of the injured partner that potentially contributed to their relationship becoming more vulnerable to an affair (e.g., deficits in emotional responsiveness, excessive negativity, prolonged absences, or significant emotional or behavioral problems), it is important that such factors be examined without blaming the injured partner for the participating partner's response of engaging in an affair. It is also important to prepare both partners to see that no amount of understanding may result in the affair "making sense"—and that the affair may always seem to some extent "irrational" or "unfathomable."

Finally, either partner may exhibit characteristics that render collaborative exploration of contributing factors more difficult—e.g., poor affect regulation that makes such discussions too threatening to pursue; inability to process or conceptualize psychological or interpersonal phenomena; persistent externalization of responsibility for one's own behaviors; or excessive tendencies toward guilt or caretaking that detract from the other partner's exploration of his or her own contributions to the affair. In such cases, couple-based interventions throughout Stage 2 need to be integrated with individual interventions targeting partners' own characteristics detracting from the goals and therapeutic processes essential to this stage.

Therapeutic Components

Exploring Factors Potentially Contributing to the Affair   We have previously articulated a comprehensive organizational framework for exploring a diverse range of factors potentially contributing to the context of an affair or influencing one or both partners' subsequent responses (Allen et al., 2005). The major domains of factors to explore in Stage 2 include (a) aspects of the relationship, such as difficulty communicating or finding time for each other; (b) external issues such as job stress, financial difficulties, or conflicts with in-laws; (c) issues specific to the participating partner such as his or her beliefs about marriage, or his or her social development history; and (d) issues specific to the injured partner such as his or her developmental history, or his or her relationship skills. In each domain, these factors are considered for their potential role as predisposing or precipitating influences leading up to the affair, factors impacting maintenance of the affair and eventual discovery or disclosure, and influences bearing on partners' subsequent responses or recovery.

These sessions exploring the context of the affair typically are conducted in two ways. Depending on the couple's level of skill and their motivation to listen to and understand each other, these sessions can take the form of structured discussions between the partners as they attempt to understand the many factors that potentially contributed to the affair. The therapist intervenes as necessary to highlight certain points, reinterpret distorted cognitions, or draw parallels or inferences from their developmental histories that the partners are not able to draw themselves. However, if the couple's communication skills are weak, if either partner is acutely defensive, or if they are having difficulty understanding each other's positions, then the therapist may structure the sessions so that they are more similar to individual therapy sessions with one partner, while the other partner listens and occasionally is asked to summarize his or her understanding of what is being expressed.

The therapist also looks for patterns and similarities between what the partners have reported in their individual histories and the problems they are reporting in their own relationship. It is in this exploration that the treatment borrows most heavily from insight-oriented approaches. Understanding how past needs and wishes influence an individual's choices in the present is a critical element to understanding why the individual chose to have an affair, or how the injured partner has responded to this event. Often, the decision to choose an affair as a possible solution to present problems is influenced by strategies that have worked in the past, or by developmental needs that were not met in the past. For example, a woman who was repeatedly rejected sexually in early adolescence and young adulthood, and consequently sees herself as unlovable and undesirable, may be particularly vulnerable to choosing a sexual affair to resolve her feelings of rejection and abandonment in her marriage. Directing both members of the couple to explore these influences helps them to gain a deeper understanding of each other's vulnerabilities and may help promote a greater level of empathy and compassion between them.

Constructing a Shared Narrative   After examining potential contributing factors across diverse domains, the therapist's task is to help the couple integrate the disparate pieces of information they have gleaned into a coherent narrative explaining how the affair came about. Achieving a shared understanding of how the affair came about is central to partners' developing a new set of assumptions about themselves, each other, and their relationship. This goal can be accomplished in several ways. As one, the therapist can explain to the couple that this is the next task and ask each partner to prepare for the next session by trying to "pull it all together," including a focus on the (a) relationship issues, (b) outside issues impacting their relationship, (c) individual issues related to the participating partner, and (d) individual issues related to the injured partner that contributed to the context within which the affair occurred. The couple and therapist then discuss their fullest understanding at the next session.

Alternatively, each partner can be asked to write a letter for the next session (similar to the task in Stage 1 described earlier) in which each person describes now in a fuller and softened manner what he or she understands to be these relevant factors. As a result of such issues arising from discussion of the affair, the therapist and the couple discuss what aspects of their relationship may need additional attention and how this can be accomplished in order to help them avoid future betrayals. In this respect, the therapy begins to move from a focus on the past to a focus on the present and future of the relationship.

Some couples seeking therapy following an affair move quickly into Stage 2 work, having already managed the initial turmoil following disclosure or discovery reasonably well on their own. Gwen and Mark were such a couple. They did not seek therapy until three months after Mark disclosed his affair to Gwen. Mark had already ended his affair before revealing it, but found his guilt disrupting virtually all his interactions with Gwen. Gwen had felt profoundly hurt by Mark's disclosure, but the couple had pledged to "move on" and put Mark's affair behind them. Several months later, when it became clear to both spouses that unresolved feelings threatened their ability to recover the intimacy they had enjoyed previously, Gwen suggested getting help.

> In their first therapy session, Gwen described how she had struggled to make sense of her husband's affair. If nothing else, Mark had always been someone she could count on. From the earliest days of their relationship he had been sensitive and caring.
>
> Over the next two months, their therapist helped them to examine factors in and outside their relationship that had rendered their marriage more vulnerable. Mark and Gwen talked about the distance

that had gradually grown between them as Mark's success at work drew him away from home, and Gwen's involvement with the children sometimes kept her from being with him. Mark was reluctant to complain about any of the shortcomings in their marriage, and struggled with his feelings of remorse and shame. He was reluctant to examine any explanations that might make it "easier" to understand, because he explicitly did not want it to be "easy" for him. The couple's therapist supported Mark's wish to be "accountable," but also helped Mark to understand that accountability involved looking at all the factors—including those for which Mark may have had less influence or even awareness. Their therapist's clear distinction between "reasons" and "excuses" proved helpful to both spouses. Mark gradually struggled through his guilt to confront long-standing issues involving his own lingering self-doubts that had their roots back in adolescence. He had to confront and shed himself of these before he could fully embrace the goodness of his relationship with Gwen.

Gwen did not simply "get over" Mark's affair after developing a better understanding of his own needs that had contributed to it. She continued to hurt. But Mark's affair became less terrifying to her, less like a random act that could repeat itself, and less like a response to something fundamentally wrong about herself. By examining what aspects of himself had contributed to his affair, Mark also seemed better able to understand what had happened as a way of making sure it did not happen again. He could now recognize his occasional feelings of loneliness in the marriage more easily; moreover, using new emotional expressiveness skills acquired in therapy, he was able to convey these feelings in ways that helped Gwen to feel needed rather than criticized, and both of them to regain the closeness they each desired rather than drifting further apart.

STAGE 3: MOVING ON

Even after a therapist helps a couple to contain the initial negative impact of an affair and then guides them through a systematic appraisal of potential contributing factors, either partner can remain mired in the past or indecisive about the future. Injured partners' hurt, anger, or fear of future betrayals may persist or episodically resurface in intense or destructive ways. Participating partners may also struggle with unrelenting guilt, unresolved resentments toward their partner that potentially contributed to the affair originally, or lingering attachment to the outside affair partner or ambivalence about remaining in the marriage.

Keith had tried to get over Judy's affair, but continued to struggle. Her brief relationship with a business consultant had devastated him. After ending her affair, Judy had moved out because she was not sure she wanted to remain married to Keith. Now, six months later, they had slowly pieced their lives back together and restored a reasonably peaceful home. Their two young children seemed relatively unscathed, as though nothing had happened.

But something had happened—and both Keith and Judy felt keenly aware of the lingering distance between them. Judy had expressed deep remorse for the hurt she had caused Keith, and she pledged never again to use an affair as a way of dealing with her own loneliness in the marriage. Keith had also accepted some of his own responsibility for Judy's loneliness and various ways he had taken her and their marriage for granted. Through months of couple therapy, they had learned better ways of approaching decisions and had implemented critical changes in how they shared responsibilities in the home.

But emotional and physical intimacy still eluded them. Keith seemed less engaged in their lovemaking, and physical closeness other than intercourse was rare. Every now and then his residual hurt erupted in anger. Judy dared not criticize anything that Keith did or left undone—because it risked his responding with, "If I'm not good enough—why don't you just find someone else like before?" Later he would apologize, but his harsh words continued to sting and Judy pulled away if Keith tried to hold her.

Their therapist also felt at a loss. The couple had survived Judy's affair and had worked to understand much that had contributed to it. They had initiated important changes in their marriage. But something vital was missing—and both the couple and their therapist recognized this. What would it take for both Keith and Judy to move on?

Treatment Challenges and Strategies

Once therapeutic efforts in Stage 2 have been completed or approach a point of diminished new information, the therapist needs to help partners move on emotionally—either together or apart. When therapists or couples talk about "moving on," "forgiving," or "letting go" they often mean different things—in terms of both what it would look like at the end and what it would take to get there. When helping couples to recover from infidelity we define *moving on* as comprising four key elements: (1) Each partner regains a balanced view of the other person and their relationship; (2) they commit not to let their hurt or anger rule their thoughts and behavior toward the partner or dominate their lives; (3) they voluntarily give up the right to continue punishing the partner for his or her actions or demanding further restitution; and (4) they decide whether to continue in the relationship based on a realistic assessment of both its positive and negative qualities.

Treatment strategies in Stage 3 emphasize helping partners examine their personal beliefs about forgiveness and how these relate to their efforts to move on from the affair. Additional strategies encourage integration of everything partners have learned about themselves and their relationship—well beyond the affair—to reach an informed decision about whether to continue in their relationship or move on separately. For couples deciding to move on together, interventions emphasize additional changes partners will need to undertake either individually or conjointly to strengthen their relationship and reduce any influences that potentially render it more vulnerable to another affair in the future. If one partner or the other reaches an informed decision to end the relationship, the couple is helped to implement that decision in order to move on separately in ways that are least hurtful to themselves and others they love—particularly their children.

It is important during Stage 3 that therapists not try to bring about their own preferred outcome, but that they also not abdicate responsibility for ensuring that all relevant information is considered by both partners in pursuing a thoughtful decision about how to move on. Similarly, the therapist needs to strike a balance between respecting partners' personal values and beliefs about forgiveness while also challenging ways in which partners' beliefs may interfere with moving on in an emotionally healthy manner. Some couples risk remaining ambivalent about their marriage for years—draining themselves of the energy required to nurture and strengthen their relationship while avoiding the challenges of pursuing healthier alternatives either alone or in a different relationship. Therapists need to balance patience with a sometimes tortuous decisional process against actively engaging partners in reaching decisions that allow them to move forward.

Therapeutic Components

Discussion of Forgiveness   Four basic aspects of forgiveness are discussed with the couple: (1) a description of the forgiveness model, (2) common beliefs about forgiveness, (3) consequences of forgiving and not forgiving, and (4) addressing blocks to forgiving, or "moving on." For example, partners may report difficulty with forgiveness out of beliefs that forgiving their partner is "weak" or is equivalent to declaring that what happened is acceptable or excusable. Or partners may equate forgiving with forgetting, or with rendering oneself vulnerable to being injured in a similar way in the future. Addressing such beliefs by exploring whether one may forgive and yet also appropriately hold the partner responsible for his or her behaviors may result in the couple developing a new conceptualization of forgiveness that feels more possible for them to achieve.

Similarly, the therapist often must explore "blocks" to forgiveness. Couples who have reasonable beliefs about forgiveness may still experience resistance to forgiving, and it is important for the therapist to examine those issues that prevent the couple from moving forward. One such issue may be that one spouse is still dominated by anger about his or her partner—for example, because of perceived power imbalances following the affair or failure to regain an adequate sense of safety in the relationship. In such cases, the anger may serve a protective function for the angry spouse. Alternatively, the anger may point to unresolved relational questions or violated assumptions that were not explored or resolved in earlier stages. Sometimes difficulty moving beyond anger toward forgiveness reflects lingering resentments from the affair not based on current dynamics in the marriage. In such cases, using motivational interviewing techniques (Miller & Rollnick, 2002) to help the angry partner examine the costs and benefits of continuing in this position versus actively working to put the anger and the event behind him or her may be useful. Additional strategies for helping clients forgive are also detailed in a manual on forgiveness therapy (Enright & Fitzgibbons, 2000).

Exploration of Factors Affecting Their Decision to Continue Their Relationship   In this final stage of treatment, couples are encouraged to use what they have learned about each other and their marriage to decide whether their relationship is a healthy one for them or not. In our work with couples, we emphasize an important distinction between "forgiveness" and "reconciliation." That is, couples who have successfully negotiated the forgiveness process may still decide to dissolve their relationship based on their new understandings of themselves. In these cases, the therapist strives to help partners separate without intense anger and resentment toward each other. To this end, couples are encouraged to ask themselves separately—and then to discuss together within the sessions—a series of questions that the therapist designs to help them evaluate their relationship. These questions focus on whether each partner is willing and able to make individual changes needed to preserve the relationship and help it be rewarding; whether as a couple they can work together effectively as a unit for the family; and whether they are willing to make needed changes in interacting with the outside world (e.g., patterns at work, interacting with other people) that might be related to the affair.

> Keith and Judy, the couple described earlier, recognized that they could not continue to interact in the same ways they had during the first six months following Judy's disclosure of her affair. Keith acknowledged that his angry outbursts toward Judy were exacting a cumulative toll and eroding any remaining closeness in their marriage. In a tearful but decisive session, he acknowledged feeling terrified of losing Judy following her affair but unable to express this for fear of seeming weak to her or his friends; in addition to expressing his hurt, Keith's anger reflected misguided efforts to project an image of strength. Keith also confessed to a reluctance to relinquish his status as the injured party in their marriage and the leverage this afforded him when he and Judy disagreed on issues. Keith resolved

to take more responsibility for dealing with residual feelings of hurt and insecurity in the marriage. He announced his wish for their marriage to continue and resolved to renew his efforts toward this goal.

Keith's declarations had a liberating effect on Judy. She continued to struggle with remorse and shame over her affair, but she also recognized that these feelings had blocked her abilities to experience joy and laughter with Keith—something they had both missed. She reassured Keith that she did not expect him to "get over" his hurt but also acknowledged that his continued anger had driven her to seek refuge alone rather than reach out for comfort. Keith and Judy each vowed that they would not forget Judy's affair—but instead would use that painful experience to prize what they had nearly lost and since restored, and would continually take steps to protect their marriage from future trauma.

Sometimes couples work successfully through the first three stages of this affair-specific treatment but, as a consequence of their efforts, recognize enduring individual or relationship issues that could potentially benefit from continued therapeutic work. For example, the couple may have identified significant stressors from child rearing as a vulnerability factor contributing to the affair, but still struggle toward acquiring more effective, collaborative parenting strategies. Or the challenges of balancing dual careers may warrant continued therapeutic interventions as the couple wrestles with decisions around child care or potential relocation to a new community. Alternatively, one or both partners may recognize long-standing relationship patterns that have their developmental origins from earlier relationships and seek to explore these more intensely in individual therapy; quite commonly, however—especially when the couple therapy has been successful—individuals express a preference to pursue these issues in conjoint sessions with their partner as a way of promoting increased understanding and opportunities for empathic joining within the marriage.

At other times when reaching the end of Stage 2, partners may conclude that critical factors contributing to the affair cannot be resolved and may determine that the best decision for them is to end their relationship and move on separately. When either partner concludes after careful consideration of all the relevant information that continuing their relationship is not in their best interests, we work to help them dissolve the relationship in a manner that is least hurtful to the two of them and to others involved in their lives—including children, other family members, and friends.

GENERAL CONSIDERATIONS IN RESPONSES TO AFFAIRS AND IMPLICATIONS FOR TREATMENT

Each couple presents their own unique challenges when affairs occur. However, there are some frequent complicating factors that the clinician should be attuned to when working with couples surrounding infidelity.

Psychopathology

As with most couple treatments, a high level of psychopathology is a poor prognostic indicator for successful recovery (Snyder & Whisman, 2003). This problem may be particularly true when the participating partner engages in affairs because she or he has antisocial or narcissistic traits and believes she or he is above social norms and mores. Such thinking communicates to the injured partner that the participating partner is at risk for additional affairs, particularly if lacking remorse or demonstrating persistent defensiveness about the affair. In this instance, a goal of treatment is to ensure that the injured partner becomes fully aware of this pattern of behavior and is able to make a good decision about whether to continue the relationship.

Individual psychological problems among injured partners also complicate treatment. Some injured partners have preexisting difficulties with affect regulation. These couples become difficult to work with due to the need to contain negative affect that dominates sessions and the couple's life outside of treatment. If the injured person generally struggles with regulating negative feelings, the strategies described in Stage 1 of treatment can be useful for these situations; so too may be the strategies for promoting forgiveness described in Stage 3. For couples in which one or both partners have long-term, extreme difficulties with affect regulation, we have developed a couple-based intervention to address such difficulties (Kirby & Baucom, in press).

Comfort With Affect

Not all affair couples present with chaotic, emotionally charged, negative interactions. Indeed, we have found avoidance of conflict to be a major relationship characteristic associated with the development of an affair in many couples. Not surprisingly, this same general reluctance to address conflict often continues after the discovery of the affair. Such couples might easily agree to forgive each other, particularly if the affair has ended, without addressing the critical issues described in this treatment. Strategies to address this discomfort with affect were discussed earlier regarding Stage 1 interventions. However, it may also be important to address the developmental source of this problem in Stage 2 of therapy, particularly if avoidance of conflict is a major contributing factor to the affair. Often, these individuals have had either direct or vicarious experiences with intense emotions in the past that had frightening or devastating outcomes. Thus, a major therapeutic task would be exploring these fears and the consequences of continued avoidance, and creating an explicitly safe environment for the expression of negative affect.

Level of Commitment

A higher level of commitment to the relationship typically leads couples to work harder in treatment and to be more willing to engage in emotional risk-taking within therapy. However, an initial ambivalence about the relationship is not necessarily a prognostic indicator of treatment failure. Ambivalence at the beginning of treatment does not preclude the couple's ability to try to improve and understand their relationship in order to come to a good decision about whether to continue with the marriage, and in fact is often quite understandable in light of the presenting issue. It is often helpful to frame this ambivalence as such in order to normalize these feelings.

On the other hand, as the treatment progresses, one may find that the issue of commitment in the treatment of infidelity is related to a developmentally based fear of intimacy or feelings of being "trapped" in a stable relationship. Attachment theorists describe a pattern of attachment that is characterized by approach-avoidance (e.g., Hazan & Shaver, 1987). Individuals with this pattern may need intimate relationships and seek them out, yet fear them to such an extent that they find it difficult to feel safe in long-term intimate relationships. Affairs may then serve as a means to create a safe level of distance from their partners (Allen & Baucom, 2004). In this case, the participating partner may need adjunctive individual treatment targeting this issue before the couple's relationship is able to recover.

Differences in Affair Patterns

Reactions to a one-night stand may be quite different from the same person's reactions to the discovery of a long-term emotional and sexual extramarital involvement, and various types of affairs have different implications for the continuation of the couple's relationship. In addition, empirical research by Glass and Wright (1985) found that affairs in which there is both emotional and sexual involvement are more predictive of couple dissatisfaction than either of these types alone. Affairs in which both types of involvement are present are likely to be more disruptive to the relationship and require a greater amount of time and processing for the couple to address pertinent issues adequately.

Similarly, a history of repeated affairs has implications for treatment. If the injured partner has been through the process several times before, the participating partner's expressions of remorse and protestations of good behavior may ring hollow. Not surprisingly, it will be more difficult for the injured partner to take the emotional risks required to rebuild trust and intimacy in the relationship. Indeed, it may be the therapist's task to help the injured partner realistically evaluate if she or he should even take those risks.

Finally, in extending this model to couples for whom the affair is ongoing, interventions during Stage 1 of the treatment would be expanded to work toward a decision to end or suspend interactions with the outside person as a basis for continuing with further interventions. Often, participating partners are reluctant to end an affair that has been ongoing for some time and that provides emotional as well as physical intimacy—

particularly if the marital relationship is currently dominated by emotional distance or conflict. Demanding that the participating partner terminate the outside affair relationship immediately and completely may prematurely precipitate that partner's decision to end both the therapy and their marriage. At the same time, it is important that the therapist clearly communicate that any continuation of the outside relationship on either an emotional or sexual level will preclude the couple's ability to recover stability in their own relationship and evaluate whether they can restore trust and intimacy in the long term. Hence, in situations involving an ongoing affair, the therapist should work to (a) promote the participating partner's agreement to limit or suspend involvement with the outside person on an intermediate basis, (b) construct a tentative timeline for reaching a more permanent decision about whether to end the outside relationship, and (c) assist both partners in defining specific ground rules for how they will interact with each other, as well as with others outside their relationship, during the interim.

EMPIRICAL FINDINGS FROM A REPLICATED CASE STUDY OF THIS COUPLE-BASED AFFAIR-SPECIFIC INTERVENTION

We have previously presented preliminary evidence for the efficacy of this treatment approach in a replicated case study of six couples recovering from infidelity (Gordon, Baucom, & Snyder, 2004). In four couples, the wife was the injured partner and the husband was the partner participating in the affair; for the remaining two couples, these roles were reversed. All couples completed treatment and a 6-month follow-up assessment.

Consistent with anecdotal literature, the majority of injured partners entering this treatment initially showed significantly elevated levels of depression and symptoms consistent with a post-traumatic stress disorder (PTSD). Concern with emotional regulation and struggles to understand their betrayal dominated. Relationship distress was severe; feelings of commitment, trust, and empathy were low. By termination, injured partners demonstrated gains in each of these areas. Most importantly, gains were greatest in those domains specifically targeted by this treatment, such as decreases in PTSD symptomatology and mastery over successive challenges of the forgiveness process. Treatment effect sizes were moderate to large and generally approached average effect sizes for efficacious marital therapies not specifically targeting couples struggling from an affair.

Participating partners in this study exhibited as a group only modest disruption of individual functioning in terms of depression or anxiety, but displayed moderately high levels of overall dissatisfaction with their marriage. Although the average reduction in marital distress was modest for the participating partners, the treatment was not without impact on them. When describing the impact of treatment, participating partners expressed that the treatment was critical to (a) exploring and eventually understanding their own affair behavior in a manner that reduced likely reoccurrence, (b) tolerating their injured partners' initial negativity and subsequent flashback reactions, (c) collaborating with their partners in a vital but often uncomfortable process of examining factors contributing to the affair, and (d) deferring their own needs for immediate forgiveness until a more comprehensive process of articulating the affair's impact, exploring its causes, and evaluating the risks of reoccurrence had been completed.

Overall, this study provided preliminary evidence for the efficacy of this treatment in helping most couples to recover and move on from an extramarital affair. Although many of the techniques used in this intervention have been promoted elsewhere in the clinical literature, this study was the first to provide empirical evidence for the success of these procedures. Based in part on these empirical findings, as well as our clinical experience implementing this approach with scores of couples recovering from infidelity, we have developed a self-guided manual for couples struggling to recover from an affair (Snyder, Baucom, & Gordon, 2007). This resource provides couples with a conceptual framework for understanding their experiences and assists them in moving through successive stages of dealing with the initial impact of the affair, arriving at a shared formulation of how the affair came about, and reaching an informed decision for how to move on—either together or separately. Structured exercises guide partners through each stage. Although the exercises are written in a manner that encourages both injured and participating partners to work through each stage collaboratively, either partner can use this resource individually or in conjunction with individual or couple therapy. A companion clinician's manual for treating couples recovering from infidelity will also be available (Baucom, Snyder, & Gordon, in press).

SUMMARY

For couples, an extramarital affair constitutes one of the most difficult relationship experiences from which to recover. For therapists, couples struggling with issues of infidelity are among the most difficult to treat. Effective treatment—and optimal recovery—require an integrative approach that (a) recognizes the traumatic impact of an affair, (b) builds relationship skills essential to initial containment of trauma and effective decision making, (c) promotes partners' greater understanding of factors within and outside themselves that increased their vulnerability to an affair and influence their recovery, and (d) addresses emotional, cognitive, and behavioral processes essential to forgiveness and moving on—either together or separately. The integrative treatment approach described here is the first conjoint therapy designed specifically to assist couples' recovery from an affair to garner empirical evidence of its efficacy. Additional clinical trials with diverse clinical populations are currently under way.

REFERENCES

Abrahms Spring, J., with Spring, M. (1996). *After the affair: Healing the pain and rebuilding trust when a partner has been unfaithful.* New York: HarperCollins.

Allen, E. S., Atkins, D. C., Baucom, D. H., Snyder, D. K., Gordon, K. C., & Glass, S. P. (2005). Intrapersonal, interpersonal, and contextual factors in engaging in and responding to extramarital involvement. *Clinical Psychology: Science and Practice, 12,* 101–130.

Allen, E. S., & Baucom, D. H. (2004). Adult attachment and patterns of extradyadic involvement. *Family Process, 43,* 467–488.

Amato, P. R., & Rogers, S. J. (1997). A longitudinal study of marital problems and subsequent divorce. *Journal of Marriage and the Family, 59,* 612–624.

Atkins, D. C., Baucom, D. H., & Jacobson, N. S. (2001). Understanding infidelity: Correlates in a national random sample. *Journal of Family Psychology, 15,* 735–749.

Baucom, D. H., Snyder, D. K., & Gordon, K. C. (in press). *Treating infidelity: An integrative approach to resolving trauma and promoting forgiveness.* Guilford Press.

Beach, S. R., Jouriles, E. N., & O'Leary, K. D. (1985). Extramarital sex: Impact on depression and commitment in couples seeking marital therapy. *Journal of Sex and Marital Therapy, 11,* 99–108.

Brown, E. (1991). *Patterns of infidelity and their treatment.* New York: Brunner/Mazel.

Cano, A., & O'Leary, K. D. (2000). Infidelity and separations precipitate major depressive episodes and symptoms of nonspecific depression and anxiety. *Journal of Consulting and Clinical Psychology, 68,* 774–781.

DiBlasio, F. A. (2000). Decision-based forgiveness treatment in cases of marital infidelity. *Psychotherapy, 37,* 149–158.

Enright, R. D., & Fitzgibbons, R. P. (2000). *Helping clients forgive: An empirical guide for resolving anger and restoring hope.* Washington, DC: American Psychological Association.

Enright, R. D., & the Human Development Study Group. (1991). The moral development of forgiveness. In W. Kurtines & J. Gewirtz (Eds.), *Handbook of moral behavior and development* (pp. 123–152). Hillsdale, NJ: Erlbaum.

Epstein, N. B., & Baucom, D. H. (2002). *Enhanced cognitive-behavioral therapy for couples: A contextual approach.* Washington, DC: American Psychological Association.

Freedman, S. R., & Enright, R. D. (1996). Forgiveness as an intervention goal with incest survivors. *Journal of Consulting and Clinical Psychology, 64,* 983–992.

Glass, S., & Wright, T. (1985). Sex differences in type of extramarital involvement and marital dissatisfaction. *Sex Roles, 12,* 1101–1120.

Glass, S., & Wright, T. (1997). Reconstructing marriages after the trauma of infidelity. In W. K. Halford & H. J. Markman (Eds.), *Clinical handbook of marriage and couples interventions* (pp. 471–507). Chichester, UK: Wiley.

Gordon, K. C., & Baucom, D. H. (1998). Understanding betrayals in marriage: A synthesized model of forgiveness. *Family Process, 37,* 425–450.

Gordon, K. C., Baucom, D. H., & Snyder, D. K. (2004). An integrative intervention for promoting recovery from extramarital affairs. *Journal of Marital and Family Therapy, 30,* 213–231.

Gordon, K. C., Heyman, R. E., & Slep, A. M. S. (2006, November). *Revisiting Othello: Examining the links between infidelity and domestic violence.* Paper presented at the meeting of the Association for Behavioral and Cognitive Therapies, Chicago.

Hargrave, T. D. (1994). *Families and forgiveness: Healing wounds in the intergenerational family.* Philadelphia: Brunner/Mazel.

Hazan, C., & Shaver, P. (1987). Romantic love conceptualized as an attachment process. *Journal of Personality and Social Psychology, 52,* 511–524.

Janoff-Bulman, R. (1989). Assumptive worlds and the stress of traumatic events: Applications of the schema construct. *Social Cognition, 7,* 113–136.

Janus, S. S., & Janus, C. L. (1993). *The Janus report on sexual behavior.* New York: Wiley.

Kirby, J. S., & Baucom, D. H. (in press). Integrating dialectical behavior therapy and cognitive-behavioral couple therapy: A couples skills group for emotion dysregulation. *Cognitive and Behavioral Practice.*

Laumann, E. O., Gagnon, J. H., Michael, R. T., & Michaels, S. (1994). *The social organization of sexuality.* Chicago: University of Chicago Press.

Lusterman, D. D. (1998). *Infidelity: A survival guide.* Oakland, CA: New Harbinger.

Miller, W. R., & Rollnick, S. R. (2002). *Motivational interviewing: Preparing people for change* (2nd ed.). New York: Guilford Press.

Pittman, F. (1989). *Private lies: Infidelity and the betrayal of intimacy.* New York: Norton.

Reibstein, J., & Richards, M. (1993). *Sexual arrangements: Marriage and the temptation of infidelity.* New York: Scribner's.

Resick, P. A., & Calhoun, K. S. (2001). Posttraumatic stress disorder. In D. H. Barlow (Ed.), *Clinical handbook of psychological disorders* (3rd ed., pp. 60–113). New York: Guilford Press.

Rowe, J. O., Halling, S., Davies, E., Leifer, M., Powers, D., & van Bronkhorst, J. (1989). The psychology of forgiving another: A dialogal research approach. In R. S. Valle & S. Halling (Eds.), *Existential-phenomenological perspectives in psychology: Exploring the breadth of human experience.* New York: Plenum Press.

Snyder, D. K. (1999). Affective reconstruction in the context of a pluralistic approach to couples therapy. *Clinical Psychology: Science and Practice, 6,* 348–365.

Snyder, D. K., Baucom, D. H., & Gordon, K. C. (2007). *Getting past the affair: A program to help you cope, heal, and move on—together or apart.* New York: Guilford Press.

Snyder, D. K., Heyman, R., & Haynes, S. N. (2005). Evidence-based approaches to assessing couple distress. *Psychological Assessment, 17,* 288–307.

Snyder, D. K., & Whisman, M. A. (Eds.). (2003). *Treating difficult couples: Helping clients with coexisting mental and relationship disorders.* New York: Guilford Press.

Whisman, M. A., Dixon, A. E., & Johnson, B. (1997). Therapists' perspectives of couple problems and treatment issues in the practice of couple therapy. *Journal of Family Psychology, 11,* 361–366.

Worthingon, E. L. (Ed.). (2005). *Handbook of forgiveness.* New York: Routledge.

NOTES

1. *Editor's note:* For a review of the effect of infidelity on children, please see Chapter 13.

CHAPTER 7

Forgive and Forget

A Comparison of Emotionally Focused and Cognitive-Behavioral Models of Forgiveness and Intervention in the Context of Couple Infidelity

HEATHER B. MACINTOSH, JOANNE HALL,
AND SUSAN M. JOHNSON

INTRODUCTION

"Forgive and forget." These are the words voiced by those who espouse the letting go of emotional distress and anger toward those who have hurt us. These are the words voiced by those who find the intensity of this distress and anger to be uncomfortable, unbearable, unacceptable. These are the words voiced by those who would like to make problems go away so that life can be "normal" again. This aphorism is based upon the belief that forgiveness is an intrapsychic phenomenon over which one has conscious and voluntary control; that it is a choice. But how can we make this forgiving and forgetting happen in the context of couple infidelity where one's basic assumptions about oneself and one's safety and intimacy in the relationship are shattered in a million tiny pieces? How can one "choose" to "forgive and forget" when one's entire world has been shaken? The goal of this chapter is to compare two models of couple therapy in the context of infidelity, Emotionally Focused Therapy for Couples and Cognitive-Behavioral Marital Therapy, and discuss how these interventions approach the idea of "forgiveness."

DEFINITIONS OF INFIDELITY

Infidelity is a common presenting issue for couples in counseling (Atkins, Baucom, Eldridge, & Christensen, 2005). Couple therapists report that 50%–65% of couples are in therapy because of infidelity (Atkins, Baucom, & Jacobson, 2001). According to Allen, Duncombe, Harrison, and Marsden (2004), between 30% and 60% of men and 20% and 50% of women will have an affair over the course of their marriage.

Of the many definitions in the literature, Johnson (2005) defines infidelity as any action that is perceived and/or experienced as a hurtful betrayal of trust or a threat to a relationship; it is any action that undermines the stability of a couple's attachment bond (Johnson, 2005). Primarily, infidelity has been viewed, in the literature, through the eyes of clinicians. Empirical investigations have been limited by definitional issues (most studies narrowly define infidelity as heterosexual, extramarital intercourse), research design challenges (design flaws—hypothesized infidelity and sample limitations), and contradictory results (Blow & Hartnett, 2005a, 2005b). As a result, current research results are "not particularly helpful to the practicing clinician" (Blow & Hartnett, 2005a, p. 183). The focus of empirical research, then, has been on infidelity definitions, predictors, and specific risk factors (Olson, Russell, Higgins-Kessler, & Miller, 2002; Treas & Giesen, 2000), rather than on providing a context with which to understand the impact of infidelity on couple relationships and the efficacy of therapeutic treatments to address the issues arising from an affair (Blow & Hartnett, 2005a, 2005b; Johnson, 2005). To date, there are few studies that assess the process and outcome of couple therapy in the context of infidelity (Atkins et al., 2005; Gordon, Baucom, & Snyder, 2004; Johnson, 2005; Johnson, Makinen, & Millikin, 2001). Therefore, despite being a common and devastating experience for individuals and couples and one of the most complex and challenging presenting problems for couple therapists, there is little empirical guidance for therapists as they work to assess the impact of infidelity and determine an appropriate course of therapeutic action (Atkins et al., 2001; Blow & Hartnett, 2005a, p. 183; Gordon, Baucom, & Snyder, 2005; McCullough, Pargament, & Thoresen, 2000).

IMPACT OF INFIDELITY

Internal working models of the other are based on our learned expectations of how the other will behave and respond to our distress and need (Kobak &

Hazan, 1991). Committed couple relationships have, by and large, a moral and contractual agreement to exclusivity and carry with them an implicit understanding that the other will provide us with love, support, comfort, and care (Atkins et al., 2005; Treas & Giesen, 2000). There is an expectation of sexual and emotional monogamy in committed couple relationships (Allen et al., 2005; Boekhout, Hendrick, & Hendrick, 2003). In "committing" to another, conventional wedding vows use language that affirms this belief "to have and to hold from this day forward, for better, for worse; for richer, for poorer; in sickness and in health; in joy and in sorrow; to love and to cherish, and to be faithful to you alone, as long as we both shall live." We trust and believe that the other will provide a secure safe haven, especially during times of distress; this is part of our secure internal working model of both our couple relationship and our committed partner (Johnson, Makinen, & Millikin, 2001).

Infidelity shatters our fundamental relational beliefs and our individual and couple identity is called into question. The wound is at both an individual and relational level (Winek & Craven, 2003). The interpersonal and intrapersonal effects of infidelity are reported to range from detrimental to devastatingly traumatic and include rage, shame, depression, trauma responses such as intrusive thoughts and feelings, challenges with concentration and affect regulation (Beach, Jouriles, & O'Leary, 1985; Cano & O'Leary, 2000; Gordon et al., 2004; Johnson et al., 2001).

When a partner violates the trust and expectation to protect and not to betray or abandon their partner, the natural response would be to feel and experience extraordinary pain and hurt. This violation leads to feelings of vulnerability; a loss of identity, self-respect, and sense of purpose; and our internal working models are dramatically affected and altered (Case, 2005; Johnson, 2005; Spring, 1996). Our understanding about self and other no longer "fits" and security is damaged; we have to incorporate new information about the self and other (Johnson et al., 2001; Kobak & Hazan, 1991). The violation of trust shatters secure attachment, the relationship is experienced as insecure, and the emotional shock and distress can cause distorted thinking about self, the other, and the environment. Distress is maintained as it is the new standard for the internal working model. This is complicated by the fact that the other is experienced as the cause and solution to the pain (Gordon & Baucom, 1998). Relationships fall into distress and are at risk of dissolution and further conflict without intervention. Couples come to therapy because they cannot forgive and have tried to make themselves forgive and forget to save their relationship without success; they need effective, well conceptualized intervention to assist them in getting through this devastating relational trauma.

INDIVIDUAL MODELS OF FORGIVENESS

Popular culture ideas and early theoretical models of forgiveness often stem from an intrapsychic, religious, or "turn the other cheek" based model. These models emphasize the need of the injured to turn the other cheek and simply forgive as this would be the "right" thing to do. They are centered within a framework of denial of the needs of the self in favor of the needs of the other. These ideas have spawned individual focused models of forgiveness that favor the moralistic ideal of harboring no ill will toward those who cause us harm, regardless of the personal price; it will all be accounted for on judgment day. This framework suggests that forgiveness is a choice, an individual rather than relational process, and that one can, in fact, achieve this goal of manipulating one's emotions and memory to forgive and forget that which has been experienced as a trauma. These models of forgiveness are highly unsatisfying and leave those who simply cannot perform these feats of emotional and cognitive manipulation as failures and those who have injured them outside of the model in terms of their responsibility for engaging in an interpersonal process of forgiveness. These models are similarly unsatisfying for couple therapists who sit with couples dealing with the traumatic impact of infidelity on their relationships, where the injured partner longs to be able to simply make him- or herself forgive, forget, and move on in the relationship but who is instead dealing with intrusive, painful memories and thoughts of his or her partner in the arms of another and who simply cannot make him- or herself trust his or her partner again.

Primarily, then, intrapsychic models, such as those posited by Enright and Fitzgibbons (2000), McCullough, Worthington, and Rachal (1997), and McCullough et al. (2000), that focus on the intrapsychic/intrapersonal process of forgiveness emphasize the individual nature of the process, and leave the relational elements outside of the process. Enright and Fitzgibbons define forgiveness as a willingness to "abandon resentment and related responses (to which they have a right), and endeavor to respond to the wrongdoer based on the moral principle of beneficence, which may include compassion, unconditional worth, generosity, and moral love (to which the wrongdoer, by nature of the hurtful act or acts, has no right)" (p. 29), negative judgment, and indifferent behavior toward one who unjustly hurt us, while fostering the undeserved qualities of compassion, generosity, and even love toward him or her.

Enright and Fitzgibbons further emphasize that people should "rationally determine" (p. 29) what has happened to them and actively forgive through willfully abandoning resentment and related responses. It is noted that while the injured person has a right to their negative feelings and that pardoning is different from forgiving in this model, the goal is that they strive to respond outside of those emotions and with a "rational" approach toward their injurer using the moral principle of beneficence, which may include compassion, making an effort to see their injurer as a person innately worthy of respect, mercy unwarranted by the actions of their injurer, and moral love characterized by concern and respect to which the wrongdoer, by nature of the hurtful act or acts, has no right but is offered. The focus here is on intellectualized processing, moralistic drives, and favoring compassion over holding the injurer responsible for their injuring.

These theorists do not posit that the injured person will not feel anger or hurt, but rather that they must resolve these feelings by finding within themselves benevolence, compassion, and moral love toward their injurer. Neither do they fail to understand that the injured person's relationship and attachment to the injurer and their response to their actions have an impact whether or not the injured person is able to forgive (Enright & Fitzgibbons, 2000; McCullough et al., 1997; McCullough et al., 2000). However, this definition and process of forgiveness places the responsibility squarely on the shoulders of the injured; it implies that he or she who cannot or will not apply these moral principles to their injurer is somehow immoral and removes the responsibility for healing intra- and interpersonally from the injurer. Not surprisingly, Enright's therapeutic intervention that arose from this model has only been studied in individual psychotherapy in populations such as persons who are experiencing anger toward someone and incest survivors, not couples (Freedman & Enright, 1996; Hebl & Enright, 1993).

Similarly, McCullough et al. (1997) proposed a model that attempts to provide a theoretical connection between empathy, forgiveness, and behavioral responses toward one's injurer and is based heavily upon Bateson's (1990, 1991, cited in McCullough et al., 1997) research on empathy: the human capacity for altruism—and the way that it motivates one to care for or help another. These authors suggest that empathy leads to the motivation to care for others, which is associated with the human capacity for altruism, and these altruistic motivations produce forgiveness, which is conceptualized as a "motivational transformation" (McCullough et al., 1997, p. 323) that inhibits revenge seeking or ongoing estrangement from the injurer on the part of the injured and impels letting go and building connection. Thus, these authors relied heavily upon the conceptualization of empathy as being a crucial facilitating condition for overcoming an injured person's initial tendency toward negative or destructive behavioral responses to an injurer after an interpersonal offense. Forgiving is hypothesized to help the injured person to let go of self-protective behavioral and emotional responses that would further damage relationship and impels the injured person to pursue relationship-constructive responses. This model focuses on the responsibility of the injured rather than the injurer's responsibility, or the relational-interpersonal process of forgiveness in the context of an injurer taking responsibility for their actions and an active role in the process of reconciliation. The focus is on the intentional, motivated, and conscious behavioral response of the injured person in the absence of a relational process. Once again, there is an assumption that people can make conscious choices about what to feel and how to respond to those feelings.

These authors argue that altruistic motivation toward a stranger would differ from that toward a partner, being more complex and affected by feelings of previous positive attachment-related experiences. Thus, empathy for a partner offender may lead the injured partner to care that their offending partner feels guilt and distress for actions that have hurt them and the relationship; empathy may lead the partner to care that the offender is alone because they have hurt their relationship; empathy may lead the partner to feel a "yearning" (McCullough et al., 1997, p. 323) to once again have positive contact with the offender. In the process, the ongoing empathy for the offending partner may overshadow their infidelity and, according to McCullough et al., lead "to the set of motivational changes that we have defined as forgiving" (p. 323). Forgiveness promotes behaviors that are "relationship-constructive" (p. 333) and releases desire for behaviors that are self-protective but relationship-destructive (p. 333).

Neither of these conceptualizations of forgiveness assists the couple therapist in working with a couple dealing with the trauma and destruction of infidelity: the overwhelming emotions, the shattered trust, the unbearable and uncontrollable intrusive thoughts and memories of your partner with another, and the impossibility of forcing oneself to forgive and forget. These conceptualizations are just that, theoretical ideas that do not translate into clinical reality as those practitioners who work directly with the betrayer and the betrayed experience; infidelity is a relational trauma that occurs within the context of an ongoing co-created relational dynamic in which both members of a couple participate and both must actively work toward healing and change. A useful model of forgiveness for working with couples dealing with infidelity must be transferable to clinical situations where persons cannot force themselves to think, feel, and behave how they "should."

COUPLE-ORIENTED MODELS OF FORGIVENESS

Currently, there are two couple therapies that have received consistent empirical validation. Cognitive Behavioral Marital Therapy (CBMT) and Emotionally Focused Therapy for Couples (EFT) have been extensively validated and both have developed theoretical models for intervention in the context of infidelity (Gordon, Baucom, & Snyder, 2000; Johnson et al., 2001). In CBMT this model is explicitly defined as a model of intervention promoting forgiveness in the context of infidelity, whereas in EFT infidelity is defined as a traumatic injury to the primary attachment relationship of the couple and forgiveness is thought to occur within the process of Attachment Injury resolution (Gordon et al., 2000; Johnson, 2005; Johnson et al., 2001).

INTEGRATIVE CBMT AND INSIGHT-ORIENTED MODEL

Gordon et al. (2000) articulated an integrated theoretical model of forgiveness intervention for use with couples in the context of infidelity based upon empirical research and clinical observation (Gordon & Baucom, 1999). This model and a study examining its process and outcome through a replicated case study will be reviewed in depth. This theory similarly criticizes current theories of forgiveness for their overemphasis on the betrayed individual without considering the relational dynamics and issues that form the context for any forgiveness intervention. They define forgiveness within this model as "a process consisting of three stages, each of which has cognitive, behavioral, and affective components . . . that may unfold relatively separately from the dyadic interactions" (Gordon & Baucom, 1998, p. 1). At the same time, the actions of the participating partner may impact this process and either exacerbate the emotional reactions or facilitate recovery (p. 13). This model emphasizes the parallels between the process of forgiveness and the process of recovering from an emotional trauma and propose a three-stage model that parallels a stage model of recovery from trauma: (1) exploring the impact; (2) the search for meaning; (3) recovery (Gordon & Baucom, 1998, 2003; Gordon et al., 2000, 2004).

These theorists understand that forgiveness in the context of infidelity is not just a response to a traumatic event but is an interpersonal trauma. Because of this interpersonal context, there are cognitive, emotional, and behavioral consequences that are specific to the relationship that have to be addressed before the process is complete. Forgiveness is understood to involve the complex interaction between the person forgiving, the person being forgiven, and the dyadic interaction between the couple. There is no stipulation for partners to reconcile for forgiveness to occur. They define three components to forgiveness. These include the development of a realistic, nondistorted, balanced view of the relationship; being released from being controlled by negative affect toward the partner; and a decreased desire to retaliate or punish the partner (Gordon & Baucom, 1998, 2003; Gordon et al., 2000, 2004). For further exploration of these stages, please see Snyder, Baucom, and Gordon, Chapter 6, this volume.

Empirical Support for the Model

Utilizing a case study replication methodology, Gordon, Baucom, and Snyder (2004) examined the process and outcome of their model of forgiveness with six couples dealing with the impact of infidelity in their relationships. Therapists were provided with an unpublished treatment manual with specific goals and scripts for each session. As predicted, these couples presented with a high level of couple distress, disrupted assumptions about their relationship and partner, and trauma symptoms in one half of the injured partners while the majority of the injuring partners displayed anxiety and emotional dysregulation. At the beginning of treatment couples' responses to measures assessing commitment, trust, and empathy were low as well as exhibiting disruptions in positive assumptions about themselves, their partners, and the relationship (Gordon et al., 2004). By the end of therapy, trauma symptoms and relationship distress did decrease with an effect size comparable to those of other studies assessing the efficacy of couple therapy outside of the context of infidelity. However, the average number of sessions provided was 26 over 6 months and this was not deemed adequate by the couples. Essentially, the authors suggested that couples were at the point of beginning to address their long-standing relationship difficulties having addressed the infidelity and determined their commitment to move forward and rebuild their relationship.

Thematically, in Stage 1, couples with high levels of emotional dysregulation were those who found it the most difficult to progress through this treatment. Writing letters was considered to be a helpful technique for exploring and expressing emotional distress and couples who were less able to establish mutually agreed upon boundaries showed less improvement through treatment (Gordon et al., 2004). Teaching communication skills was associated with higher levels of success in dealing with difficult issues, and those couples who were dealing with high levels of emotional dysregulation were less able to generalize these skills to their interactions outside of sessions. The authors indicated that these couples also exhibited frequent crises that were managed through developing strategies for addressing the crisis if it was determined to be "legitimate" (Gordon et al., 2004).

In Stage 2, during the process of exploring contextual factors, it was clear that these couples had in common a history of many stressors outside of the relationship. These included moves and job stress and avoidance of conflict in the injuring partner, making them vulnerable to seeking support and solace from others with the additional risk factor for the injuring partner of fearing conflict due to conflict and other dysfunction in the family of origin (Gordon et al., 2004).

In Stage 3, it is reported that couples were supported in integrating Stage 1 and Stage 2 and coming to an "informed decision" (Gordon et al., 2004, p. 216) about continuing their relationship. Couples were coached through the process of examining and reconstructing beliefs about the relationships although this process is not explicated clinically save that further exploration is required if there are challenges in moving past this stage. Written exercises and handouts are used to look at issues of relationship viability, commitment, and change and forgiveness and to develop problem-solving skills.

Overall, outcomes suggest moderate treatment gains and thematic analyses suggest that couples did benefit from the processes involved in this intervention. However, the authors noted that couples indicated to researchers at termination that they did not feel that they had had the opportunity to address chronic or long-standing relationship issues beyond the specific forgiveness intervention.

EMOTIONALLY FOCUSED THERAPY (EFT): ATTACHMENT INJURY RESOLUTION MODEL

The EFT Model

EFT is a short-term, structured approach to the repair of distressed relationships. A clear theoretical framework on adult love is invaluable to the couple therapist. It not only helps us understand partners' wounds and difficulties and how they impact a relationship, it offers a map to effective intervention (Johnson, 2003). Without such a framework it is often difficult to delineate the key elements of negative events and the key change events necessary to remedy them. Attachment theory is one such framework with which to view the impact of infidelity on couple relationships.

Feeling secure with a loved one increases a person's ability to tolerate and cope with traumatic experiences. The attachment system is evolution's way of maximizing possibilities for survival in a dangerous world. Humans have survived millennia by being social beings that provide a safe haven and secure base for their loved ones from which to explore and learn about the world (Bowlby, 1969; Johnson, 2002). Secure attachment creates resilience in the face of terror and helplessness and a natural arena for healing. Isolation and a lack of secure attachment add to our vulnerability, exacerbate traumatic events, and are actually wounding in themselves. It is also hard to develop an integrated, confident sense of self without secure connections to significant others.

Attachment has also been described as a "theory of trauma" (Atkinson, 1997) to denote that isolation and separation are extensively aversive experiences for humans, especially in times of vulnerability. Affect is the music of the attachment dance (Johnson, 1996). The loss of affect regulation as a result of trauma can be expected to play havoc with close relationships.

Attachment theorists suggest further that there are only very few ways to regulate the powerful emotions that arise when the security of a bond is threatened. In the case of infidelity, it is possible that the injured partner can, if the threat is manageable, if the extramarital involvement was minimal, and if the offending partner takes responsibility and offers caring, openly approach the offending partner for soothing contact and reassurance—behavior typical of a secure attachment, thus reducing the threat to the security of the bond. If the threat is perceived to be more serious, however, or if the relationship was not experienced to be a safe haven before the injury, then the injured partner may either hyperactivate attachment anxieties and protests, or try to deactivate needs and fears through numbing out and defensive avoidance. If injured partners are extremely fearful of both depending on and losing their partner, these partners may swing between anxious clinging and avoidant responses. For example, an injured partner might angrily protest her hurt and her partner's defensiveness and push for him to respond in a conciliatory way, but if he then responds or initiates contact, she would immediately withdraw and shut him out. As she vacillates between anxious proximity seeking and defended distancing, her partner becomes more withdrawn. Attachment theory offers a map to the emotional realities and responses of such partners. This allows the therapist to empathize effectively and create meaning frames that capture and order this experience.

The experience of infidelity as an attachment trauma or injury often results in disorganization and chaos in the relationship with the injured partner experiencing emotional responses characteristic of post-traumatic responding such as hypervigilance, intrusive thoughts and memories, and numbness (Johnson et al., 2001). Herman (1992, p. 35) describes the "indelible imprint" of the traumatic moment; memories and emotions connected to the infidelity that simply will not let the injured partner be free to live in the present and respond openly to whatever apologies, responsibility taking, or soothing that may be available from the offending partner. While numbing and avoidance can be self-protective in the face of the overwhelming emotional consequences of trauma (van der Kolk & McFarlane, 1996), they can also be highly destructive to relationships as they prevent connection and engagement, which interferes with the process of healing from the attachment injury (Johnson et al., 2001).

Internalized models of self and other are created from repeated interactions with those who matter most to us. The model of the other as a dependable attachment figure, who places the partner in a position of primacy in their attachment hierarchy, is seriously compromised by events such as affairs. This model has then to be reconstructed in couple sessions. When a client asks, "How can I ever trust you again?" what she is asking for is a clear narrative, an explanation of how the affair occurred and was dealt with, so that her partner may again become known and predictable. Models of self are also threatened by these events. An injured partner might blame herself for her partner's behavior and, in her despair, conclude that she is indeed unlovable or deficient or he would not have turned to another. Many partners who believe that they are "strong" and should instantly end a relationship with an unfaithful partner struggle with their experience of vulnerability and helplessness. The EFT therapist is prepared for these responses and actively helps the client work through these fears and self-recriminations.

Attachment theory posits that the key feature of a secure bond is mutual emotional accessibility and responsiveness. This principle then guides the EFT therapist when he or she is helping the couple to make sense of the affair, deal with their emotions, deal with the task of forgiveness, re-create trust and the beginnings of a renewed, more secure bond. Attachment theory and the principles of humanistic therapy on which EFT is based (Johnson, 1996; Johnson & Denton, 2002) suggest that there is no purely behavioral or predominantly cognitive way of healing the hurts and injuries of events such as affairs. The strong emotions that arise must be accepted, dealt with, and then used to create specific kinds of responsive healing interactions—the kinds of interactions that are typical of the main change event in EFT, entitled a softening (Johnson, 1996), where partners are emotionally engaged, accessible and responsive to each other, and so can comfort and soothe each other, providing an antidote to hurt and helplessness.

Infidelity may be experienced as one of many hurts in a relationship and may be addressed, as are other hurts, in the De-escalation stage by placing it in the context of the attachment history of the relationship and of specific and general negative cycles of interaction. For example, one partner may become overwhelmed by anxiety and interrogate the "guilty" partner, who then becomes inundated with shame and hopelessness and withdraws, leaving his partner still overwhelmed. This kind of specific cycle usually parallels the couple's general way of dealing with difficulties and their general negative cycle of, for example, attack/withdraw. In this first stage of therapy, partners are encouraged to move beyond reactive surface emotions and access their more basic attachment-oriented emotional responses and express them to their partner. This occurs in relation to the infidelity as well. De-escalation is considered accomplished when both partners can see and name the cycles of distress and insecurity in their relationship and view these cycles as a main part of the problem. They can also then begin to address their significant hurts and fears in the relationship. If some form of infidelity is a relatively minor hurt it is then addressed as part of the usual interventions in EFT. If infidelity is more significant and is experienced as a traumatizing abandonment and/or betrayal, the injured partner's anguish and lack of trust will create impasses in Stage 2 and block the change process. These injuries must then be addressed in a more focused fashion and are seen as specific attachment injuries.

Attachment Injuries

An attachment injury is defined in the EFT literature as a violation of trust resulting from a betrayal or from an abandonment at a moment of intense need or vulnerability. It is a wound that violates the basic assumptions of attachment relationships. An attachment injury is similar to a "traumatic flashback." When a partner does not respond in "reparative, reassuring" ways or when the injured partner "cannot accept reassurances," the injury is complicated (Johnson et al., 2001). Beliefs, assumptions, and experiences have to heal and be reconstructed on personal and interpersonal levels (Johnson, 2005). The "disorganizing" and "overwhelming" feelings and experiences "must be dealt with for the relationship to survive" (Johnson, 2005, p. 19). Infidelity does not have to mean the end of a relationship; however, it must be acknowledged, tended to, and resolved for the relationship to heal.

These wounds are difficult to deal with and often create an impasse in the process of healing the relationship. It is the attachment significance that is the core of the trauma, not the particular incident that occurred. For a particular partner a sexless emotional connection may be just as traumatic as an affair that involved a deeper sexual relationship. As a result of an infidelity or attachment injury, an injured partner may be absorbed by anger, grief, and attachment fear, where everything leads into these emotions and there seems to be no way out; the partner could never be trusted again.

The concept of attachment injuries was first formulated during the study of key change events in EFT, particularly Stage 2 softenings. A blamer softening event occurs when a blaming spouse asks for his/her attachment needs for comfort and caring to be met from a position of vulnerability. This results in interactions of mutual accessibility and responsiveness and more secure bonding. In some cases, as the EFT therapist set up a softening event, where a previously hostile partner begins to risk being vulnerable and reach for a now available and more responsive other, the more vulnerable partner would suddenly move back to a very defended position. He or she would then refer to a particular abandonment or betrayal, announcing that because of this remembered event he or she would "never again" risk being vulnerable to the other. A series of small EFT studies are in progress to confirm the major steps in the resolution of these injuries in Stage 2 of EFT. Resolution involves more than simple "forgiveness" as understood to be a cognitive letting go; is also intrapsychic and interpersonal to the point where reconciliation is achievable and completed softening events lead to more emotional engagement and a sense of secure bonding. The major interventions used in the resolution of these injuries are presently being studied and are hypothesized to be the same as those that facilitate softening events (Bradley & Furrow, in press), namely, heightening of key emotional responses, framing attachment needs, and shaping emotional engagement with the partner.

The key stages identified in the resolution of injuries, including infidelity, are as follows:

1. A partner describes an incident, such as the discovery of an affair, in which he/she felt betrayed, abandoned, and helpless, experiencing a violation of trust that damaged his/her belief in the relationship as a secure bond. The incident is experienced as an acutely painful trauma and has stayed actively alive and present as an intrusive and arousing memory that continues to plague them. In response to the intensity of emotion and pain, the partner defensively discounts, denies, or minimizes the incident and his/her partner's pain and moves to a withdrawn, defensive stance.

2. With the therapist's help, the injured partner stays in touch with the pain of his/her injury and begins to explicitly articulate its impact and its attachment significance. Newly formulated or denied emotions frequently emerge at this point. Anger often evolves into clear expressions of hurt, helplessness, fear, and shame. The connection of the injury to present negative cycles in the relationship becomes clear. For example, a partner says, "I feel so wounded. I just smack him to show him he can't just wipe out my hurt. This has changed everything—I'm not sure of anything anymore. How can I let him close? I can't, even when he says he is sorry" (Johnson, 2005).

3. The partner, supported by the therapist, begins to be able to hear and understand the significance of the trauma of the infidelity to the partner and to understand this in attachment terms as a reflection of his/her primacy in the attachment hierarchy of the injured partner,

rather than as simply a reflection of his/her personal inadequacies or "crimes." With this new understanding, the offending partner is more able to stay out of the defensive, withdrawn position and acknowledge the injured partner's pain and suffering and elaborate on how the infidelity evolved for him/her, so that his/her actions become clear and understandable to the injured partner.

4. The injured partner then tentatively moves toward a more integrated and complete articulation of how the infidelity occurred and what it entailed. With the help of the therapist, this narrative is now made clear and organized. It encapsulates the loss, attachment fears, pain, and longings. This partner, supported by the therapist, allows the other to witness his/her vulnerability.

5. The injured partner is also now able to be more emotionally engaged and acknowledge his/her own responsibility in the evolution of the infidelity and express empathy, regret, and/or remorse in an emotionally engaged and clearly understood manner.

6. The injured partner can now, then, finally risk being open and trusting enough to ask for the comfort and caring from his/her partner which were unavailable at the time of the affair, the discovery of the infidelity, or the couple's previous discussions of the infidelity.

7. The offending partner is freed up from the guilt, shame, and defensiveness that they experienced prior to the beginning of this resolution and is able to respond in an open caring manner that soothes, reassures, and acts as an antidote to the traumatic experience of the attachment injury. The partners are then able to construct together a new narrative of the injury. This narrative is ordered and includes, for the injured partner, a clear and acceptable sense of how the other became involved with another person and how this relationship has now been resolved.

The couple then go on to build more trusting, open, and emotionally healing interactions that renew and repair the bond between them and are able to move into the third, consolidation phase of EFT.

Support for the Model

Johnson et al. (2001) outlined the process of the Attachment Injury Resolution Model with couples dealing with attachment injuries and offered a case study that discussed both the clinical process and outcome of a couple dealing with an attachment injury related to the husband's lack of emotional availability during the wife's miscarriage and the traumatic impact that this breach of connection had on their relationship. This qualitative investigation of a single case of the process and outcome of the Attachment Injury Resolution model from beginning to end initially demonstrated the veracity of the model for this one couple and pointed in the direction of the importance of further study.

The first empirical study of the model was undertaken following this case study analysis (Makinen & Johnson, in press). In this study, 24 couples who self-referred with a known attachment injury were followed through the process of EFT using the Attachment Injury Resolution model explicitly during Stage 2 when couples encountered the predicted challenges at moving into softening events. Process and outcome measures were used to assess both the efficacy of the intervention and the clinical application of the proposal model of change and resolution. The types of attachment injuries were diverse but many involved overt infidelity or Internet sex/dating. The couples were offered, on average, 13 sessions of EFT. Of these 24, 15 were rated as resolved at the end of the study. Resolution was identified by statistically significant improvements on a measure of relationship satisfaction and forgiveness, while they also demonstrated higher levels of sharing and positive emotion in their interactions and lower levels of blaming and withdrawal in key sessions. The couples who were not rated as resolved at the end of the study were characterized by more compounded injuries of a longer duration and frequency, and required more sessions than were offered in this study to achieve resolution. These improvements in relationship health and well-being through the process of EFT have remained stable over a 3-year follow up (Schnare, Makinen, & Johnson, 2006).

A further assessment of the process and outcomes of the Attachment Injury Resolution model analyzed taped sessions of one resolving and one nonresolving couple to assess the pathway of change predicated by the model (Naaman, Pappa, Makinen, Zuccarinin, & Johnson-Douglas, 2005). The resolved couple did follow this expected path and followed the seven steps of the model. The injuring partner took full responsibility for the injury and expressed sincere remorse, the couple demonstrated higher levels of experiential depth in sessions, and the therapist was able to move this couple through the process of EFT into a softening event resulting in the resolution of the injury. Contrarily, the nonresolved couple did not adhere to the model due to their highly entrenched negative interaction cycle, which included volatility and an extended period of time to achieve deescalation of their cycle. In particular reference to the model of resolution, during the withdrawer reengagement process, the "injured partner refused to risk exposing any vulnerability or expressing any need" and was very adamant about her refusal to trust her partner unless he proved himself worthy of trust over time (Naaman et al., 2005). As such, this couple did not complete Stage 2 of the steps of EFT or any of the steps of the Attachment Injury Resolution Model. In keeping with Makinen and Johnson (in press), this couple evidenced compound attachment injuries and the injured partner was also "carrying over" (Naaman et al., 2005) unresolved attachment-oriented traumas from earlier in her life.

In summary, preliminary evidence suggests that the Attachment Injury Resolution Model for facilitating forgiveness and resolution of relationship distress in the context of infidelity shows strong promise. This promise is evident in both positive treatment outcomes and initial validation for a clinically replicable process of intervention. This model is clearly articulated in steps that allow clinicians to utilize the model with clarity and confidence with couples dealing with infidelity-related distress and challenges in maintaining deescalation and achieving softening events in EFT.

CBMT and EFT Models and Processes: A Comparison

Both the CBMT and EFT models of resolution of couple distress in response to infidelity have received some initial validation. CBMT has been initially assessed using a case replication with six couples and other work is in process (Gordon et al., 2004), while EFT has been examined in terms of both outcome and process through qualitative case study, replicated case study, and empirical assessment of process and outcome in a study of 24 couples. Positive results from this empirical study have remained stable after three years (Schnare et al., 2006). CBMT has not demonstrated stable treatment effects but initial findings are positive. Additionally, both models have identified through early studies that couples dealing with compound injuries, multiple past challenges, difficulties with affect regulation, or early interpersonal traumas in one or both partners pose certain challenges to the process of resolution that will require the addition of sessions beyond that which would be suggested by the model.

Both the EFT and the CBMT theoretical models of forgiveness in the context of infidelity can be characterized as interpersonal models. Neither places the emphasis for forgiveness in the hands of the injured partner and both identify the clear requirement of both partners to engage in the process of resolution rather than assuming that the injured partner will somehow find a way to "forgive and forget" without being supported through this interpersonal process of resolution hand and hand with the offending partner. Both the EFT and the CBMT theoretical models to the approach to forgiveness in the context of infidelity agree that it is vital to work couples through the process of exploring the impact of the infidelity, finding an explanation for the event, and developing a clearly articulated narrative that involves both partners taking responsibility for their role in the development of relationship factors implicated in the affair. Both models also agree on the putative violation of infidelity on the working models of self and other. While EFT explicitly uses the language of Attachment Theory to ground the model in empirically supported theory, CBMT uses language that could be understood within the framework of Attachment Theory without explicitly referring to this model of understanding the underlying context for the violation of assumptions about self and other in the context of infidelity. Thus, these two theoretical models posit similar positions in terms of the nature of the violation and the process of resolution. It is in the clinical application, translating theory into practice, where the differences begin to emerge.

Clinically, EFT presents a well-articulated model with clear clinically applicable steps with which clinicians can approach the process of Attachment Injury Resolution with their couples who are struggling with the impact of an affair. CBMT also divides their clinical approach into stages that mirror the theoretical model. However, their stages are not clearly articulated in terms of clinical process but rather are the resultant outcomes from the clinical process; that is, they identify the required outcomes for the various stages of the process but do not clearly articulate how to get there. This is not helpful to clinicians who may have a felt sense of where they need to get to with clients but need more clearly articulated clinical guidance with which to approach their clinical work with these challenging couples. However, authors state that a clinical manual is in preparation and these more clearly articulated clinical steps may be contained in this guide for clinicians.

Another significant difference between the CBMT and the EFT clinical models of resolution of relationship distress caused by infidelity is how emotion is viewed within the process. For EFT, intense emotional distress is assumed to be a part of the experience of both parties, the injured partner, in particular. That emotional distress is understood within the attachment framework as relating to the threat to the primacy of the attachment bond and the violation of basic attachment-related assumptions about the safety and availability of the partner and the relationship. As such, the exploration and articulation of these strong emotions is considered to be an essential first step in the process. It is through this process that the offending partner comes to more clearly understand the impact of their actions and the injured partner is more able to feel heard and validated and to begin to dispel the traumatic intensity around these unprocessed emotions. Eventually, it has been shown, these emotions dissipate and become a part of the clearly articulated narrative of the whole traumatic experience of the infidelity that lives in the memory of the couple as the move forward into building more trust and health in their relationship. To control or deny the emotions would be to deny and invalidate the experience of the injured partner and stall the process of resolution by not allowing for the completion of the first and necessary step, which is a precursor for the resolution process. It is when the couple is able to complete the Attachment Injury Resolution model and move into a completed softening event as they move toward building trust and commitment that EFT can behaviorally mark the occurrence of forgiveness, moving forward. CBMT marks forgiveness by the self-report of the injured partner.

CBMT takes a different approach to the intense emotions of the injured partner. They recommend a containment and management of affect approach where didactic psychoeducation and highly scripted "effective" communication is espoused (Gordon et al., 2004). With some couples, this containment approach extends to holding separate sessions with the injured partner to assist him or her in containing their affect and helping the injured partner write a letter to the offending partner outlining their response to the infidelity.

This letter is written apart from their partner, edited by the therapist and then read by the offending partner in a session separate from the injured partner. This high level of choreography around the disclosure of the emotional impact of the infidelity on the injured partner suggests a preference for a contained approach to processing the emotion of the wounded partner. From the perspective of outcomes, containing such intense affect may allow for a short-term appearance of resolution; but will this emotion arise at a later time, perhaps in response to future perceived failures by the partner that lead to an explosion of unresolved emotional distress? The review of an initial study (Gordon et al., 2004) discusses emotion extensively and describes the need to differentiate between "legitimate" and illegitimate crises in couples undergoing treatment post-infidelity. This again suggests an approach to dealing with the emotional intensity and chaotic distress of these couples that is focused on containment and management rather than processing and resolving.

Essentially the difference between EFT and CBMT is a difference between exploring, expanding, processing, and resolving; and containing and managing emotion and experience. In the long run, the containing and managing approach of CBMT will not allow for effective and long-standing resolution. Given the traumatic nature of the emotions associated with infidelity, affect regulation is an issue to be addressed directly with couples. However, does this mean that an affectively activating therapeutic process such as EFT be used with these couples? Clinicians and researchers working with trauma survivors agree that, while didactic learning is an important first level of intervention for trauma survivors, the only way to shift chronic trauma-based affective disturbances and relational expectations is through the accessing, activating, and expressing of these expectations in the context of a new and restorative relationship. EFT intervenes directly at the level of the primary attachment relationship for the survivor and creates the direct context for the development of a new emotional experience of the partner. While this may be more challenging with trauma survivors than the CBMT approach, it has the potential to be profoundly and deeply restorative for couples who, in the aftermath of a deeply processed experience of their, now, shared trauma, have begun the process of rebuilding a stronger relationship built on earned trust and the developed capacity to respond to, engage with, and soothe each other (Briere, 1997; Paivio & Nieuwenhuis, 2001).

Another difference between these two models clinically is the articulated end point of the process. CBMT ends the process with "forgiveness" and discusses the importance of then moving into additional sessions to deal with the underlying issues that may continue to pose a risk for the couple in the long term. EFT, however, sees the underlying issues as essential in the process of resolution and takes the process beyond simple "forgiveness" and into the realm of true resolution, which involves the rebuilding of trust, the resolution of past issues that may have played a role in the development of the relationship vulnerability leading to the infidelity, and the development of a new relationship built upon deep interconnectedness, healthy dependence, and mutual soothing and an ability to truly rely upon the other to be available to them as a safe base. EFT, then, does not consider "forgiveness" to be enough for resolution of distress and clearly indicates that full resolution can only come with the completion of the Attachment Injury Resolution process, which simply sets the stage for full participation in the process of EFT and the eventual softening events that lead to the healthy aforementioned new relationship.

CONCLUSION

Cognitive-Behavioral Marital Therapy and Emotionally Focused Therapy for couples are the two approaches to couple therapy that have received the highest level of empirical support. Both have been validated with couples dealing with a variety of issues and it is essential that both have a clearly articulated approach to dealing with infidelity given the high prevalence of couples presenting with this issue in clinical practice. Both CBMT and EFT have articulated a theoretical model of forgiveness in the context of infidelity that are quite synchronous and understand forgiveness to be an interpersonal process in which the offending partner must take full responsibility and the couple must develop a clear narrative of the infidelity prior to moving forward to forgiveness. However, clinically, the EFT model of Attachment Injury Resolution provides a clearer, more clinically relevant and easily followed process for clinicians that provides actual clinical steps with markers for clinicians to determine when to move to the next step. This model understands and facilitates the processing of traumatic emotion and memories and does not deny the intensity of emotional experiencing of the injured partner; the attachment relevance of this trauma is always a part of the growing discourse. Additionally, the process of EFT in the context of infidelity does not end with "forgiveness" but uses this as a stepping stone to the full resolution of couple distress, much of which may have been extant prior to the affair.

Overall, further study is required to come to deeper conclusions about which model may, clinically, provide the standard of care for couples dealing with the aftermath of the trauma of infidelity. However, initial comparisons suggest that the EFT model of Attachment Injury Resolution and change offers couples a more complete opportunity for full resolution of their relationship distress and offers clinicians clearer guidelines with which to work with these highly distressed and challenging couples.

REFERENCES

Allen, E. S., Atkins, D. C., Baucom, D. H., Snyder, D. K., Gordon, K., & Glass, S. P. (2005). Interpersonal, interpersonal, and contextual factors in engaging in and responding to extramarital involvement. *Clinical Psychology: Science an Practice, 12*(2), 101–130.

Allen, G., Duncombe, J., Harrison, K., & Marsden, D. (Eds.). (2004). *The state of affairs: Explorations in infidelity and commitment.* Mahwah, NJ: Erlbaum.

Atkins, D. C., Baucom, D. H., Eldridge, K., & Christensen, A. (2005). Infidelity and behavioral couple therapy: Optimism in the face of betrayal. *Journal of Consulting and Clinical Psychology 73*(1), 144–150.

Atkins, D. C., Baucom, D. H., & Jacobson, N. S. (2001). Understanding infidelity: Correlates in a national random sample. *Journal of Family Psychology, 15*(4), 735–749.

Atkinson, L. (1997). Attachment and psychopathology: From laboratory to clinic. In L. Atkinson & K. J. Zucker (Eds.), *Attachment and psychopathology* (pp. 3–16). New York: Guilford Press.

Beach, S. R. H., Jouriles, E. N., & O'Leary, K. D. (1985). Extramarital sex: Impact on depression and commitment in couples seeking marital therapy. *Journal of Sex and Marital Therapy, 11.*

Blow, A., & Hartnett, K. (2005a). Infidelity in committed relationships I: A methodological review. *Journal of Marital and Family Therapy, 31*(2), 183–216.

Blow, A., & Hartnett, K. (2005b). Infidelity in committed relationships II: A substantive review. *Journal of Marital and Family Therapy, 31*(2), 217–233.

Boekhout, B. A., Hendrick, S. S., & Hendrick, C. (2003). Exploring infidelity: Developing the relationship issues scale. *Journal of Loss and Trauma, 8,* 283–306.

Bowlby, J. (1969). *Attachment and loss: Vol. 1. Attachment.* New York: Basic Books.

Bradley, B., & Furrow, J. (in press). Toward a mini-theory of EFT therapist behaviors facilitating a softening event. *Journal of Marital and Family Therapy.*

Briere, J. (1997). Treating adults severely abused as children: The self-trauma model. In D. A. Wolfe (Ed.), *Child abuse: New directions in prevention and treatment across the lifespan* (pp. 177–204). Thousand Oaks, CA.

Cano, A., & O'Leary, D. (2000). Infidelity and separations precipitate major depressive episodes and symptoms of nonspecific depression and anxiety. *Journal of Consulting and Clinical Psychology, 68*(5), 774–781.

Case, B. (2005). Healing the wounds of infidelity through the healing power of apology and forgiveness. *Journal of Couple & Relationship Therapy, 4*(2/3), 41–55.

Enright, R., & Fitzgibbons, R. (2000). *Helping clients forgive: An empirical guide for resolving anger and restoring hope.* Washington, DC: American Psychological Association.

Freedman, S. R., & Enright, R. D. (1996). Forgiveness as an intervention goal with incest survivors. *Journal of Consulting and Clinical Psychology, 64,* 983–992.

Gordon, K. C., & Baucom, D. H. (1998). Understanding betrayals in marriage: A synthesized model of forgiveness. *Family Process, 37,* 425–449.

Gordon, K. C., & Baucom, D. H. (1999). A forgiveness-based intervention for addressing extramarital affairs. *Clinical Psychology: Science and Practice, 6,* 382–399.

Gordon, K. C., & Baucom, D. H. (2003). Forgiveness and marriage: Preliminary support for a measure based on a model of recovery from a marital betrayal. *American Journal of Family Therapy, 31,* 179–199.

Gordon, K. C., Baucom, D. H., & Snyder, D. K. (2000). The use of forgiveness in marital therapy. In M. McCullough, K. Pargament, & C.E. Thoresen (Eds.), *Forgiveness: Theory, research, and practice* (pp. 203–227). New York: Guilford Press.

Gordon, K. C., Baucom, D. H., & Snyder, D. K. (2004). An integrative intervention for promoting recovery from extramarital affairs. *Journal of Marital and Family Therapy, 30*(2), 213–231.

Gordon, K. C., Baucom, D. H., & Snyder, D. K. (2005). Treating couples recovering from infidelity: An integrative approach. *Journal of Clinical Psychology, 61*(11), 1393–1405.

Hebl, J. H., & Enright, R. D. (1993). Forgiveness as a psychotherapeutic goal with elderly females. *Psychotherapy, 30,* 658–667.

Herman, J. L. (1992). *Trauma and recovery: The aftermath of violence from domestic abuse to political terror.* New York: Basic Books.

Johnson, S. M. (1996). *The practice of emotionally focused marital therapy: Creating connection.* New York: Brunner/Mazel (now Brunner/Routledge).

Johnson, S. M. (2002). *Emotionally focused couples therapy for trauma survivors: Strengthening attachment bonds.* New York: Guilford Press.

Johnson, S. M. (2003). The revolution in couples therapy: A practitioner-scientist perspective. *Journal of Marital and Family Therapy, 29,* 365–384.

Johnson, S. M. (2005). Broken bonds: An emotionally focused approach to infidelity. *Journal of Couple & Relationship Therapy, 4*(2/3), 17–29.

Johnson, S. M., & Denton, W. (2002). Emotionally focused couples therapy: Creating secure connections. In A. Gurman & N. Jacobson (Eds.), *Clinical handbook of couple therapy* (pp. 221–250). New York: Guilford Press.

Johnson, S. M., & Makinen, J (2003). Posttraumatic stress. In D. K. Snyder & M. A. Whisman (Eds.), *Treating difficult couples* (pp. 308–329). New York: Guilford Press.

Johnson, S. M., Makinen, J. A., & Millikin, J. W. (2001). Attachment injuries in couple relationships: A new perspective on impasses in couples therapy. *Journal of Marital and Family Therapy, 27*(2), 145–155.

Kobak, R. R., & Hazan, C. (1991). Attachment in marriage: Effects of security and accuracy of working models. *Journal of Personality and Social Psychology, 60*(6), 861–869.

Makinen, J. A., & Johnson, S. (in press). Resolving attachment injuries in couples using EFT: Steps toward forgiveness and reconciliation. *Journal of Consulting and Clinical Psychology.*

McCullough, M., Pargament, K., & Thoresen, C. (2000). The psychology of forgiveness, history, conceptual issues, and overview. In M. McCullough, K. Pargament, & C. Thoresen (Eds.), *Forgiveness: Theory, research, and practice.* New York: Guilford Press.

McCullough, M., Worthington, E., Jr., & Rachal, K. (1997). Interpersonal forgiving in close relationships. *Journal of Personality and Social Psychology, 73*(2), 321–336.

Naaman, S., Pappas, J. D., Makinen, J. A., Zuccarini, D., & Johnson-Douglas, S. (2005). Treating attachment injured couples with emotionally focused therapy: A case study. *Psychiatry: Interpersonal & Biological Processes, 68*(1), 55–77.

Olson, M., Russell, C., Higgins-Kessler, M., & Miller, R. (2002). Emotional processes following disclosure of an extramarital affair. *Journal of Marital and Family Therapy, 28*(4), 423–434.

Paivio, S. C., & Nieuwenhuis, J. A. (2001). Efficacy of Emotion Focused Therapy for adult survivors of child abuse: A preliminary study. *Journal of Traumatic Stress, 14,* 115–133.

Schnare, R., Makinen, J. A., & Johnson, S. M. (2006). *Resolving attachment in couples: A three year follow-up study.* Unpublished manuscript, University of Ottawa.

Spring, J. (1996). *After the affair: Healing the pain and rebuilding trust when a partner has been unfaithful.* New York: HarperCollins.

Treas, J., & Giesen, D. (2000). Sexual infidelity among married and cohabitating Americans. *Journal of Marriage and the Family, 62,* 48–60.

van der Kolk, B., & Fisler, R. (1995). Dissociation and the fragmentary nature of traumatic memories: Overview and exploratory study. *Journal of Traumatic Stress, 8,* 505–525.

van der Kolk, B. A., & McFarlane, A. (1996). The complexity of adaptation to trauma: Self-regulation, stimulus discrimination, and characterological development. In B. A. van der Kolk (Ed.), *Traumatic stress: The effects of overwhelming experience on mind, body, and society* (pp. 182–213). New York: Guilford Press.

van der Kolk, B. A., Perry, C., & Herman, J. (1991). Childhood origins of self-destructive behavior. *American Journal of Psychiatry, 148,* 1665–1671.

Winek, J., & Craven, P. (2003). Healing rituals for couples recovering from adultery. *Contemporary Family Therapy, 25*(3), 249–266.

CHAPTER 8

The Affair as a Catalyst for Change

EMILY M. BROWN

INTRODUCTION

People shriek and cry when they are confronted with an affair. Almost never do they realize that it might be the best thing that ever happened to them. An affair says, "Wake up! Something's wrong here." What's often misunderstood is that what's wrong is not just the affair, but the issues that led to the affair that were never addressed. In the midst of the pain, sense of betrayal, and shame, the affair can open up the opportunity to understand and resolve old toxic issues. This view is contrary to our national mythology that claims affairs are always deadly for American marriages. Friends and relatives who learn of the affair often advise the betrayed spouse to "throw the cheater out." What doesn't get discussed is the positive change that can eventually arise from an affair. "News" about positive outcomes from an affair never makes the news, however. And positive change is not dramatic—it takes time coupled with hard work.

Disclosure of an affair is a major event in a couple's history. It marks the ending of the old marriage. It turns everything—assumptions, behavior patterns, values, beliefs—totally upside down. With this level of pain and crisis,

149

deep change is a possibility—completing developmental tasks, changing dysfunctional communication patterns, and resolving other problematic issues.
But how will the affair actually be used? Will the affair be the basis for ending
the marriage abruptly? Will it be used to obsess and punish for years into the
future or to shut off emotionally? Or will it be the catalyst for resolving old
issues? To take advantage of opportunities, choices must be made. It is the
crisis that explodes, kicked off by discovery of the affair, that holds the seeds
for change.

Not knowing what else to do, many individuals and couples turn to a
therapist for help with the pain and chaos. If all we do is begin to heal the
hurt, we stop short of helping our clients find and use the opportunities that
emerge from an affair. For our clients to waste this opportunity would be a
tragedy. To help our clients, we need to have a vision of what is possible. The
opportunities flow from the unfinished business of the past, those very things
that motivated the affair in the first place. Not all couples will choose to look
at these opportunities, and very few will be able to look at them immediately
after disclosure of an affair. However, we can begin to open up the playing
field in the initial session by suggesting they make no decisions about their
marriage until they both understand how they arrived at this crisis.

Not all couples want or are willing to remake their marriage after an
affair. And not all of those marriages should be remade. Some marriages are
too far gone, some too painful, and some should never have occurred in the
first place. However, many couples are desperate for positive change. They
may not know that change is possible or how to embark on remaking their
relationship. A sorting out period is usually necessary as they consider their
next moves.

The appropriate treatment format varies with the type of affair. Couples
who want to work on their marriage or explore doing so are best served by
couples therapy. For them, the greatest opportunities lie within the couple
relationship. For those with a greater loss of self, individual therapy is the
treatment of choice, possibly with parallel couples therapy.

In the therapy process, the major factors influencing whether the affair
crisis is used productively are the client's attributes and the skills, beliefs, and
characteristics of the therapist. Outside the therapy room, but also influencing the process, are friends, family, and other professionals (such as physicians and attorneys).

WHAT INFLUENCES WHETHER SOMEONE HAS AN AFFAIR?

The most common factor leading to an affair is the lack of a strong emotional
connection between the spouses. They may never have had an emotional connection or their connection has eroded. Erosion occurs when couples don't
address their differences or their difficult issues. Some couples have made
unsuccessful attempts to bridge the gap between them. Other couples bring

unresolved issues from childhood to their marriage, such as a belief that a good wife doesn't fight with her husband, a history of fearing the next eruption, a pattern of reactive anger, or an absence of good communication skills. Some spouses believe that by verbally attacking their spouse, they are sharing their feelings. The marital past is a joint past, one in which both spouses contributed to making enough room in the marriage for an affair. Their unfinished business is usually a combination of each individual's early history and the couple's shared history.

Couples generally view the affair in terms of right and wrong, all or nothing, innocence and guilt. They rarely understand how they have set the stage for an affair. The Betrayed Spouse talks about having totally trusted the Betraying Partner until now. This type of trust usually turns out to have been blind trust, that is, trusting because of the need or desire to trust, rather than trust that develops from open communication and mutual emotional vulnerability. With disclosure, total distrust replaces total trust in our clients' eyes.

TYPOLOGY OF AFFAIRS

Affairs are not all alike. Each of the five types of affairs is characterized by a particular set of underlying issues and dynamics (see Table 8.1). These have little to do with sex per se, but with attempts (often unconscious) to resolve an existing problem. For example, the *Conflict Avoidance Affair* is an attempt to get unaddressed issues out in the open. The *Intimacy Avoidance Affair* is driven by a fear of getting too close and being too vulnerable with one's spouse. *Sexual Addiction* is a way of trying to numb pain and fill up an inner emptiness. The *Split Self Affair* represents a struggle between the rational self that tries to do things right and the neglected emotional self. The *Exit Affair* is used to end the marriage by those who have difficulty with endings.[1]

A loss of self is always a significant precipitant of an affair. Almost always this loss is of the emotional self. It may be played out by trying to appease one's spouse while withholding one's own emotions, avoiding difficult issues, or becoming a workaholic. Reactive anger is another common pattern. These patterns usually develop in childhood, either inculcated by parents or developed as ways of coping with problematic situations.

- Patterns such as never fighting or always taking care of others (seen in the *Conflict Avoidance Affair* and the *Split Self Affair*) may be viewed by self and others as positive attributes rather than as related to a loss of self.
- *Intimacy Avoiders* learned early to fear being emotionally vulnerable so they cut off their positive emotions with provocative or withholding behavior.
- An overreliance on the rational self to the exclusion of the emotional self is another pattern learned early in life that involves a major loss

Table 8.1 Typical Characteristics by Type of Affair

	Conflict Avoidance	Intimacy Avoidance	Sexual Addiction	Split Self	Exit
Gender of straying partner	male or female	male and female	male	male	female or male
Age of straying partner	20s and 30s	20s and 30s	any	40 and up	any
Length of marriage before affair	less than 12 years	less than 6 years	0 years	20 or more years	less than 15 years
Theme of affair	avoid conflict	avoid intimacy	individual feels empty	family and shoulds vs. wants	avoid facing ending of marriage
Duration of affair	brief	brief	brief	2 or more years	6 months to 2 years
Level of emotional involvement in affair	minimal	minimal	none	great	some
Presenting affect of straying partner	guilty	angry and chaotic	grandiose and/or seductive	depressed	uninvolved
Presenting affect of betrayed spouse	angry but extra-nice	angry and chaotic	denial	depressed	angry

	conflict is deflected	continual conflict	separate lives	troubled communication	straying partner uninvolved, spouse angry
Interaction pattern of couple					
Who presents for therapy	straying partner or couple	couple	straying partner or spouse	couple, straying partner, or spouse	couple or spouse
Primary treatment mode initially	couple	couple	individual	individual	couple
Prognosis for resolving issues	very good	very good	poor	good	good
Probability of divorce	low	low	low	above average	extremely high
Best outcome	solid marriage	solid marriage	family in recovery	revived marriage or divorce	resolve issues of ending marriage
Worst outcome	other affairs or divorce	other affairs or divorce	damaged family and public humiliation	empty shell marriage or divorce	unresolved loss

© *Emily M. Brown, 1990, 2001*

of self. The affair taps into the neglected emotional self and this pattern is at the heart of the *Split Self Affair*.

- The *Sexual Addict* feels empty inside and engages in addictive behavior in an attempt to fill the aching emptiness.
- In the *Exit Affair*, the spouses are afraid to take responsibility for deciding what to do about their deteriorating marriage. Being unable to face one's fears reflects another loss of self.

COUPLE ATTRIBUTES

The very fact that it has taken an affair to get the marital problems into the open indicates how stuck the marriage has been. The therapy process can make a crucial difference for many couples dealing with an affair. The mix of what couples bring to the therapy process and what the therapist offers will influence the outcome.

Couples vary along the following lines:

- Underlying motivations for the affair: Based on my clinical experience, the affair with the best prognosis for positive change in the marriage is the *Conflict Avoidant Affair*. It usually occurs earlier in the marriage, while there is still some emotional connection between the spouses. The next best prognosis is for *Intimacy Avoidant Affairs*, but since intimacy issues go deeper, positive changes are more difficult to make and take longer. A number of these couples give up along the way. For those *Conflict Avoiders* and *Intimacy Avoiders* whose marriage ends, the affair still provides an opportunity for individual change. *Split Self Affairs* have a much lower prognosis for positive change in the marriage, but a very good prognosis for positive change in the betraying partner. Some *Betrayed Spouses* use this opportunity to make positive changes, but they are less likely to do so if the *Betraying Partner* leaves the marriage. The *Exit Affair* is generally a statement that the marriage is over, and is accompanied by the expectation that the new relationship will make everything right. Motivation to work on changing the self is rarely on the agenda for the betraying partner, but the betrayed spouse often makes good use of therapy.
- The couple's past emotional connection: Couples who have had an emotional connection with each other, especially those who still have some connection, are more likely to choose to work on the marriage and to follow through with that choice.
- Level of maturity of the partners: Greater maturity is generally associated with choosing to work on the marriage, except when one spouse, usually the Betraying Partner, has done some growing and the other spouse has not. Commonly in Split Self Affairs, the affair

has awakened the Betraying Partner's emotional self but the Betrayed Spouse stays mired in obsessive behavior rather than learning to access the emotional self. With other affairs, the struggle with one's self in deciding whether or not to end the marriage can be a growth process in itself. Those spouses who need to be right, or who refuse to engage in dialogue with the partner, are not engaging in a growth process and often don't see the need to do so. If they don't make changes that lead to a better balance, the couples therapy may lead to a decision to end the marriage.

- Willingness to examine self and make changes in own behavior: Initially the Betraying Partner is usually more willing to examine his or her emotions and behaviors than the Betrayed Spouse. When the Betrayed Spouse's obsession is replaced with an understanding that both made room in the marriage for an affair, that spouse's self-examination has already begun.

- Desire to maintain the marriage: At first, many couples don't know whether they want their marriage to continue or not. After the Betrayed Spouse's obsession with details of the affair has been curbed, a sorting out process is in order. If both spouses want the marriage to continue, they are likely to work toward making that happen. When only one spouse wants the marriage to continue, chances for the marriage are poor.

- Resiliency: Resiliency comes from both nature and nurture. The challenge of dealing with an emotionally devastating experience seems to bring out the best in some people. For example, some soldiers return from combat feeling enhanced. Psychologists who are studying post-traumatic growth say, "We're talking about a positive change that comes about as a result of the struggle with something very difficult. It's not just some automatic outcome of a bad thing."[2]

THERAPIST ATTRIBUTES

The attitudes, values, and skills that the therapist brings to the process will make a difference in the outcome for the couple. Therapists vary along the following lines:

- Willingness to address the emotionally difficult issues: Secrecy, obsessive behavior, and intense pain are part of the picture with affairs. The effectiveness of the therapy process depends to a significant degree on whether the therapist stays present and focused as clients struggle with these difficult issues or whether the therapist backs off from intense emotions. Being present allows us to listen to all the layers of communication—tone of voice, body language, what is said, what is not said—and to fully respond.

- Integrity: Secrecy and lies are at the heart of an affair. Therapists differ as to whether the hidden affair should be surfaced. Some collude, knowingly or naively, with secrecy between the spouses, thinking that the truth would be too painful for the uninformed spouse. Other therapists, myself included, find it impossible to be effective with an elephant hiding under the rug. Those who collude are probably apprehensive about the intense emotional response that they will need to deal with following disclosure of an affair, just as the Betraying Partner is. However, if the Betrayed Spouse learns that the therapist knew of the affair and kept the secret, the therapeutic relationship is mortally wounded. It is not the therapist's job to disclose the affair, but to prepare the Betraying Partner to do so.[3] In couples' therapy, there are relatively few circumstances, such as the potential for suicide or domestic violence, when disclosure of an affair is not indicated. In these situations, individual therapy is the preferred modality. The effective therapist is one who confronts evasive behavior of any sort. Confrontation can be done gently, without blame but with persistence.
- Being nonjudgmental: Couples' therapists create problems for themselves and their clients when they are judgmental. As one Betrayed Spouse said of a prior therapist, "She's on his back, saying 'why did you do that,' 'don't you know how much you've hurt her,' and so on, and part of me is cheering her on. But I know that what she's doing is not helping us." Therapists who are judgmental about an affair are reinforcing the Betrayed Spouse's obsession and increasing the polarization between the spouses. A right/wrong stance eliminates the potential for positive change. Therapists who truly understand that both spouses set the stage for an affair find it much easier to remain nonjudgmental, thus opening up the therapy process.
- Experience of the therapist: Experience levels vary among therapists. The more experience in working with difficult and complex couples' issues the better the outcome. Inexperienced couples' therapists are likely to get caught up in the Betrayed Spouse's obsession about the affair, encourage acceptance of premature apologies from the Betraying Partner—or throw up their hands! Experienced therapists resist the temptation to make decisions for the couple. They see their role as helping the couple understand how they got to this point, and as facilitating their struggle with self and other so that they are better equipped to make their own decisions.

COUPLES WORK AFTER AN AFFAIR

What is our role in helping our clients use the affair as a catalyst for change? It is to take our clients through a process of growing up—not just healing the wounds of infidelity but helping them resolve old issues and learn new behaviors. It is helping them realize that they don't have to shape their behavior to fit someone else's style or desires; they don't need a third party to make them feel good, it is okay to be who they are. It is also about making choices, about owning responsibility for choices and behaviors. It is about integrity. To take advantage of opportunities, choices must be made. The work is theirs to do, but we can lend hope, encouragement, clarity, and a sense of the possibilities for transformation.

A few clients seek help individually when they are considering an affair. Others come individually for help with disclosure. Most arrive as couples when the affair has been discovered or disclosed. Pain, shock, guilt, fury, and obsession with the betrayal are the norm. They are raw, and exhausted. *Devastation* is the word that is most often used by Betrayed Spouses. The Betraying Partner is at wit's end. At this early stage their choices involve how to address the pain, devastation, and guilt, who should be told what, and whether to work on the marriage. Except with *Exit Affairs*, a decision about the marriage is premature.

As therapists, we need to be able to sit with their mix of raw emotions and stay emotionally present, and to distinguish between genuine emotions and verbal noise and clutter. It's all too easy to get caught up in the clutter. Our role at this point is to calm them, to let them know that their reactions are normal, that they need to take time to untangle why this has happened, and that we will help them.

At each phase of recovering from an affair there are opportunities to be had and choices to be made. Let's look at what's going on during each phase of the process, identify the choice points, and consider how we can help the couples we work with make lemonade instead of becoming lemons. It is during these steps that our interventions as therapists can have the most impact.

Disclosure

Once an affair occurs, the question arises of whether to disclose it. Therapists disagree about the necessity to disclose. Some believe that disclosure will be hurtful, damaging to the marriage, or even lead to divorce. Other therapists (myself included) believe that honesty between spouses is essential for intimacy. By coming to us for help, our clients are saying they want change. If the affair is hidden it cannot serve as a catalyst for change. A choice point for our clients is whether or not to tell the spouse of an affair. Our job is not to tell the client that she must tell or shouldn't tell, but to take her through a process of deciding whether to tell. Sorting out whether to tell has to be done in individual sessions.[4]

Obsession, Emotions, and Reframing

It bears repeating that after disclosure, pain, shock, fury, and obsession are the norm. The Betrayed Spouse wants all the details about the affair. The

Betraying Partner feels guilty and doesn't want to talk about the affair. They are at an impasse. It's easy to let the verbal noise and clutter about the affair take over. However, focusing on the affair is a dead end. *Our task is to take the affair off center stage and get the real issues onto center stage, which is easier said than done.* Fear is usually a factor when issues have not been addressed. Fear of intimacy, of abandonment, of conflict, and of pain and powerlessness are common. Therapists need to provide an environment that feels safe enough for clients to risk getting beneath the presenting problem of the affair.

The Betrayed Spouse has a choice between obsessing about the affair or experiencing her own pain. The Betraying Partner has a similar choice: whether to focus on his own guilt and desire for forgiveness or on hearing the Spouse's pain. Both have to decide whether to work on the marriage or not. (They are not yet ready to decide whether to stay in the marriage.) The therapist's role in this phase is to help both spouses explore their ambivalence and to help them see alternatives to their prior patterns of behavior.

Many clients don't know how to access their emotions. Therefore, the therapist's central task is teaching them how to pay attention to their own emotions and how to voice them, rather than stuffing their emotions or acting them out. *It is the emotional self that has everything to say about seeing and seizing the opportunities that are presented by an affair.* Of course, it's not possible to do this while the obsession continues. One of the major interventions for getting the obsession under control is helping the Betrayed Spouse pay attention to what he is feeling in the moment. You might ask, "What are you feeling, this moment?" A typical response is, "I feel that she's really not being honest with me." This response is a thought and not a feeling. You might pursue the feeling by asking, "How do you feel when you think she's not being honest with you?" or "What is your physical self feeling right now?" Help the client understand the difference between thoughts and feelings, and how to connect bodily reactions to emotions. Common words that pertain to feelings about an affair include *pain, hurt, fear, helpless, powerless, guilty. Anger* is also a word that comes up frequently. Help the client learn that anger is a secondary feeling and what you want to hear is the primary feeling under the anger.

The Betrayed Spouse needs our help to reach under the anger (the anger is a secondary emotion) and find the primary emotion, usually pain, fear, and/ or powerlessness. We need to make sure we don't reinforce the anger. This will only further fuel the obsession. Anger and obsession preclude all future opportunities. We can help the Betraying Partner to hear the spouse's pain and acknowledge it. This begins the work of accessing his emotional self.

Another choice that clients make in this early phase is whether to own their own responsibility for helping set the stage for the affair. An aspect of this is identifying behavior patterns that need changing. The therapist can facilitate this step by reframing the affair as a marital problem, and reframing dysfunctional behaviors as attempts to cope with a problem. Dealing with obsession and reframing the affair go hand in hand. The reframe takes the attention off the affair and opens opportunities for change on the part of both spouses.

To explore what each contributed to making space for the affair, ask each in a couple's session what attracted them to the other. Help the couple identify what brought them together, how those positives shifted over time, what was going on when things were shifting, and what each said to each other about the shifts. Most often little or nothing was said about what was really happening although they may have argued about surface matters. Identify each one's contribution to the marital evolution and from this information fashion a statement that incorporates each spouse's contribution to setting the stage for the affair.

> Brian and Jennifer had been married for 14 years when he had an affair. In the reframing process, I stated, "Brian, when you inherited the family business, you had so much to do that you came home later and later, and you were pretty well exhausted when you were home. Jennifer, you felt hurt and disappointed that Brian didn't have time for you, but you swallowed it because you knew how hard he was working, and you were busy with the kids anyway. Sounds like both of you backed off from each other, you both felt lonely, and neither of you said much about it. So there was a big space in the middle of your marriage—big enough for an affair." When Brian and Jennifer agreed that this was the case, I framed the work to be done as learning to talk to each other about what each is thinking and most importantly, what each is feeling. Reframing the affair as a marital problem enables both to work toward change.

During the course of therapy we also looked at how not talking about their feelings served them as children in their families of origin. So in addition to reframing the affair, we reframed their dysfunctional behaviors as necessary coping skills in childhood, although not useful now. Reframing normalizes rather than castigates. It offers a different perspective than the one of guilt and blame, one that makes it easier to let go of obsessive thinking. Reframing can elicit an "aha" moment as in "I never thought of it that way." And it serves the purpose of lessening guilt about problematic behaviors of the past. Feeling guilty is appropriate only up to the point where it leads to constructive change. Too much energy spent on guilt leads to endless ruminating, or depression. With less attention to blame and guilt, people are freer to work toward positive goals. When the work on reframing falters and the obsession recurs, again help the Betrayed Spouse access and stay with the underlying emotions until calm enough to get back to the reframing task. Reframing the problem as belonging to both clients creates safety in the therapy process. It is in the reframing process that the real issues start to open up. No longer is one spouse the innocent victim and the other an evil wrongdoer. Until this reframing is done, couples work cannot proceed because the problem is viewed as belonging only to the Betraying Partner. The reframe is also empowering—since both share responsibility for setting the stage for the affair, each has the power to change those behaviors that contributed to the problem.

In the process of getting the obsession under control and the reframe in place, the work on the underlying issues has already started. Positive opportunities start to be visible, although we may see them before our clients dare to dream they are there. The early phase of therapy lasts roughly from 3 to 6 months. Some couples drop out when the hard work of changing behavior appears on the horizon but many get to work on changing their dysfunctional patterns.

Old Baggage

In reframing the affair, clues are often given about family of origin issues. Make some space for getting a good family history. In doing so you can highlight significant details and tie together threads that seem to be related. Current opportunities will flow from the unfinished business of the past, those very things that motivated the affair in the first place.

> Alan and Janet met in school. After a long friendship, they married and went westward, escaping the reach of their families. They had kids and went to grad school simultaneously. Both coped by being rational, building a professional life, and overdoing for their children. Little time was available for fun or socializing. Their unwritten "contract" was that Janet wouldn't get emotional so Alan didn't get anxious.

What was the personal, couple, and family of origin history of each that set the stage for Alan's affair? Both had grown up with very difficult family situations. Alan's family was repressive, unemotional, and physically abusive—"for his own good." He had learned to be a rock in the face of physical abuse. Janet's family was loaded with sexual abuse and secrecy. She had been fondled once at the age of 11 but after that experience was able to stay out of harm's way although others in her family were not that fortunate. Each was the kid in the family of origin who was going to make it despite the crazy backgrounds.

They agreed that Alan had lost his emotional self and Janet had overridden her emotional self. I commented that the skills they had learned in order to protect themselves as children, while essential then, were dysfunctional now. Both agreed on the importance of developing their emotional selves before making any big decisions. Thus the primary goal of therapy became emotional growth with secondary goals of understanding what had gone wrong and eventually deciding what to do with their marriage.

In addition to "old baggage" from childhood, there is always baggage that has accrued during the marriage. Alan wanted Janet to be there for him, but was afraid to let her in for fear his emotions would be suppressed. Control issues played out, as Alan continued to insist that nobody impose anything on him, although he responded when they did. Then he would pull away.

Janet's reaction to Alan's withdrawal was to push him to talk and to explain and justify her requests rather than express her emotions—thus both were in a double bind. I framed Janet's job now as learning to identify her emotions, feel them, and give voice to them. Alan's job I framed as dealing with his anxiety: feeling it, talking about it, riding it out, and knowing that the harm that he fears is not really about Janet but goes back to childhood. The Betrayed Spouse's "gatekeeping" behavior needs to be monitored. When it continues inappropriately, it needs to be addressed, along with other control issues. The therapist can encourage the Betraying Partner to stand up and be heard, rather than silently resent the leash. At the same time, the therapist can surface the underlying issues that make control so important for the Betrayed Spouse. Those issues go deeper than the affair.

When the childhood issues go deep, individual therapy for each spouse can be a crucial adjunct to couples work. Unaddressed experiences such as physical or emotional abuse, PTSD, or early loss of parents clearly call for individual therapy in addition to any couples work. In many cases this individual work is necessary before starting couples work.

Rebuilding Trust

The next phase, rebuilding trust, requires each spouse to take responsibility for one's own changes and to let go of attempts to change the spouse. Individual change goes hand in hand with changing the dynamics of the marriage. The focus is on connecting emotionally and addressing deeper issues. Opportunities abound for learning how to negotiate with each other and how to set boundaries. Each issue, each difference or disagreement provides a chance to try out new behavior. Honesty is always an issue and is best addressed moment by moment, as choices are made and information is, or is not, conveyed to the spouse. Therapists need to hold the clients' feet to the fire so that they don't avoid dealing with emotionally laden issues, especially those issues that have been taboo in the past.

In this phase the affair resurfaces again. With the therapist's help, talking about the affair can be productive. The talk isn't just about the affair—it is another, deeper look at how the marriage got off track emotionally. The Betrayed Spouse may begin sharing the deep pain about the affair. The Betraying Partner who listens to his spouse's pain will resonate and reach out with his own pain. They can connect through their pain. From there it is possible to talk at a deeper level, probably deeper than ever before.

> Because Brian was afraid of losing Jennifer, he began working on developing and sharing his emotional self. Jennifer worked on giving up her role as protector of Brian by paying more attention to her emotions and voicing them. As Jennifer began to convey the extent of her pain to Brian, he responded sometimes with empathy and sometimes with irritation. He also began to talk about his pain at hurting

Jennifer so badly. Their shared pain was the key element in renewing their long lost emotional connection.

Each partner may be impatient with the other when needed changes do not proceed quickly—and significant change never happens quickly. At the same time, a deeper understanding of what led to the affair is possible. Misunderstandings about what the other partner wanted or expected can be cleared up. With each issue there is an opportunity for changing the way the couple addresses it. The therapist is active, helping them learn to negotiate differences, make choices, set boundaries, share emotions, and change expectations. The process runs up and down, hot and cold. Some couples drop out along the way.

Trust is never the same after an affair. Blind trust is no longer possible. However, informed trust is a possibility. This is trust without naivete, trust that is based on experience. Informed trust allows noticing and addressing factors that don't fit. Implied is the sense that problems and betrayals can be faced, and that the ability to take care of one's self is necessary and present. Lingering distrust when there is no longer a reason for it indicates that the Betraying Spouse fears she cannot take care of herself. She probably has always looked to others for validation. Learning to self-validate so that she can trust herself to handle whatever situation presents itself will be an important part of therapy.

Toward the end of the rebuilding phase, decisions about the marriage begin to come to the fore. When change is not an outcome of this crisis, the marriage may continue along its old pathways or it may end. However, the opportunity for insight, change, and renewed strength will be lost. If one spouse has made significant changes and the other has not, or if the emotional connection is not revived, chances are that the marriage will end. When both spouses have grown as individuals and joined together in remaking their marriage they are likely to have a stronger bond and a more vital marriage than ever before.

Forgiveness

The last phase of the process is choosing to forgive. (Many of our clients would like this to come first.) Since both spouses contributed to setting the stage for the affair, both need to request forgiveness for their contribution, and each needs to respond from the heart. When couples are truly ready to ask for forgiveness they usually know what they want to say to each other. The therapist may need to do little other than provide them with the space to do so. If the desire for forgiveness is premature, the therapist can highlight the work that remains to be done first. Forgiving the self is another part of the forgiveness process. *Forgiving is not forgetting, but allows the affair to be moved from center stage to a place in the couple's history.*

The end of couples therapy comes during this phase, usually soon after the spouses have forgiven each other. Comments by clients at the end of therapy speak to the transformation that can occur following an affair.

Jennifer stated, "I hated her and I still don't like her (the third party) but I'm really grateful to her. We've got a much better marriage now than we ever would have had without the affair. It was a wake-up call." Brian said, "I never thought we'd be able to make it after what I did, but here we are knowing that we love each other and are going to be with each other and it's the best it's ever been!"

Forgiveness is also important for those whose marriage does not continue, but it may come later, after the marriage has ended.

WORKING WITH INDIVIDUALS AFTER AN AFFAIR

Betrayed Spouses in *Exit Affairs*, and those whose partner does not want to participate in therapy, often seek individual therapy. They are more likely to see themselves as victims than do Betrayed Spouses in other types of affairs or those whose partner agrees to therapy. They too need help in moving beyond obsession, seeing their role in making room for an affair in their marriage, reclaiming their emotional self, and rebuilding their lives. The work is much the same, but lacks the counterpoint of the spouse's view. Thus, the therapist needs to inquire along the way about the spouse's perspective and behavior.

For *Split Selves*, individual work is often the treatment of choice. These people have been so weighted down with overwhelming responsibilities from a very early age that they have never fully developed their emotional selves.

> Gary, for example, shouldered the responsibility for his alcoholic and promiscuous mother at the age of 7 when his stepfather left. He married Beth who had been taught that her emotions were not to be trusted. Gary and Beth's marriage centered on doing what was supposed to be done, with some affection but no intimacy. Gary's affair with Marie (a Split Self Affair) offered a glimpse of how it feels to connect emotionally. Because he couldn't make a choice between Beth and Marie, he came to therapy. We worked on differentiating his thoughts and feelings, and on accessing and paying attention to his feelings, particularly powerlessness. Gary began to get clarity about what boundaries he wanted to set and how to set them without explaining and justifying everything. The responses he got gave him additional perspectives on each relationship. His goal shifted from deciding who was the right woman to reclaiming his integrity. Integrity is more than honesty; it is also about integrating the emotional and rational selves. The affair with Marie opened the door for Gary to develop his neglected emotional self, integrating his heart with his mind. Gary says, "It had to happen. Neither of us was happy. Taking some time to be by myself and deal with myself made all the difference: I grew up."

THE COUPLES THERAPIST'S ROLE WITH AFFAIRS

Affairs have always been lightning rods for negative judgments. What doesn't get attention is the positive change that can arise from an affair. "News" about positive outcomes of an affair *doesn't make the news*. Thus, many of us grew up believing that affairs were shameful, or worse, unforgiveable. However, as therapists, being nonjudgmental is crucial, especially with affairs. When the rest of the world seems to be judging one or the other spouse, or both, we are of most help by keeping focused on our clients' emotions and needs without being judgmental or imposing decisions on them. The effective therapeutic approach is framing the affair as a marital problem, rather than as a good-spouse-gone-bad/innocent-victim situation.

We know that when marriages are troubled or on a collision course, something is bound to happen. An affair, even though incredibly painful, is not the worst that can happen. If we therapists can see the affair as a catalyst for positive change we can help our clients identify and explore the opportunities for change that come with each choice or decision. Clients feel encouraged and work harder when the therapist provides hope that the future can be different. We also need to hold our clients strictly accountable for their choices and their decisions, rather than letting anything slide. We are not just confronting issues here, but modeling appropriate relationship behavior.

To work with affairs, the therapist has to be able to invite the pain of each spouse and sit with them as they experience it. It's crucial to be able to differentiate pain from obsession, and genuine emotions from the verbal noise and clutter about the affair. Pain comes across very differently than loud and angry accusations and inquisitions. Teasing out and listening to the underlying emotions that need to be heard, especially those that venture into forbidden territory, is life-affirming for our clients. One of the most important interventions is to be emotionally present ourselves. Equally important is teaching clients how to access their emotions, label them, and be emotionally present themselves.

Some therapists struggle with their role in working with affairs. A therapist may have a personal belief that couples should stay together. This may not mesh with the couple's need to explore what is right for them. A therapist's underlying belief that "cheaters should be thrown out" also limits the couple's options. It is important that therapists are aware of any biases that may limit the work and inform the clients of them. If there is a current or recent affair in the therapist's life, it's usually better not to take these cases for now.

Honesty is always an issue when working with affairs, for therapists as well as clients. Some therapists avoid addressing the hidden affair out of a misdirected desire to protect a client from pain. This gives a mixed message to the client about honesty. The therapy is also limited by the avoidance of pain on the part of the therapist.

In these days of managed care, we are asked to put band-aids on our clients' wounds when clients are in the midst of major surgery working on restructuring themselves and their lives. Working with affairs is not short-term work. Real change takes time. Couples can expect to take a minimum of one to two years to make significant changes in their lives. The timetable is much the same for individuals. Since many clients hope that therapy will work magic, and work it quickly, it's helpful to reorient their expectations about the time and the effort involved.

OUTCOMES

By the time couples therapy ends, many Betrayed Spouses state that despite the pain, the affair was the best thing that happened to them. They know that without the affair, their marriage would have continued to slide—or plummet—into oblivion. The affair was the wake-up call that prompted action.

Other individuals and couples decide that there isn't enough of an emotional connection and move toward separation. This too can be a positive decision when it's arrived at in the process of resolving old issues and reclaiming the self.

The outcomes of an affair that matter most have to do with healing childhood wounds, reclaiming the cut-off parts of self, and learning to nurture one's inner self, rather than whether the marriage ends or the affair ends. When the affair serves as a catalyst for developing the emotional self, the individuals will be able to arrive at decisions about their marriage and their lives that are right for them. The major outcome is not the status of the marriage but the integrity that the individuals involved bring to their lives.

REFERENCES

1. For more information on types of affairs, see Emily M. Brown, *Patterns of infidelity and their treatment* (2nd ed.), Philadelphia, PA: Brunner-Routledge, 2001.
2. Lawrence G. Calhoun & Richard G. Tedeschi, University of North Carolina, as quoted in Michael E. Ruane, From wounds, inner strength: Some veterans feel lives enlarged by wartime suffering, *The Washington Post,* Nov. 26, 2005, p. A1.
3. For a full discussion of how to approach the hidden affair, see Brown, *Patterns of infidelity and their treatment.*
4. For guidance on the sorting out process, see Brown, *Patterns of infidelity and their treatment.* See also Emily M. Brown, *Affairs: A guide to working through the repercussions of infidelity,* San Francisco: Jossey-Bass, 1999. This latter publication helps clients sort through disclosure and other issues.

PART III

The Impact of Infidelity on Couples and Families From Different Social, Cultural, Generational, and Sexual Perspectives

CHAPTER 9

Cyber-Infidelity

RONA SUBOTNIK

"Cyber-affairs occur when a partner in a committed relationship uses the computer or Internet to violate promises, vows, or agreements concerning his or her sexual exclusivity" (Maheu & Subotnik, 2001, p. 100). The cyber-affair has forced therapists as well as their clients to look differently at infidelity because many issues resulting from the new technology differ from those in off-line relationships.

For the purpose of simplicity in this chapter, the husband has been designated as the unfaithful partner, even though it could be the reverse. The terms *cyber-affair* and *cyber-infidelity* will be used interchangeably and reflect that understanding.

The treatment of extramarital infidelity is challenging for the therapist, because the couple must directly address not only the affair as well as pre- and post-affair issues but also the high degree of emotional reactivity after discovery of the affair. The unusual aspects of a computer affair with an unknown person only add to the distress that accompanies the discovery. The wife is just as devastated as if it had been a traditional affair, that is, one conducted off-line involving actual physical contact. In fact, she sometimes feels even worse because she thinks of herself as competing with a faceless person—a phantom—and that she is losing the competition.

Cyber-infidelity might begin innocently in a chat room devoted to some common interest, or deliberately pursued on a site that promotes affairs, offering ways to meet others, or connecting people with similar sexual interests. Interactions on-line can be viewed on a *continuum* according to the degree of involvement with the other person. These interactions can proceed from a regular exchange that increasingly becomes very important to each. The desire to meet on-line may then increase and become more obsessive. The high point of one's day is being on-line with the cyber-lover, so one looks forward to the rendezvous, fantasizes about the other, and saves stories to share. They begin typing sexual text messages to one another that move them along the continuum. They reach a point where they exchange sexually stimulating words to bring each other to orgasm. Their interactions might not be just text, but include two-way video cameras so they can transmit photos of their bodies to each other. They can see one another posing sexually or masturbating in real time. This is known as "cybering."

However, the cyber-affair may be part of a larger picture. The husband may be behaving in a sexually compulsive manner. He may have many affairs on-line as well as off-line, his on-line visits may be mainly to sexual sites, and he may spend significant amounts of time in these activities. This is different from meeting a woman on-line and conducting a cyber-affair. He is sexually addicted and uses the Internet for sexual stimulation and release.

IS IT THE AFFAIR OR IS IT ADDICTION?

It is important for the therapist, in creating a treatment plan for cyber-infidelity, to distinguish the person who is sexually addicted from the person who is having an affair on-line but is not sexually addicted. In the first case, the addiction is the primary problem to be treated, and like other addictions must become the chief focus in treatment. Addiction is better treated by a specialist with experience in that area.

In the second case, the infidelity is addressed similarly as a traditional affair, but with recognition of the part the computer plays. In both cases, however, underlying issues, such as anxiety, depression, or childhood trauma, must be dealt with.

There are three characteristics that all addictions have in common. The first is loss of control over the ability to stop the addictive behavior whether it is use of drugs, alcohol, food, or on-line sexual pursuits. The second is that the behavior continues despite dire consequences in his personal, professional, or social life. The third characteristic is preoccupation with the addictive behavior (Schneider, 2001).

The sexual addict has unresolved emotional issues and unmet needs that cause him pain. He believes his greatest need is sex. The addiction cycle starts with thoughts of sex. He repeatedly finds himself in a cycle that includes preoccupation with his sexual needs as his anxiety rises, some type of sexual release, and finally guilt and remorse until the cycle begins again (Carnes,

1992). Essentially, the addictive person has lost control over his addiction, just like the person addicted to alcohol or drugs.

The behavior could include visiting pornographic Web sites, shopping for sexual paraphernalia, and numerous other sexual sites that are available on the Internet. In 1998 MSNBC surveyed the use of the Internet in its sexual survey, *Sexuality on the Internet: From sexual exploration to pathological expression* (Cooper, Scherer, Boies, & Gordon, 1999). Of 9,177 respondents, 8.5% were found to be sexually addicted; 20% of individuals visited sexual sites during regular working hours. Consequently, therapists are seeing more problems related to online sexual behavior (Cooper, Scherer, Boise, & Gordon, 1999). To understand this development of a sexual affair with someone unseen and unknown, we must understand the attraction of the Internet and the enormous effect it is capable of exerting on individuals.

ATTRACTIONS OF THE INTERNET

The Internet can be an ongoing "party" where people can meet without many of the barriers that are found off-line. The doors are always open and everyone is invited.

Triple A Engine

The Internet is driven by a "Triple A Engine," defined as accessibility, affordability, and anonymity, which together act like a "turbojet," increasing the speed and intensity of interactions (Cooper, 1998). Such speed allows individuals to connect faster than if they were meeting off-line, and they can progress rapidly along the continuum.

Accessibility   The Internet phenomenon of accessibility allows individuals to connect with large numbers of others very quickly, in a manner that cannot compare with any other off-line activity. There are Internet sex shops with merchandise for any taste, service sites offering all types of erotica including bestiality, and easy access to explicit texts and images available on-line anonymously with no questions asked (Fisher & Barak, 2000).

There are no international boundaries to prohibit connecting with others. Not only does this increase the chance of finding a partner, but it can enhance the sense of intrigue. One's "dream lover" may be just one click away; and if the party isn't going well, another click can literally end the connection.

Affordability   The cost of this Internet "party" is reasonable, in most cases just the Internet Service Provider (ISP) fee and, depending on the site, another small user fee. On the other hand, financing a "night on the town" in the real world can be high, when one considers the cost of transportation, dinner, drinks, a concert or show, the dress or suit, and hairstyling.

Anonymity   In this case, the on-line "party" can really be a masquerade. A person can come in disguise and pretend to be someone else. The anonymity frees people to be whomever they want to be or to experiment by trying new roles. Of course, there is a decided disadvantage to not being sure who one's Internet partner really is. One can lie about age, sex, race, religion, occupation, marital status, or any other facts of his life. It can be like wearing a mask and interacting with someone who may also be in disguise.

The Internet makes it easier today than in the past for a married person to reach out to another, with a reduced chance of detection. He does not have to leave his home, or account for unexplained absences and mysterious charges on his credit card bills. He can have a cyber-affair while his wife is asleep in the next room. In addition to these components, the Internet offers an immediate exit, a quick getaway.

Although accessibility, affordability, and anonymity are the initial attractions of the Internet, once contact has been made with an individual, there are other aspects that maintain one's interest in these pursuits, as described in the following sections.

Psuedo-Intimacy   Individuals report a strong feeling of closeness or intimacy that develops with others on-line. Yet this profound on-line closeness is not true intimacy, but psuedo-intimacy, one of the paradoxes of the Internet (Maheu & Subotnik, 2001). It has the potential to become a major threat to the marriage. Individuals report that they are shocked at how quickly such a feeling of closeness is experienced with someone they have never really met. Yet, *true intimacy* can develop only when two people interact with each other *in the real world*, where they can see each other's weaknesses, vulnerabilities, and self-doubts. In this way, they find that even with such knowledge they can still care and respect their partner. Not only can one's vulnerabilities be masked by individuals who are not being truthful, but by the projection of one's individual needs in such a way that they lose objectivity.

Loss of Objectivity   While one may feel free to act differently on-line when protected by the anonymity of the Internet, another process may be operating that contributes to the experience of closeness. The Internet becomes the "blank screen" upon which an individual can read meanings into the text that will satisfy his or her own emotional desires. For example, a person who feels her needs are not being met in her marriage may feel they are being met from her virtual encounters with her cyber-lover. From what she reads into the text she may perceive him as the one who will rescue her from her unhappy situation. She may have unresolved issues from childhood and feel that her cyber-romance provides what was missing from her early life experiences. For example, he can become the caring parent she never had, just by what she reads into what appears on the screen.

Additionally, the informational cues that are seen in off-line face-to-face meetings are missing in Internet exchanges. These are voice tone, body language, and facial expressions. Because they are missing from the text communication of the Internet, misinterpretation can easily occur. For example, someone may be writing tender words to his on-line lover while reading his mail or eating a pizza. His on-line lover doesn't see what he is doing, only what he writes. She can interpret his words without the benefit of seeing and hearing him, and then can imagine him the way she desires him to be.

Much can be hidden on-line. When couples live in the same geographical area, they have a shared knowledge of the attractions and meeting places. This can give them information about each other's interests. Because the cyberlover most likely lives in a different geographical area, some of the places he mentions may not give clues that could be valuable in understanding one another. For example, she may not know that he frequents a gambling club because the name of the club doesn't indicate its purpose. If she knows the purpose of the club, she would then be able to discuss the role gambling plays in his life.

Another concern about Internet affairs is that the nature of the affair prevents the lovers from receiving feedback from friends that might be enlightening about the character of their cyber-lover. Often the friends can see problematic behaviors that one of the cyber-lovers cannot.

On-line, people are perceived largely by what they write. In the real world, one's perception of others is typically formed from how they look, what they wear, their personality, and those with whom they associate. Many who don't find acceptance in the real world may find it on-line, where they are judged by their words and thoughts. For example, such acceptance is often reported by overweight individuals who report being repeatedly rejected off-line, but not on-line (Maheu & Subotnik, 2001). The absence of a physical body provides an illusion of whom we are on-line, if not in the real world. This is due to the disembodiment aspect of the Internet in which we are known by our thoughts and how they are expressed rather than by our appearance.

Loneliness   The Internet is used by some as a technological solution for their social or emotional loneliness. Such a need can be mitigated by going on-line to "hook up" with others, attend an "all-night" party, or find a lover. For many, loneliness needs are satisfied when contact is achieved on-line. For some, their life on-line becomes a parallel world with a strong emotional pull—but with real-world consequences. One such consequence is cyber-infidelity. A parallel world may be built on a "house of cards" that could come tumbling down. The emotional pain will not be *virtual*—it will be *real*.

Time   People experience time differently on-line than in the real world. Time seems to be deceptive. As a result, relationships move quickly along the continuum, or can end suddenly without forewarning. People lose track of time, and experience it as going quickly. They may have spent eight hours on-line but they experience it as much less. Time affects communication and the reactions to it. Receiving five off-line notes in a 24-hour period from a lover may seem like an intrusion but the same number of e-mails does not. Communication can occur sporadically, but not be perceived in that way. An individual may feel he has his lover's attention, but actually the e-mail may have been written at different times during the day among other activities and transmitted even later (Maheu & Subotnik, 2001).

Immediate Reinforcement   While the Internet provides satisfaction for issues such as loneliness, acceptance, and the desire to experiment with new behaviors, individuals can also look to their computer for instant gratification of other needs. For many, it is orgasm. The gratification does nothing to actually solve their problems, but provides a release for the anxiety that has begun to build.

Yet the orgasm, so reinforcing for other users, may not be desired by the sexual addict who wants to maintain the high level of sexual excitement as long as possible. The orgasm signals the end of this euphoric state and a return to the problems from which he is trying to escape (Schneider, 2001).

COMPONENTS OF TRUE LOVE

Love, being subjective, is difficult to define, but becomes even more so as it pertains to the Internet. The components of true love are *passion, intimacy*, and *commitment*, each being one leg of a triangle (Sternberg, 1988). This concept allows for flexibility in defining subtypes, as well as more objectivity in understanding the complexity of personal relationships. It can also be adapted to Internet relationships.

Passion is the motivational component. It usually peaks early in a relationship and can reach great heights dramatically, but can drop off quickly. It has been likened to a state of intoxication.

Intimacy is the emotional component and involves aspects of closeness, trust, and safety. It grows more slowly, levels off, and can reach heights similar to passion.

The third component is *commitment,* which is the cognitive component. It grows slowly over time. It is at first a short-term promise to love someone, which then becomes a long-term promise to maintain that love.

TYPES OF AFFAIRS

In 1953, Alfred C. Kinsey startled the world with his survey showing 26% of women and 50% of men reported having had an affair (Kinsey, Pomeroy, & Martin, 1953). The Janus Report in 1993 (Janus & Janus, 1993) places the figure at 26% for women and 35% for men. Shirley Glass (2003) reports 25% for women and 44% for men. Lower figures of 11.6% for women and 22.7% for men were reported in *Sex in America* based on the National Health and Social Life Survey (Michael, Gagnon, Laumann, & Kolata, 1994). Internet statistics have not been reported, but the ease with which people can now meet others on-line may show an increase of such affairs in the future.

Four types of affairs have been identified: the serial affair, the fling, the romantic love affair, and the long-term affair (Subotnik & Harris, 2005). It is possible to view Internet affairs using this model as well (Maheu & Subotnik, 2001). Affairs are seen on a *continuum* according to the degree of emotional connection the spouse has to the lover. Knowledge of the type of affair gives the therapist information about the degree of difficulty the spouse will have ending the affair and about the possible outcomes. The greater the degree of emotional connection to the lover, the more difficult it is for him to give up the affair. Additionally, the more the affair satisfies his psychological needs, the more difficult it will be to end the infidelity.

The Serial Affair   Typically, this is a series of one-night stands, or of many affairs, or a history of visiting prostitutes. It is characterized by no emotional connection to the lovers. These infidelities can occur over many years in the marriage. The affairs aren't serious, but the behavior is. Such a person involved in serial affairs is a poor-risk partner (Subotnik & Harris, 2005).

The Internet is very alluring to the poor-risk partner because he has access to large numbers of individuals and very little will be asked of him in return. The poor-risk partner has little to give in a relationship. He is usually narcissistic, has an inability to tolerate closeness, may have serious emotional problems, and could have a history of poor interpersonal relationships starting from childhood. He may have been sexually, physically, or emotionally abused as a child. The accessibility, affordability, anonymity, and low accountability of the Internet are very appealing to him, as is the possibility of the quick escape. He finds the use of the Internet an ideal way to relieve his anxiety, but his victim is often deceived because of the pseudo-intimacy experienced on-line.

The Fling   Although this type of affair moves further along the continuum, there is little emotional connection to the lover. For some, there may be just one fling or a few during the course of his marriage. The Internet is a place where a fling can easily develop and be maintained for a while. He may have accidentally met someone in a chat room or when actually looking for some diversion. Typically, an individual having a fling believes it will not intrude upon his married life. The belief that the risk of detection is low on the Internet, that the environment is free from sexually transmitted diseases, and that no paper trail of bills is made leads to a sense of safety.

What starts out as a fling can, in some cases, change in character and move further along the continuum to become a romantic love affair.

The Romantic Love Affair   After repeated contacts with each other on-line, Internet factors such as the feeling of closeness, acceptance without actual physical contact, the loss of objectivity, the different experience of time, and the immediate sexual release and gratification, one or both may experience their on-line relationship as a romantic love affair.

This is a very serious affair in terms of its immediate threat to the marriage. The wife reacts with the same emotional reactivity on discovering an Internet affair as an off-line one, but in addition she is confused. Some wives feel that their strong reactions are out of proportion to the fact that the lovers have not met and have not actually had a physical relationship. Some deny or rationalize their feelings, because it is difficult for them to believe such an affair can develop. It seems to many like "science fiction." She is devastated and her feeling intensifies when she realizes how very serious the relationship is and how important the cyber-lover is to her husband. The therapist can validate her experience rather than deny or minimize it.

In romantic love affairs, the lovers typically feel a decision must be made about their relationship. In the case of cyber-lovers, their decision is whether to meet off-line. However, in many cases, by this time the cyber-lovers have already met off-line. When this occurs, it is no longer a cyber-affair, but a traditional one that is supported by on-line contact. Although they may continue having cyber-sex, they now know each other and the Internet becomes a way to communicate. The husband who stays in the marriage often becomes depressed because of the decision not to be with his lover. The wife, on the other hand, must watch her husband recover from a depression brought on by his decision to end his relationship and stay in his marriage. The woman who never knows about the affair may not be able to comprehend the reason for the depression her husband is experiencing.

Yet, there are men who cannot make a decision to actually meet their cyber-lover. If the affair continues, it can move along the continuum.

The Long-Term Affair   In a traditional affair, when the couple cannot reach a decision for whatever reason, including ambivalence, the affair can move along the continuum to become long-term. It may, in some ways, be like a parallel marriage, such as the secret affair of the American hero, Charles Lindbergh. He had three children with Brigitte Hesshaimer, a young Munich milliner, while he was married to Anne Morrow Lindbergh. Long-term affairs can continue on-line as well and also have the potential to become a parallel life.

In relating the types of affairs to Sternberg's triangular model of love, passion is the single component in both the serial affair and the fling. For serial lovers, multitudes of affairs provide an escape from anxiety and may be an indication of sexual addiction. Internet affairs are most likely to be serial affairs or flings. When passion and intimacy are present, the individual believes the relationship is a romantic love affair because of the *psuedo*-intimacy experienced on-line. It is not true intimacy as Sternberg described it. Because real intimacy cannot be experienced on-line, true love is not attainable in cyber-affairs despite the fact that people may feel very emotionally close to each other on-line. It takes *commitment,* which is the last part to develop, to complete the triangle.

The ramifications of each category are significant for the marriage. Most importantly, the affair can be experienced differently for each of the individuals (Subotnik, 2005). It becomes more complicated, for example, when one person feels the affair is a *fling,* and the other feels it is a *romantic love affair.*

In addition to the Internet affair, another kind has been described in which there also is no physical contact. This is the *emotional affair.*

The emotional affair is one in which a couple has *not* been sexually intimate, but a sexual chemistry and emotional intimacy have developed between them (Glass, 2003). They obsess about one another and can be very close to crossing the line and having a sexual affair. Such affairs are seen with increasing frequency in the workplace (Glass, 2003). Although it seems an emotional affair could develop on-line, it is the intimacy, not emotional intimacy that presents the problem.

DIFFERENCES BETWEEN CYBER-AFFAIRS AND TRADITIONAL AFFAIRS

It is easier to conduct a cyber-affair than a traditional one because one can meet a large number of individuals in a relatively short time, and with a reduced chance of discovery. On the surface, it appears to satisfy needs such as loneliness, excitement, and anxiety reduction, or the desire for instant gratification. It requires little or no advance preparation.

A traditional affair, by comparison, can be difficult to conceal not just from the spouse and children, but also from co-workers and friends. It requires careful attention to organization and planning, and results in guarded behavior. Life takes on a more clandestine aspect because the chance of discovery is greater than in an Internet rendezvous. For example, the computer screen can be instantly "minimized" if someone walks into the room. There are many possible explanations for such activities, while in a traditional affair the husband will find it difficult to explain his being seen with another woman, as well as credit card bills for hotels, gifts, and secretive phone calls.

The Danger Zone

There are signs that an individual who is in a monogamous relationship may be in a Danger Zone that could lead to infidelity (Maheu & Subotnik, 2001).

1. *Meeting people on sites that are designed for dating or sexual contact.* Individuals often minimize this behavior by saying that it isn't serious and they are just having fun. After all, they rationalize, they don't

even know this person. Yet the time, energy, money, and emotional connections are diverted from their primary relationship to those they meet on these sites.

2. *Reacting with tension to sexual discussions on-line.* This is similar to the reaction found in new relationships when there is excitement and a feeling of intoxication of what "could be."

3. *Discussing sexual topics with someone on-line.* This seems safe because of the distance and the anonymity. Yet, paradoxically, it feels dangerous while seeming intimate.

4. *Experiencing and/or sharing erotic fantasies or daydreams involving this person.* When this occurs, the individual moves further away from reality and begins to incorporate the on-line attraction into his/her everyday life. This increases the danger and the threat to the marriage.

5. *Hiding the Internet behavior from a spouse.* The on-line relationship now holds a prominent place in the life of the individual and must be kept secret because of its importance. In other words, it becomes something that cannot easily be given up, and thus must be hidden.

6. *Feeling shame, guilt, or fear about this behavior.* These are the feelings that arise when so much time is spent hiding on-line activities. It is cheating the marriage, so shame and guilt accompany the secret life on-line. The fear comes from the threat of discovery.

7. *Spending more time talking with this new individual on-line than with one's spouse.* At this point, the time on-line becomes the highlight of the day and every opportunity to be on-line is sought. A feeling of closeness is being shifted away from the marriage and into the on-line relationship.

8. *Having intense thoughts about the new person when having sex with one's spouse.* The on-line relationship is now intruding on the most physically intimate area of the marital relationship and indicates the desire to be having sex with the on-line lover.

If the contact goes on to become an affair, the relationship will be supported by those characteristics of the Internet that make it conducive to secrecy and excitement, while the marriage is adversely affected.

STAGES OF AN AFFAIR

Affairs can proceed in fairly predictable stages from the initial attraction to finding an answer to the future of the relationship (Subotnik, 2005).

Attraction is the first stage, when they meet on-line. It can be one's screen name or the text of the message that creates the appeal on-line. Physical appearance is not the attraction at first. Flirting by the use of language is the major device sustaining the attraction. The text message can convey charm, mystery, sensuality, and a promise of excitement to come. It can be directly stated, or implied. It is the allure, the "hook." The couple may chat privately if the site has accommodations such as instant messaging, or they may move on to exchanging e-mails. As the relationship develops and is established, they describe themselves to each other and soon feel as though they are a couple. By this time, they have probably shared their real identity. It may not be until they are more involved that they discover, or realize, the other's marital status, but at that point this new information does not deter them. The relationship is new, and they are dedicated to making these meetings a most wonderful part of their week.

The Honeymoon is the second stage, with its feeling of intoxication. It is the passionate stage of the affair. By now the couple is sexually involved and obsessing about each other. The secrecy nurtures the obsession. Living with a spouse and suppressing thoughts of the lover and the affair typically results in an increased level of arousal (Layton-Tholl, 1999). They start to plan their next meeting and think of what they want to do, to say, and how it will feel to be together. Even though it is a virtual affair, it feels as exhilarating as if it were happening in real time.

The Honeymoon Stage lasts until it transitions to the next stage, in which one starts to talk seriously about meeting off-line. At this point, the relationship can begin to show instability and the couple is at the next stage, which is turbulent.

Disequilibrium is the next stage, characterized by arguments about their future together and whether or not they will meet off-line. Promises are made and broken, deadlines are set and passed, ultimatums issued and ignored, and no definite time is set for their next meeting. If he agrees to meet off-line, this does not mean he will leave his marriage for her. It depends on his feelings regarding his marriage. Meeting depends on his ability to get away, the cost of travel, his emotional health, his expectations, his intentions, and how he experiences this affair.

He may be a poor-risk partner, emotionally impaired, or a sex addict. *Anyone agreeing to meet off-line must be aware that it is possible to meet a sexual predator* (Maheu & Subotnik, 2001; Tarbox, 2000).

An Answer is the last stage, the point where an ending to the search for an answer is reached. They can continue their affair on-line, end their affair, or meet off-line.

RESOLUTION OF THE INTERNET AFFAIR

Before the therapist proceeds with treating the issue of cyber-infidelity, the degree of depression, anxiety, guilt, and homicidal, suicidal, or violent behavior must first be assessed and attended to, as in other treatments, and must continue to be monitored throughout the treatment.

Typically, couples are seen together. Sometimes there may be one or two individual sessions early in their treatment. Conjoint sessions are a way to replace secrecy with openness and honesty.

The major question that must be answered at this time is whether the unfaithful spouse has already given up the affair or will do so. His answer to the question of giving up the affair will provide the first indication of what the affair means to him. The couple must understand there is to be absolutely no contact between the husband and his lover. If the husband will not end the affair, there are a few choices. One is to work together with the couple for a short time to see if any progress can be made. Another is to refer him to a different therapist to see why he will not give up the affair, while the wife works with you or another therapist. If the issue is resolved satisfactorily, they can continue couples therapy to deal with the affair.

The path to recovery typically proceeds in four stages that can meld one into the other. Sometimes there is a temporary regression, but in general these are the categories that emerge in resolving the infidelity and all its ensuing problems (Maheu & Subotnik, 2001).

STAGE 1. COPING WITH EMOTIONS

The difficulties with the treatment of infidelity are due to the high degree of emotional reactivity with which couples typically present. This must be reduced before proceeding to individual and marital issues, rebuilding trust, restructuring the marriage, and providing as many safeguards as possible so that there is not a repeat of infidelity.

Her Reaction   The wife's emotions are intense and can be shock, disbelief, rage, depression, and anxiety. The discovery of an affair is traumatic, and she experiences the betrayal as an emotional abandonment. She feels she has lost her "specialness" to him and their marriage has lost its innocence. Her reaction to the betrayal will continue for some time. She will be particularly distressed by her obsessive thinking about the affair, which can be quite disturbing, typically described by women as "going crazy."

His Reaction   He also has an emotional reaction. He may experience guilt, shame, anxiety, and depression. He is often shocked at the intensity of her response. At first, he may deny his behavior, then minimize it, and finally acknowledge it.

The husband's reaction is crucial. If he shows remorse, shows empathy for his wife, gives up the affair, and is willing to help in resolution of the problem, the outcome can be a good one. If, on the other hand, he shows no remorse or empathy and chooses to be minimally involved in the counseling, the outcome most likely will not be a positive one.

His degree of ***narcissism*** is important to recognize. It is possible that he is a poor-risk partner and could be dealing with issues of sexual compulsivity or a personality disorder, in which case there is significant individual work as well as couples work to be done.

The Therapist   The first rule for the therapist is not to get caught up in the clients' emotional reactivity, regardless of how egregious the behavior may appear. One of the best strategies for reducing this reactivity is to maintain an impartial or neutral position. If this is not done, the therapist can easily become enmeshed in their system and may be seen as being in collusion with one of the individuals. There can be no partiality or it will feel like a two-against-one situation.

The therapist stands outside of the family system and acts as a coach, consultant, and investigator. The therapist asks many questions. This moves the couple from being reactive to becoming more thoughtful and observant and they soon begin the work of understanding their family's emotional process. Thus, the therapist remains in contact, but does not get drawn into their system (Bowen, 1978).

The second very effective strategy in reducing the emotional reactivity is to have the clients talk to each other "through the therapist" (Bowen, 1978). This means that the couple does not address one another, but instead speaks to the therapist. The therapist will ask each their view and be impartial, not taking sides. The therapist is in control of the session and brings calmness to the room as the clients realize that each will have the opportunity to speak. He will ask many questions as he tries to understand their family. Clients listen more attentively when the other speaks and, consequently, their responses are less defensive and less aggressive.

This approach also shows the willingness of the therapist to hear and try to understand the facts from the point of view of each of the individuals. This not only provides a model of empathy for the couple but also translates into an interest for each in what the other thinks.

When anxiety is reduced, symptoms are as well (Titelman, 1998), and more in-depth work can be accomplished.

Use of the Computer   His use of the computer must change. The first step is to place it in plain view in a public room. The client can use an Internet Service Provider (ISP) that prevents access to sexually explicit Web sites, or he can buy software for that purpose (Putnam & Maheu, 2000). Additionally, software should be purchased that will block certain senders. Keeping an open log of the time spent on-line and sites visited, and sharing all folders and files is an additional step in eliminating the secrecy that is part of the affair. The log will help not just in dispelling the secrecy, but in the accountability of time that is often lost track of when one is on-line. There should be an understanding of how much time is permitted on the computer and an agreement about what hours the computer can and cannot be used. For example, the computer may not be used after 10 or 11 o'clock in the evening and not before 7 in the morning. Family pictures or mementos can be kept beside the computer as a reminder of the consequences of cyber-sex to those loved ones (Delmonico, Griffin, & Carnes, 2002).

Cyber-Addiction   If the client is sexually addicted, the therapist can help patients and their families understand that cyber-sex can be an addiction. People often can understand addiction to a substance such as alcohol or drugs, but find it difficult to believe someone can be addicted to a behavior. Yet, some behaviors can actually change the neurochemistry of an individual in much the same way a drug can, releasing chemicals from within rather than from an external source such as alcohol or drugs (Schneider & Weiss, 2001).

Individuals can move progressively on a continuum from being at risk, to abuse, and finally to addiction. Treatment for cyber-sexual addiction will depend on the type of user he is (Delmonico, Griffin, & Carnes, 2000; Cooper, Delmonico, & Burg, 2000).

Obsessive Review   The wife can be helped with her obsessive review of the affair by assigning regularly scheduled times for this review and decreasing review sessions as indicated (Subotnik & Harris, 2005) Thought-stopping techniques, such as visualizing a stop sign or snapping a rubber band worn on the wrist, can be used when thoughts come to her outside of the agreed-upon session for review. Assurances to her that the obsession is part of the healing process are helpful, and that it will decrease in frequency and intensity as the infidelity becomes part of their history.

Anger Management   She can also be helped to manage her anger in such standard ways as "journaling," the unmailed letter, exercising, meditation, use of relaxation techniques, and participating in positive activities that she enjoys. For some people, strategies such as pillow punching and journaling are helpful, but for others the anger can reach intolerable levels and so instructions to discontinue them should be given should this occur. The wife needs to be aware of those activities that are self-soothing to her and to be encouraged to do them.

The Love Letter   The husband becomes a part of the healing process by participating in the assignments. One effective assignment is for the therapist to ask him to write a love letter to his wife, one to which he gives careful thought. She is instructed to read the letter when doubts arise and for some this prevents escalating emotions (Subotnik & Harris, 2005).

"Talk Time"   Because she has so many questions and he feels that he never knows when the next "attack" will occur, the concept of a regularly scheduled time to talk reduces his anxiety and helps her to know that she has a forum to discuss her concerns. The schedule of these meetings is correlated to their needs. The couple is taught guidelines for discussing the issues and the communication skills necessary for this to succeed (Maheu & Subotnik, 2001; Subotnik & Harris, 2005).

Family Meetings   As part of restructuring their marriage, they are instructed to plan for fun (Weil, 1993). This must be done both as a couple and as a family. At this time, the concept of an additional meeting for all the family members is introduced so that they can begin to make plans and function as a unit once again. They are instructed not to discuss infidelity on their "fun" evenings together as a couple because of the adverse reactions they may have. Now they have established a forum that will continue after this issue has been resolved.

Cognitive Therapy   The use of cognitive therapy is very helpful in reducing emotional reactivity, but most importantly it helps the couple separate the thinking process from the emotional process. Teaching clients how to identify the 10 cognitive distortions and how to challenge them (Burns, 1980), and how to understand what statements they make that represent a belief system rather than objective fact using the A + B = C scheme (Ellis, 1975), are self-help strategies couples can do on their own. Thus they feel less powerless when strong emotions seem to overwhelm them. It helps them clarify their thinking and minimize their reactivity.

The second benefit is that challenging distortions in thought is very effective in breaking down defense mechanisms such as denial and rationalizations and cognitive distortions such as minimizing.

STAGE 2. SEARCHING FOR UNDERSTANDING

When the reactivity has been reduced, they can begin to understand the affair in relation to themselves as individuals and as a couple. It is also a time when communication skills can be honed so that they can effectively exchange information.

Current Stressors   It is productive to look at individual and family issues for stressors over the two years prior to the cyber-affair, including individual and family transitions and their family life cycle. There is much to explore, such as losses, health issues, finances, roles of children and in-laws, mid-life issues, infertility, partner's expectations, and the loss of dreams. The definition of a transition as "an event or non-event resulting in a change" of assumptions about oneself and the world is an excellent description of situations that can cause pain (Schlossberg, 1981, p. 43; 1984, p5). This is useful in helping them understand their situation and learn to develop more appropriate strategies for dealing with change.

Past Stressors   Creating a ***genogram*** with the client is extremely valuable because of the generational history obtained and the knowledge of the family emotional system. The genogram is a graphic representation of people, events, and dates by use of symbols to delineate the family history (McGoldrick & Gerson, 1985). Family patterns will emerge, as will the means of coping with stress, attitudes toward infidelity, and nodal points. This information will help the couple understand his motivation for infidelity. The information elicited provides much of the framework for developing interventions and will help the clients understand their family system and its relationship to the current problem. Once they understand this process, they will become more accustomed to thinking this way and may experience less reactivity to issues that arise in the future.

Another benefit of the genogram is the understanding that each of the couple develops for the other as they learn the effects of generational influences. This creates intimacy and empathy, some of which may have been previously lacking. It also is a pool of information the therapist can explore, and which will result in a better understanding of their family life and those implications for the future.

STAGE 3. RECONSTRUCTING THE RELATIONSHIP

The couple has the opportunity to make changes in themselves and in the relationship. With their new information, their relationship can become stronger than before the affair. At this point, they continue their genogram work and continue to discuss in session their anxieties and issues that concern them. Current problems and misunderstandings are worked on.

"Talk Time," the regularly scheduled meeting for discussing the current problems and for addressing future issues as they arise, can begin at this point. Certain rules need to be agreed upon regarding time and procedure. The meeting should be held at a convenient time and rescheduled only if absolutely necessary. There should be no interruptions like phone calls or leaving the room to check on something. It is time-limited to one hour, with each person taking a turn speaking and bringing up an issue. Each issue should take about 15 minutes of discussion time. To ensure understanding, paraphrasing each other is important. The couple should know that not all problems will be resolved at this time and that thinking about them for the next meeting is an option. Having this time set aside prevents arguments arising at other times because the couple has a mechanism set in place.

With a regularly scheduled meeting, there is less of a tendency to bring up issues spontaneously, and thus the couple has a decreased chance of ending up in an argument. If the couple has children, a separate but shorter Family Meeting (previously described) can be held with the children to decide on family plans, distribution of chores, and future outings. In general, it can be a forum, where they can contribute and feel part of the family process. By now the couple has reached an understanding of each other, their relationship, the influences of their family-of-origin, and their own family emotional system. Additionally, they have had time to learn and practice effective communication skills. It is now time to move toward making the infidelity a part of their shared history.

STAGE 4. FINDING CLOSURE

Closure means putting the affair to rest, being willing to close that door even though the affair will always be part of their shared history. This can come about if all the previous work has been carefully done. It varies, but can take nearly two years or more to accomplish.

The Apology   The unfaithful spouse may apologize hundreds of times, but typically the apology will not be accepted until all the therapeutic work is done and they have come to this point. Closure includes an apology that must be sincere and contrite, with recognition of the effect the affair has had on the spouse and the family. It includes a promise to be faithful, to make only appropriate use of the computer, and to keep communication open so that concerns can be addressed as they appear. It also may mean an apology to other family members who have been hurt by the affair.

Couples who discuss their views on infidelity with each other before their marriage are less likely to be unfaithful (Lawson, 1988). Therefore, this is also a time now for them to make an *infidelity contract* with each other stating their expectations and how to communicate any concerns they may have individually or as a couple.

Rituals and Gifts   Closure, in general, is helped by incorporating a shared ritual (Imber-Black, Roberts, & Whiting, 1988) relevant to the issues, one with meaning to the couple. At this time, some couples decide to renew their marriage vows; others have written something of significance to the other.

Asking couples, as they approach this point, to think of a way to mark the end of their recovery will bring creative ways that are very individualized and meaningful for them (Subotnik & Harris, 2005). For many, such a marker may include gifts of jewelry and special vacations. Others have bought a painting that represented something special from their years together; another got a puppy because it seemed like a new beginning. One couple bought rings that fit together, but detached one for each of them, and another couple found an object for their home that signified love from another culture. People can be very creative in their selection of something as a symbol of their feelings for each other and their belief in their future.

Forgiveness   Not everyone will be able to forgive a spouse for infidelity. Forgiving the infidelity does not mean condoning it or minimizing its impact. Research on forgiveness shows that it is beneficial to one's health to let go of high levels of sustained anger (Luskin, 2002). Yet people differ in their need to forgive. Some can do it more easily because of their religious principles; some want to forgive but cannot; some let go of anger, but cannot easily forgive. It is important to recognize and respect that some people will be unable to forgive even though they work hard on restructuring their marriage. A couple can move forward *without* forgiving. They can be most helped when they understand one another through exploration of the stresses prior to the infidelity and knowing more about themselves from a generational view by the use of a genogram. They may have more empathy for their partner because of the latter. They also need to have good communication skills, a forum for talking over problems, the family meeting, and ways to cope with anger.

While they may not be able to forgive, they usually benefit from understanding the reasons the infidelity occurred, and by developing relationship skills. The path to forgiveness is made easier by understanding.

CASE STUDY

Problem

At Jean's request, she and her husband, Bob, have an appointment with a therapist to discuss Bob's on-line activities. On three occasions, Jean had discovered Bob at their computer in the middle of the night. Each time she expressed surprise at seeing him there and noted that he was just as surprised at seeing her. He quickly "minimized" the screen and swiveled his chair around abruptly to face her. She questioned his nocturnal use of the computer, and although each time he gave her a reason, she said that she felt something was not quite right about it.

After 20 years of marriage, Jean felt she knew her husband and became convinced that he was hiding something from her despite his repeated denials. To relieve her anxieties about Bob's behavior, Jean called a national computer service specializing in searching the hardware for hidden files. However, her anxieties were not relieved, but elevated even more when she discovered that Bob was having an affair on-line.

Subsequent interviews revealed the following:

Current Stressors

Jean and Bob had been married 20 years and had a 17-year-old son. Bob and his son had been very close and Bob was anticipating his son's entrance to a college thousands of miles away with a combination of pride and sadness. Bob was a master carpenter and worked from his home workshop. He had few friends as his work was isolating except for visits to stores to buy materials for the job. Jean was attending college to get a degree in business and was also very preoccupied with care for her aging and ailing mother. Jean and Bob both acknowledged that they had grown apart in the last few years. They had little time for socializing and keeping up friendships. They occasionally go out for dinner as a family and they regularly attend church on Sunday mornings.

Genogram

Jean's genogram of her family-of-origin showed that she has always assumed responsibility for chores and for helping with the care of her younger sister, Sue.

Jean felt because of her father's death early in her life, she grew up being self-reliant and became a major source of support for her mother, a pattern that continued today. At present, Jean assumed responsibility for the care of their mother with little help from her sister. In addition to taking college classes towards her degree, Jean works part-time. Her religion had been a source of comfort and Bob's behavior on-line was in conflict with her religious and moral values.

Bob's genogram showed him to be the youngest of three brothers. His father worked very long hours and his mother took over many responsibilities that were expected of fathers. Bob grew up considering his mother to be strong and capable. His parents are both deceased. Although he keeps in phone contact with his brothers, they live quite a distance from him, and so they seldom see each other.

It became evident that the family-of-origin pattern of a strong woman taking on responsibilities with little help from others has been repeated in this nuclear family. Bob's loneliness can be understood by the isolating character of his work, the preoccupation of his wife with other concerns, his lack of personal contact with friends and close family members, and the coming departure of his son for college many miles away. He used the Internet to help him cope with his loneliness and found that he was very quickly emotionally involved with Lisa, a woman he didn't even know.

Bob is very remorseful about his on-line relationship with Lisa even though he first denied the significance of it. After the discovery of the cyber-infidelity, he wanted to end that relationship. He was shocked at Jean's reaction to the relationship since he had never even met or intended to meet Lisa.

Therapeutic Intervention

Bob needed to end his on-line relationship with Lisa and did so with an e-mail explaining the situation. He had to be firm about no future contact whatsoever and apologized to her for the deception about his marital status. The e-mail was sent in Jean's presence. The therapist allowed each to "talk through" her as one way to reduce Jean's emotional reactivity. This not only served to calm them so that they could begin to work on their problems, but also helped to model communications skills and to develop empathy for one another.

Computer Use

The computer was moved to a public room.

Rules were set up limiting computer time.

A log for signing in when using the computer was placed next to the computer.

Family pictures were also placed on the computer table.

Software was purchased that blocks certain senders and Lisa's name was placed on the blocked list.

They found an Internet Service Provider that records visits and prohibits unauthorized sites.

Individual Interventions   Bob was encouraged to be in more frequent contact with his brothers, to contact former friends and to meet them for lunch, and to become more active in church activities.

Jean was encouraged to join a support group for caregivers and to meet with her sister regularly to go over details of her mother's condition and to find ways for her to participate in the care giving.

Couple Interventions   Jean's perception that this was an affair, despite Bob's denial, was validated by the therapist. Their cognitive distortions, such as her overgeneralization, future predictions, denials, rationalizations, and minimizations were challenged. Jean and Bob established a regular meeting time and were encouraged to have time alone each evening to talk on "non-problem" areas, to have evenings out for dinners, and to plan events they both enjoy.

They were taught communication skills, coping skills such as journaling, relaxation techniques, and self-nurturing behaviors. Jean was helped with her obsessive review by scheduling a time for it, learning how to thought-stop, and reading a love letter that Bob had written her when she had doubts about his devotion to her.

Bob acknowledged Jean's feelings of betrayal and hurt. He apologized and promised to use their meetings as a time to discuss his feeling and needs. Jean acknowledged and apologized for her role in their growing apart. Together they made plans to be more active socially and to plan visits to their son at college in the future. Most importantly, they will try to break the old patterns of behavior now that they understood their genogram.

SEXUAL ADDICTION TREATMENT

If the cyber-infidelity is a consequence of sexual addiction, the treatment is based on an addiction model. Addiction treatment involves the entire family, since his behavior can adversely affect his spouse as well as his children. A survey of 91 women and 3 men showed that the partner feels betrayed, abandoned, shamed, and angry as well as many other emotions. On-line sexual activities were the cause of separation and divorce in over 22% of those surveyed (Schneider & Weiss, 2001). It is interesting to note that the reactions are similar to those in off-line affairs.

A treatment plan for addiction addresses the use of the computer as a first order change, similar to those previously described in "Use of the Computer." If these steps are not effective, complete restriction of the use of the Internet is a last resort (Delmonico, Griffen, & Cairns, 2002). In addition to the steps outlined in the above section entitled "Resolution of the Internet Affair," the sex addict must regularly attend a 12-Step group. He must find a sponsor and fully participate in the program (Schneider, 2002). The sex addict may need complete abuse screening and psychological health assessment by appropriate testing (Delmonico et al., 2000).

FINDING MEANING

Finding meaning from such an experience (Frankl, 1963) is an important part of healing from a trauma. This concept can be applied to infidelity because it is so devastating to the individual (Subotnik & Harris, 2005).

Individuals can use their experiences to reach out to others as a way of finding meaning. Peggy Vaughan is such a person. She has authored many books on the subject of infidelity, become a lecturer on this subject and moderator of her Web site http://www.dearpeggy.com. Vaughan takes a systems view in terms of the role of affairs and society. "We need to acknowledge our role in perpetuating affairs and take more responsibility for dealing with factors that support affairs" (Vaughan, 1989). With such a view, she founded and administers *Beyond Affairs Network* (BAN), a nationwide self-help support group. Through her work, she has helped thousands of others.

Meaning can come to a couple in very personal ways as well, from a new understanding of each other and the value they now place on their relationship. This can result in an increased capacity for empathy, not just for their partner, but for others and other situations as well. They can view themselves differently from the lessons learned.

Resolution of the problem can result in a stronger marriage and benefit the generations that follow, both by changing the family's emotional process and teaching coping skills to handle anxiety.

REFERENCES

Bowen, M. (1978). *Family therapy in clinical practice*. New York: Jason Aaronson.

Burns, D. (1980). *Feeling good*. New York: William Morrow.

Carnes, P. (1992). *Out of the shadows*. Center City, MN: Hazelton.

Cooper, A. (1998). Sexuality and the Internet: Surfing into the new millennium. *Cyberpsychology & Behavior, 1*(2), 181-187.

Cooper, A., Delmonico, D. L., & Burg, R. (2000). Cybersex users, abusers and compulsions: New findings and implications. In A. Cooper (Ed.), *Cybersex: The dark side of the force* (pp. 1–34). New York: Brunner/Mazel.

Cooper, A., Scherer, C. A., Boies, S. C., & Gordon, B. L. (1999). Sexuality on the Internet: From sexual exploration to pathological expression. *Professional Psychology: Research and Practice, 30*(2),154-164.

Delmonico, D. L., Griffin, E., & Carnes, P. (2000). Treating on-line compulsive sexual behavior: When cybersex is the drug of choice. In A. Cooper (Ed.), *Sex and the Internet: A guidebook for clinicians* (pp. 147–167). New York: Brunner-Routledge.

Ellis, A. (1975). *A new guide to rational living*. North Hollywood, CA: Wilshire Books.

Fisher, Q. W., & Barak, A. (2000). On-line sex shops: Phenomenological, psychological, and ideological perspectives on Internet sexuality. *Cyber Psychology & Behavior, 3* (4), 575–589.

Frankl, V. E. (1963). *Man's search for meaning*. New York: Washington Square Press.

Glass, S. (2003). *NOT "just friends": Protect your relationship from infidelity and heal the trauma of betrayal.* New York: The Free Press.

Imber-Black, E., Roberts, J., & Whiting, R. (1988). *Rituals in families and family therapy.* New York: Norton.

Janus, S., & Janus, C. (1993). *The Janus Report on Sexual Behavior.* New York: Wiley.

Kinsey, A. C., Pomeroy, W. B., & Martin, C. E. (1953). *Sexual behavior in the human female.* Philadelphia: W. B. Saunders.

Lawson, A. (1988). *Adultery: An analysis of love and betrayal.* New York: Basic Books.

Layton-Tholl, D. (1999). Extramarital affairs: The link between thought suppression and level of arousal. *Dissertation Abstracts International, Series B: The Physical Sciences & Engineering, 60*(5-B), pp. 23–48.

Luskin, F. (2002). *Forgive for good: A proven prescription for health and happiness.* New York: Harper Collins.

Maheu, M., & Subotnik, R. (2001). *Infidelity on the Internet: Virtual relationships and real betrayal.* Naperville, IL: Sourcebooks.

McGoldrick, M., & Gerson, R. (1985). *Genograms in family assessment.* New York: Norton.

Michael, R., Gagnon, J. H., Laumann, E. O., & Kolata, G. (1994). *Sex in America.* New York: Warner Books.

Putnam, D., & Maheu, M. (2000). On-line sexual addiction and compulsivity: Integrating web resources and behavioral telehealth in treatment. In A. Cooper (Ed.), *Cybersex: The dark side of the force* (pp. 91–112). New York: Brunner/Mazel.

Schlossberg, N. (1981). A model for analyzing human adaptation to transitions. *The Counseling Psychologist, 9*(2), 2–18.

Schlossberg, N. (1984). *Counseling adults in transition.* New York: Springer.

Schneider, J. P. (2000). Effects of cybersex addiction on the family: Results of a survey. In A. Cooper (Ed.), *Cybersex: The dark side of the force* (pp. 31–58). New York: Brunner/Mazel.

Schneider, J. P., & Weiss, R. (2001). *Cybersex exposed: Simple fantasy or obsession.* Center City, MN: Hazelton.

Sternberg, R. (1988). *The triangle of love: Intimacy, passion, and commitment.* New York: Basic Books.

Subotnik, R. (2005). *Will he really leave her for me?* Avon, MA: Adams Media.

Subotnik, R., & Harris, G. (2005). *Surviving infidelity: Making decisions, recovering from the pain* (3rd ed.). Avon, MA: Adams Media.

Tarbox, K. (2000). *Katie.com: My story.* New York: Plume.

Titelman, P., Ed. (1998). *Clinical applications of Bowen family systems therapy.* New York: Haworth Press.

Vaughan, P. (1989). *The monogamy myth.* New York: New Market Press.

Vaughan, P. (1999). Dear Peggy. Peggy Vaughan answers questions about extramarital affairs. La Jolla, CA: Dialog Press.

Weil, B. (1993). *Adultery, the forgivable sin.* New York: Birch Lane Press.

CHAPTER 10

Infidelity

A Multicultural Perspective

RICHARD C. HENRIKSEN, JR.

"Infidelity is a breach of trust that signifies a lack of faithfulness to a moral obligation to one's partner"

(Treas, 2003, p. 895)

Intimate relationships provide opportunities for the development of an emotional commitment between two people. One of the challenges faced by many couples is the occurrence of deception in the relationship. One of the most challenging deceptive activities couples face is infidelity.

The complexity of intimate relationships and the effects of infidelity on intimate relationships require therapists to look at how infidelity affects intimate relationships from a variety of perspectives. Intimate or committed relationships are no longer viewed as just the existence of a marriage between a man and a woman. Today, intimate and committed relationships also take place between men and women who are in heterosexual and homosexual partnerships, married and unmarried couples, couples who choose to live together and create families with children, and couples who have decided to date each other exclusively, to name a few. Society has also affected how intimate relationships are defined through the creation of marriage laws. Massachusetts is the first state to legally recognize marriage between two men

191

or two women, while many states have recognized common law marriage between a man and a woman for decades.

INFIDELITY DEFINED

Blow and Hartnett (2005a) found in a study of infidelity literature that there is no consensus on the definition of infidelity. Additionally, defining infidelity is made more complex when the diversity of intimate or committed relationships is taken into account because of different norms and expectations of the partners. For purposes of this chapter, the simplified definition of infidelity presented by Penn, Hernández, and Bermúdez (1997) will be used: "Infidelity is unfaithfulness between partners in a relationship" (p. 169).

INFIDELITY RESEARCH

Blow and Hartnett (2005a) in their methodological study found that there is little research related to infidelity involving couples that are not heterosexual, middle-to-upper class, married, and Caucasian. They also pointed out the importance of recognizing that infidelity may have different meanings from culture to culture and relationship to relationship. Abraham, Cramer, Fernandez, and Mahler (2003) noted that emotional infidelity is often more distressing to women than men while sexual infidelity is often more distressing to men than women. These differences are based on beliefs about the emotional commitment couples make to each other. Because the roles of men and women are often different from culture to culture, hypotheses concerning the complexity of infidelity from diverse perspectives become complicated due to the value placed on fidelity from culture to culture. Penn et al. (1997) noted that therapists should always take into account the unique cultural meanings of infidelity when working with ethnic minority couples, which includes recognizing religious perspectives on infidelity. The purpose of this chapter is to provide an overview of infidelity from a multicultural perspective and to provide suggestions for working with diverse couples who are experiencing problems with infidelity.

MULTICULTURAL PERSPECTIVES ON INFIDELITY

Understanding infidelity from a multicultural perspective is limited because of the dearth of literature focusing on diverse cultures (Abraham et al., 2003; Blow & Hartnett, 2005a; Penn et al., 1997). Available studies also provide limited utility because of the low number of culturally diverse participants and the lack of consistent results involving the magnitude of infidelity among different racial groups (Blow & Hartnett, 2005b). Issues of infidelity from a multicultural perspective are also challenging because the culture of one partner may be different from the culture of the other partner, resulting in a conflict concerning the role of relationships outside of committed relationships. For example, Treas (2003) noted that *la casa chica,* or little house is a Latin American custom whereby married men also have another partner and family. In China, where polygamy is illegal, some Chinese businessmen maintain a mistress in her own apartment. In honor-based Arab societies, where female chastity is highly valued, families may feel obligated to put to death a wife who has committed adultery. Finally, in parts of Africa, casual sexual relationships outside of marriage are acceptable on the part of both men and women. Treas also noted that in Western societies that have a Christian foundation there is less tolerance for relationships outside of marriage. Even though Western societies tolerate premarital sex and homosexual sex, strong disapproval of extramarital sex continues to be a dominant viewpoint. However, the above viewpoints are not valued by all members of the cultural groups identified.

Counselors are cautioned not to fall into stereotypical thinking based on the very limited information presented in this chapter (Young & Long, 1998). Counselors are always cautioned to look at each couple individually and to allow the couple to share their narrative, informing the therapist of their basic morals, values, and beliefs. Because there is so little research available to discuss infidelity as it is related to diverse cultural groups, this discussion will be limited to religion, African Americans, Hispanic Americans, Asian Americans, and gay and lesbian relationships. Rather than providing an in-depth discussion, the following information will serve as an overview.

Religion

With this ring I said of our love I would sing.
'Twas proclaimed of each other to be faithful, trusting and true.
Alas, as it turned out, such could only be said of you.
Others may look at the infidelity I've wrought to one, to all;
The pain, the shame that I've brought
And thus judge my life by my actions, both large and small…

Ralph Weaver, 1999

Religion and spirituality are often recognized as integral parts of the personal identity of members of minority groups and the general population. The United States Census Bureau (2005) reported that, in 2000, more than 50% of the American population made reference to a belief in religion/spirituality. The moral teachings of many religions serve as the foundation for what is right in relationships and often lead to negative psychological consequences for those who choose to violate those moral teachings. Penn et al. (1997) noted that for those whose religious beliefs include Catholicism, Islam, Protestantism, and Eastern philosophies, infidelity is for the most part discouraged, but there can be exceptions based on culture. For example, Eastern philosophy holds that filial piety (commitment to and respect for one's family of origin) is a guiding principle in marriage. Demonstrating this commitment and respect in marriage requires the birth of male children. Historically it was permissible for a husband to divorce his wife or to engage in extramarital affairs so that a boy might be born resulting in the maintenance of the family bloodline (Penn et al. 1997). However, guilt and shame are often found as the outcome of infidelity for many people whose lives are impacted by religious beliefs as demonstrated by Weaver's (1999) verse.

Penn et al. (1997) made several observations concerning religious perspectives on sexual relationships. In Catholicism, the purpose of marriage is procreation. Because of this belief, chastity is expected of men and women before marriage, and fidelity is expected after marriage. In Islam, marriage is viewed as the union between two families, and thus marriages are often arranged. The family's honor rests upon the chastity of women, but polygyny (the practice of having more than one wife or female mate at one time) may be allowed. In Protestantism, marriage is sacred, with God serving as the central focus of the union. There is a clear ban on infidelity for both men and women. In each of these religions, sexual relationships outside of marriage are unacceptable for men and women and are viewed as grounds for divorce.

> Jean and Luis have come to see a marriage counselor after six years of marriage because Jean caught Luis having a sexual liaison with another woman. Jean and Luis are married with two children. They are both of Hispanic heritage and Catholic. They were married in a Catholic church and have come to counseling because they are concerned about what would happen if the church found out about Luis's affair. They say they love and care about each other but find it difficult to have intimate sexual relations. Luis says he is a man and needs sex and, if he can't get it at home, he will find it elsewhere.

How would you work with this couple? What would be your starting point? How will you remain neutral? These and many other questions point out the difficulty of providing multicultural couples counseling when infidelity is what brings the couple to seek help. In this vignette, it would be important to understand the influence of religious beliefs on the couple and the influence of culture on the marital dyad.

Penn et al. (1997) provided several therapeutic implications that apply to couples from all religious backgrounds and could provide a sound basis for the provision of counseling services. First, it is important to take a "one-down" position where the couple is viewed as experts on their religion. In the case of Jean and Luis, it would be important for the counselor to discover the role religion plays in their relationship and in their individual lives. Second, therapists should be open to discussing religious sanctions for infidelity because this might be the basis for what brought the couple to counseling.

Luis has violated his marriage vows and, on the face of things, appears not to care. However, if the counselor has insight into the role religion plays in Luis's life, the counselor can encourage Luis to talk about the sanctions he will face due to his infidelity. Third, therapists should be willing to address feelings of loss, guilt, and shame for breaking the holy vows of marriage. In the case of Jean and Luis, it is necessary to understand the role *Machismo* (Ehlers, 1991; Villereal & Cavazos, 2005) plays in how Luis makes decisions. Because of his cultural background, Luis might find it difficult to admit the loss, shame, and guilt he is experiencing because it could make him appear less of a man. It would be important for the counselor to help Luis discuss these issues while preserving his manhood. Finally, therapists should obtain consent for release of information from the couple so that the counselor can discuss the case with the couple's religious leader so that appropriate interventions can be determined. Because Jean and Luis have already indicated that they are concerned about how the church would respond to Luis's infidelity, it would be important for the counselor to ensure the couple's confidentiality and only seek consultation related to understanding the church's view on infidelity and how infidelity would impact the couple's standing in the church.

Therapists should be aware of the need for some couples to maintain confidentiality so as not to lose face in their religious institutions. It is most important that therapists include a discussion of religion with all couples to determine the importance of religion in their relationships. This can be particularly important for couples who have not married because they may experience shame and guilt for not being married yet engaging in sexual activity.

> Robert is Catholic and Ditza is Jewish. They have been married for 13 years but have been having difficulties for the past five years. Ditza has found out that Robert has been having an affair off and on for the past two years but has promised that it is now over and wants to work on his marriage.

The case of Robert and Ditza presents a growing trend in relationships of interfaith couples (marriage or dating between individuals of different religions; Greenstein, Carlson, & Howell, 1993). The challenges of interfaith relationships is most pronounced when the couple has one Christian partner and one Jewish partner (Chintz & Brown, 2001; Eaton, 1994; Greenstein et al., 1993; Sussman & Alexander, 1999) due to the different set of beliefs based on religious ideology. Additionally, how infidelity is faced based on religious beliefs can vary based on the religion of each partner, the commitment to religious traditions, and the role that marriage, gender roles, religious expression, communication, and problem solving play in each religion (Eaton, 1994). For example, both Catholics and Jews value family and recognize that a commitment to marriage is made before God. Divorce is not always an option for either partner but instead a working out of the couple's problems is most desirable. However, because divorce is becoming more commonplace the commitment to working through problems must be assessed for each couple. Yadgar (2006) pointed out that as feminism has grown in the Israeli Jewish community so has the independence of Jewish women and their willingness to make decisions that can include divorce.

Working with Robert and Ditza requires counselors to learn how the couple's religious beliefs are incorporated into their relationship. Farbman (2004) pointed out that infidelity has typically been viewed as a non-Jewish problem but with the Americanization of the Jewish faith there has been a rise in infidelity. Farbman also pointed out that at the root of recovery for a Jewish person is the need to grow as a couple spiritually. This can be a complex process because of the two different religious beliefs of the couple. In contrast, infidelity is viewed as a sin in the Catholic Church because of the belief that sexual interaction is for the purpose of procreation. The focus of change, from a Catholic perspective, is on repentance. While both partners' religious beliefs take a different approach to working with issues of infidelity, in the case of Robert and Ditza, divorce is frowned upon, which allows counselors to focus on ways to help the couple heal and work through issues resulting from the infidelity.

Farbman (2004) provided a framework for counseling Jewish couples where infidelity has occurred, which would be appropriate for this couple. The process begins with asking the party who has committed the infidelity (a) if he or she has owned up to the infidelity to the other party, (b) if he or she is genuinely contrite, and (c) if he or she is committed to a lifelong investment in the relationship. With a commitment to the relationship and a willingness to work on the relationship, the couple can then focus on healing. This begins with dealing with the pain and fallout from the infidelity. The couple then focuses on improving communication skills, meaning that they learn how to listen so that they can respond to each other. Next, the couple seeks to clarify and better understand what they need from each other. They work to regain trust and begin to spend quality time with each other. Finally they share the spiritual centers of their lives with each other striving to integrate transcendent values such as a relationship with God. Counselors may seek the assistance of a rabbi and priest to help in this area. This plan has the potential to be beneficial to the couple because the focus is on the couple and their desire to stay together.

Because the interfaith population has traditionally been small and is only beginning to grow, there is little literature available concerning strategies for counseling and no literature was found discussing strategies for counseling when infidelity has occurred. Counselors must therefore gain a clear understanding of each partner's religious beliefs, their commitment to religious traditions, how they incorporate religious practices into their relationship, and how they view their religions as strengths. With this information, the couple can establish a plan to strengthen the relationship and work through issues related to infidelity.

African Americans

Since the days of slavery, sexual intimacy between African American men and women has been mired in complexity. Bowleg, Lucas, and Tschann (2004) noted that the sexual behavior of African American women and men is rooted in the "sociohistorical context of slavery and institutionalized racial and economic oppression" (p. 71). Penn et al. (1997) also suggested that vestiges of slavery contribute to instances of infidelity along with "the impact of racism and discrimination, economic hardships, and imbalanced sex ratios (i.e., the high number of African-American women per African-American men)" (p. 173). Norment (1998) reported that women engage in sexual activity outside of marriage for a variety of reasons including a self-esteem boost, emotional neglect, revenge, excitement, seduction and romance, "sugar daddy" search, sexual deprivation, and the "little woman" syndrome. However, even with this knowledge, there is little research available to understand the sociocultural factors of sexual behavior in intimate and committed relationships among African Americans.

The available literature suggests that African Americans value fidelity but also experience differences for men and women. Eyre, Auerswald, Hoffman, and Millstein (1998) noted that fidelity management within African American nonmarried couples "is based on a stated or implied promise to be faithful. This promise, which is reciprocal, introduces a moral accountability between partners" (p. 396). Aborampah (1989) also noted that tension and conflict arise in African American couples when partners or spouses cannot accommodate the extradating behavior or extramarital behavior of the other partner or spouse. The notion of the double standard, that is, extramarital sex by men is often condoned while it is frowned upon when committed by a woman, also brings tension to African American couples. However, Bassett (2005) noted that African Americans project more anger over sexual infidelity than over emotional infidelity, suggesting that intimacy and commitment in relationships remains important.

> Joe has been living with his girlfriend Jolene for 15 years. He has recently started having problems with his son and has stopped talking to Jolene. Jolene believes that Joe has emotionally left the relationship and does not understand why he does not talk to her. She is concerned about their relationship and the impact that it is having on their son. Joe says that things are okay but does not look at Jolene. Joe and Jolene have come to counseling for help with their son and to work on their communication issues.

Research suggests that many African American couples seek counseling for issues surrounding their children rather than for issues related to marital difficulties (Ho, 1987; Penn et al., 1997). Boyd-Franklin (1989) suggested that, in addition to children being the basis for obtaining counseling, several other issues can also lead African American couples to seek professional assistance: (a) traditional marriage counseling, (b) unmarried couples with long-term live-in relationships who are now having problems, (c) premarital therapy, (d) a couple in crisis, and (e) couples seeking divorce mediation.

In the above case, Joe had engaged in an extrarelationship affair. He has become estranged from his girlfriend and is taking out their difficulties on his son. Because of the challenges African American couples face when trying to keep relationships intact, counselors and family therapists need to develop a clear strategy designed to engage both partners in the therapeutic process. Helping Joe believe that his views of the relationship are important could help keep him engaged in the therapeutic process. This is critical because African American men often believe that their views are not considered because, historically, African American women have been viewed as heads of households even when the couple is married (Boyd-Franklin, 1989).

Boyd-Franklin (1989) pointed out that African American men are often resistant to therapy, which results in the need to begin therapy with the wife or partner. African American men's resistance to therapy could be affected by previous discrimination, lack of trust in institutional systems, and feelings of defeat, humiliation, and powerlessness due to the expectations that men should be able to meet the needs of their spouses. Many African American men also believe that they are not treated fairly, and this results in a lack of trust, which is necessary for an effective therapeutic process (Boyd-Franklin, 1989; Ho, 1987). Boyd-Franklin suggested several activities that could bring African American men into the therapeutic process. First, counselors and marriage and family therapists need to keep in mind that they are working with a dyadic system. It is appropriate to reflect the reality that many men are reluctant to engage in relationship therapy and to realize that this will often help normalize the partner's feelings. Second, it is important to understand the nature of the partner's resistance to therapy and to figure out strategies that will lead to his becoming involved in the couple therapy process. Forcing the male partner to come to therapy should be avoided but, if this is done, the therapist should work to develop a positive relationship with him. Third, therapists should make an attempt to talk to the male partner directly. Therapists should avoid using the wife or mate as a go-between but should encourage the wife or mate to let her partner know that the therapist will be calling. Fourth, therapists might have to rely on the partner's curiosity to rise, as a result of changes taking place, to seek his place in the therapeutic process. This can take time, resulting in the need for the therapist to display patience. Finally, if the therapist has been seeing the female spouse for individual sessions, it would be important to see the male partner for individual sessions prior to seeing the couple together in order to level the playing field. Once the couple appears for therapy together, it would be necessary to employ a therapeutic process that will meet both their individual and relationship needs.

Working with Joe and Jolene requires the counselor to gain an understanding of the role and functions of men and women from each partner's perspective. Completing a genogram helps both the counselor and the couple gain insights into their beliefs about the fidelity of their relationship and the roles each is expected to fill (Penn et al., 1997). In this case, infidelity is not clearly identified, but it is apparent because Joe has emotionally and cognitively left the relationship. Counselors need to help the couple to open up and have honest communication. It would also be necessary to help the couple make a commitment to counseling and to saving the relationship by establishing a no escape contract (each partner would commit to attending sessions and neither would threaten to leave the relationship). Focusing on helping the couple learn ways to meet each other's needs could help save the relationship and help them overcome the effects of infidelity.

Intercultural/Interracial Couples   The notion that people get married because they love each other is magnified by those who enter intercultural or interracial relationships (relationships between people from two different racial/ethnic groups, such as a Mexican American and a Korean American, and different national or religious backgrounds; Ho, 1990). These couples often bring "cultural differences into an intimate confrontation" (Waldman & Rubalcava, 2005), such as when one partner confronts the other partner about infidelity. Cultural differences often result in the two seeing the issue from two different perspectives that are not necessarily congruent with each other. The result is often increased difficulty coming to a solution of the problem. Little research is available for helping intercultural/interracial couples who seek help with relationship difficulties (Bakken & Huber, 2005). Counselors should work to understand the cultural perspectives of each individual and seek to help them find a resolution to the problem based on their values and beliefs and their commitment to the relationship.

Hispanic Americans

> Juan and Maria have been married for 25 years, and both report that the marriage has been very good until about three years ago when Juan found out that Maria was having an affair. Juan works two jobs, six days a week and spends little time with Maria. Maria stated that she feels shame because of her infidelity but could not find a way to get love and affection from her husband.

The Hispanic culture is varied across many countries including Mexico, Cuba, Puerto Rico, and Argentina. There are a variety of languages and many similar and different cultural beliefs. Penn et al. (1997) also noted that the term "Hispanic" also encompasses native peoples from the Americas, Caucasian emigrants from Europe, and people of African descent who arrived as slaves and remained in many Latin American countries. Family is viewed as one of the most important aspects of life in many Hispanic cultures and provides the foundation for many marriages.

Penn et al. (1997) and Ho (1987) indicated that Hispanics' expectations of marriage are bound to underlying gender role expectations. Ho noted that "the hierarchical role of male dominance and female submission rooted in Spanish customs defines the husband and wife relationship" (p. 128). Men have traditionally been the dominant members of couples and have served as providers and protectors of families. They are typically hard working, dignified, and "macho." Women have traditionally been submissive, homemakers, and caretakers. However, in the home women often have more decision-making responsibility with the male role often being a public perception.

Hispanics often place interdependence over independence and cooperation over competition. There is also a deep sense of family loyalty where children play important roles in the marriage. Families also have a deep sense of loyalty, commitment, obligation, and responsibility (Penn et al., 1997). Ho (1987) also indicated that because of the strong sense of family loyalty and the influence of religion, there are low divorce rates among Hispanic families.

Like other cultural groups, there are several factors that affect infidelity within Hispanic couples. Most Hispanic couples marry believing that both partners will be faithful to each other throughout the marriage. However, Ho (1987) pointed out that there is some expectation that the husband will someday have an affair. He also pointed out that this behavior is not formally accepted, but oftentimes the wife will pretend that it does not exist, try to win her husband back, or be thankful that the husband provides for the family. However, levels of assimilation and acculturation may affect their views of infidelity. Ho also noted that, if the wife has a sexual affair, she will often be viewed negatively. Counselors need to remember that much of the preceding is a generalization and that a thorough understanding of the couple is necessary in order to assess the effects of infidelity on them.

The challenge to helping a couple such as the one in the case example that began this section is that there is scant literature available for helping Hispanic couples experiencing infidelity. Complications also occur because Hispanic couples often seek to keep their marital problems private. While many of the suggestions provided for helping couples overcome problems of infidelity can be applied across cultures, Ho (1987) provided several suggestions for helping Hispanic couples. First, the couple should be helped to feel safe and to trust the counselor and not feel judged. Second, individual sessions would help to determine both partners' perceptions concerning infidelity and their commitment to the marriage. Additionally, counselors should "be aware of gender roles, acculturation level, and expectations of primacy" (Penn et al., 1997, p. 183). Finally, with all couples, counselors should explain the therapeutic process, expectations, and possible outcomes of therapy. Following these guidelines proved beneficial to Juan and Maria and allowed them to address their issues and find solutions.

Asian/Pacific Americans

> Chang and Takeyo have sought help with marital difficulties they
> are currently experiencing. Chang is currently having an affair
> that Takeyo objects to. Chang believes that it is okay and says that
> Chinese women have always tolerated affairs and she just needs to
> remember that he is married to her and that his affair is just about
> sex. Chang is a recent immigrant to the United States, while Takeyo
> is a fourth-generation American.

In many cultures, the roles of men and women vary. This is particularly
noticed in Asian American cultures, which include people from China, Japan,
Korea, Southeast Asia, the Pacific Islands (Penn et al., 1997), Thailand, Viet-
nam, Cambodia, Laos, and Indonesia (Ho, 1987). Even though these cultures
differ in many ways, they also have many similarities. Because there are differences based on language, history, and social and economic issues, it is
important for counselors to make note of the differences between cultures
and of several important factors that should be considered when counseling
Asian/Pacific American couples. These factors include a careful evaluation
of the Asian/Pacific American couple, geographic origin of the couple, birth-
place of the couple, generation in the United States, and the social class of the
couple in the country of origin and the United States (Ho, 1987). Based on the
level of assimilation and acculturation of the couple, these factors could help
the counselor decide upon the interventions necessary to help the couple. In
the case of Chang and Takeyo, it would be important to address the issues
related to the differences in their assimilation and acculturation levels and
how that has impacted their views of the marital dyad. From there, importance is placed on determining their willingness to work on defining a marriage that would be acceptable to both with the goal of achieving fidelity.

Sexuality in Chinese culture has historically been viewed as a natural urge
(Chang, 1999). Sex with the right person at the right time was not viewed as
a sin or moral weakness. Extramarital affairs, therefore, have often been kept
invisible because of Chinese women's historical tolerance of their husband's
sexual affairs. However, in recent decades Taiwanese women have become
leery of *waiyu* (extramarital affairs), which has led to increasing divorce
rates even though research has not shown a connection between divorce and
infidelity (Chang, 1999). In other Asian American cultures (i.e., Chinese,
Vietnamese, and Cambodian), violence against women who have had extramarital affairs has been justified by men (Yoshioka, DiNoia, & Ullah, 2001).
The above points out the double standard related to infidelity; however, there
is very little research into the role of infidelity in Asian couples and in relation
to treatment of couples where infidelity has occurred.

Helping Asian American couples can be complex due to many factors, the
most pronounced being the type of Asian American couple presenting for help:

(a) recently arrived immigrant couples, (b) immigrant-American couples, and (c) immigrant-descendant couples (Ho, 1987). Providing counseling services should include a complete assessment of the couple's needs and readiness for counseling. Ho noted that it is important to assess the couple's readiness for conjoint marital therapy, to emphasize the social moral explanation of marital disharmony rather than focus on the emotional aspect of the couple's relationship, to challenge the couple's willingness and ability to collaborate to find solutions to their current problems, and to teach the couple the skills necessary for negotiation. While these suggestions can help the couple learn to talk about and act upon the many possible solutions to their problems, it is important to remember that little research is available that provides effective practices for assisting Asian/Pacific Americans with issues of infidelity.

Asian cultures also include India, Pakistan, and Sri Lanka. In these regions, there are different cultural beliefs and traditions concerning infidelity and the belief that infidelity has occurred can lead to accusations and interrogations to murder (De Silva & De Silva, 1999; Kumar & Kanth, 2004; Peedicayil et al., 2004). Kumar and Kanth pointed out that in India the mere suspicion that a married woman has committed sexual infidelity can lead to bride burning, which often results in death.

In Sri Lanka, treatment for couples experiencing marital discord often occurs in hospitals, clinics, and medical school settings. Many of the cases discussed by De Silva and De Silva (1999) involved couples who were also receiving help for other issues besides infidelity. For example, the following case is given to reflect the challenges faced by a couple in which the husband suspects that his wife is having affairs.

> Mr. B, a Sinhalese Buddhist man of 40 years of age, was brought by a friend to the clinic. He had been married to his second wife, a woman 14 years younger than himself, for 9 years. She was Sinhalese and Christian. Throughout the marriage, he suspected and accused her of having affairs. A daughter was born 3 years ago, and he maintained that the child was not his (p. 118).

This case resulted with the husband engaging in behaviors toward the wife that included interrogation, picking quarrels, checking (physically looking at the wife's vagina to see if she had engaged in intercourse), imposing restrictions on her movements, and physical assault. It should also be noted that in this case Mr. B also had problems with alcohol consumption. This case is complicated because Mr. B suspected that his wife was committing infidelity and these suspicions may have been exacerbated by his alcohol use. In counseling this couple, there would be several issues that would need to be discussed. First, Mr. B's alcohol use would need to be treated, secondly and probably more importantly, the safety and security of his wife and child would need to be assured. Finally, issues related to religious beliefs would need to be discussed especially in light of the fact that they are of two different religious backgrounds. The case of Mr. B points out many of the complexities of working with couples from a cultural perspective.

The issue of violence against women who are accused of or suspected of engaging in acts of infidelity can also lead to violence in other countries such as India. In a study conducted by Peedicayil et al. (2004), the researchers noted that the main risk factors for women who experienced moderate to severe violence during their pregnancies included the husband accusing his wife of having an affair and the husband engaging in an affair. The risk of violence to women makes issues of infidelity more complex because of the need to help ensure the safety of the wife. Note should also be made that no research was found that provided resources or methods of treatment for couples who are experiencing difficulties due to infidelity from this region of Asia, which points to the need for research to assist this population. However, change is occurring in India as it relates to Indian women and sexuality.

Chopra (2006) stated that marriage was redefined in urban India in 1991 following the India liberation movement. Current Indian moves reflect this modern view of marriage. Pearson (2005a) has focused on the changes taking place in Indian movies. He pointed out that a new wave of Hindi-lingo movies is beginning to grow in India and that the movies include subjects long viewed as taboo, which include infidelity, women's sexual enjoyment, and homosexuality. Pearson also points out that the growth in Hindi-lingo movies covers all of Asia and has also garnered a sizeable market in the United Kingdom. Note should also be made that this growth in movies with sexual content is mostly supported by younger generations but remains taboo with older generations, and as an overseas phenomenon is primarily due to the increasing use of technology (Pearson, 2005b). These changes in Indian culture will bring about different views of infidelity and will challenge counselors to remain up to date on the ever changing view of Indians and their relationships. Chopra (2006) pointed out how modern marriage looks little like traditional marriage in India and how marriage now includes altered gender roles, satellite relationships, geographical separations, where one partner lives in one country and the other partner lives in another country, and divorce. This has led to the development of marriage counseling in India and a renewed research focus on the effects of infidelity on couples and the skills necessary for effective counseling.

Gay and Lesbian Relationships

Like all other cultural groups, gay and lesbian couples experience both the joys and pain of committed and long-term relationships. Carl (1990) also noted that "gays and lesbians approach relationships with the same preconceptions as prevail in the heterosexual world" (p. 47). However, Carl also noted that it is more difficult to function as a same-sex couple than as a heterosexual couple because of societal pressures. One of the significant restrictions that society has placed on same-sex couples is the inability to get married. Currently 40 states have enacted laws that define marriage as occurring between a man and a woman, with Vermont being the first state to recognize "civil unions" between same-sex couples while maintaining marriage as occurring between a man and a woman. Seventeen states have enshrined the heterosexual definition of marriage in their state constitutions, with 19 states considering doing the same. Massachusetts was the first state to establish a law recognizing same-sex marriage following a court decision requiring the state government to do so (Peterson, 2005). The result of defining marriage as occurring between a man and a woman has made it difficult to understand the effects of infidelity on same-sex couples. However, the majority of same-sex couples seek to maintain monogamous relationships even in light of the lack of a societal recognition of their relationships (Barret & Logan, 2002). The likelihood that infidelity could harm a gay couple and even lead to the breakup of the couple was noted by Blumstein and Schwarz (1983), who reported that gay couples that remained monogamous for the first two years were more likely to remain together than couples who did not remain monogamous.

When helping gay and lesbian couples work through issues related to infidelity, Barret and Logan (2002) suggested several tips that could help develop an atmosphere where effective counseling could take place. These tips include the expectation of language differences (i.e., use of the term "partner") and the notion that counselors should expect diversity that may require the counselor to revise traditional notions of relationship counseling, make assumptions explicit, expect HIV issues to surface, and celebrate relationships.

Counselors should always keep in mind that when assisting gay and lesbian couples, where infidelity has occurred, one important factor is to keep in mind that the relationship is experiencing difficulty and that you are there to help the couple overcome their problems in the relationship. Counselors also need to avoid stereotypical thinking concerning gay and lesbian couples. Effective work with gay couples also requires counselors to look at the intersection of sexual orientation, racial/ethnic group identity, and religion as it affects each of the partners in the relationship. Issues of gay male and lesbian relationships are discussed further in separate chapters within this text.

COUNSELING IMPLICATIONS

Counseling multicultural populations in the area of infidelity is complex due to the impact of cultural beliefs. The scarcity of literature related to diverse populations provides little assistance to therapists who seek opportunities to be of help to couples in crisis over infidelity. Counselors need to be careful not to use stereotypical thinking when working with couples of diverse backgrounds due to the many factors that could influence the thinking of the couple and the counselor.

This chapter provides an overview of many of the challenges facing counselors who are providing services to couples of diverse cultural backgrounds who are experiencing the effects of infidelity. One glaring point becomes clear. There is a need for research that will assess the range of infidelity within diverse cultures and the effects of infidelity on these couples, and provide suggestions for interventions that have been shown to exhibit positive outcomes. This chapter is but a beginning in the understanding of this problem and should serve as the basis for continuing research.

REFERENCES

Aborampah, O.-M. (1989). Black male-female relationships: Some observations. *Journal of Black Studies, 19*(3), 320–342.

Abraham, W. T., Cramer, R. E., Fernandez, A. M., & Mahler, E. (2003). Infidelity, race, and gender: An evolutionary perspective on asymmetries in subjective distress to violations of trust. In N. J. Pallone (Ed.), *Love, romance, sexual interaction: Research perspectives from current psychology* (pp. 211–224). New Brunswick, NJ: Transaction.

Bakken, L., & Huber, T. (2005). Ego development at the crossroads: Identity and intimacy among Black men and White women in cross-racial relationships. *Journal of Adult Development, 12*(1), 63–73.

Barret, B., & Logan, C. (2002). *Counseling gay men and lesbians: A practice primer.* Pacific Grove, CA: Brooks/Cole.

Bassett, J. F. (2005). Sex differences in jealousy in response to a partner's imagined sexual or emotional infidelity with a same or different race other. *North American Journal of Psychology, 7*(1), 71–84.

Blow, A. J., & Hartnett, K. (2005a). Infidelity in committed relationships I: A methodological review. *Journal of Marital & Family Therapy, 31*(2), 183–216.

Blow, A. J., & Hartnett, K. (2005b). Infidelity in committed relationships II: A substantive review. *Journal of Marital & Family Therapy, 31*(2), 217–233.

Blumstein, P., & Schwarz, P. (1983). *American couples.* New York: William Morrow.

Bowleg, L., Lucas, K. J., & Tschann, J. M. (2004). The ball was always in his court: An exploratory analysis of relationship scripts, sexual scripts, and condom use among African American women. *Psychology of Women Quarterly, 28*(1), 70–82.

Boyd-Franklin, N. (1989). *Black families in therapy: A multisystems approach.* New York: Guilford Press.

Carl, D. (1990). *Counseling same-sex couples.* New York: Norton.

Chang, J.-S. (1999). Scripting extramarital affairs: Marital mores, gender politics, and infidelity in Taiwan. *Modern China, 25*(1), 69–99.

Chintz, J. G., & Brown, R. A. (2001). Religious homogamy, marital conflict, and stability in same-faith and interfaith Jewish marriages. *Journal of the Scientific Study of Religion, 40*(4), 723–733.

Chopra, A. (2006). Sex, turmoil, infidelity, divorce: That's Bollywood. *The New York Times,* July 30, p. 14.

De Silva, D., & De Silva, P. (1999). Morbid jealousy in an Asian country: A clinical exploration from Sri Lanka. *International Review of Psychiatry, 11*(2/3), 116–121.

Eaton, S. C. (1994). Marriage between Jews and non-Jews: Counseling implications. *Journal of Multicultural Counseling & Development, 22*(4), 210–214.

Ehlers, T. B. (1991). Debunking marianismo: Economic vulnerability and survival strategies among Guatemalan wives. *Ethnology, 30(1)*, 1–14.

Eyre, S. L., Auerswald, C., Hoffman, V., & Millstein, S. G. (1998). Fidelity management: African-American adolescents' attempts to control the sexual behavior of their partners. *Journal of Health Psychology, 3*(3), 393–406.

Farbman, S. (2004). *Back from betrayal: Saving a marriage, a family, a life.* South Boardman, MI: Crofton Creek Press.

Greenstein, D., Carlson, J., & Howell, C. W. (1993). Counseling with interfaith couples. *Individual Psychology, 49(3-4)*, 428–437.

Ho, M. K. (1987). *Family therapy with ethnic minorities.* Newbury Park, CA: Sage.

Ho, M. K. (1990). *Intermarried couples in therapy.* Springfield, IL: Charles Thomas.

Kumar, V., & Kanth, S. (2004). Bride burning. *Medicine, Crime, and Punishment, 364(1)*, 18–19.

Norment, L. (1998). Infidelity II: Why women cheat. *Ebony, 54*(2), 148–152.

Pearson, B. (2005a). Some like it hot: New wave producers find a market for risqué movies. *Variety, 398*(6), pp. A1, A4, A8.

Pearson, B. (2005b). Zee leads race to capture diaspora. *Variety, 398*(6), p. A6.

Peedicayil, A., Sadowski, L. S., Jeyaseelan, L., Shankar, V., Jain, D., Suresh, S., et al. (2004). Spousal physical violence against women during pregnancy. *International Journal of Obstetrics and Gynecology, 111*(7), 682–698.

Penn, C. D., Hernández, S. L., & Bermúdez, J. M. (1997). Using a cross-cultural perspective to understand infidelity in couples therapy. *American Journal of Family Therapy, 25*(2), 169–185.

Peterson, K. (2005). 50-state rundown on gay marriage laws. Retrieved May 3, 2006, from http://www.stateline.org/live/ViewPage.action?siteNodeId=136&languageId=1&contentId=15966

Sussman, L. M., & Alexander, C. M. (1999). How religiosity and ethnicity affect marital satisfaction for Jewish-Christian couples. *Journal of Mental Health Counseling, 21*(2) 173–185.

Treas, J. (2003). Infidelity. In Ponzetti, J. J., Jr. (Ed.), *The international encyclopedia of marriage and family relationships* (2nd ed., pp. 895–901). New York: Macmillan Reference.

United States Census Bureau. (2005). *Statistical abstract of the United States: 2005.* Washington, DC: United States Census Bureau.

Villereal, G. L., & Cavazos, A., Jr. (2005). Shifting identity: Process and change in identity of aging Mexican-American males. *Journal of Sociology & Social Welfare, 32*(1), 33–41.

Waldman, K., & Rubalcava, L. (2005). Psychotherapy with intercultural couples: A contemporary psychodynamic approach. *American Journal of Psychotherapy, 59*(3), 227–245.

Weaver, R. (1999). With this ring: Part II. Retrieved from http://users.nti.net/abundantlife/2excerpt/poem_3withthisring_II.htm.

Yadgar, Y. (2006). Gender, religion, and feminism: The case of Jewish Israeli traditionalists. *Journal for the Scientific Study of Religion, 45*(3), 353–370.

Yoshioka, M. R., DiNoia, J., & Ullah, K. (2001). Attitudes toward marital violence. *Violence Against Women, 7*(8), 900–926.

Young, M. E., & Long, L. L. (1998). *Counseling and therapy for couples.* Pacific Grove, CA: Brooks/Cole.

CHAPTER 11

Male Couples and Monogamy
Clinical and Cultural Issues

MICHAEL SHERNOFF

While many male couples are sexually exclusive, others have honestly nego-tiated a nonmonogamous relationship. In order to do effective clinical work with male couples, therapists have to be open to moving beyond traditional theories inherent in family and couples therapy regarding extradyadic sex. One way of achieving this is to recognize countertransference, which is often based on cultural biases regarding monogamy. This chapter reviews the research on male couples and sexual exclusivity and suggests a variety of ways that therapists can be better prepared to work with male couples around the issue of sexual exclusivity and nonexclusivity.

One challenge for many therapists working with male couples, no matter their sexual orientation, is the issue of nonmonogamy. Sexual nonexclusivity may challenge fundamental assumptions that "affairs," or extra-relationship sex without any emotional attachment, are symptoms of troubled relation-ships and are always a form of "sexual acting out." Scheinkman (2005) is concerned about the ways that affairs are thought about and approached clini-cally as well as theoretically. She suggests that a large part of the hegemonic response by most American mental health professionals to sex outside a com-mitted relationship has to do with an inability to approach this issue through a multicultural perspective. Her position is that using a multicultural lens to examine outside sex would provide a flexibility "to address the multiple values, meanings and to take into account nuances of specific situations, that would permit the individuals involved in an affair choice and self-determination in matters of secrecy and truth-telling" (pp. 227–228).

COUNTERTRANSFERENCE

Clinical work with couples is ripe with the potential for countertransference. D. Davies (personal communication, May 6, 2005) suggests a number of useful questions for therapists to consider, which if left unexamined could adversely affect therapeutic work with couples (see Table 11.1). I urge readers to keep these questions in mind, and ask yourself if your responses to any of the questions change as you read this chapter.

It is easy for therapists to use whatever choices they have made about how they conduct their own relationships as the standard of normalcy and health by which to gauge all others. In addition to demonstrating questionable clinical skills, assumptions about whether any couple should or should not be sexually exclusive reveal a basic lack of clinical curiosity.

Table 11.1 Questions for Therapists to Ask Regarding Countertransference in Dealing With Monogamy

Do I feel monogamy is better than nonmonogamy? If so, why?

Do I feel nonmonogamy is more "progressive" or evolved than monogamy? If so, why?

Do I place a different value on sex outside of a committed relationship? If so, why?

What are my feelings about "recreational sex"? Do I believe that it is immature, less "evolved," or less meaningful than sex between people who are committed to each other?

Do I believe that heterosexual relationships and sex is "normal" and healthy while same-sex love and sex is not? If so, why?

What might be the issues for me if my partner had sex with someone else? What do I value in my own personal and sexual relationships?

Is a current sexual relationship necessary for my partnership or marriage to be called a relationship? Why?

How open am I with my partner about my sexual likes, desires, and fantasies?

Are there things I hear about my clients' sex lives and relationships that make me envious, nervous, or uncomfortable?

How does any couple define "sex"?

How might any of the above issues and my reactions to them influence my clinical work and therapeutic neutrality?

Note: From Davies (2005).

MALE COUPLES' SEXUAL DIVERSITY

One of the biggest differences between male couples and heterosexual couples is the cultural difference regarding sexual exclusivity. There is research that documents that some male couples are sexually exclusive (Advocate Sex Poll, 2002; Blumstein & Schwartz, 1983; Bryant & Demian, 1994; Kurdek & Schmitt, 1985/86; LaSala, 2004). As Johnson and Keren (1996) note: "Monogamy seems to be hardwired into spoken and culturally sanctioned norms for heterosexual relationships. The gay community's normative acceptance of casual sex, anonymous sex and nonmonogamy in couple relationships represents a dramatic departure from heterocentric norms and values" (pp. 238–239). Negatively judging those who choose negotiated nonmonogamy without assessing its motivations and functionality reflects contemporary heterosexual cultural biases as well as a lack of clinical sophistication and acumen.

Research conducted prior to the onset of AIDS showed that many gay men were in couples in which both members agreed to be sexually nonexclusive (Blumstein & Schwartz, 1983; Kurdek & Schmitt, 1985/86; McWhirter & Mattison, 1984). Later studies conducted in Australia, Europe, and the United States confirmed that a large percentage of male couples were not monogamous (Bringle, 1995; Bryant & Demian, 1994; Elford, Bolding, Maguire, & Sherr, 1999; Hickson et al., 1992; Kippax, Crawford, Davis, Rodden, & Dowset, 1993); Wagner, Remien, and Carballo-Dieguez (1998, 2000), Crawford, Rodden, Kippax, and Van de Ven (2001), Davidovich et al. (2001), Halkitis, Zade, Schrem, and Marmor (2004), and LaSala (2004) found that even two decades into the AIDS pandemic, fear of becoming infected with HIV has not caused a sizable increase in monogamy among male couples. Yet, in one post-AIDS study, 70% of men in male couples reported being in a monogamous relationship, and would view any sex outside the relationship as a betrayal of commitment and an impediment to intimacy (Campbell, 2000).

PROFESSIONAL HETEROCENTRISM

Heterocentrism is defined as assumptions and processes embedded in mainstream society and institutions that imply human beings are naturally heterosexual and that heterosexual lifestyles are the normal standard against which those of lesbian, gay, and transgender people should be compared in order to be understood and evaluated (Herek, 1998). In the mental health fields, heterocentrism occurs when theories or research based on heterosexuals are automatically assumed to apply to gays, lesbians, bisexuals, and transgender people, or when heterosexuality is assumed to be a better psychological adjustment even though the research evidence does not support that conclusion (Gonsiorek, 1991). I suggest that one major area of heterocentrism within the mental health field is reflected in the lack of theoretical and practical sophistication that many therapists bring to the issue of sex outside of a committed relationship.

Even after homosexuality was removed from the American Psychiatric Association's list of diagnosed mental disorders, mental health professionals such as psychoanalyst Charles Socarides (1978) have portrayed gay men (and lesbians) as deeply disturbed people simply by virtue of being homosexual. One of the most often cited examples of homosexual men not being as developed or mature as "normal" heterosexual men is the supposed inability of gay men to form long-term, stable, and committed relationships. Socarides and other heterocentric therapists cited the high incidence of nonmonogamy to support their belief that gay men's loving relationships are inherently unstable, and used such terms as "narcissism" and "pre-oedipal relatedness" to describe a different cultural norm than that of the majority of opposite sex couples. Socarides' position assumes that for a relationship to be loving and committed it must be monogamous (which is his personal cultural bias). The gay men's community evolved an easier acceptance of nonmonogamy than the mainstream world. That doesn't mean gay men suffer from psychopathology, arrested development, or immoral values (though of course these are as prevalent among gay-identified men as among heterosexual men), only that honest, negotiated nonmonogamy in and of itself is not indicative of any characterological disorder, psychopathology, or relational dysfunction.

POSSIBLE EXPLANATIONS FOR NONMONOGAMY AMONG MALE COUPLES

Kipnis (2003) and Mitchell (2002) encourage professionals to refocus from the almost exclusive impact of affairs to a broader framework that starts with the emotional forces that are often but not exclusively associated with desire that contribute to why some individuals feel the need to have sex outside a committed relationship. Bettinger (2005b) suggests that therapists need to bring an anthropological and cross-cultural understanding to modern human sexuality in order to be open to what is actually a range of variations that appear to be consistently and often inevitably occurring in contemporary relationships of whatever sexual orientation.

The high levels of nonmonogamy among male couples may be attributed to at least three factors. Gender differences impact and create dynamics between male couples that account for an acceptance of nonmonogamy, which is mitigated in opposite sex couples by how women are socialized. Green and Mitchell (2002) suggest that in general men tend to be more oriented than women toward a recreational approach to sex and tend to be less monogamous. Bettinger (2005b) suggests that the higher degree of nonmonogamy among men as opposed to women might be genetically hard wired, as it is evident in all human cultures throughout history. Taking this anthropological perspective may provide an understanding that helps question any of the "moral" issues that often cloud discussions about monogamy. The immediate move to pathologize all forms of nonmonogamy demonstrates a lack of understanding of human mating and sexuality.

LaSala (2004) also discusses gender differences regarding sex when he notes: "It is believed that men, in contrast to women, are more likely to cognitively separate love from sex (Banfield & McCabe, 2001; Duncombe & Marsden, 1999), and though investigators disagree as to the causes (biology, social conditioning, or a combination of both), available findings seem to reflect this tendency" (p. 406). An additional dynamic at play is simply that some male couples may be more realistic about the limitations of sexual exclusivity when combined with a committed love relationship. "Since sexual minority couples have been for the most part excluded from acceptance by the mainstream social institutions, many have made a close examination of how society operates and in response, created their own values system. Seeing that monogamy does not work for a sizable minority of heterosexual couples, many have elected not to take on the patriarchial and capitalist notion of a partner as a possession" (D. Davies, personal communication, May 6, 2005).

FAMILY AND COUPLES THERAPY

Johnson and Keren (1996) describe how even supposedly liberal branches of the mental health field, such as family therapy, often use judgmental terms such as "triangulation," "difficulty with intimacy," and "male objectification" to try to come to terms with nonmonogamy. Some therapists assume that gay men are avoiding intimacy by triangulating other men into their relationship. This is a valid clinical concern and one that needs to be explored with any couple that is discussing the issue of sexual nonexclusivity.

Not specifically addressing the sexual orientation of the people involved, Murray Bowen (who never addressed same-sex couples in any of his writings) wrote that when tensions arise between two people in an intimate relationship, there is a tendency to engage outsiders, resulting in an emotional triangle that deflects tension and stabilizes the original couple (Kerr & Bowen, 1988). Though the partner who has extra-relationship sex gets some of his or her needs met, the unresolved conflict between the partners, in combination with the outside sexual relationship, has the potential to increase the primary couple's distance and exacerbate the difficulties they are having, increasing the likelihood that the more distant member of the triangle is at high risk for developing symptoms and/or the primary relationship is at risk for disintegrating (Kerr & Bowen, 1988). The traditional family therapy notion is that the result of "triangulation" is always destructive to the individuals involved and that the primary relationship is based on an unexamined acceptance of mainstream society's moral code, not upon a careful assessment of how a particular sexual liaison or affair outside of a marriage may in fact have the potential to stabilize a particular relationship in positive ways that contribute to the longevity of the primary dyad. For years, gay-affirmative family and couples therapists tried to reconcile traditional theories of family and couples therapy with the primarily happy nonmonogamous male couples they were seeing (Cheuvront, 2004; Green, Bettinger, & Zacks, 1996; Green & Mitchell, 2002; Greenan & Tunnell, 2003; Kurdek & Schmitt, 1985/86). The point is that nonmonogamy is not inherently unhealthy or a sign of dysfunction when it is openly discussed and mutually agreed upon by all parties involved.

Couples therapy with male couples should offer a place where the following highly fraught issues can be discussed:

- How does each man feel about the fact that they are currently monogamous, not sexually exclusive, or are considering becoming not sexually exclusive?
- Why might each partner want to be monogamous or nonmonogamous?
- What are the potential benefits as well as liabilities of monogamy and nonmonogamy for these men at the current time?
- What are their underlying fears and concerns about how it will change their lives and relationship if they decide to open up their relationship?
- How might any change impact on their intimacy?
- What ethical and practical considerations does either have regarding emotional safety, physical health, and honesty?

Luis and Peter are a white couple of 10 years in their early 40s. They had started dating 10 years ago and moved in together a year later, settling into a satisfying, loving, monogamous relationship. Both were HIV-negative, prosperous, and well-integrated as out gay men in their workplaces, with their extended families, and in the community. They described a good balance of time together and apart, equitable distribution of housework and financial responsibility, and a strong network of friends. During our first consultation I found myself waiting for the other shoe to drop—perfectly happy people don't come to therapy.

When I asked how I could help them, they both tensed up. Peter shot Luis a look and said, "The thing is, I still find Luis really sexy, but we're not having sex as often as we used to. I mean, we still have sex, but it's not like it was, and it seems to be getting, you know, even more . . . I don't know . . . I guess I worry that maybe he's not as turned on to me. Am I beginning to lose him?"

Luis's eyes widened. "It's not you. It's me. I mean, I don't know what it is, but it's not that." Both of them felt their sex life was becoming increasingly stale and boring, but neither one had felt safe nor comfortable talking about what was happening. "It's too loaded," said Peter. "I'm afraid of hurting his feelings or hearing something I don't want to hear from Luis. But it's starting to make us—or me, anyway—wonder if we're really going to last as a couple. That is so terrifying."

When they told me they had sex at minimum twice a month, I responded that many couples would envy that frequency after 10 years together, and they were pleasantly surprised to hear it. We talked about their sexual expectations, and how aging could also account for some of the reduced feelings of passion. They both reflected that they didn't seem to daydream or fantasize about sex as much as they did when they were younger, and allowed that this might explain some of the loss of passion they were both experiencing. Peter seemed relieved to hear that there was a reasonable explanation for why their sex life seemed so dull, but Luis still looked miserable. When I asked him what he was feeling, he hesitated and then looked at Peter and said, "I've felt too guilty even thinking this to actually suggest it, but I've been wondering what it might be like to open up the relationship." Peter paled, put his head back against the sofa cushions, and stared at the ceiling like a doomed man.

In the long, stunned silence that followed Luis's suggestion, I felt the session come alive. We were getting to the taboo subject that both men probably had been dancing around for some time. Often, my gay clients come in to work on sexual problems in their relationships and it emerges that both partners assumed the other one was having sex outside the relationship, but neither one felt safe openly discussing it or negotiating it. This had not been the case for these men who had remained sexually exclusive during the course of their relationship. My role with Peter and Luis was to help them air their feelings about nonmonogamy and to make it safe and acceptable for them to discuss this potentially explosive topic without guilt, judgment, recriminations, or expectations about what was best for them. Neither man would look at the other. I said, "Luis, I respect you for having the courage to raise this in front of Peter. It's important to talk about it." I asked Peter how he felt. He immediately said, "I don't want that. I've thought about it. But I don't think we can handle it. If we do it, we'll end up divorcing." This conversation provided the field to begin our therapeutic journey together.

DEFINING MONOGAMY

How sex is defined varies enormously. In his research, LaSala defined sexual behavior as oral sex, anal sex, or mutual masturbation (personal communication, July 1, 2005). He explained that many gay youth define sex only as anal intercourse, and getting naked, having oral sex, or mutually masturbating was not "really" sex but was considered "hooking up." I have worked with male couples in monogamous relationships who considered cyber sex, or even masturbating to pornography as a violation of a monogamous agreement. Other couples have an agreement that mutual masturbation with other men without any touching is not a violation of their agreement to remain sexually exclusive. Some couples permit sexual three-ways, and this is not viewed as a breach of their monogamous agreement. The point is that when working with couples, clinicians need to explicitly ask how each person defines sexual behavior and how their definitions fit into the agreement they have or are in the midst of trying to negotiate.

NONMONOGAMY MAY NOT BE INFIDELITY

Nonmonogamy challenges many basic assumptions about love and commitment. Some heterosexual therapists (e.g., Charny, 1992), referring only to heterosexual couples, suggest that sex outside a primary relationship is *always* a sign that the primary relationship is troubled. Indeed, there is some research suggesting that sex outside a male couple's relationship may be related to dissatisfaction about the partnership (Bell & Weinberg, 1978; Kurdek & Schmitt, 1985/86; Saghir & Robins, 1973). Yet, subsequent studies find no significant differences in relationship quality or satisfaction between samples of sexually exclusive and nonexclusive male couples (Blasband & Peplau, 1985; Kurdek, 1988; LaSala, 2004, in press; Wagner et al., 2000). For therapists who work with male couples, it is always useful to inquire about whether or not the couple is monogamous, and how they negotiated whatever understanding they have about sex with outside partners.

Male couples may be sexually exclusive either for certain periods of their relationships, or for the duration of their relationships (Blumstein & Schwartz, 1983; Bryant & Demian, 1994; Crawford et al., 2001; Kippax et al., 1993; Kurdek & Schmitt, 1985/86; Shernoff, 1995; Stulberg & Smith, 1988). There is research confirming that nonmonogamy in and of itself does not create a problem for male couples when it has been honestly negotiated. A majority of male couples studied did not believe that sexual nonexclusivity threatened their relationship and differentiated between negotiated sexual nonexclusivity and infidelity (Blumstein & Schwartz, 1983; McWhirter & Mattison, 1984; Mendola, 1980; Silverstein, 1981). This research all took place prior to AIDS, which changed the potential impact that a sexual infidelity could have upon a relationship. Wagner et al. (2000) found that in the second decade of AIDS, both monogamous as well as self-described "open" male couples demonstrated higher levels of relationship quality and lower levels of psychological distress compared to couples who had not negotiated nonmonogamy but reported secret outside sexual activity. Thus, not surprisingly, male couples who were honest with each other about whether or not they were sexually exclusive had happier and healthier relationships. LaSala (2004, in press) confirmed that using the Dyadic Adjustment Scale (Spanier, 1976, 1989) there was no discernible difference in relationship satisfaction or quality between couples who had negotiated nonmonogamy or were monogamous. Yet, his research did find that supposedly sexually exclusive male couples where one or both were having clandestine outside sexual liaisons scored lower in terms of relationship satisfaction and contentment.

Psychologist Robert-Jay Green's observations are that whenever a partner's dishonesty about staying sexually exclusive is discovered it has a much more negative effect post-HIV than it did prior to the onset of the epidemic. "Probably ANY kind of lying in couple relationships is having a much more negative effect on gay couples since the advent of HIV because one's life sometimes depends on one's partner's honesty. But it's probably more destructive when the lie concerns sex" (personal communication, April 26, 2005).

Observations from my practice agree with Green's statement. In the past several years, I have seen numerous couples in a crisis due to one of them having unprotected sex outside of their supposedly monogamous relationship. The potential of having contracted HIV, and possibly passing it on to one's partner, certainly contributed to the intensity of the crisis. Davies (personal communication, May 6, 2005) notes that he has seen the risk of HIV sometimes becoming triangulated into the relationship when there has been an infidelity even when no unsafe sex occurred outside the relationship. Thus the partner who has "been cheated on" sometimes uses his fears of HIV as a defense from either fully experiencing or discussing feelings of hurt, betrayal, and distrust that the discovery of an infidelity has produced. This dynamic needs to be probed for when it is appropriate to do so.

Terms and definitions are slippery areas, and it is dangerous for a therapist to assume he or she understands what specific words mean to any particular couple until definitions are elicited. For example, "fidelity" may be used by male couples differently than by heterosexual couples. Generally, heterosexual couples use the term "fidelity" synonymously with "monogamy." If the male couple has explicitly agreed to be sexually exclusive, then fidelity has the identical meaning for them. Coleman and Rosser (1996) discuss that though a majority of male couples are not sexually exclusive, they are in fact emotionally monogamous. Describing these kinds of couples LaSala (in press) has coined the expression "monogamy of the heart."

For many male couples, "fidelity" means "honesty," and for those who are not sexually exclusive, "fidelity" means the emotional primacy of the relationship, and definitely means abiding by whatever rules the couple has agreed upon for how liaisons outside the relationship will be conducted. For example, two men may live together and jointly own property, share a rich social and emotional life, celebrate holidays together, and be integrated into each other's families. This couple may or may not still be sexually active with each other. There may be an understanding that one night of the week they are each permitted to have a night of sex with another person. Perhaps there is an agreement that includes more than just sex outside the relationship and permits affairs. These are only some of the possible ways that male couples may set up how they will be sexually nonexclusive while remaining committed to each other.

VARIETIES OF SEXUAL NONEXCLUSIVITY

One way of categorizing male couples is in regard to characteristics of sexual exclusivity/nonexclusivity. Male couples appear to fall into one of the following categories:

- The sexually exclusive couple
- The sexually nonexclusive but unacknowledged open relationship
- The primarily sexually exclusive relationship
- The sexually nonexclusive and acknowledged open relationship
- Nonsexual partners

As a therapist working with male couples, I routinely explore how each member of the couple feels about monogamy and whether the couple has explicitly discussed the issue. If they have reached an understanding about how sex outside the partnership will be handled, asking about this can elicit important information about the couple's decision-making process and values as well as clarifying any possible confusion or miscommunication that may have occurred. It's not uncommon for couples to come to therapy in crisis because one member of the couple has either had sex or had an affair outside of a supposedly monogamous relationship, or one man wants to open the relationship up to outside sexual partners and the other doesn't, fearing that this may mean a diminishing emotional attachment.

HELPING COUPLES DECIDE

It is important for therapists working with male couples wrestling with whether or not to be nonmonogamous or with the impact of nonmonogamy on their relationship to be alert to the fact that power issues have the potential to come up in negotiating nonmonogamy, much like they do when negotiating any other highly charged issue (Greenan & Shernoff, 2003; Morin, 1999; Shernoff, 1995; Shernoff & Morin, 1999). Several couples have consulted with me where one was pushing for a sexually open relationship, and his partner was feeling pressured into going along so he wouldn't end up losing his spouse. When therapy has been able to get both men to look at issues that range from power imbalances between them to emotional vulnerability, the couple is more likely to find a satisfying way to keep their erotic fires lit and their trust and communication strong. At the very least, once these conversations are begun about power and how it is played out in the sexual realm, couples can approach the issue of whether or not to be monogamous with increased clarity about why they are at this place in their relationship at this time, and what options they wish to explore.

Therapists working with couples who are considering changing their relationship from monogamous to sexually nonexclusive need to remind the men that it is naive and unrealistic to think that changing the rules will not have an important and possibly irreversible impact on their relationship. For instance, if they have an open relationship and go out to have sex immediately after a fight, then most likely the two of them will not revisit the issue that prompted the argument, and it will reemerge only with increased intensity at a later point.

It is useful for a therapist to dispense certain cautions to a couple grappling with whether or not to open their relationship sexually. It is crucial that neither use sex outside the relationship to avoid issues that are occurring between the partners. It is often a good idea for a therapist to predict the likelihood of one or both using outside sex as a way of avoiding resolving a situation that resulted in an argument or fight. I often ask the couple to discuss this now so that it won't be a surprise when it happens and to brainstorm possible responses to that potential situation. If a relationship is falling apart, opening it up sexually will not save the relationship; it will only hasten its demise and cloud the real reasons why things are not working. To try and ensure the emotional fidelity of the partnership, some couples decide that one-time-only sexual encounters are fine, but it is not permissible to see anyone more than once. Speaking to this point Davies (personal communication, May 6, 2005) suggests that for couples who are not seeking anything beyond outside sex, avoiding using the word "date" to refer to these encounters is sometimes a useful strategy.

There is an additional caution that is important to mention. Many couples choose sexual nonexclusivity as a way of adding some spice and excitement to a dwindling and increasingly less exciting sex life. For some male couples, what winds up happening is that the only really exciting sex they have is either with an outside partner or with each other only when a third person is present. Some couples cease having any sexual contact with each other at all, and still think of themselves as life partners. If the goal is to keep having an exciting and interesting sex life with one's partner, then it is important that neither person invest all of his sexual creativity and energy only in outside liaisons. If their goal is to have a hot sex life with each other and that is not happening, the couple will need to work on that whether or not they open up their relationship sexually.

Morin (1999) feels that a couple has a very good chance of adjusting to the change from monogamous to nonmonogamous if at least some of the following conditions exist:

- Both partners want their relationship to remain primary.
- The couple has an established reservoir of good will.
- There is minimal lingering resentments from past hurts and betrayals.
- The partners are not polarized over monogamy/nonmonogamy.
- The partners are feeling similarly powerful and autonomous.
- Each partner has an independent support system, so that neither is only dependent on the other as an emotional and social resource.
- The partners have a higher than average tolerance for change, confusion, anxiety, jealousy, and other extremely uncomfortable feelings.
- The couple is merely bored but very secure with each other.

The above are all issues I explore with couples who arrive in my office questioning whether or not to open their relationship.

POLYAMORY

Polyamory literally means many loves (Anapol, 1997). Bettinger (2005) states that "some gay men in committed relationships have other sexual relationships which involve a degree of emotional intimacy, commitment and/or longevity" (p. 98). My clinical experience is that some male couples are polyamorous and may form a variety of relationships that are often overlapping and sometimes become their primary families of choice. Speaking to this reality, Bettinger reports that "the sexual and romantic mating patterns of gay men are more complex than domestic partnership connotates. The lack of monogamy results in some gay men having primary and secondary partners. There may be more than one primary or secondary partner" (p. 98).

Bert and Ted had been partners for 14 years when they consulted me. They reported feeling more in love with each other than at any time in their relationship. Both feel that their sex life has steadily improved over the years, and is more exciting and satisfying now than ever before. They were sexually nonexclusive for only a short time, which ended as the AIDS crisis began to escalate. Both have tested negative to HIV antibodies. With the onset of AIDS, they have decided to discontinue any independent extra-relationship sexual activity. The reason they sought counseling was that about 4 months previously, while out dancing, they ran into Michael, a man with whom Ted had occasionally had sex. All three went home together that night. They have been spending Saturday nights together dancing and going home for exciting "threesomes" once or twice a month since. They agree that the relationship with Michael is much more than merely sexual. The previous week they had all admitted to being in love with one another, and had begun discussing whether or not Michael should move in with them. After three sessions of our discussing how expanding their relationship and home to include Michael might affect them, I suggested that we ask Michael to join us for a form of "prenuptial" counseling. We worked together for six months during which time these three men used therapy as a place to help them talk through a variety of emotional and practical issues including

- How would they be ready to decide whether or not they were ready to live together?
- If they decide to live together, will they all share a bedroom or have separate bedrooms?
- What would the rules be if any of them wanted to have sex outside of the relationship?
- How were they going to ensure legal protections for all of them if they decided to merge their finances or buy property jointly?
- What steps do they each need to take to strike the right balance of togetherness and autonomy?

They all agreed that in spite of the increased complexity, there were definite benefits to having a polyamorous relationship. Interestingly, one of the benefits they cited to forming this kind of a relationship was security. When one partner was not available emotionally or physically, there would always be a third person to turn to for support. Bert and Ted shared their concerns about learning not to exclude Michael and no longer relying entirely on one person for all of their needs.

After six months, during which time Michael moved in with Bert and Ted, we reduced the frequency of sessions to once a month and continued them for another year. During one session Bert suggested, "Although there is the heightened opportunity for conflict, there is also another set of eyes and ears to help and understand what the basis of conflict truly is. So often in a traditional couple the partners become so overwhelmed by what they 'think' the problems are that they do not take the extra effort to really look deep inside and see what might be the true underlying problem." Michael reported, "The feeling of security with two, amazing men laying on either side of you when you are feeling weak or vulnerable is unmatched by anything that I can think of. Wrapped in their warmth and love keeping the world away. I am not sure that I can ever be one-of-two again."

NEGOTIATING OPEN RELATIONSHIPS

One important aspect to keeping a nonmonogamous relationship healthy is explicit and clear communication between the partners in order to establish a set of rules or guidelines for both to follow that set the parameters about how sex outside the relationship is to be conducted. Hickson et al. (1992) and LaSala (in press) both give examples of specific rules that couples may establish while negotiating nonmonogamy. Often I find myself called upon to help couples honestly articulate what each of their needs and comfort levels are regarding what rules will result in creating emotional and physical safety regarding sex outside the primary relationship. Infidelity within this context means breaking the rules that the couple has agreed upon for how sex outside the primary relationship is conducted (Shernoff, 1995).

Examples of the kinds of rules that some couples set up regarding non-monogamy may include

- Always use a condom for anal sex outside the relationship
- No anal sex with outside partners
- No affairs
- Don't ask, don't tell
- Full disclosure
- No sex with friends
- No sex in the couple's home
- Sex in their home is allowed, but not in their bed
- Mutual participation in the outside sexual relationships (three-ways or group sex)

This list is obviously only suggestions of some of the rules couples may wish to explore in order to figure out whether nonmonogamy is viable for them and if so how they can come to a mutually acceptable set of rules that best meet their particular needs and comfort level. It is important for the therapist to remind the couple that the rules can always be revisited and revised as either partner feels the need. For example, if the couple has decided that sex outside the relationship is permitted when either partner is traveling, and one man steps outside the relationship when both men are in their home city, this would constitute a sexual infidelity.

FOUR AGREEMENTS ON CONDOM USE

In the worst-case scenario, couples never directly talk about what they are going to do sexually either with each other or with any potential outside partners. AIDS has necessitated that conversations about condom use and safer sex become part of every male couple's discourse, and should be an issue that therapists inquire about of all male couples they work with.

Crawford et al. (2001) suggest that agreements regarding anal sex within and outside a relationship can be classified as such:

- None—where men have no agreement with their partner about how anal sex will be conducted either between them or with outside partners.
- No unprotected anal intercourse—where the men have agreed always to use condoms with each other and outside partners or to abstain from anal sex entirely with each other and outside partners.
- Negotiated safety—which will be described in detail further on in this chapter.
- Unsafe—where the men agree not to use condoms either sometimes or all the time within the relationship and where (a) one of the men is HIV-positive and the other is uninfected, or the HIV status of one or both partners is unknown; or (b) both men have the same HIV status but there is not any agreement about not engaging in anal sex without condoms outside the relationship.

STAGE OF RELATIONSHIP AND SEXUAL RISK-TAKING

Male couples living in the age of AIDS need to balance different desires, sexual tastes, and levels of comfort regarding what sexual risk-taking, if any, is acceptable and how the couple decides whether or not to be sexually exclusive. Thus, monogamy in the age of HIV and AIDS is an even more important issue to be discussed openly than it was historically. How these issues are raised, discussed, and negotiated are indications of the emotional climate created in the couple's daily interactions and shared emotional life. Hendrick and

Hendrick (1983) and Brehm (1985) both suggest that relationship dynamics vary depending on the developmental stage of the relationship. As Hays, Kegeles, and Coates (1997) note, "It is reasonable to expect that the factors contributing to high-risk sex at early stages of relationships may differ from those associated with high-risk sex in relationships of longer duration" (p. 322). Research on unprotected sex by gay men in relationships found that gay men's sexual behaviors become increasingly risky as they progress (Hays et al., 1997).

NEGOTIATED SAFETY

Why would relationship longevity increase partners' willingness to take sexual risks? The answer lies primarily in the fact that the longer male couples stay together, the more likely they are to develop trust and better communication; also, the more likely they then may attempt the delicate negotiations around sexual nonexclusivity and sexual safety. It is important to differentiate between not having safer sex and having sex that places the individual at risk for transmitting HIV. "Men in mutually monogamous, HIV-negative concordant relationships are not at high risk for transmission of HIV if they only have sex with each other—even if they have unprotected anal intercourse" (Hoff et al., 1997).

"Negotiated safety" (Crawford et al., 2001; Kippax et al., 1993; Kippax, Noble, & Prestage, 1997) is an agreement between two HIV-negative men to get ready to stop using condoms with each other. They only have safer sex with each other when mutual testing at least several months after either partner's most recent high-risk encounter shows that both men are uninfected. Once this has been established, nothing unsafe is permitted with outside partners. While there may be varieties of negotiated safety agreements, the most commonly accepted one is as follows: The only time the men do not use condoms is when they have sex with each other, making this an acceptable safer sex option. They agree not to have unprotected sex outside the relationship; if either partner does so, then he must immediately inform his partner prior to their having sex again. They then agree to resume using condoms until subsequent HIV tests prove that the partner who had unprotected sex is still negative (freedoms.org.uk, 2002).

Willis and Larry were both HIV-negative African American attorneys in their mid-30s, and had been a couple for 3 years. They had just bought an apartment together prior to our first consultation, and came to therapy to talk about how living together was affecting their relationship. Among the issues they raised was the possibility of stopping their use of condoms with each other, since they had been monogamous for the past 2 years and since each had recently retested negative for HIV.

Willis said that one of the reasons he wanted a monogamous relationship with another HIV-negative man was so that they could forget about safer sex.

Willis described how neither he nor Larry had ever had anal sex without a condom, nor experienced anyone ejaculating in their mouths, and the prospect of both was exciting. Larry agreed that being in a sexually exclusive relationship with a man he loved provided them with the perfect opportunity to expand his sexual boundaries while not having to worry about HIV (or other STDs). "Having that latex barrier between us seems like such a metaphor for our love and relationship not being able to grow any stronger or closer," Larry said. When I asked them why the issue of condoms had come up now, Larry explained that until he was ready to commit to not having sex with anyone else, which had only happened in the past few months, he did not even want to open up the condom conversation, though they had come very close to not using one on several occasions. It was after the last time that they had physically flirted with not using one that he finally began to talk with Willis about this issue. Their initial conversation about wanting to have unprotected sex had prompted them to go together and get retested. When I asked Larry what he meant by having physically flirted with not using one, he told me that they had "gone inside for a few good pumps, but pulled out way before the point of no return." I told them that this was known as "dipping," and many men used it as a method of keeping anal sex without condoms safer than "going all the way." They both grinned and nodded.

QUESTIONING DEFINITIONS

Having worked with numerous couples who have elastic definitions of monogamy, I knew that there was the possibility that, like many male couples, Larry and Willis might be practicing what San Francisco psychologist Jack Morin has labeled "modified monogamy." Morin defines modified monogamy as when a couple values monogamy, and strives to be monogamous. At the same time, the men recognize that the goal of monogamy may not be realistic or achievable, so the couple devises certain accommodations that reflect the tension between their desire to be sexually exclusive and practical realities (Morin, 1999). One example of "modified monogamy" is when a couple who define themselves as sexually exclusive, together have sex with a third person or a group of other people. With Morin's work in mind, I asked if their definition of monogamy encompassed having sex together with another person or with other people. At this point, they became noticeably uncomfortable. I commented on their squirming, and asked what it was a response to. In an uncharacteristically sheepish manner, Willis asked: "Are we monogamous if we occasionally have played together with another guy?" I asked if they had done that, and when both nodded affirmatively, I responded: "The rules and definitions of your sexual relationship are up to you to decide. But this raises an important issue about safer sex that we need to talk about."

I proceeded to explain the concept of "negotiated safety," and provided them with the URL of a British organization's Web site that has prepared a sample negotiated safety agreement (freedoms.org.uk, 2002). I suggested that they download the agreement and spend time talking about all the issues raised in the questionnaire. They did this prior to our next session and the next few visits were spent discussing all of their feelings about the issues that the questionnaire raised for each of them.

Willis said, "While we're talking about condoms, what about Dan?" Dan was a semi-regular third partner, also HIV-negative, they occasionally invited into their bed. Willis wanted to know if there was a point at which they could stop using condoms with Dan. Hearing this, Larry became angry. "Are you nuts? If he's screwing around with us, we can only assume there are other men he's sexual with as well. Even if he tells us he's uninfected, I, for one, am not willing to trust either my health or yours to some other guy. I don't even want us to go there."

At first, Willis was taken aback by the intensity of Larry's response. "I was just thinking out loud," he told Larry.

"I know how your brain works," Larry told him. "The only way I will agree to take the condoms off with you is if you promise me that you will never again raise the issue of going bareback with anyone other than me, even if it's someone we both know well and play with." When I asked Willis how Larry's position made him feel, he thought for a few moments and eventually smiled. "I feel like you are my main man and are really looking out for me and us. I love it! You've got yourself a deal." He said this in a flirtatious way.

CONCLUSION

The internalization by male couples of the mainstream norms of romance and coupledom is often in conflict with gay cultural realities. Male couples are constantly bombarded by gay cultural pressures to have lots of hot sex, with and without their partner. With almost all male couples that arrive in my office with issues about diminished sexual satisfaction in their relationship, I normalize the reality that for many couples the sexual intensity does indeed diminish over the years. But then, I also use a concept first articulated by San Francisco psychologist Jack Morin (1999) by asking them, "What is wrong with a steady supply of good warm sex when hot sex is not happening?" This often opens up frank conversations about each of their expectations about sex with each other and the numerous options for addressing sexual dissatisfactions, one of which is negotiated nonmonogamy.

The first step for therapists to be effective with male couples is to recognize whatever levels of discomfort they may have about homosexuality and love between men. Next, they also have to be honest about whether they will be able to achieve a clinical neutrality with male couples who are discussing issues that pertain to ways of being sexual and structuring a relationship that may be alien or distasteful to them. Green and Mitchell (2002) discuss how therapists need to take the position that neither monogamy nor nonmonogamy is good or bad, adaptive or maladaptive in and of itself. The task of the therapist is to engage couples in conversations that lead them to decide for themselves whether sexual exclusivity or nonexclusivity is functional or dysfunctional for the relationship and the individuals involved.

Psychiatrist Mark Epstein (2001) suggests that therapy should ideally help individuals and couples to accept what is true about themselves and, working from there, help people to find their own meaning in their lives and relationships. These thoughts seem particularly relevant for therapists working with any couple, regardless of sexual orientation.

ACKNOWLEDGMENTS

Author's note: I wish to thank my colleagues Michael Bettinger, Michael LaSala, Robert-Jay Green, and Dominic Davies for reading early drafts of this article and providing useful feedback.

REFERENCES

Advocate sex poll. (2002). *The Advocate, 869*, pp. 28–43.

Anapol, D. (1997). *Polyamory: The new love without limits*. San Rafael, CA: Internet Resource Center.

Banfield, S., & McCabe, M. (2001). Extra relationship involvement among women: Are they different from men? *Archives of Sexual Behavior, 30* (2), 119–142.

Bell, A. P., & Weinberg, M. M. (1978). *Homosexualities: A study of diversity among men and women*. New York: Simon & Schuster.

Bettinger, M. (2005). Polyamory and gay men: A family systems approach. *Journal of GLBT Family Studies: Innovations in Theory, Research and Practice, 1(1)*, 97–116.

Blasband, D., & Peplau, L. (1985). Sexual exclusivity versus openness in gay male couples. *Archives of Sexual Behavior, 14(5)*, 395–412.

Blumstein, P., & Schwartz, P. (1983). *American couples: Money, work & sex*. New York: William Morrow.

Brehm, S. (1985). *Intimate relationships*. New York: Random House.

Bringle, R. (1995). Sexual jealousy in the relationships of homosexual and heterosexual men: 1980 and 1995. *Personal Relationships, 2*, 313–325.

Bryant, A. S., & Demian, R. (1994). Relationship characteristics of American gays and lesbians: Findings from a national survey. *Journal of Gay & Lesbian Social Services, 1(2)*, 101–117.

Campbell, K. (2000). *Relationship characteristics, social support, masculine ideologies and psychological functioning of gay men in couples*. Unpublished doctoral dissertation, California School of Professional Psychology, Alameda (cited in Green & Mitchell, 2002).

Charny, I. W. (1992). *Existential/dialectic marital therapy: Breaking the secret code of marital therapy*. New York: Brunner Mazel.

Cheuvront, J. P. (2004). Couples, imagined. In A. D'Erocle & J. Drescher (Eds.), *Uncoupling convention: Psychoanalytic approaches to same-sex couples and families* (pp. 43–68). Hillsdale, NJ: Analytic Press.

Coleman, E., & Rosser, B. (1996). Gay and bisexual male sexuality. In R. Cabaj & T. Stein (Eds.), *Textbook of homosexuality and mental health* (pp. 702–721). Washington, DC: American Psychiatric Press.

Crawford, J., Rodden, P., Kippax, S., & Van de Ven, P. (2001). Negotiated safety and other agreements between men in relationships: Risk practice redefined. *International Journal of STD & AIDS, 12 (3),* 164–170.

Davidovich, U., de Witt, J., Albrecht, N., Geskus, R., Stroebe, W., & Coutinho, R. (2001). Increase in the share of steady partners as a source of HIV infection—A 17 year study of seroconversion among younger and older gay men. *AIDS, 15,* 1303–1308.

Duncombe, J., & Marsden, D. (1999). Love and intimacy: The gender division of emotion and "emotion work": A neglected aspect of sociological discussion of heterosexual relationships. In. G. Allan (Ed.), *The sociology of the family: A reader* (pp. 91–110). Malden, MA: Blackwell.

Elford, J., Bolding, G., Maguire, M., & Sherr, I. (1999). Sexual risk behavior among gay men in a relationship. *AIDS, 13,* 1407–1411.

Epstein, M. (2001). *Going on being: Buddhism and the way of change . . . A positive psychology for the West.* New York: Broadway Books.

Freedoms.org.uk (2002). http://www.freedoms.org.uk/advice/air/air02.htm

Gonsiorek, J. (1991). The empirical basis for the demise of the illness model of homosexuality. In J. C. Gonsiorek & J. D. Weinrich (Eds.), *Homosexuality: Research implications for public policy* (pp. 115–136). Newbury Park, CA: Sage.

Green, R., Bettinger, M., & Zacks, E. (1996). Are lesbian couples fused and gay male couples disengaged? Questioning gender straightjackets. In J. Laird & R. Lifton (Eds.), *Lesbians and gays in couples and families* (pp. 185–230). San Francisco: Jossey-Bass.

Green, R. J., & Mitchell, V. (2002). Gay and lesbian couples in therapy: Homophobia, relational ambiguity, and social support. In A. S. Gurman & N. S. Jacobson (Eds.), *Handbook of couple therapy* (3rd ed., pp. 546–568). New York: Guilford Press.

Greenan, D., & Shernoff, M. (2003). Do open relationships work? Gay couples and the question of monogamy. *Psychotherapy Networker, 27,* 71–75.

Greenan, D., & Tunnell, G. (2003). *Couple therapy with gay men.* New York: Guilford Press.

Halkitis, T., Zade, D., Shrem, M., & Marmor, M. (2004). Beliefs about HIV noninfection and risky sexual behavior among MSM. *AIDS Education and Prevention, 16 (5),* 448–458.

Hays, R. B., Kegeles, S. M., & Coates, T. (1997). Unprotected sex and HIV risk-taking among young gay men within boyfriend relationships. *AIDS Education and Prevention, 9,* 314–329.

Hendrick, C., & Hendrick, S. (1983). *Liking, loving & relating.* Monterey, CA: Brooks/Cole.

Herek, G. (1998). *Stigma and sexual orientation: Understanding prejudice against lesbians, gay men, and bisexuals.* Thousand Oaks, CA: Sage

Hickson, F. C., Davies, P. M., Hunt, A. J., Weatherburn, P., McManus, T. J., & Coxon, P. (1992). Maintenance of open gay relationships: Some strategies for protection against HIV. *AIDS Care, 4(4),* 409–419.

Hoff, C., Stall, R. D., Paul, J., Acree, M., Daigle, D., Phillips, K., et al. (1997). Differences in sexual behavior among HIV discordant and concordant gay men in primary relationships. *Journal of AIDS and Human Retrovirology, 14,* 72–78.

Johnson, T. W., & Keren, M. S. (1996). Creating and maintaining boundaries in male couples. In. J. Laird & R. J. Green (Eds.), *Lesbians and gays in couples and families: A handbook for therapists* (pp. 231–250). San Francisco: Jossey-Bass.

Kerr, M., & Bowen, M. (1988). *Family evaluation: An approach based on Bowen theory.* New York: Norton.

Kipnis, L. (2003). *Against love: A polemic.* New York: Pantheon Books.

Kippax, S., Crawford, J. M., Davis, M., Rodden, P., & Dowset, G. (1993). Sustaining safe sex: A longitudinal study of a sample of homosexual men. *AIDS, 7 (3),* 257–263.

Kippax, S., Noble, J., Prestage, G., Crawford, J. M., Campbell, B., Baxter, D., et al. (1997). Sexual negotiation in the AIDS era: Negotiated safety revisited. *AIDS, 11(2),* 191–197.

Kurdek, L. A. (1988). Relationship quality of gay and lesbian cohabitating couples. *Journal of Homosexuality, 15(1),* 85–99.

Kurdek, L., & Schmitt, P. (1985/86). Relationship quality of gay men in closed or open relationships. *Journal of Homosexuality, 12(1),* 85–99.

LaSala, M. (2004). Extradyadic sex and gay male couples: Comparing monogamous and nonmonogamous relationships. *Families in Society: The Journal of Contemporary Human Services, 85,* 405–412.

LaSala, M. (in press). Monogamy of the heart: A qualitative study of extradyadic sex among gay male couples. *Journal of Gay and Lesbian Social Services.*

McWhirter, D., & Mattison, A. (1984). *The male couple: How relationships develop.* Englewood Cliffs, NJ: Prentice-Hall.

Mendola, M. (1980). *The Mendola Report: A new look at gay couples.* New York: Crown Books.

Mitchell, S. (2002). *Can love last? The fate of romance over time.* New York: Norton.

Morin, J. (1999). When hot monogamy isn't happening, consider plan B. *In the Family, 4 (1),* 12–15.

Saghir, G. B., & Robins, E. (1973). *Male and female homosexuality: A comprehensive investigation.* Baltimore: Williams & Wilkins.

Scheinkman, M. (2005). Beyond the trauma of betrayal: Reconsidering affairs in couples therapy. *Family Process, 44,* 227–244.

Shernoff, M. (1995). Male couples and their relationship styles. *Journal of Gay & Lesbian Social Services, 2 (1),* 43–58.

Shernoff, M., & Morin, J. (1999). Monogamy and gay men: When open relationships are a therapeutic option. *Family Therapy Networker, 23 (1),* 63–71.

Silverstein, C. (1981). *Man to Man: Gay couples in America.* New York: William Morrow.

Socarides, C. W. (1978). *Homosexuality.* Northvale, NJ: Aronson.

Spanier, G. (1976). Measuring dyadic adjustment: New scales for assessing the quality of marriage and similar dyads. *Journal of Marriage and the Family, 38 (1),* 15–28.

Spanier, G. (1989). *Manual for the Dyadic Adjustment Scale.* North Tonowanda, NY: Multi-Health Systems.

Stulberg, I., & Smith, M. (1988). Psychosocial impact of the AIDS epidemic on the lives of gay men. *Social Work, 33 (3),* 277–281.

Wagner, G., Remien, R., & Carballo-Dieguez, A. (1998). "Extramarital" sex: Is there an increased risk for HIV transmission? A study of male couples of mixed HIV status. *AIDS Education and Prevention, 10 (3)*, 245–256.

Wagner, G. J., Remien, R. H., & Carballo-Dieguez, A. (2000). Prevalence of extradyadic sex in male couples of mixed HIV status and its relationship to psychological distress and relationship quality. *Journal of Homosexuality, 39(1)*, 31–46.

CHAPTER 12

Lesbian Couples
The Infidelities of Women,
Sexual and Otherwise

BEVERLY BURCH

Is infidelity a different experience in any way for lesbians than for other couples? Heartache, anger, a sense of betrayal, a difficult recovery—the fundamental human responses to infidelity are the same. But in this postmodern era, we know social context is everything. Therapists who work with lesbian couples need two kinds of knowledge: how to work with the incendiary experience of infidelity and how to understand the varieties of what may be considered infidelity by one couple, but not by another. I'll discuss this second issue first because it forms the backdrop for understanding that infidelity is subject to redefinition for all couples and has particular nuances in lesbian relationships.

PART I: WHAT IS INFIDELITY?

If the word means betrayal rather than nonmonogamy—and I think it does—then we can never assume the answer to be obvious. The story of marriage reveals an evolution over time, from arranged marriages, child marriages, polygamy, and implicitly sanctioned nonmonogamy for some—mostly men—to our current norm of heterosexual monogamy. What's defined as fidelity and infidelity profoundly shapes one's emotional response to it. If the husband is tacitly allowed to sleep with other women, does the wife feel the same as she would in a culture that explicitly condemns it? In a polygamous marriage does a woman consider her husband unfaithful when he sleeps with another wife? In either situation a woman might feel hurt or jealous, but jealousy does not necessarily equal a sense of betrayal. The notion of infidelity as betrayal is culturally determined as well as emotionally laden.

The word "infidelity" is not morally neutral: infidelity is a serious breach in most heterosexual marriages and it's usually also seen as a violation of ethical norms. Couples who are dating may view infidelity as wrong and hurtful but not necessarily as the same kind of transgression as in a marriage. "My girlfriend cheated on me" doesn't quite equal "My wife cheated on me." And people are likely to respond with, "Better you found out now than when you're married."

Legal limbo leaves gay and lesbian relationships with a lack of social definition. Are we perpetually dating? If we live together, are we the same as a straight couple who *chooses* not to get married? Does the norm of monogamy simply transfer to homosexual relationships, who can make no legal commitment, have no traditional ceremony in which they promise to "cleave only unto one another"? We lack given rules, we have no social contract to accept or reject.

A common view of gay relationships, especially male ones, is that they are less concerned with monogamy, less judgmental about "infidelity." Perhaps this view has historical accuracy but as gay relationships find more legitimacy, the question of monogamy seems to be changing. I have no formal data here, but my experience is that this is shifting with time, that there's a higher value on monogamy now. Between women, monogamy has traditionally been esteemed, even if the question has to be settled, not assumed. These differences are real, but we can resist the impulse to simplify the complex. Lesbian and gay relationships evolve structures in response to social constraints. As with all cultural differences, therapists must beware of transfering normative assumptions to every relationship.

Alternative Family Structures

Some lesbian couples live in a matrix of supportive relationships that gives meaning to their special status. In my therapy practice I frequently see examples of this matrix: There are several women with very close ties to an ex-lover, one whose children have a legal parental relationship with another woman—like an extended family relationship—and another whose close friend helps her raise her two children. In lesbian families at least one parent is not a biological parent. Parenting is understood as a psychological relationship as much as a biological one. In *Reinventing the Family* (1994) Laura Benkov writes:

> Families don't exist as independent units within which intimacy unfolds unto itself. Instead, life in every family is shaped as surely

by surrounding cultural discourse and institutions as it is by idiosyncrasies of each family member. A question like "Who is the mommy?" reflects the meeting of the world outside and the world within. The ideas that prevail in society profoundly influence how we each construct and feel about our families and our roles within them. (p. 145)

For lesbians the "society around them" is multilayered: the dominant culture, their families of origin, and lesbian and gay culture. Many lesbian families develop nontraditional structures. These situations complicate the question of fidelity without ever transgressing sexual boundaries. The following case illustrates the complexities of a supportive matrix.

Jennifer, an interior designer, and Zoe, an architect, met on a joint project that required them to consult frequently. They became good friends, then began a love affair when Zoe left her husband. Eventually she moved with her two daughters into the home of Jennifer and Jennifer's 7-year-old son, Max. Jennifer's ex, Marsha, is also Max's mother and considers herself, Jennifer, and Max still a family even though they separated when Max was 2.

Jennifer juggles these two families. She's tied to the threesome of herself, Max, and Marsha. Max is used to this arrangement, including joint vacations and holiday celebrations with both of his mothers. Jennifer and Marsha's finances are still entwined. Marsha drops by for dinner sometimes, and Max moves between the nearby houses of his two mothers on an ever-changing schedule.

Zoe can make no sense of this. She and her husband, Jeffrey, had a traumatic divorce. He remains hurt and angry. It's not easy for them to cooperate as parents to their two girls, who spend half the week with him and half with her. She can't imagine continuing the kind of family life that Jennifer and Marsha have. She presses Jennifer to make some rules with Marsha, not to give her such free access to their home, and to end vacations with each other.

Jennifer resents and resists Zoe's demands. She's loyal to Marsha—they helped and protected each other through single motherhood after their separation. Marsha dates occasionally but hasn't found anyone else. Jennifer feels it would be a betrayal of Marsha and wrenching for Max if she changed the rules. She can handle two families if Zoe can get past her jealousy. She'd love for them all to be an extended family, doing things together.

Zoe says she's the betrayed one. She assumed the relationship with Marsha would change when she moved in. She doesn't worry that Zoe and Marsha have lingering romantic or sexual feelings, but their continuing closeness seems like some version of infidelity.

In *Unbroken Ties: Lesbian Ex-lovers*, Carol Becker (1988) documents the enduring bonds that characterize many lesbian relationships after a breakup:

> To varying degrees, lesbian ex-lovers retain their ties to one another after their breakup and use these bonds to rebuild their lives. An ex-lover remains an important part of a woman's evolving identity: as a woman, as a lesbian, and as a participant in intimate relationships. (p. 211)

Social and family support for lesbians is not guaranteed after a breakup. Support isn't always there when marriage ends, but the larger social view of what divorce means is at least secure. No one treats the marriage as if it didn't exist or didn't mean something important. For a lesbian, a breakup may even meet with relief from her family of origin, especially if it rekindles hope that she will now, finally, find a man. Where is she to turn except to her own community, even to her ex? "Despite the unresolvable differences that resulted in their breakup, lesbian ex-lovers remained connected by an overriding common cause—that of combating negative stereotypes of themselves, their relationship and their lifestyle" (Becker, 1988).

Kath Weston's (1991) study of gay families echoes this view:

> Former lovers' ... inclusion in families we choose was far from automatic, but most people hoped to stay connected to ex-lovers as friends and family .... This emphasis on making a transition from lover to friend while remaining within the bounds of gay families contrasted with heterosexual partners ... for whom separation or divorce often meant permanent rupture of a kinship tie. (p. 11)

Jennifer and Zoe have a "cross-cultural" relationship, Jennifer coming from a lesbian culture that tolerates different boundaries, Zoe coming from a heterosexual one that finds these odd and threatening. Even if she and Jeffrey were friendly, Zoe can't imagine taking a vacation with him. She would never expect Jennifer to accept such closeness. Are she and Jennifer essentially married or not, she asks?

If Zoe had previously been in a lesbian relationship she might still dislike having Marsha around so much. Ex-lovers are not necessarily welcomed into the picture any more than in-laws are. But they are like in-laws for many lesbians; they're the people you inherit when you enter a relationship. These ties are not incomprehensible or equivalent to being unfaithful. Many times new lovers do gradually accommodate their partner's ex. As one woman new to lesbian relationships said to me in an interview for an earlier book (Burch, 1993) on lesbian relationships:

> I'm not like other lesbians, for example, because I don't have ex-lovers. They're all male. That's a really big thing .... You know there's this stuff about lesbians having extended families, and when we're

old we'll all be sitting on the porch rocking with our ex-lovers ....
This weekend we were with some friends who've been lesbian for at
least 15 years, and one of them said to me, "My God, you don't have
ex-lovers!" It was like I was missing my right arm. (p. 94)

A therapist working with a complex family like Jennifer's and Zoe's needs
an open mind. Once, when divorce was uncommon, we couldn't imagine that
blended families were viable, yet now they're a routine part of couples therapy
work. Step-families can be immensely challenging, but we understand that
each one has to find its own way, has to figure out what arrangements work
for them. Because we know the potential harm to children of divorce from
loss of one parent or from ongoing conflict, we can imagine that close ties
between ex's may even be good for children.

With extended lesbian families the trick is also to side-step normative
assumptions. Listening to Zoe's sense of betrayal, I feel empathy. Listening to
Jennifer's fears of altering her relationship with Marsha, I also feel empathy.
When Zoe insists that Jennifer's relationship with Marsha reflects a lack of faithfulness to her, I ask: How? In what specific ways? We try to work from there.

By holding each woman's subjective experience in the room, I implicitly say both views are legitimate. Somewhere in the course of our work I let
them know that my experience with complicated family systems tells me they
can work, with effort and commitment. Lesbian couples need mirroring and
validation by therapists even more than heterosexual ones do since they don't
find it in the broader culture. They are the ones to decide if this arrangement
must change or if it's ultimately untenable.

Open Relationships

Then again, there is real nonmonogamy. In *American Couples* (1983), the only
large study of heterosexual, lesbian, and gay relationships, Phillip Blumstein
and Pepper Schwartz found that the large majority of lesbians prefer monogamy.
But some do choose an open relationship. The sense of sexual liberation in lesbian and feminist communities at least nominally allows them choice. Again,
there's no formal data here, but my experience is that lesbians place a higher
value on monogamy as they find a more accepted place in mainstream culture. Views of nonmonogamy tend to change with age as well, younger couples
making more tentative commitments or wanting to experiment with relationships. Still, how do we draw the line between dating, commitment, and formal
commitment or marriage when comparing gay and straight relationships?

Couples who sanction nonmonogamy, or an occasional affair, may establish their own rules to limit the threat to their primary relationship. Tolerance can turn out to be in theory only, however. Actual affairs sometimes
cause one partner to decide nonmonogamy no longer works. All of us, gay and
straight, are steeped in the romance of a "one and only" that permeates our
culture. Nonmonogamy may be "natural" to the human species, but it seems

viable only within a culture or community that is thoroughly acclimated to it. For women it tends to be especially difficult, gay or straight (Blumstein & Schwartz, 1983).

> For four years Suzanne and Brigit maintained a very sexual and open relationship. Brigit traveled frequently in her work; they both felt these imposed separations kept their erotic life lively—missing each other was like an aphrodisiac. Neither wanted to slip into the "companionate marriage" that relied on common interests rather than passion as a bond. They viewed this as an easy trap for lesbian relationships. Both agreed from the beginning to an open relationship with the understanding that each could have some kind of sexual "liaison," a term they preferred to "affair," when Brigit was away. No ongoing liaisons: If either felt a full-blown affair was imminent, she'd stop seeing the other person.
>
> Suzanne liked having so much time as an essentially single person. Before Brigit she had a number of lovers. She saw herself as fundamentally nonmonogamous and doubted she'd ever manage a long-term relationship. This arrangement with Brigit seemed perfect, the best of both worlds. Although there was stress and distress—many midnight conversations and urgent phone calls—it was exciting, worth it all.
>
> Brigit was more dubious. She agreed to the arrangement because it intrigued her. Her work did keep her away and she loved how passionate they were on her return. She indulged in the occasional liaison on the road, something she'd never considered in her former relationship. The built-in limits of her out-of-town adventures made her feel safe, but Suzanne's in-town liaisons worried her. So far they'd worked things out, but she felt the strain.
>
> Over time Brigit's grown weary and even wary of their agreement. She's considering a job change. Does their relationship require that she have a job involving travel? She's beginning to want more companionship with Suzanne, even at the price of less passion. She knows she can't tolerate Brigit having liaisons indefinitely nor while she's in town.
>
> Suzanne doesn't want to change things. She feels betrayed; they founded their relationship on an understanding: It's not fair for Brigit to change the rules! But she's also deeply attached to her now. She wants the relationship to last. This conflict seems impossibly daunting.

Even when a couple hasn't agreed on nonmonogamy, lesbians tend to be more open about it than married people do. Blumstein and Schwartz (1983) write:

> The interesting thing here is that marriage itself makes couples more deceptive. Couples who marry have traditionally sworn to "forsake

all others," and it is rare that couples change the agreement, even if they do not always live up to it. Because most nonmonogamous husbands and wives have broken their contract rather than revised it, they are forced into dishonesty. (p. 270)

Revising that contract would be difficult, of course, and likely grounds for divorce. But revising it the other way, back to monogamy, is equally challenging. Brigit and Suzanne's dilemma is a common endpoint of nonmonogamy. An open relationship is hard to sustain over time and difficult to change into a monogamous one. It may seem strange that Suzanne's the one to feel betrayed, but again, betrayal is defined by context not by absolutes. Suzanne must get past this sense of betrayal to accept a change in the rules. But does she want to?

More frequently now, lesbian and gay couples do marry, if not legally at least making a personal and/or spiritual commitment. They rent a hall, a florist, a caterer, musicians, and photographers. They invite friends and family, hire a minister, and exchange rings and vows. Vows are of their own creation, like more and more heterosexual couples. There is no way to know whether the vows typically involve promises of fidelity since they are private and unstudied. Perhaps faithfulness is simply assumed, as it is for heterosexuality.

The possibility of legal marriage dangles on the horizon. As the definition of marriage evolves to include gay relationships, its bond of monogamy will likely add weight to most lesbians' wish for mutual commitment. I expect, however, that the gay community, hardly a homogeneous or unified entity, will still tolerate open relationships more than heterosexual ones do. At the same time, such a hard-won legal right will be taken very seriously by many and may move the communal ethic further toward monogamy.

Open relationships usually announce this understanding at the beginning of therapy—then look to see if the therapist accepts their views. Some therapists believe too strongly in the impossibility or unsoundness of nonmonogamy or interpret it in terms of individual or systemic pathology. Others simply have a moral aversion to it. I believe therapists have an obligation to be transparent about issues like this. It may be necessary to say "I'm not the best therapist for you. I don't think nonmonogamy works."

My personal view is that open relationships are tough, that in the end most couples founder on the shoals of jealousy or one person falls in love with an affair—a particular vulnerability for lesbians. I tell clients that my experience has led me to this conclusion, although I've seen exceptions. If they are committed to making nonmonogamy work for them, I'm very willing to help. But it seems fair to let them know I have concerns; they're free to seek a more optimistic view.

For a couple such as Brigit and Suzanne, embracing different needs is especially challenging. Relationships resist changing. Over time they may succeed, but there's usually opposition or reluctance, then a sense of betrayal, resentment, and anger. We see heterosexual couples go through these stages as they try to renegotiate gender roles. Deeply held patterns and beliefs don't budge easily. Brigit and Suzanne finally separated, with a great deal of unhappiness and mutual blame. Suzanne believed monogamy wasn't the route for her and continued to resent Brigit's efforts to change things. Brigit felt she'd tried, but an open relationship held no real future for her.

Emotional "Affairs"

Another complication on traditional monogamy is the depth of friendship some women have outside of a primary relationship. A woman may have a close friendship that leaves her partner threatened or jealous. No matter if the friendship is nonsexual, the knowledge that one's lover is very close to someone else—with possible feelings of attraction, admitted or not—can feel too much like infidelity. Yet lesbian culture supports friendships like these.

For centuries the culture of women has sanctioned "romantic friendships." Carroll Smith-Rosenberg's (1975) now-classic study of letters between women, *The Female World of Love and Ritual: Relations Between Women in the Nineteenth Century*," reveals astonishing confessions of love, passion, and intimacy between women who were surely never lovers—in fact most of them were married. This tradition of intimacy and strong emotion in friendship reflects women's acculturation. It may also reflect something innate in women or a consequence of our family structures. For whatever reasons, many women, both heterosexual and lesbian, have friendships that occupy a place of prominence in their lives, friendships that in some ways seem to come first or affect their availability to partners at times.

Husbands may find these friendships perplexing, relieving (fewer emotional demands on them!), or threatening. But the threat is rarely sexual. In a lesbian relationship the line is not so clear. Though there may be no sexual transgressing, the possibility can't be ruled out. Even without that, partners feel justified in being jealous. It *feels* like an affair, an emotional affair.

> Ruth and Lucie have been together 24 years and have a daughter who's a junior in high school. Ruth's a nurse on an intensive neonatal unit where infants don't always survive. Her work is demanding and sometimes traumatic. She's very close to Roxy, another neonatal nurse who shares the emotional stress of their work. She and Roxy get together frequently for a drink or a meal. They spend time on the phone with each other. They go skiing and cycling together.
>
> Lucie's developing her own business. She works long hours when clients need her, but there are also lulls when she's not busy. She's grown to dislike Ruth's friendship with Roxy more and more. She feels she has to schedule time with Ruth around Roxy's plans. It's clear to her that they share interests she and Ruth don't have. What's

hardest is how they don't have the kinds of arguments she and Ruth have.

Ruth thinks Lucie is unnecessarily jealous of Roxy. They have years of security with each other, share a home and a child. She and Roxy don't find it easy to make social plans due to their respective family and work demands. Lucie doesn't love long intimate talks; Roxy does. Lucie doesn't like sports; Roxy does. She no longer presses Lucie to do those things with her because Roxy will do them. Shouldn't Lucie be relieved? There's nothing sexual between her and Roxy and never will be, she insists. Lucie should be more generous about their time.

The blurred line between lovers and friends may be confusing. Weston (1991) writes:

> When I asked interview participants if they were currently involved in a relationship, a few were uncertain how to answer. Of those who hesitated, the women wondered whether they should count primary emotional bonds as relationships in the absence of sexual involvement, while the men wondered whether to include routinized sexual relationships that lacked emotional depth and commitment. (p. 140)

Lucie may trust Ruth, may believe Ruth won't sleep with Roxy. But the friendship occupies the same place an affair might; it stirs up similar feelings. She senses competition between herself and Roxy. At the same time she doesn't feel legitimate protesting a friendship. It makes her look possessive, even to herself. In *After the Affair*, Janis Abrahms Spring (1996) writes:

> Women have affairs to experience an emotional connection they feel is lacking in their primary relationship. They stray in search of a soul-mate, someone who pays attention to their feelings and encourages meaningful conversation. . . . Women who stray often develop a close friendship with their lovers before they become sexually involved.

Lesbian couples value intimate friendships in their own right. They may also treat them as stabilizing forces: Rather than threatening the primary relationship, friendships keep it balanced. Many writers observe an internal pull in lesbian relationships: They can be so relationship centered that a sense of fusion develops between the women. At first fusion is welcomed, but eventually it becomes its own problem, stifling individuality and eroticism (see Burch, 1997). Relationships that don't tolerate close outside friendships are then suspect. But what happens when the friendship competes with the primary relationship instead of balancing it. Is that infidelity?

Intimate friendships do sometimes turn into affairs. The threat can never be completely dismissed. Lucie's jealousy is easy to understand. Even without sex, Roxy's friendship is compelling for Ruth. It also highlights what's lacking for Ruth with Lucie. In that sense, is it as symptomatic of problems as an affair would be? Or is it just a natural outcome of a woman's tendency to seek closeness and intensity in friendships? Both could be true.

Therapy helped by focusing on issues in their relationship, much as if there were an affair. Recognizing each woman's legitimate feelings didn't require treating the friendship as illicit, however. In their long history together Ruth always had closer friends than Lucie did. Lucie began to see that for years she'd neglected their relationship in favor of work. The threat of Roxy made Ruth's feelings of deprivation more real to her. Ruth continued to be close to Roxy but as she and Lucie also got closer the tension over their friendship eased.

PART II: PSYCHOTHERAPY AND INFIDELITY

The tasks of psychotherapy with a lesbian couple after an affair are similar to those of any couple: naming the injury, expressing the hurt and anger, learning what it means, figuring out the future, and going forward with healing if the couple hopes to survive. The partners begin to recognize that they are forever on new ground. Work with a lesbian couple has its own flavor, however, because they are two women, not a man and woman or two men.

> Sarah and Mickie have been together 13 years. They've been through illness, career changes, family loss, and geographical moves. Both are religious and share a life of social and moral commitment. They're sensitive to each other's vulnerabilities. They rarely fight; in fact they're very careful with each other, too careful.
>
> Sarah returned to graduate school to prepare as a minister a few years ago. Between work and classes she didn't spend much time at home. Mickie tried to be selfless, but she was lonely. Her only protest about Sarah's absence came as a complaint that she did all the housework now, all the cleaning and cooking. Ultimately she decided it was a reasonable imbalance, given the demands on Sarah's time.
>
> To fill her empty hours Mickie spent a lot of time with their church's women's group. Sarah realized Mickie was getting close with Anna, another woman in the group. Mickie admitted she found a degree of emotional intensity with Anna that Sarah couldn't offer now. Sarah was actually relieved. She felt guilty being away so much. She liked Anna herself and thought Mickie's relationship with her a great thing.
>
> After Sarah finished school she and Mickie recognized how their relationship had suffered and came to therapy. It became clear that Sarah's lack of focus at home had hurt more than their division of labor. Slowly they began talking about Mickie's disappointments.

Sarah noticed that Mickie no longer went to the women's group and didn't see Anna any more. Mickie shrugged this off at first, then finally admitted she and Anna had had an affair which ended when Sarah finished school. She felt shame and remorse, a sense of guilt toward both of them.

Sarah was stunned. An affair seemed completely out of Mickie's character. She was openly furious with her and felt a painful loss of innocence. She didn't think good people did things like that. With the help of therapy, Mickie was able to do that most painful thing: hear how much she'd hurt Sarah, neither denying nor excusing herself. In the first weeks after the disclosure, Mickie listened a lot and expressed her deep remorse. Her open admission that she'd betrayed her own ideals as well as Sarah's were extremely helpful. It took a while, but Sarah forgave her. Then they began to look again at what Mickie had been through while Sarah was preoccupied with her work and school.

The meaning of the affair was difficult for both of them: not simply that Mickie felt abandoned, but that their way of dealing with things was to sweep trouble nobly aside. The hard work of the therapy, even more than the aftermath of the affair, has been to accept the inevitability of conflict. Mickie especially finds it difficult to be honest if she thinks Sarah will be upset. Emotional honesty seems hurtful. The irony of that view is apparent, yet she resists the discomfort.

During the past year of working on their mutual tendency to avoid conflict, more old anger and disappointment have come out. Sarah periodically reexperiences anger over the affair. Mickie stumbles and delays talking when she's unhappy about something Sarah's doing. They fight more now, and sometimes doubt if this can really be a good relationship. Their view of relationship is definitely tarnished, yet they're closer and more sexually intimate than they've been for years.

Whose Side Are You On?

Gay relationships have the burden—and benefit—of lacking clear norms or rules of relationship, as I hope I've shown. A therapist can be pulled into the role of arbiter here, asked to weigh in on the morality of affairs, to validate the sanctity of relationship or to provide the missing rules. Supporting the couple to find their own answers to these issues requires a neutral voice. When a woman discovers her partner has slept with someone else, unsanctioned, she feels what most people feel: a violation of trust, injury to their intimacy, anger that it happened, confusion about what it means. The therapist should probably also be confused about what it means, that is, not presume to know.

Some therapists believe an affair signifies lack of commitment to the relationship and to the therapy (Jacobson & Christenson, 1996). This is an easy assumption, and often true, but not always. I worked for months with a woman who was having an undisclosed affair. Her commitment to the relationship, however, was not a question. As the individual therapist, not the couple's therapist, I knew she was committed to the relationship, unclear herself about why she sometimes slept with this other woman, and guilt-ridden about it. She wanted to sort these matters out herself before she could talk to her partner.

Illicit affairs usually signal something amiss, but like any issue, its meaning needs to be revealed not assumed. We try to position ourselves in neutral: We assume there are two sides to the problem, two different meanings, two contributions to its creation and its resolution. Not that partners always play equal or symmetrical roles: There's individual responsibility. Still the difficulties are mutually created except in extreme cases. But our neutrality can be severely challenged.

> Joanna and Caroline came to therapy on the heels of Joanna learning that Caroline was having an affair with one of their friends. The friend's partner discovered a letter, a confession ensued; she called Joanna in fury and told her the whole story. Caroline was shocked to be caught in the act, so to speak, but unrepentant. Joanna was devastated. She wept through the entire first session, asking "How could you?" again and again. She had no idea how to cope with this. She loved Caroline, didn't want to break up, but couldn't imagine trusting her or being intimate with her again. Caroline seemed unmoved. She denied nothing, even said she was sorry to end the affair because it meant a lot to her, even though she didn't want to break up with Joanna.
>
> By the next session Joanna looked worse: she wasn't eating or sleeping. The life she thought she had with Caroline was a sham; she knew there'd be no going back to what she once believed about their relationship. Caroline, however, just wanted an end to the accusations. She asked Joanna to recognize that she'd been unhappy: they were no longer passionate and Joanna was preoccupied with work. She offered Joanna nothing by way of regret or concern and asked me to understand this.

In the face of Joanna's shock and undeniable sense of betrayal, I couldn't empathize with Caroline's request. It might have been reasonable later, but her timing was bad. With Joanna in so much pain, Caroline seemed the picture of coldness and self-absorption. I wondered how there could be no apology, no words of concern for Joanna if she hoped to stay with her. In other words, my sympathies were with Joanna and I struggled against judgment. Only the belief that there must be more to this picture protected me from taking it at face value.

In time I learned that Joanna typically prevented Caroline from talking about problems by becoming emotional. For 2 years Caroline had asked

Joanna to come to therapy. Joanna would get very upset until one of them changed the subject. Repeatedly having her overtures avoided left Caroline feeling more hostile than open to Joanna (see Gottman, 2001). Caroline no longer read Joanna's tears as signs of pain but as unwillingness to engage. If I'd reflexively sided with Caroline in these first highly charged sessions, Joanna might have given up on the therapy and maybe on the relationship. I assured her that her concerns were vital and we would take them seriously, but I asked her to wait.

The injured person's pain usually has to be seen as legitimate first. That priority doesn't mean the therapist holds the woman who strayed more blameworthy or is blind to her pain; it simply recognizes that the partner is in a state of emotional emergency. The pull to assign blame can be intense, especially from the injured one—and sometimes even from the transgressor. Once the therapist trips over the line into judgment, it's hard to return to neutrality. The consulting room veers toward being a courtroom and the partners toward being entrenched adversaries. To help couples talk to each other with honesty, we advocate for both.

Committed or Not?

Most couples come to therapy with the hope of surviving the disclosure; sometimes, however, another agenda lurks that may not even be conscious— a desire for help in leaving and/or help breaking this news. When a therapist finds that reconciliation isn't progressing, the real work may be separating.

> Sasha recently confessed that she just ended an affair, but she hopes to salvage her long relationship with Ariel. Ariel's reeling from the news, angry, unsure if she can stay with her or forgive her, but she agrees to therapy. The relationship is the first long-term for each of them. The emotional stakes are high.
>
> In therapy there are painful disclosures by Sasha: she loves Ariel but their sexual relationship has faded into oblivion. Ariel finds it difficult to talk about sex, and Sasha has protected her by not insisting. Sasha also believes that once passion has dimmed, not much can be done.
>
> Ariel takes this crisis as a wake-up call. With great discomfort and vulnerability, she begins to talk about her sexual issues. I see the possibility of movement. Ariel admits she's very cautious sexually, that she feels almost too vulnerable to bear talking about it. We make some headway there. But Sasha is curiously disengaged. At home she avoids being intimate or even talking about sex. After a time the therapy feels stalemated.
>
> Ariel visits an old college friend for a week. After this week apart, Sasha is even more distant. Finally she spills the truth: she doesn't want to go on with Ariel. She believes their relationship

really ended before the affair, she just wasn't able to admit this to herself, much less to Ariel. The time apart gave her clarity— she wants to be friends not lovers. Ariel feels triply betrayed: first the affair, then the painful exploration of her sexual issues, now abandonment and the news that Sasha hasn't been committed to working things out with her. Even though Sasha pleads to remain friends, Ariel says she feels like a fool for having believed her. She can't bear to be around her now.

The poignant outcome of this therapy felt like a failure to everyone. Ariel's sense of being deceived by Sasha is the most human of feelings. For a long time I also believed Sasha meant to work things out. But as Ariel and I discussed in a follow-up session (I offer couples individual follow-up sessions when a relationship has ended in therapy), the alternative to being sometimes fooled is to be forever mistrustful. Deception stings bitterly, but it doesn't reflect some failing of the self. Yes, at some point distrust is warranted and trust becomes foolhardy. But hard territory has to be crossed before that point is reached.

Ariel and Sasha had years of being trustworthy for each other. Sasha's intense difficulty in realizing she needed to end their relationship led to the affair and then to the ambiguity of their therapy. However agonizing (and it was agonizing) for Ariel, Sasha's dishonesty was a failure to face hard truth, not chronic untrustworthiness. How could Ariel be expected to accept this? Her fury was warranted. The need for distance was wise. But not the self-blame.

I hoped she would eventually feel that it's better to trust one's history with someone than to replace it with constant suspicion. Otherwise she wouldn't heal from this loss or hope for a future relationship. This understanding would necessarily take a long time, but I wanted her to consider its possibilities.

For her part, Sasha had long concluded that they would never have a good sexual relationship again. Their lack of passion seemed like a shameful secret: They weren't really lovers any more, just pretending to be. That many couples, gay and heterosexual, have difficulty keeping their sexual connection alive and satisfying was unknown to her. Approximately 20% of married couples have a no-sex marriage and another 15% have infrequent sex (McCarthy & McCarthy, 2003). [We don't have figures for lesbian and gay couples; many are still closeted.]

In our sex-conscious culture, low sexual frequency seems embarrassing. That it's a common problem is not widely known. Many couples subscribe to the idea that passion is either easy or it's impossible. Like being "in love," desire is treated as a yes or no state, not as something that waxes and wanes, something that relationships strengthen or neglect. That therapy can help to re-find passion seemed unlikely to Sasha because she'd never questioned her beliefs about it. By the time she revealed her conviction that sex was over for them, she was already out of the relationship emotionally.

The Changed Future

Even for a couple who navigates the rough waters of an affair, things are not the same afterwards. That's the bad news and the good news. Usually something needed to change. Not by having an affair of course—it's one of the hardest ways to make changes. But if a couple survives to the point of deeper understanding, renewed trust, and revived intimacy, they have a future ahead of them.

First, though, is mourning the old, forever lost relationship. A poem by Eloise Klein Healy expresses how we hope this isn't true, while we know it is.

THE ELEMENTS

Fire for anger, water for change,
earth for stability, wind? well,
who knows what wind is about?
In life, they mix so. Like that day,
I was taking a shower
with my lover and she told me
she was sleeping with
her ex-lover again. Wasn't
a fire supposed to leap
out of me, or wasn't water
there to drown the flames,
or wash her clean of betrayal?
Wasn't the hillside out the window
there to settle me, inform me
of the underlying design
and long term balance in things?
Wasn't some wind going to blow
those words away and leave us
soapy and sweet smelling
in that shower, just about to
towel off, have a drink,
cook dinner and read a little?
Wasn't my love for her supposed to mean
I could step into the same river
over and over again?

How one gets through the affair and what the future becomes is determined by what the affair and its aftermath ultimately mean. If they didn't talk to each other honestly, can they now? If they were avoiding sexual issues, have they begun to face them? Did recovery require some tenacity they didn't know they had? A discovery of personal resilience? Did it bring a sadder-but-wiser view of love? Rebalance dependency and independence? As with many hardships, they may learn profound things about themselves. Not an experience they'd choose, but sometimes people gain surprising benefits from hard times.

The story of love and long-term relationship *is* one of hard times as much as of romance and happiness—news we keep resisting. I've never seen a long-term relationship or a marriage, an essentially sound and rewarding relationship, that didn't also have at least one long period of crisis—a really difficult struggle and a time of deep unhappiness. Many have more than one. These crises are a crucible in which the couple learns whether they're still viable, whether what they have together is worth it. They will end the relationship there or they will go on, perhaps more securely or perhaps with scar tissue, but definitely altered.

When couples are full of doubt about whether recovery is possible, I tell them this has been my experience. It's the part of the story of love that's usually left out. Therapy is often the place where unpleasant truth is encountered, but it can also be an experience of survival, with happier prospects for the future.

Because human relationships are difficult, and long-term intimacy especially so, we are poorly prepared by a popular culture that suggests love is all there is. Many couples come to therapy convinced that they *shouldn't* go on because they fight too much, don't have sex enough, don't talk openly enough, or suffer some other failure that makes them fall short of the idealized view of relationships in popular literature, music, and movies. They believe theirs is a fundamentally flawed relationship. The disclosure of an affair can feel like the worst of these failures.

Couples bat around the words "healthy" and "unhealthy" as accusations. There's the idea that a person is weak or too dependent if she doesn't leave after an affair. It's news to couples that many relationships, maybe most, experience major problems or disappointments. Each couple lives with its guilty little secrets, sure that hardly anyone else has these problems and that almost everyone else is happy. Our job as therapists is to convey implicitly that this is a human dilemma, not the province of the "dysfunctional."

How someone interprets an affair may be determined by family history. When a parent has been unfaithful, especially chronically so, it's not just the spouse who is hurt. As one woman said:

> By 15 or so, I was aware of my father's affairs. They affected me as well as my mother. My father had issues about women because his mother abandoned the family when he was 10. I understand him better now, but I have to say that infidelity is also unfaithfulness to one's children and causes damage to everyone in the family.

When this woman discovered her partner's affair, she felt confirmed in her early belief that no relationship can be relied on. The idea that trust can be reestablished seemed like an empty dream. This was the second time she'd been with a woman who had a secret affair. Did her conviction play an unconscious role in her choice of lovers? Don't we all hope to relive the past but make it come out differently?

Another woman with a similar family history went in a different direction:

I don't believe in open marriage and could never have an affair. My lover and I have talked about this a lot. Anyone can be tempted and find the opportunity. Sheila got very close to a co-worker in our fourth year together. They ended up sleeping together when their whole agency went on retreat. But when she came back she told me right away. She used honesty like a brake. I was so upset. Some basic cynicism in me came out first. But in the end I trusted her honesty. She knows I can't go that route. She's promised me it won't happen again. Each of us wishes to be loved in some singular way. Not that that's always real, but you have to respect the need for it.

This woman's story suggests how important honest disclosure can be in healing. Not that disclosure is always the right or best choice. Honesty with one's self is probably the most important factor and sometimes confession is more about seeking absolution than it is about reparing damage. In that sense, confession can be rather selfish. But having an affair discovered rather than revealed usually makes the healing more difficult. There's the affair and then there's the dishonesty. The length of an affair, the circumstances, the person of the lover, and the point in the relationship when it occurs add to the sense of injury.

CONCLUSION

Every couple holds its own tacit or explicit understanding of what their relationship should be. Will they be a tightly knit, best friends, intimate-in-all-ways couple? Do they tolerate, even prefer, a degree of independence or emotional distance? How do they value romance, passion, and sexuality? Might they be good companions but perhaps not so passionate? Will they be career-bound, putting the relationship second to work? Do they tolerate conflict, keep important outside friendships, hold close relations with extended family, or not? Do they want children? Are children their primary bond? The work of a relationship requires sorting out these unnamed concerns.

Psychotherapists are liable to bias in these areas and others. We do not always examine our beliefs if they seem normative. But we cannot be without beliefs and opinions: We need norms for our work to make sense. Allowing clients to know our beliefs when they're relevant—that is, transparency—is sometimes the only ethical stance. But we can also keep learning, trying to understand the ever-changing structures of relationships, and the reality of differences between people.

REFERENCES

Becker, C. (1988). *Unbroken ties: Lesbian ex-lovers*. Boston: Alyson Publications.

Benkov, L. (1994). *Reinventing the family: The emerging story of lesbian and gay parents*. New York: Crown.

Blumstein, P., & Schwartz, P. (1983). *American couples*. New York: William Morrow.

Burch, B. (1993). *On intimate terms: The psychology of difference in lesbian relationships*. Chicago: University of Illinois Press.

Burch, B. (1997). *Other women: Lesbian/bisexual experience and psychoanalytic views of women*. New York: Columbia University Press.

Gottman, J. (2001). *The relationship cure*. New York: Three Rivers Press.

Healy, E.K. (2007). The elements. In *The islands project: Poems for Sappho* (pp. 48–49). Los Angeles, CA: Red Hen Press.

Jacobson, N., & Christensen, A. (1996). *Integrative couple therapy*. New York: Norton.

McCarthy, B., & McCarthy, E. (2003). *Rekindling desire*. New York: Bruner-Routledge.

Smith-Rosenberg, C. (1975). The female world of Love And Ritual: Relations between women in the nineteenth-century America. *Signs* 1(1): 1–30.

Spring, J. A. (1996). *After the affair*. New York: HarperCollins.

Weston, K. (1991). *Families we choose*. New York: Columbia University Press.

CHAPTER 13

"An Affair to Remember"

Infidelity and Its Impact on Children

CATHERINE FORD SORI

While there is research that examines the topic of marital infidelity (e.g., Glass & Wright, 1992; Hertlein & Skaggs, 2005), including cyber sex (e.g., Mitchell, Becker-Blease, & Finkelhor, 2005; Nelson, Piercy, & Sprenkle, 2005; Schneider, 2003), and several scholars have provided guidelines to treat couples for infidelity (e.g., Brown, 1991, 2001; Glass, 2002; Lusterman, 1998; Pittman, 1989; Pittman & Wagers, 1995), there is a paucity of research on the effects of affairs on children and only a few authors discuss at length the impact of infidelity on children and offer ways to help them (e.g., Brown, 1991, 1999, 2001; Kaslow, 1993; Lusterman, 2005a; Pittman, 1989). This seems to reflect findings that children are largely excluded from family therapy (Johnson & Thomas, 1999; Korner & Brown, 1990), and suggests that children are often not included in treatment following parental infidelity.

Yet countless children are impacted by parental infidelity, often with long-term negative effects. Estimates of the frequency of parental affairs vary (see Glass & Wright, 1992; Kaslow, 1993; Laumann, Gagnon, Michael, & Michaels, 1994), and it is unknown what percent of adults who engage in affairs have children. However, since many affairs occur at various transition points in the life cycle (Pittman, 1989), such as after the birth of the first child, at midlife, or after the children leave home, it is highly probable that a large percentage of these couples have children. Surveys among therapists who treat couples found that infidelity was rated as one of the most difficult issues to treat, with clinicians often feeling they lack the training to intervene effectively (Whisman, Dixon, & Johnson, 1997). Amato and Rogers (1997) report that infidelity is the most frequently listed cause of divorce. These facts call for more research and discussion on how to treat couples as well as all the children who are impacted by affairs.

Any type of affair—emotional, physical, Internet, or philandering—has the potential to seriously harm children. This chapter will examine how children are impacted by affairs through a developmental and theoretical lens, and offers some suggestions for assessing and treating children and their families.

One of the basic needs of children is for their parents to provide a sense of security, which all children crave (Lusterman, 1998, 2005a). Even though children may rebel against parental authority, they need to look up to their parents and believe in their wisdom (Lusterman, 1998). Children see their parents as models of good behavior (Lusterman, 2005a), and look to them to model values, moral judgment, and what it means to be a good spouse and parent. Lusterman (2005a) states, "When their parents fall short of these qualities, they experience discomfort, disillusion, confusion, and, at times, despair. The manifestations of these problems may differ by age, developmental differences, gender, and culture" (p. 1440).

What Happens in the Family When There Is an Affair

Secrets and lies   Secrets and lies are part of the fiber of affairs, and knowing that a parent lied repeatedly can have devastating effects on children (Lusterman, 2005b). Pittman (1989) points out how important the stability of both the marital relationship and the family are to children, and how disorienting secrets can be because they create distance among family members. Pittman states, "Children who experience secrecy and lies cannot trust what they are told; they become insecure and dependent" (p. 260). Brown (1999) discusses how children worry when they sense unexplained emotional tension or behavioral changes in the family that they don't understand, and states that the long-term "legacy of family secrets is difficulty trusting those close to you" (p. 172).

While children may accidentally discover that a parent is involved in an affair, some parents share the secret with a child (Duncombe & Marsden, 2004), sometimes even including a child or adolescent in a tryst (see Lusterman, 1998), such as a lunch date. Secrets are most harmful when a parent confides an affair to a child and swears the child to secrecy (Lusterman, 2005a; Pittman, 1989). This rupture in the generational boundaries can be highly detrimental to a child's development, even though children may relish the sense of power that results from such a coalition (see Kaslow, 1993).

Triangulation, coalitions, and loyalty conflicts   When there is stress between two people it is natural to triangulate in a third party to alleviate stress (Bowen, 1978). According to Papero (1995), triangles comprise three relationships, each consisting of two people, and are characterized by "shifting alliances and reactive processes. The communication from one to another about yet a third affects the sensitivity, perception/interpretation, and behavior of each" (p. 15). Either partner may triangulate a child in the marital relationship when there is infidelity. The wronged parent may burden a child by seeking an alliance with the child against the infidel. For example, Siegler (1994) describes a child who stated:

> "Daddy says you don't love us anymore. He says you're selfish, and you only love your boyfriend, Matthew. He says that *he* loves us better because he didn't want the family to get all broken up. He wants us all to stay together. The divorce is all your fault" (pp. 136–137).

Children may be openly contemptuous of the unfaithful parent, or may align with the wronged parent and simply dismiss the infidel (Reibstein & Richards, 1992).

This puts a child in a loyalty conflict that is often born out of a parent's revenge and fear of losing the children to the infidel (Lusterman, 1998). Parents' fear of abandonment by the children may be so strong that it leads them to confide in a child or align with the child against the unfaithful spouse (Brown, 1991). Brown states:

> Abandoned parents who involve the children in their obsession about the affair don't trust that their children love them. They act as if they expect the children to abandon them as well. Sharing the obsession with the children, however, is one of the most damaging things a parent can do. Such a stance asks the children to betray the other parent. This in itself is hostile and intrusive. (p. 249)

Such a spouse may lean on their child, demanding much time and attention, which can inhibit children's ability to separate and develop normally. Especially if the child is an adolescent, too much physical closeness can be uncomfortable and have undertones of sexuality that may be experienced as "seductive and repulsive" (Lusterman, 1998, p. 163). Efforts to alienate a child from the infidel parent can have negative effects that last a lifetime, and many children will cut off from the "bad" parent in order to support their hurting and "wronged" parent.

Sometimes *both* parents attempt to triangulate children by asking them to keep secrets. One parent may confide his affair to a child, while the other may reveal that she suspects her husband is being unfaithful (see Lusterman, 1998, p. 162). A child who is sworn to secrecy by both parents is in a most untenable position and may be overburdened with feelings of confusion, guilt, betrayal, and disloyalty. The triangles (see Bowen, 1978) that are formed when a child is asked to keep information about infidelity a secret from the other parent or from siblings must be a primary target of therapy.

Many clinicians who counsel only the couple when there is infidelity may work with triangles, such as the triangle formed by the spouses and the affairee; or the infidel and his or her mother and father; or the infidel, his or her unfaithful parent, and the affairee (Moultrup, 2005). However, few look at the triangles that are formed when a child is asked to carry the secret of an affair. These triangles include at minimum: (1) child, infidel, uninformed other parent; (2) child, infidel, affair partner; (3) child, sibling (who may or may not know the secret), infidel; and (4) child, siblings, uninformed parent. Each of these potential interlocking triangles (see Lusterman, 2005a) needs to be addressed in family therapy with the goal of extricating the child from the role of secret-holder and helping the spouses to deal directly with each other regarding issues relating to the affair as well as other marital issues that need to be addressed.

HOW AFFAIRS AFFECT CHILDREN

Children have various reactions to affairs. These reactions vary according to whether the affair is hidden or known, and according to the age of the children.

Children's Reactions to a Hidden Affair

Even when a parent attempts to hide an affair from a spouse or children, children may react to the underlying tension and sense something's wrong (Reibstein & Richards, 1992), and may suspect an affair. Brown (1999) discusses several reactions children may have to an affair that one or both parents have attempted to keep hidden from them, including (1) silence; (2) acting out behaviors; (3) reactions to a loyalty conflict that might include somatic complaints or depression; (4) trying to be perfect; (5) attempting to protect or align with a weak parent; (6) escaping from the home; and (7) self-destructive behaviors (pp. 173–174). These behaviors may reflect the stress a child is picking up on from a hidden affair.

Reactions When an Affair Is Acknowledged

While some believe that affairs are not necessarily harmful and may even be beneficial to a couple's relationship (e.g., Reibstein & Richards, 1992), and relationships may indeed be strengthened when couples work through issues related to both the affair and any problems in the relationships, children never benefit from parental infidelity. Although it is certainly helpful for children to witness their parents addressing difficult problems, and they may ultimately benefit from seeing their parents in a more open, honest, and committed relationship, an affair shatters a child's sense of security and trust that their world is safe and predictable. Case states that "an affair is often 'crazy-making' for the betrayed partner due to the loss of consistency, predictability and safety" (2005, p. 52). Children's experience of an affair may parallel that of the betrayed parent. When parents' stories are contradictory, children often lose trust in and respect for *both* parents (Duncombe & Marsden, 2004). Siblings may split and align with different parents according to who they feel was to blame, affecting sibling relationships for years to come (see Duncombe & Marsden, 2004).

These effects have both short- and long-term consequences for children, although the effects are mediated by individual factors (such as the child's age and stage of development, temperament, and resiliency), family factors (e.g., if the affair ends and parents work on their issues, the level of parental hostility and conflict, if the infidel moves in with the affairee), cultural factors (such as the level of acceptance of the affair), contextual factors (e.g., the reactions of extended family and friends, and the amount of support available), and the losses incurred (e.g., divorce, financial status, having to move or change schools). Brown (2001) lists some of the long-term risks for children, including "diminished self-esteem and problems with trust and intimacy, which can extend for generations" (p. 282). Older children may believe the affair and subsequent divorce has ruined their lives and question how they could ever marry (Duncombe & Marsden, 2004), fearing their lives are destined to imitate that of one of their parents: that they will be cheated on, or that they may have an affair.

Children's Emotional and Cognitive Reactions

In general, children are impacted by an affair in two ways: by what happens between their parents and subsequently to their family, and how the affair shakes up their own beliefs about their parents and the values they have been taught. Children will be upset by open fighting or silent hostility, by parental depression, anxiety, preoccupation (with either the unfaithful spouse or the affair partner); by loyalty conflicts, and by any perceived threat to the continuation of the marriage (see Reibstein & Richards, 1992). "Anxiety is contagious" according to Lusterman (2005a, p. 1442), and children often mirror parental anxiety (see Stone Fish, Jensen, Reichert, & Wainman-Sauda, 2000) and/or depression (see Kaslow, Mintzer, Meadows, & Grabill, 2000). Once an affair is out in the open the family may be thrown into great turmoil. Parents may fight bitterly, hurtling insults and tossing blame, often with little awareness of how children are bombarded as they are caught in the crossfire. Children want to see their parents "as models of what is right. Seeing them as almost godlike. . . . When parents fall short their children experience discomfort, disillusion, and confusion" (Lusterman, 1998, p. 159). When children become aware of the lies that have been part of the infidelity, they may begin to question their parent's honesty in other areas, such as the morals, values, and any religious training that they have received. This can be especially problematic for adolescents who have a heightened awareness of their sexuality and may react to a parent whose behavior contradicts his or her teachings.

When an affair receives publicity or creates a public uproar, children's lives become even more complicated (Reibstein & Richards, 1992). This can occur when friends or family members take sides or blame a parent, or when friends at school or in the community learn of the affair. This brings to mind some of the sexual scandals that have plagued politicians and their families in recent years. The shame associated with a public scandal is perhaps the most treacherous of all waters for children to navigate, especially when parents are preoccupied with saving face by denying the allegations (leaving children extremely confused), and are not emotionally or psychologically available to help their children cope with the shock, gossip, and public humiliation.

Divorce and conflict As children struggle to make sense of parental infidelity they often worry about the future of their family. Their biggest worries are if their parents will divorce and, if they do, what will happen to the children (Lusterman, 1998). While there is little research on the effect of affairs on children, there is ample research on the impact of divorce and parental conflict on children, and many believe that children's reactions to infidelity are similar to those experienced in a divorce (e.g., Duncombe & Marsden, 2004; Reibstein & Richards, 1992; Wallerstein & Kelly, 1980).

According to Kelly (1993), many of the problems seen in children of divorce actually *preceded* the divorce, and likewise problems in the family prior to the discovery of an affair can negatively impact children. It has been well documented that conflict between parents is detrimental to children (Amato, 1994), and of course this would include fighting about an affair. Kelly (2000, p. 964) points out that it is specific factors in parental conflict that harm children, including (1) the severity of the conflict; (2) the frequency of the conflict; (3) how hostile or abusive the conflict is; (4) if and how conflict is resolved; and (5) if a child has buffers, such as a warm relationship with one parent or outside support. Hecker and Sori (2006) believe the goal for children who are caught in the middle of parental conflict is to help them disengage from the parents' marital problems and resume their normal life, free from adult stressors. Psychoeducation is useful for parents to understand how their fighting and attempts to form coalitions negatively harm their children. Children also benefit when clinicians work with parents not to fight openly and to improve their conflict resolution skills (Hecker & Sori, 2006).

An affair may indeed be "a symptom or outcome of the marital unhappiness that leads to marital breakdown and divorce rather than the cause" (Duncombe & Marsden, 2004, p. 192). If the affair was preceded by an unhappy or conflictual marriage, the children are likely to be more distressed. However, not all affairs are the result of problems in a marriage. Some affairs have their seeds in a parent's individual issues, such as a sexual addiction, the need for titillation and excitement, a personality disorder or psychopathology, or a midlife crisis. These parental problems also impact children.

General reactions Pittman (1989) points out that those children whose parents are fighting about an affair and feel their family is threatened "can develop virtually any physical or emotional symptom" (p. 262). Children are likely to exhibit more severe symptoms when a parent is openly hostile or contemptuous, asks the child to keep a secret about the affair, or confides inappropriate details of the affair. Reactions can be divided into two overall categories: *Externalizing* behaviors (e.g., aggressive or destructive behaviors) and *internalizing* behaviors (e.g., children are anxious, depressed, or withdrawn; see Achenbach, 1992). Externalizing behaviors may include defiance, anger, challenging parents, arguing with siblings and/or peers, hyperactive behaviors, stealing, running away, fighting at school, or lying. Older children may use alcohol, drugs, or sex to act out. Children who internalize their reactions may become depressed, anxious, have trouble sleeping, have nightmares, exhibit regressive behaviors, cry easily, have difficulty concentrating in school and a drop in grades, or experience appetite changes or weight loss. While these are some general reactions that may occur, responses often vary according to the age of the child, and research is needed in this area.

Young children Lusterman (1998) points out that young children do not yet have the language skills to articulate complex feelings or give voice to their inner experiences, so they tend to express their distress through their behavior. They are likely to show their insecurity by regressing back to how they behaved at a younger age. Some may become clingy, develop physical illnesses, or have temper tantrums, while others may attempt to become the "perfect child" (Lusterman, 1998, p. 166). Yet young children's cries for help and their need for time and attention may be overlooked by parents who are preoccupied with the drama of an affair (Reibstein & Richards, 1992). When these needs are neglected by parents who are engrossed with an affair, children may feel bewildered, believe that they are to blame, and fear they are no longer loved by their parents (Duncombe & Marsden, 2004). According to Pittman (1989), small children "may exhibit anxiety symptoms, with clinging, bed-wetting, thumb-sucking, firesetting, temper tantrums, night terrors—in fact, anything that seems an appropriate response to the fear that their family is about to be wiped out" (p. 262).

Middle childhood While older children may also regress (Pittman, 1989), they now have the language to express some of their emotions (Lusterman, 1998). They are more aware that the tension in the home could lead to divorce, and worry about how their lives would change if that should happen (Lusterman, 1998). These children may withdraw or act out in an effort to get their parents' attention, stop the affair, or at least prevent a divorce. They may shoplift, vandalize, get into fights, run away, act "hyper," threaten suicide, or set fires to their homes (Lusterman, 1998; Pittman, 1989). Lusterman sees this extreme behavior as children "attempting to make themselves seem so disturbed that their parents will realize that they must stay together" (p. 167).

Pre-adolescent and adolescent children   Older children and adolescents are more apt to learn of a parent's affair and be asked to keep secrets, or to be drawn into the conflict and expected to choose sides (see Duncombe & Marsden, 2004). Children who are pulled into loyalty conflicts and alliances with one parent against another, usually the one they blame for the problems, often experience much anger and resentment.

Affairs are especially difficult for adolescents for two reasons, according to Lusterman (1998). First, they are at the stage of cognitive development that allows them to see the big picture and to think abstractly. They can critically examine the rules and values that they have been taught and asked to live by, and adolescents are highly sensitive to any hypocrisy in parents. Lusterman states, "Woe is the parent who asks an adolescent to do as he says, rather than as he acts—or even worse, the parent whose actions are opposed to his or her stated values" (1998, p. 167). Brown (1999) states that "When a parent falls off the pedestal it changes children's whole conception of who their family is and thus, their sense of who they are" (p. 178). This has implications for the task of identity development, as well as moral development, especially in adolescents.

The second reason that an affair is particularly hard for adolescents is their awareness of their own sexuality (Lusterman, 1998). They may experience problems when confronted with their parents' sexuality at a time when they are dealing with their own emergent sexuality, and they may see an affair as a violation of the generation gap (Duncombe & Marsden, 2004). Adolescents want parents to be role models of a secure relationship where sex remains within the boundaries of the couple (Lusterman, 1998).

Adolescents frequently attempt suicide or hurt themselves in some way, trying to get the parent to leave the affair and focus on them (Pittman, 1989). They are, in effect, asking the parent to choose between them and the affair partner. Pittman points out that "if the parent doesn't give up the affair for them, children feel unloved and betrayed. These children are asking, 'Who is more important? Your child or your affair?'" (p. 262). If the parent refuses to leave the affairee the child can feel abandoned and truly be suicidal (Pittman, 1989). While some adolescents may exhibit externalizing behavior as described above, Reibstein and Richards (1992) point out that the effects on older children or adolescents may be more subtle; "their trust and belief in stable partnerships might be shaken, or their need for refuge in a relationship of their own creation might be forged at that point" (p. 179). Fairy tale beliefs about romance, marriage, and living happily ever after may be deeply shaken (Pittman, 1989), and adolescents may react with withdrawal, depression, despondency, or anger (see Duncombe & Marsden, 2004, p. 190).

When adolescents become either solicitous of one parent or furious with another, they are experiencing a regressive pull back into their parents' relationship "just at the time they were moving out into the world" (Brown, 1999, p. 178). They may "question the values and expectations they were relying on to guide them as they left home" (Brown, 1999, p. 178). These children can feel like the foundation has been knocked out from under them. Leaving home may be difficult if an adolescent is worried about what will happen to a depressed, dependent parent who is left behind (Brown, 1999).

Adult children   Brown (1999) reports that adults whose parents had affairs when they were children experience problems with secrets and an ability to trust, "unresolved anger and pain, disregard for their own feelings, family schisms, relationship problems, and confused boundaries" (p. 182). Adult children who take sides may cut off from the infidel parent, refusing to let their children have any contact with that grandparent, especially if he or she marries the affairee. When the wronged parent's life remains organized around a past affair, he or she stays preoccupied with the betrayal and is vengeful, demanding allegiance from adult children against the unfaithful parent; adult children will have issues of trust and loyalty that cannot help but affect their own marriages and children. Some become very cynical and their outlook on relationships may change so drastically that they may hesitate to marry (see Lusterman, 1998, p. 166), wondering if they are destined to live out their "family scripts" and repeat the mistakes of their parents (Byng-Hall, 1995; Reibstein & Richards, 1992).

Pittman (1989) believes that one of the most common effects of a parent's infidelity is the likelihood that the child will grow up to have affairs. He points out that the environment of children who grow up with the chaos, secrets, deceits, and threats to stability that accompany many affairs is not much different from the environment of children of alcoholics. He states, "Children are not likely to grow up normally surrounded by dishonesty, disorientation, gender obsessions, or the temporary insanity and fugue states of high romance" (Pittman, 1989, p. 267). Adult children may identify with either the parent who was unfaithful, the parent who was a "victim," or the affairee. Thus, they may have affairs, marry someone who is unfaithful, or become involved in affairs with someone who is married. They need to learn to love and trust in order to be a better spouse and parent than their parents were (Pittman, 1989).

Moral and religious development   Children go through stages of moral development (Kohlberg, 1963), and Fowler (1995) argues that there is a strong correlation between moral development and religious development. But parental infidelity can affect both the moral and religious development of children. For example, Kaslow (1993) describes an 18-year-old boy who was trying to adapt to a half brother, his father's son from an affair, who had come to live with them. The son blurted out that his father had raised him by the Ten Commandments and had taught him that sex outside of marriage was wrong. Kaslow states: "He had been in shock since they learned about his dad's affair and about Jose's existence and found it almost impossible to reconcile his dad's behavior with his teachings. He felt ashamed, depressed, baffled and hurt" (1993, p. 21). This affair created a moral and spiritual crisis for this boy who had to grapple with what he had been taught in the face of his father's incongruent behavior.

Attachment   Johnson (2005) uses an attachment framework to discuss how an affair threatens attachment bonds in couples. She states,

> A secure attachment is based on a sense that you exist and are prized in the mind of the other, that you can depend on the other when you need him/her and that this other will cherish and protect rather than reject or abandon you. When this sense is shattered there is a traumatic loss. (p. 19)

Secure attachment bonds are essential to develop a positive model of self (Johnson, 2005), yet children's feelings may mirror the wronged parent's experience of abandonment and subsequent attachment injury (see Johnson, 2002) when there is an affair. Children may even experience a double attachment trauma: They may feel abandoned by both a parent who is wrapped up in an affair and may physically leave, and by the other parent who is preoccupied with his or her own trauma and grief. For this child there might be no reassurances, safety, comfort for the pain, or help making sense of the fundamentally disorganizing events (see Johnson, 2005). Children may exhibit symptoms similar to those reported by adults who develop symptoms of post-traumatic stress reactions in response to an affair (Glass, 2002; Glass & Staeheli, 2003), such as angry outbursts, physiological reactivity, or difficulty sleeping (see Lusterman, 2005a, 2005b). Children may become over-attached to one parent and insecurely attached to the other. These attachment injuries have far-reaching effects as children grow up and attempt to form long-lasting attachments (Brown, 2001).

Losses and grief   All family members experience losses that must be grieved following an affair. The infidel may need to grieve an affair that has ended or is coming to an end (Case, 2005). The wronged spouse who is grappling with the reality of the affair and the depth of the lies and deception needs to grieve the loss of trust and the relationship that he or she thought was there. And if the relationship cannot be repaired and they decide to divorce, both spouses need to grieve the loss of the marriage.

Children are affected by grieving parents (see Biank & Sori, 2006), especially by parents who are so wrapped up in their own grief or ongoing affair that they cannot support them. They may have no one to help them cope and make sense of everything. Children also need to grieve the loss of safety, security, and their previously "normal" family life. They may experience numerous secondary losses if there is a divorce and they will live with one parent and only "visit" the other (who may be living with the affairee), or if they have to move and change schools, leaving friends and all that is familiar behind. The worst losses occur when a child is abandoned by or cut off from the unfaithful parent. If they are abandoned by that parent's extended family they lose important kinship relationships that could have helped to buffer them.

Children need protected space to grieve these losses and to adjust to changes in their lives (Brown, 1999). This process is hindered when a parent prematurely involves children with the affair partner. Brown cautions parents who are living with the third party not to pull children into this "volatile triangle" (p. 181) by forcing children to interact with the affair partner. She believes that children need about six months before they should have any contact with an affairee, and she recommends that parents develop a plan for gradual contact *based on the needs of the children*—not the parents' neediness or jealousy, or on an affairee's insistence on being recognized (Brown, 1999).

Children of philanderers   Children of philanderers may experience many of the effects discussed above; but in addition they are living in a family characterized by an addiction. Many philanderers also have addictions to alcohol (Brown, 1999) and use sex with numerous partners to "numb their inner pain and fill up the emptiness inside, much as alcoholics use alcohol" (Brown, 1999, p. 9). Some of the wives of sex addicts accept their outrageous behavior, put on a brave front, and take responsibility that they should not (Brown, 1999). Hence, both parents become poor role models for their sons and daughters.

Philanderers may be either male or female, although they are most often men (Pittman, 1989). Lusterman (2005a) states that "womanizers are generally personality-disordered men, usually narcissistically deprived" (p. 1447), and that unlike conjoint treatment for affairs, philanderers need many individual sessions to work on their personal issues that lie at the heart of their womanizing. Philanderers may claim that they have a wonderful marriage and can't seem to understand the detrimental effects of their behavior on spouses and children (Kaslow, 1993). According to Pittman (1989), these men are obsessed with gender and gender stereotypes, and view women as trophies or property for men to own. Treatment for these families is difficult and complex.

This leads to the obvious question of how children of both genders might be affected by a parent who is a philanderer. Boys are at risk when fathers seek an alliance with their sons, bragging about their escapades, and asking sons to hide the affairs from their mother (Lusterman, 1998; Pittman, 1989). Sons may be recruited to actively cover up affairs and provide philandering fathers with alibis for their trysts. These sons often experience loyalty conflicts, a sense of duty and protectiveness toward the mother, and an ambivalent alliance with the father. They are at risk to grow up to become philanderers (Pittman, 1989, p. 262). But if sons learn of their father's philandering from someone other than the father, they may be repelled by this behavior and feel protective toward their mother (Lusterman, 1998; Pittman, 1989). The daughters of philanderers are also at risk to either have affairs or marry womanizers (Lusterman, 1998, p. 164).

Culture   No discussion on infidelity is complete without examining cultural influences on affairs that can impact children. Snyder (2005) discusses how social norms regarding infidelity vary across cultures. For example, Lusterman (2005a) describes a case where a distressed 16-year-old Asian client who suspected her father was having an affair could not tell her mother because this would be seen as a sign of great disrespect in her culture. Kaslow (1993) discusses how men in some cultures divide women into two categories: "Madonnas," the "good" respectable women men should marry to bear their children; and "whores," or "bad" sexual temptresses whom men pursue to seek the decadent sex that is not suitable with a Madonna wife.

From this we see the importance of exploring clients' cultural backgrounds, individual attitudes, and beliefs about extramarital sex. Children learn both explicitly and implicitly what an affair means in their culture and in their family. These beliefs and attitudes influence children's gender roles and how they view power, love, and fidelity in relationships. We should not judge clients but should be culturally sensitive, and help clients explore what legacies they want to leave their children as they deal with an affair.*

ADDITIONAL CONSEQUENCES OF AFFAIRS

Aside from the trauma of learning of parental infidelity and witnessing the subsequent marital conflict that often follows, there can be other serious consequences with which parents and children must grapple. It is not uncommon for a child to be born from an affair, whom the father will have to support. This can mean the loss of time, attention, and resources for the children of the marriage. The affair child may grow up with great financial and emotional insecurity, ashamed of his or her second-class status, feeling "not as good as" the father's children by his marriage. These children may be used as leverage by an affair mother who tries to get the married infidel to leave his wife. She may also blackmail the father by threatening to disclose the existence of the child to his wife or children (see Kaslow, 1993, for an excellent discussion on affair children).

Sometimes the affair partner even convinces the spouse to take the child into the family and raise it with their other children (Kaslow, 1993). If blackmail doesn't work the mother may offer to give up custody, or a father may not like how his child is being raised and take the child after paying the woman off. Kaslow (1993) discusses some of the dynamics of these families and the effects on the affair child (who may be resented by the nonbiological parent and half siblings, and be grieving the loss of a biological parent), as well as on the emo-

---

* *Editor's note*: Please see Chapter 10 for a discussion of the impact of culture on infidelity.

tions of siblings that may be overlooked as the family attempts to reorganize and adapt to the presence of a child of an affair. Children may experience shame and humiliation if the story of their half-sibling becomes known, resentment at the attention the child receives, and anger at one or both parents.

Suicide is another serious consequence that can occur when a child is born of an affair. Kaslow (1993) describes a case where a mother gave birth to a biracial baby after an affair. Her husband and children were shocked, but were all trying to work through the humiliation and anger when the mother, increasingly despondent, took her own life. The children were left to make sense of the event and to cope with grief and abandonment issues, while trying not to blame an innocent child for their mother's death.

I have supervised several cases where a spouse learned of an affair after being diagnosed with an STD or learning the infidel had AIDS. This can have far-reaching effects when the spouse is pregnant and the health of the unborn child is jeopardized. Another phenomenon is when a parent has a secret second family (Reibstein & Richards, 1992, p. 134). This can shake a child's world and profoundly affect his/her sense of reality.

ASSESSING CHILDREN

Expert panelists in a study by Sori and Sprenkle (2004) agreed that children should *not* be included in sessions when sensitive topics, such as adult sexual issues, are being discussed. However, panelists in this study also stressed that children need to be included in therapy at some point to assess the effect of the problems on them (Sori, 2006c; Sori & Sprenkle, 2004). It is important to assess the child in the context of the family along several dimensions. These include the following:

- How was the child functioning *before* the affair at home and at school (academically, psychologically, socially, and emotionally)?
- What was the quality of the marital relationship *before* the affair became known?
- How did the family function prior to the affair?
- What has the child been told, how, by whom, and how did the child respond?
- What do family members and friends know about the affair? How did they react?
- Are there any parent-child coalitions in the family?
- How contentious are the parents, and are they working toward either a reconciliation or a cordial divorce?
- How is each parent coping and functioning in their roles, and how available are they to meet the child(ren)'s needs?
- What other stressors are this child and family experiencing; is this a multi-crisis family (see Minuchin, Colapinto, & Minuchin, 1998)?

- What sources of outside support are available and being utilized by the child and the parents?
- How extensively has the child's daily life been impacted, and what losses have been incurred? How are these losses being grieved?
- Does the child have contact with both parents, and has the child been given time to adjust to the changes without pressure to interact with an affairee?

CONSIDERATIONS ON DISCLOSURE

Disclosing to a spouse   Clinicians should help clients consider the possible effects on children when an affair is disclosed to a partner. Secrets can indeed be harmful, but it is prudent to assess the possibility that a wronged spouse might become violent, physically abusive, suicidal, or even homicidal (see Lerner, 1993, p. 172). For example, care should be taken when disclosing to a spouse who has an alcohol or drug abuse problem, is depressed, suicidal, has a history of violence or abuse, or has a psychological disorder. The possibility that the wronged partner may seek revenge directly on the spouse or through the children should be carefully explored and considered in helping clients decide whether to disclose, or in developing a disclosure plan.

Disclosing an affair to children   Parents often err in one of two ways in deciding to reveal an affair to children (Brown, 1999). They may hesitate to burden their children, or believe children are clueless and show no signs of distress. "They are afraid their kids can't handle knowing, that they'll be devastated, that their grades will go down. They also feel ashamed and worry that telling the truth will irretrievably damage their relationship with the child" (Brown, 1999, p. 172). Other parents go to the opposite extreme—especially if the affair partner is leaving the marriage: "They insist that the children should know how untrustworthy and awful the other parent is. Both approaches are seriously flawed" (Brown, 1999, p. 172).

Privacy versus secrecy   In helping parents decide how much to disclose to children it is important to discuss the differences between privacy and secrecy. A *secret* is something that may be shared with some people or withheld from others (Lusterman, 2005a). Information kept within the family or within the couple subsystem may be considered *private*. A secret is something that cannot be spoken about, but people may declare that an aspect of their life or a topic is private, which they choose not to discuss (Lusterman, 1998). To lie and tell children who are worried or stressed that "everything is fine" is creating an *environment of secrecy*. It may be better for parents to admit there is a problem, but that it is private—just between mommy and daddy—at least for the time being (Lusterman, 1998).

Parents need to carefully consider how relevant the disclosure of an affair is to children, according to Lusterman (1998). Lusterman believes it may not be appropriate to tell young children about sexual unfaithfulness, but may be more prudent to explain that the parents have been fighting quite a bit lately, and that they are trying to work it out and are going to a therapist to help them get along better. However, parents may decide to offer more information to an adolescent who is questioning or struggling to understand what is happening, or is stressed about relationship issues (Lusterman, 1998).

The ultimate test is always the question of *what is in the best interests of the children* (Lusterman, 1998). When a parent shares information about the other parent's affair to win the allegiance of a child, this is a boundary violation "making something best kept *private* a *secret*" (Lusterman, 1998, p. 168). Parents should evaluate how mature a child is, how he or she might respond to the news, and how they can minimize the negative effects and best help the child survive the crisis (Lusterman, 1998).

In General, Don't Tell Children

There is a strong consensus in the field that it is probably better for parents *not* to disclose an affair to children. Siegler (1994) suggests that parents should try to shield their children from the knowledge of problems that have nothing to do with them, such as extramarital affairs and sexual issues. This position is supported by research by Sori and Sprenkle (2004), where expert panelists reached consensus that children should not be included in family sessions when parents are discussing adult sexual issues. These findings suggest that parents should use extreme caution in deciding to disclose parental infidelity to children unless it seems necessary.

According to Lusterman, "Unless there is pressing need" (1998, p. 169), or a child believes a parent is having an affair (Lusterman, 2005a), it is generally not advisable to tell children about an infidelity. Younger children may know something is amiss, but cannot really comprehend the concept of infidelity, and any decision about what to tell children must consider the child's level of development (Lusterman, 2005a). Parents should not burden children with adult information they do not understand or are not ready to hear (Lusterman, 2005a). Glass and Staeheli (2003) believe that parents should tell their children as little as possible about an affair. They see two exceptions to this position: (1) if a child has overheard the parents discussing the infidelity or has found evidence of an affair; or (2) if the child is likely to learn about it in the news or from outsiders (Glass & Staeheli, 2003, p. 329).

But children do need to be told something. If not, they will use their imagination, and often what they imagine is worse than reality. They may blame themselves for the problems they sense in the family. But if everyone has been discreet and it is unlikely that children will learn of the affair, children might simply be told that their parents are having marital problems (Lusterman,

1998) or have adult problems that are making it difficult for them to love each other or get along (Siegler, 1994).

However, often parents are *not* discreet (Siegler, 1994). Children may have overheard whispered accusations, may have discovered the affair for themselves, or overheard others talking about it. Siegler is correct in suggesting, "Once a child has picked up clues about the problems in the marriage, it's best to offer her a chance to ask her questions and to construct a narrative that helps her to understand what has happened" (p. 137). This may or may not mean explaining one parent has had an affair.

GUIDELINES ON DECIDING TO TELL CHILDREN

The following are some criteria to guide parents in making decisions about telling a child about parental infidelity. In general, children should probably be told under the following circumstances:

There is a probability the child will find out   This might occur if parents have discussed the affair when children are home (see Siegler, 1994, p. 137), if it is even remotely possible that the affair partner might call the house, if the affair is known to anyone outside the family, if the affairee is a close friend or relative, if children of both the infidel and affairee go to the same school or know each other (see Brown, 2001), or if there is the possibility of gossip or a public scandal. Brown (1999) states:

> If *anyone* else knows about the affair, if there is the *slightest* chance a child might hear about it, or the parent is living with the third party, then children need to hear about the affair from their parents. You can prevent the additional betrayal of allowing your child to bump into the affair accidentally. (p. 175)

Parents should also consider what the legacy of the secret might be (Brown, 2001).

A child is born of the affair   Sometimes parents may think they can shield children from this knowledge, but Kaslow (1993) offers several cases where children eventually learned they had a half-sibling, either from a phone call from the mistress, or when the mistress gave up custody to the father and the child came to live with the family. Children who learn they have a half-sibling who was kept hidden for several years experience a compound sense of betrayal, distrust, and anger that can be quite damaging and affect their ability to form trusting relationships as adults. In addition, parents should consider children's rights to know that they have another sibling.

The child is an adolescent   Adolescents are especially attuned to sexual innuendos and may have guessed what is wrong, even when parents have been very discreet. Do not assume that the child is ignorant or doesn't suspect. An adolescent may have overheard parents fighting and sense it is about an affair, they may have found clues, or even seen the affair partners together (see Brown, 2001; Siegler, 1994). What they worry about the most is whether the marriage will survive (Brown, 2001). They deserve the opportunity to ask questions and receive honest, age-appropriate answers.

The affair parent is moving in with the affairee   Brown (1999) believes that when this occurs children need to know where and with whom the parent will be living. However, extreme care should be taken not to expose children to the affairee until they have had time to adjust to the losses and changes in their lives.

HOW TO TALK WITH CHILDREN ABOUT AN AFFAIR

When children are aware of problems in the family, their experiences need to be validated. They need to be told something, and what, how, and by whom they are told is crucial. What is said and the manner in which the information is conveyed, as well as who is included and excluded in these initial conversations, has tremendous influence on how the children make sense of the affair and its implications.

Clinicians should work with parents to decide what to tell children as soon as possible (Brown, 2001). Parents may need to plan with the therapist what to say, and how to stay calm when talking with children. If possible, it is best if both parents talk to the child. Parents need to keep the child's best interest at heart, and children should not be put in the position of having to take sides.

GUIDELINES FOR TELLING CHILDREN IN
AN AGE-APPROPRIATE MANNER

Parents should not give children details that they don't need to know, or that are beyond their ability to comprehend (see Cole, 1999; Duncombe & Marsden, 2004), and children should then be given an opportunity to share their reactions and ask questions. They need to know if parents are working to improve the marriage and work through the affair issues, if they are in therapy, if they are planning to separate and divorce, or if they honestly don't yet know what is going to happen (Brown, 1999). Children also need to be reassured that they are and always will be loved (Duncombe & Marsden, 2004). Above all, "they need their parents to face the real issues rather than hold the children hostage in a war that cannot be won" (Brown, 2001, p. 271).

How parents discuss problems related to infidelity is crucial. Brown (1999) believes children usually either hear too much or learn too little. Telling a child too much often invites the child to take care of the parent. But when children know something is going on but aren't given any plausible information, they feel confused and tense, with no one to talk to or no idea of how to handle the tension and situation.

The following are some recommendations for parents on talking to their children about an affair in an age-appropriate manner.

Infants and toddlers   Children this young cannot comprehend through a verbal explanation what is causing the tension they feel. Young children need physical reassurance, to be held and soothed by each parent, and less tension in the home (Brown, 1999, p. 175). Glass and Staehli (2003) suggest giving preschoolers a simple explanation, such as, "Mommy and Daddy have some disagreements that have nothing to do with you. We both still love you, so you don't have to worry" (p. 329).

Young children   Four- to seven-year-olds also do not have the cognitive development to understand infidelity, so parents of young children should not offer a detailed explanation of an affair. Brown (1999) suggests they might simply be told that one parent is upset because the other is spending a lot of time with a friend.

Middle childhood   Although children from about 8 to 11 may have some understanding of what an affair is, it is probably adequate to offer them the same explanation as younger children (Brown, 1999). Grade-school children are tuned in to both tensions and secrets, and they probably have friends whose parents are divorced, so they may fear their parents will also separate. It is important to ask children what they are aware of and what their fears are, reassuring them, if at all possible, that although the parents are having problems they want to stay together (Glass & Staehli, 2003).   If there is to be a separation, Siegler (1994) suggests telling older children (from 9 to 12) something that confirms their reality. This might be that the parents are not in love like they were when they first married. Children should be reassured that they are still loved, and parents should empathize with how difficult this is for them. They should be allowed to freely express their anger or sadness, ask questions, and be told they don't have to take sides (Siegler, 1994).

Preteens and adolescents   Children from age 12 and up can probably comprehend the meaning of infidelity. Adolescents experiencing their own sexuality are more apt to suspect an affair (Glass & Staehli, 2003). If asked directly about infidelity, without going into detail a parent might concede, "Yes, Dad got too friendly with another woman, but he realizes that he really loves me and wants us to stay together" (Glass & Staehli, 2003, p. 330). Brown (1999) suggests that they be told the truth in very simple words, such as "I'm involved in an affair with a woman at work" (p. 175).

If a parent decides to leave, adolescents may be told something that corresponds to their reality of the parents' relationship. Adolescents might be told the parents no longer love each other, or if there is a long history of conflict, that they cannot resolve their differences, and that one is involved with someone else. Of course adolescents should also be reassured that they are not to blame and that they will always be loved.

TREATMENT

Whenever a child is brought for counseling for any reason clinicians should be alert to the possibility of a secret affair. A child's symptoms may be in reaction to the tension of an undisclosed affair; the child may have accidentally learned of the affair, or been told by the infidel and asked to keep the affair secret. Tell-tale signs that might signal a hidden affair include a strong parent-child coalition, sudden unexplained changes in a child's behavior, or an air of secrecy that suggests the child might be hiding something. In any of these scenarios the child may be the ticket to getting the family in to counseling so the affair can be unearthed and addressed. Lusterman (1998) points out that a child's symptoms may be a wake-up call to a parent to end the secrecy and address both the infidelity and marital issues (p. 163).

Multi-modal approach   While children should be offered individual time where they can express their feelings without fear of upsetting their parents, family sessions can be extremely helpful early in the game to head off any developing coalitions, or to begin to extricate children from any coalitions. Other goals include removing children from the middle of parental conflict and helping them talk to their parents about the future.

If a child is holding a secret the first step in treatment may be to detriangulate the child by helping the infidel to tell the spouse, thus freeing the child from an untenable position. While much individual and marital work will follow, it is vital that children's needs be met, and this often requires a multi-modal approach. In addition to sessions with each parent and the couple, this may include individual sessions with each child, sessions with siblings, and sessions with one and/or both parents and the child(ren). Decisions on who to see should be based on the needs of individuals and the family as they progress through therapy (see Bailey & Sori, 2000; Sori, Dermer, & Wesolowski, 2006). Treatment will be more complicated when the infidelity is from a sexual addiction, especially if there are co-morbid addictions.

Theoretical Approaches

Family play therapy is a meta-theory that is developmentally well suited to children, and can be integrated with any of the major theories of family therapy, including structural family therapy (Minuchin, 1974), experiential (Keith & Whitaker, 1981), and postmodern theories (see Dermer, Olund, &

Sori, 2006). Family play therapy (Gil, 1994; Gil & Sobol, 2000; Gil interview in Sori, 2006a) offers clinicians methods to observe family interactions
and communication patterns and to assess relationships, and is beneficial to
adults as well as children. Families who are stressed or depleted often change
dramatically as they play together, and these techniques can help therapists
breathe life back into sessions (Sori, 2006a). Both the process of how families
play together and the content of their play are beneficial in assessing and
treating families with children. In family play therapy clinicians can observe
the family process: how they talk to one another, who is closer to whom,
whose ideas are utilized, and whose are ignored. Also important to note is
the family's ability to organize around a playful task, their level of enjoyment,
and how a family handles any conflict that arises (Gil & Sobol, 2000). The
content of their play (e.g., the artwork or sandtray) is often a rich metaphoric
representation of what the family is experiencing (see Sori, 2006a).

The following are some general overarching goals and guidelines for integrating individual play therapy and family play therapy in the treatment of
children who are coping with parental infidelity. Many of these interventions
appeal to children from age 6 up through adolescents and adulthood. These
approaches may be especially useful with children and families who have a
difficult time talking about issues related to an affair, as some offer nonverbal, creative methods of self-expression. Clinicians should use their judgment
on the timing of family sessions. Play activities should be stopped if parents
revert to contentious behavior, and resumed when the couple is able to focus
on the needs of the child(ren).

Goal 1: Reinforcing generational boundaries   Generational boundaries
often become blurred when an affair occurs. Parents may tell children secrets,
seeking an alliance with their children; or parents may lean too heavily on
their child(ren) for emotional support. Structural interventions that break up
coalitions and encourage parents to parent appropriately are especially helpful (Minuchin, 1974).

Integrating family play therapy interventions   Art can be especially useful
to clinicians in assessing the structure of a family following an affair. Children can be asked to draw their family doing something, and these pictures
often reveal the structure of the family and the relationships among family
members (see Sori, 1995). For example, one child whose father had moved
in with his affair partner was having trouble sleeping. In a session with her
mother she drew a picture of her family doing something. On one side of the
paper she drew her mother and herself standing close together inside their
house. On the other side of the paper she drew her father standing close to
his affair partner, and she was below them at the bottom of the page. Initially
she had drawn smiles on all the faces, but as she talked about the picture and
what it was like for her to go back and forth between the two homes, she was

able to finally express her despair. She took a black marker and drew heavy frowns over the smiles on her own and her mother's face. This activity helped the child to finally express her feelings, especially about being expected to accept the affairee when she visited dad, and her worry if her mother was okay when she was gone. The picture was useful to begin addressing the coalition between mother and child and the child's loyalty conflict, to motivate mom to reassure her daughter she was okay when she visited dad's, and to work with the father to allow his daughter time to adjust before involving her with his affair partner.

Structural enactments (Minuchin, 1974) can be conducted playfully. For example, the therapist may ask each family member to select a puppet and then use the puppets to enact a problem, and then to discuss a sensitive issue. It is often easier for children and adults alike to discuss problems indirectly, through a metaphor or using a puppet (Gil, 1994), than to directly tackle a hot topic, such as an affair. During a playful enactment the therapist may observe the process of the family as they interact, and hypothesize about the structure, boundaries, relationships, coalitions, and so on in the family.

Puppets can also be used in a more structured way in a family puppet interview (Irwin & Malloy, 1994), where families select puppets and make up a story that has a beginning, a middle, and an end, but which is not a story known to the family. Not only is the family's process revealed through this playful intervention, but the story is often a rich metaphor that reflects each family member's experience with the problem that brought them to therapy (Gil & Sobol, 2000).

I was supervising a case live that involved a separated mother and her two children, who had recently revealed the secret that "Mr. Peepers" was living in the attic. In a family puppet interview the story involved two chattering squirrels who were upset that a fox was living in a hole in their tree. The children's puppets confronted their mother's bunny puppet with "the truth" about her relationship with "Mr. Fox," and their puppets let her know that it wasn't fair for them to keep this a secret from their father. The counselor-in-training stayed in the metaphor, using the puppets to engage the mother and children in a discussion about the secret of her relationship with "Mr. Fox." This was a turning point in the case, and following this session the mother decided to ask Mr. Peepers to move out so the children weren't in a loyalty conflict over holding a secret.

Goal 2: Help children express their feelings and open family communication   Children may have a difficult time expressing their emotions or discussing their feelings either because they lack the cognitive and language development, or because there may be a "no talk" rule in the family, which is especially likely if there are secrets regarding an affair. Children need help to be able to make sense of what they are feeling, and then to articulate their reactions and pose questions to parents who are ready and able to respond.

Playful interventions are especially useful to meet the goal of helping children express their feelings and to open family communication.

Integrating play therapy and family play therapy interventions   Therapists may meet with children alone to help them first identify and then normalize their emotions regarding a parent's affair. Books or feeling charts can be used to offer children a vocabulary for emotions. Biank and Sori (2003) discuss the importance of teaching children that they can have more than one feeling simultaneously, and that there are both "inside" feelings (that we keep hidden from others) and "outside" feelings (like masks that we put on to hide the inside feelings). Children can discuss how they feel about their parent's affair, and draw their hidden inside feelings and the corresponding visible outside feelings. With children's permission these drawings can be brought back into a family session and used to facilitate an enactment between children and their parents. One child's inside feelings were of anxiety, fear, and sadness; the corresponding faces were all happy faces. Parents are often shocked to learn how their children are putting on a happy front to hide their real emotions. This activity can be useful to motivate parents to address their own problems and to recognize that their children need help in coping.

A body trace (Selekman, 2000) or body drawing (Sori & Biank, 2003a) is a useful activity to help children pinpoint physical reactions to stress and fear in their bodies. Parents who think their children are "fine" or don't know anything is going on are often surprised when their children reveal how many somatic reactions they are experiencing.

One case I supervised live consisted of Mexican-American parents and their two children, a son aged 7 and a daughter, aged 9. The father had been having a long-term affair and had two children from that relationship. The parents would fight, and the father would then leave and move in with his affair partner for a few weeks. When things would settle down he would return to his family. The children were aware that their father had a "girlfriend" and other children, and although the parents thought they were "just fine" they agreed to bring them to a session. In that session the counselor-in-training utilized Selekman's (2000) body trace, having the children lie on large sheets of newspaper ends and trace each other's bodies. They were then told they could draw in any feelings or thoughts they had that they felt in different parts of the bodies. The 9-year-old girl drew large question marks and the words "Will Daddy leave and not come home anymore?" on her stomach, head, and heart. Both children drew bright colors and symbols on various parts of their bodies that represented their "worry," "sadness," and "fear" that dad would go away and they'd never see him again. The parents were shocked and saddened to learn of the profound effect dad's affair and apparent ambivalence was having on the children. While they were talking the son went to the whiteboard and drew a heart that was broken in two, with the words "mommy" and "daddy" under each half of his heart. This session contained a defining moment for the couple, and helped the father jump off the fence. Although he decided to divorce his wife for his affair partner and her children, we were able to help him realize the importance of staying connected to his first children and of developing a workable co-parenting relationship. We were also able to help the children and their mother adjust to all the losses and changes.

Goal 3: Reduce children's anxiety   Anxiety is "catching" and anxious children often have an anxious parent. Steps should be taken to help both adults and children express their anxiety and learn ways to cope and to reduce their levels of stress. One of the most direct ways children are helped is to have parents reassure them that they are loved, will be taken care of, and that their parents are working on their problems.

Integrating play therapy interventions   In addition to talk therapy, there are playful approaches to reducing stress in children. As discussed above, therapists can have family members use puppets, for example, using an enactment where a mommy puppet reassures baby puppet that she will be taken care of and is loved. From this it is easy to have a mother hold a child, talking softly to her to soothe her stress.

Relaxation training is an excellent way to reduce stress in children and parents. "Soaring Above Stress" (Sori & Biank, 2003b) offers guidelines on using deep muscle relaxation, breathing techniques, and visualization with children. This intervention has been used extensively with children experiencing illness and loss, and is also effective with children and parents dealing with an affair. It is especially beneficial when combined with soft, soothing music, which helps to lower blood pressure, and increases the release of endorphins that promote feelings of well-being. Many children love this activity and insist one or both parents do it with them every night. This promotes better sleep, and can strengthen attachment bonds between parents and children.

Sometimes parents are not yet emotionally available to help their children cope. Violet Oaklander (Carlson & Keat, 2002) demonstrates how clay can be useful in individual sessions to unveil children's underlying anxiety. Children can pound clay while expressing their feelings; they can mold clay figures of family members, and the child can then "talk through" his clay figure, expressing his emotions to each figure. Oaklander (Carlson & Keat, 2002) also believes it is important for children to make lists of what children can do when anxious. She emphasizes that children should not repress their feelings, but experience them while doing the things on the list, such as calling a friend, shooting baskets, or journaling.

Goal 4: Adjust to changes and express their grief   Children often go through many changes in their family when a parent has an affair, especially if the parents separate. They need time and assistance in adjusting to these changes, which may include many secondary losses that need to be grieved.

This need can be overlooked and hampered by parents who are preoccupied with their own adjustment and grief issues.

Integrating play therapy and family play therapy interventions   Sand play is excellent for clients to process changes in their lives, and can be used with individual children, couples, and families. Clients may be asked to "build a world in the sand" using miniatures. Children or families could do a series of sandtrays, such as "build your world before the affair," "build your world now," and "build your world as it will be when you have worked through this problem." This last sandtray can be used from a postmodern position (see Dermer, Olund, & Sori, 2006), as families concretely depict how that world will be when trust and safety are restored. This future sandtray can be used to help families establish concrete goals, such as what steps need to be taken to build boundaries around the couple and family. The content of the sandtray is also important, as the miniatures selected often have unconscious symbolic meaning that clinicians can explore (see Sori, 2006a). The appearance of sandtrays reflects the emotional climate of the home; some are sparse or barren, with few signs of life; others appear chaotic and are crammed full of figures. Children may portray the threat they feel from an affair by having many symbols of danger with few signs of boundaries, protection, defense, or enjoyment. Both the process and content of sandtrays reveal much about the boundaries and emotional climate in the family, and offer clinicians a sense of how family life feels for children who may not be able to convey this with words.

Goal 5: Promote the utilization of outside support   Having a warm, supportive relationship with an emotionally stable caregiver helps buffer children who are at risk (Klimes-Dougan & Kendziora, 2000). Children may need support from other adults when a parent is obsessed with an affair, until the parents are able to focus on the children (Brown, 1999, p. 178). This person may be a grandparent or someone else close to the child. Klimes-Dougan and Kendziora (2000) also discuss the importance of support within the community in promoting resiliency in at risk-children. Supportive, mentoring relationships in the community may include teachers, scout leaders, religious leaders, coaches, neighbors, or extended family members. Children can also be taught new ways to cope with family stress, and parents can be helped to understand and be more supportive of stressed children.

Integrating play therapy and family play therapy interventions   Clinicians can help children identify and foster outside supportive relationships to enhance their resiliency (Klimes-Dougan & Kendziora, 2000). Biank and Sori (in press) describe an activity called "Coping Circles" where children identify who is in their circle of support, including family, friends, and neighbors. Children may list what they do with each person that helps them feel supported, and they could also draw pictures of themselves with these people.

A kinetic drawing could be integrated with Gil's (2003) idea of the play geno-gram. Children could be given a sheet of paper on which a small circle is drawn within a larger circle. The small circle represents the child, who is asked to write the names of people who support him/her in the larger circle. Next, children may select a miniature that "best represents their thoughts and feelings" (see Gil, 2003) for themselves and for each person in their circle. Clinicians might simply note the figures selected, or discuss the child's relationship with each person, what the selected figure means to the child, and how the child's figure relates to each of the other figures. It is important to notice who is represented and who is omitted, and the proximity of the placement of the figures to the child's figure. Parents can also do this "kinetic play" activity, which can help them identify who is in their own circle of support and how they might develop more supportive relationships. Parents and children may share their "kinetic play" boards with one another; this can alert parents to the child's need for more contact with some of the people represented, and can also reassure children that their parent has other people (besides the child) to turn to for support. This can begin to free children from feeling responsible for a needy, dependent parent.

OTHER TREATMENT CONSIDERATIONS

While the focus of this chapter has been on helping children within the con-text of their families, one of the best ways to help children is by helping their parents—to reduce the child's exposure to marital conflict, and to help them deal with the affair and its aftermath. This includes helping parents to commu-nicate with one another, to understand the needs of their children, and what they can do to support and help their children (Brown, 2001). Therapists may use a feminist family therapy lens to address issues of sexism, power imbal-ances, and male privilege, and to help parents take responsibility for their own behavior (see Goodrich, 1991; Goodrich, Rampage, Ellman, & Halstead, 1988; Kaslow, 1993; Walters, Carter, Papp, & Silverstein, 1988). Patterns of infidelity across generations must be explored for both partners (Bowen, 1978), and a contextual approach (Boszormenyi-Nagy & Krasner, 1986) that utilizes multi-partiality and helps partners exonerate their own parents helps to balance the intergenerational ledger. These transgenerational approaches can help free children from the intergenerational legacy of infidelity.

Apologizing and forgiveness   Treating couples for infidelity is a complex issue, but at the core of rebuilding a relationship damaged by an affair is the importance of reestablishing trust. Central to this process is the need for the affair partner to offer heartfelt, sincere apologies to the wronged partner (Case, 2005; Kaslow, 1993), which lays the foundation for the wronged partner to begin the process of forgiveness or exoneration. However, it is also impor-tant for therapists to work with the unfaithful parent toward the goal of also apologizing to the children and taking responsibility for the lies, secrecy, and behavior that have caused pain, insecurity, anger, anxiety, and other reactions in the children (see Kaslow, 1993, p. 21).

Rebuilding attachment injuries   One excellent method of helping parents help their children cope with their emotions following infidelity, and to strengthen attachment bonds that may have been injured when a child felt abandoned by a parent, is Filial Therapy (VanFleet, 1994; see interview with VanFleet in Sori, 2006b). This approach trains parents to do nondirective play therapy with their own children, and has been shown to be effective in treating a wide range of internalizing and externalizing behaviors in children.

Addressing spiritual issues   Clinicians need to explore how infidelity may have affected children's views about their religious or spiritual upbringing. This is a sensitive topic that might be introduced by doing a variation of Gil's (2003) play genogram: a spiritual play genogram (Sori, in press). Using a three-generation genogram, children individually or with parents select miniatures to represent their thoughts and feelings about each person's spiritual or religious beliefs and practices. The miniatures chosen often reveal much about how the child views his own spirituality and that of both parents. This activity can open conversation about beliefs that may have been transmitted or changed across generations, which can help ground children whose beliefs may have been shaken. Religious figures in the child's life, such as a pastor or Sunday School teacher, may also be included. This may open the door for the child to raise questions to these leaders.

SELF OF THE THERAPIST ISSUES

The topic of infidelity is an emotionally loaded issue for therapists as well as the clients that they serve. Clinicians need to be aware of their own individual and family of origin issues around affairs, and to carefully monitor their reactions to all parties involved. The expert panelists in the Sori and Sprenkle (2004) study cautioned therapists who work with children to avoid rescuing children from bad parents, and this holds true when children are caught in the crossfire of parental hostility after an affair. Sometimes there is "no one except the therapist" who can advocate for the children (Kaslow, 1993, p. 18). This points to the need for good supervision and perhaps even one's own therapy to uphold ethical standards, to maintain therapist neutrality, to deal with countertransference issues (Kaslow, 1993), and to be effective in counseling these children and families.

CONCLUSION

The best outcome for children is when parents can repair their relationship following an affair, and "perceive the affair as a warning and work seriously to resolve the underlying individual and marital problems" (Brown, 2001, p. 294). If parents do decide to divorce, the next best outcome is for them to resolve as many issues as possible, and to separate in a manner that is the least harmful to the children. Often much of the marital work may involve helping the couple to decide which course of action to take. In either event, children must be assessed to see how they are being impacted by the infidelity, and included as part of the overall treatment plan.

REFERENCES

Achenbach, T. M. (1992). *Manual for the children behavior checklist/2-3 and 1992 profile*. Burlington: University of Vermont, Department of Psychiatry.

Amato, P. R. (1994). Life-span adjustment of children to their parents' divorces. *Future of Children, 25,* 1031–1042.

Amato, P. R., & Rogers, S. J. (1997). A longitudinal study of marital problems and subsequent divorce. *Journal of Marriage and the Family, 58,* 612–624.

Bailey, C. E., & Sori, C. E. F. (2000). Involving parents in children's therapy. In C. E. Bailey (Ed.), *Children in therapy: Using the family as a resource* (pp. 475–502). New York: Norton.

Biank, N., & Sori, C. F. (2003). Feeling faces prevent scary places. In C. F. Sori, L. L. Hecker, & Associates, *The therapist's notebook for children and adolescents: Homework, handouts, and activities for use in psychotherapy* (pp. 3–8). New York: Haworth Press.

Biank, N., & Sori, C. F. (2006). Helping children cope with the death of a family member. In C. Sori (Ed.), *Engaging children in family therapy: Creative approaches to integrating theory and research in clinical practice* (pp. 245–262). New York: Routledge.

Biank, N., & Sori, C. F. (in press). Coping circles: Exploring children's ability to manage in times of stress. In C. Elias & L. Jameyfield (Eds.), *The therapist's notebook: Resources for working with children*. New York: Haworth Press.

Boszormenyi-Nagy, I., & Krasner, B. R. (1986). *Between give and take: A clinical guide to contextual therapy*. New York: Brunner/Mazel.

Bowen, M. (1978). *Family therapy in clinical practice*. New York: Jason Aronson.

Brown, E. M. (1991). Children and affairs: Issues and interventions. In E. M. Brown, *Patterns of infidelity and their treatment* (pp. 245–304). New York: Brunner/Mazel.

Brown, E. M. (1999). *Affairs: A guide to working through the repercussions of infidelity*. San Francisco: Jossey-Bass.

Brown, E. M. (2001). Children and affairs: Issues and interventions. In E. M. Brown, *Patterns of infidelity and their treatment* (2nd ed., pp. 269–295). New York: Brunner-Routledge.

Byng-Hall, J. (1995). *Rewriting family scripts: Improvisation and systems change*. New York: Guilford Press.

Carlson, J., & Keat, D. B. (2002). *Gestalt therapy with Violet Oaklander: Child therapy with the experts video*. New York: Allyn & Bacon.

Case, B. (2005). Healing the wounds of infidelity through the healing power of apology and forgiveness. In F. P. Piercy, K. M. Hertlein, & J. L. Wetchler (Eds.), *Handbook of the clinical treatment of infidelity* (pp. 41–54). New York: Haworth Press.

Cole, J. (1999). *After the affair.* London: Vermillion.

Dermer, S., Olund, D., & Sori, C. F. (2006). Integrating play in family therapy theories. In C. Sori (Ed.), *Engaging children in family therapy: Creative approaches to integrating theory and research in clinical practice* (pp. 37–65). New York: Routledge.

Duncombe, J., & Marsden, D. (2004). Affairs and children. In J. Duncombe, K. Harrison, G. Allan, & D. Marsden (Eds.), *The state of affairs: Explorations in infidelity and commitment* (pp. 187–201). Mahwah, NJ: Erlbaum.

Fowler, J. W. (1995). *Stages of faith: The psychology of human development and the quest for meaning.* San Francisco: HarperCollins.

Gil, E. (1994). *Play in family therapy.* New York: Guilford Press.

Gil, E. (2003). Play genograms. In C. F. Sori, L. L. Hecker, and Associates, *The therapist's notebook for children and adolescents: Homework, handouts, and activities for use in psychotherapy* (pp. 49–56). Binghamton, NY: Haworth Press.

Gil, E., & Sobol, B. (2000). Engaging families in therapeutic play. In C. E. Bailey (Ed.), *Children in therapy: Using the family as a resource* (pp. 341–392). New York: Norton.

Glass, S. P. (2002). Couple therapy after the trauma of infidelity. In A. S. Gurman & N. S. Jacobson (Eds.), *Clinical handbook of couple therapy* (pp. 488–507). New York: Guilford Press.

Glass, S. P., & Staeheli, J. C. (2003). *Not "just friends": Rebuilding trust and recovering your sanity after infidelity.* New York: The Free Press.

Glass, S., & Wright, T. L. (1992). Justifications for extramarital involvement: The association between attitudes, behaviors, and gender. *Journal of Sex Research, 29*(3), 361–387.

Goodrich, T. J. (Ed.). (1991). *Women and power: Perspectives for family therapy.* New York: Norton.

Goodrich, T. J., Rampage, C., Ellman, B., & Halstead, K. (1988). *Feminist family therapy: A casebook.* New York: Norton.

Hecker, L. L. & Sori, C. F. (2006). Divorce and stepfamily issues. In C. Sori (Ed.), *Engaging children in family therapy: Creative approaches to integrating theory and research in clinical practice* (pp. 177–204). New York: Routledge.

Hertlein, K. M., & Skaggs, G. (2005). Assessing the relationship between differentiation and infidelity: A structural equation model. In F. P. Piercy, K. M. Hertlein, & J. L. Wetchler (Eds.), *Handbook of the clinical treatment of infidelity* (pp. 195–214). New York: Haworth Press.

Irwin, E. C., & Malloy, E. S. (1994). Family puppet interview. In C. Schaefer & L. Carey (Eds.), *Family play therapy* (pp. 21–34). Northvale, NJ: Aronson.

Johnson, L., & Thomas, V. (1999). Influences on the inclusion of children in family therapy. *Journal of Marital and Family Therapy, 25*(1), 117–123.

Johnson, S. M. (2002). *Emotional couples therapy for trauma survivors: Strengthening attachment bonds.* New York: Guilford Press.

Johnson, S. M. (2005). Broken bonds: An emotionally focused approach to infidelity. In F. P. Piercy, K. M. Hertlein, & J. L. Wetchler (Eds.), *Handbook of the clinical treatment of infidelity* (pp. 17–29). New York: Haworth Press.

Kaslow, F. (1993). Attractions and affairs: Fabulous and fatal. *Journal of Family Psychotherapy, 4*(4), 1–34.

Kaslow, N. J., Mintzer, M. B., Meadows, L. A., & Grabill, C. M. (2000). A family perspective on assessing and treating childhood depression. In C. E. Bailey (Ed.), *Children in therapy: Using the family as a resource* (pp. 215–241). New York: Norton.

Keith, D. V., & Whitaker, C. A. (1981). Play therapy: A paradigm for work with families. *Journal of Marital and Family Therapy, 7*, 243–254.

Kelly, J. (1993). Current research on children's postdivorce adjustment. *Family and Conciliation Courts Review, 31*, 29–40.

Kelly, J. (2000). Children's adjustment in conflicted marriage and divorce. A decade review of research. *Journal of the American Academy of Child and Adolescent Psychiatry, 39*, 963–973.

Klimes-Dougan, B., & Kendziora, K. T. (2000). In C. E. Bailey (Ed.), *Children in therapy: Using the family as a resource.* New York: Norton.

Kohlberg, L. (1963). The development of children's orientations toward a moral order: I. Sequence in the development of moral thought. *Vita Humana, 6*, 11–33.

Korner, S., & Brown, G. (1990). Exclusion of children from family psychotherapy: Family therapists' beliefs and practices. *Journal of Family Psychology, 3*(4), 420–430.

Laumann, E. O., Gagnon, J. H., Michael, R. T., & Michaels, S. (1994). *The social organization of sexuality: Sexual practices in the United States.* Chicago: University of Chicago Press.

Lerner, H. (1993). *The dance of deception: A guide to authenticity and truth-telling in women's relationships.* New York: HarperCollins.

Lusterman, D.-D. (1998). *Infidelity: A survival guide.* Oakland, CA: New Harbinger Publications.

Lusterman, D.-D. (2005a). Helping children and adults cope with parental infidelity. *Journal of Clinical Psychology, 61*(11), 1439–1451.

Lusterman, D.-D. (2005b). Infidelity: Theory and treatment. In M. Harway (Ed.), *Handbook of couples therapy* (pp. 337–351). Hoboken, NJ: Wiley.

Minuchin, P., Colapinto, J., & Minuchin, S. (1998). *Working with families of the poor.* New York: Guilford Press.

Minuchin, S. (1974). *Families and family therapy.* Cambridge, MA: Harvard University Press.

Mitchell, K. J., Becker-Blease, K. A., & Finkelhor, D. (2005). Inventory of problematic Internet experiences encountered in clinical practice. *Professional Psychology: Research and Practice, 36*(5), 498–509.

Moultrup, D. (2005). Undercurrents. In F. P. Piercy, K. M. Hertlein, & J. L. Wetchler (Eds.), *Handbook of the clinical treatment of infidelity* (pp. 31–40). New York: Haworth Press.

Nelson, T., Piercy, F. P., & Sprenkle, D. H. (2005). Internet infidelity: A multi-phase Delphi study. In F. P. Piercy, K. M. Hertlein, & J. L. Wetchler (Eds.), *Handbook of the clinical treatment of infidelity* (pp. 173–194). New York: Haworth Press.

Papero, D. V. (1995). Bowen family systems and marriage. In N. S. Jacobson & A. S. Gurman (Eds.), *Clinical handbook of couple therapy* (pp. 11–30). New York: Guilford Press.

Pittman, F. (1989). *Private lies: Infidelity and the betrayal of intimacy.* New York: Norton.

Pittman, F. S., & Wagers, T. P. (1995). Crises of infidelity. In N. S. Jacobson & A. S. Gurman (Eds.), *Clinical handbook of couple therapy* (pp. 295–316). New York: Guilford Press.

Reibstein, J., & Richards, M. (1992). *Sexual arrangements: Marriage and affairs.* London: Heinemann.

Schneider, J. P. (2003). The impact of compulsive cybersex behaviours on the family. *Sexual and Relationship Therapy, 183*(3), 329–354.

Selekman, M. D. (2000). Solution-oriented brief family therapy with children. In C. E. Bailey (Ed.), *Children in therapy: Using the family as a resource* (pp. 1-19). New York: Norton.

Siegler, A. L. (1994). *What should I tell the kids? A parent's guide to real problems in the real world.* New York: Plume.

Snyder, D. K. (2005). Treatment of clients coping with infidelity: An introduction. *Journal of Clinical Psychology, 61*(11), 1367–1370.

Sori, C. E. F. (1995). The "art" of restructuring. *Journal of Family Psychotherapy 6*(2), 13–31.

Sori, C. F. (2006a). Family play therapy: An interview with Eliana Gil. In C. F. Sori (Ed.), *Engaging children in family therapy: Creative approaches to integrating theory and research in clinical practice* (pp. 69–90). New York: Routledge.

Sori, C. F. (2006b). Filial therapy: An interview with Rise VanFleet. In C. F. Sori (Ed.), *Engaging children in family therapy: Creative approaches to integrating theory and research in clinical practice* (pp. 91–116). New York: Routledge.

Sori, C. F. (2006c). On counseling children and families: Recommendations from the experts. In C. F. Sori (Ed.), *Engaging children in family therapy: Creative approaches to integrating theory and research in clinical practice* (pp. 3–20). New York: Routledge.

Sori, C. F. (in press). Spiritual play genogram. In L. Hecker and C. F. Sori (Eds.), *The therapist's notebook II: More homework, handouts, and activities for use in psychotherapy.* New York: Haworth Press.

Sori, C. F., & Biank, N. (2003a). Deflating fear. In C. F. Sori, L. L. Hecker, & Associates, *The therapist's notebook for children and adolescents: Homework, handouts, and activities for use in psychotherapy* (pp. 9–17). New York: Haworth Press.

Sori, C. F., & Biank, N. (2003b). Soaring above stress: Using relaxation and visualization with anxious children. In C. F. Sori, L. L. Hecker, & Associates, *The therapist's notebook for children and adolescents: Homework, handouts, and activities for use in psychotherapy* (pp. 25–39). New York: Haworth Press.

Sori, C. F., Dermer, S., & Wesolowski, G. (2006). Involving children in family counseling and involving parents in children's counseling: Practical and theoretical guidelines. In C. Sori (Ed.), *Engaging children in family therapy: Creative approaches to integrating theory and research in clinical practice* (pp. 139–158). New York: Routledge.

Sori, C. F., & Sprenkle, D. H. (2004). Training family therapists to work with children and families: A modified Delphi study. *Journal of Marital and Family Therapy, 30*(4), 479–495.

Stone Fish, L., Jensen, M., Reichert, T., & Wainman-Sauda, J. (2000). Anxious children and their families: Affirming courageous alternatives. In C. E. Bailey (Ed.), *Children in therapy: Using the family as a resource* (pp. 192–214). New York: Norton.

VanFleet, R. (1994). *Filial therapy: Strengthening parent-child relationships through play.* Sarasota, FL: Professional Resource Press.

Wallerstein, J., & Kelly, J. B. (1980). *Surviving the breakup: How childen and aprents cope with divorce.* New York: Basic.

Walters, M., Carter, B., Papp, P., & Silverstein, O. (1988). *The invisible web: Gender patterns in family relationships.* New York: Guilford Press.

Whisman, M. A., Dixon, A. E., & Johnson, B. (1997). Therapists' perspectives of couple problems and treatment issues in couple therapy. *Journal of Family Psychology, 11,* 361–366.

PART IV

Professional Reflections and Conclusion

CHAPTER 14

Reflections of a Master
An Interview with Frank Pittman

FRANK PITTMAN, KATIE BERMAN, AND PAUL R. PELUSO*

Dr. Frank Pittman is a psychiatrist as well as a family therapist and author with over 45 years of experience working with couples and families in crisis. Widely acknowledged as a master practitioner, his approach is both witty and incisive. Among his authored works are *Private Lies: Infidelity and the Betrayal of Intimacy* (1989) and *Man Enough: Fathers, Sons and the Search for Masculinity* (1993). If young family therapists were ever going to get past the "danger" and discomfort of speaking about infidelity, as well as effectively help their clients work through this specific problem, they had to be privy to Dr. Frank Pittman's knowledge and experience. He was kind enough to allow us to interview him via the phone and edit this chapter to be able to provide beginning, and advanced, therapists with the insight borne out of decades of working with couples in crisis. And so, it is with great hope that you find this interview to be just as insightful and helpful.

Question: *Private Lies* was published in 1991. Fifteen years later, has infidelity in couples changed, and if so, how?

---

* Note: Interview was conducted between Katie Berman and Frank Pittman on July 8, 2006, with further editing done at a later date.

Answer: Interesting question. It hasn't changed enough. People still tend to blame themselves for their partner's infidelity. The craziest attitude anybody has come up with, which is quite popular, is the idea that if someone is unfaithful, it proves that this was the wrong marriage—that the marriage was fatally flawed from the beginning and should not have taken place. Rather than seeing the infidelity as inappropriate behavior, as some character flaw on the part of the person who is messing around, the marriage is seen as wrong.

Another popular error I see a lot is the "Clintonian" notion that blowjobs don't count; that any sexual activity short of intercourse is not really a betrayal of the marriage. You wouldn't buy that, and I wouldn't buy that, but there are people who do.

Question: It is interesting that you mention those specific "errors," because I'm curious to know if you believe popular culture has anything to do with these new perceptions and definitions of infidelity. I'm thinking specifically of the "Desperate Housewives" effect, where infidelity is an extremely integral component of the show and illustrated in such a way that it is almost glorified. Are we seeing popular culture affect infidelity or at least the way couples perceive infidelity?

Answer: Yes, absolutely.

Question: If this seems to be the new trend, please clarify if both partners in the relationship share this same definition, or if it's different for the partner who gets left out and essentially, is the victim of infidelity.

Answer: It's interesting how differently people react to the things they themselves do, versus how they react to things their partners do. Forays beyond the bonds of marriage are far more threatening when your partner does them, rather than when you do them. There are levels of flirtation that people grant themselves the right to do, which they would not tolerate very well in their partner.

Question: In an interview with Baker and Jencius, you discuss the birth of *Private Lies*, and mention that the original publisher didn't want to publish the book, due to its topic being that of a *moral* issue. You didn't necessarily agree with that opinion. Please share your own thoughts on this.

Answer: He said "Infidelity is not a mental health issue. It's a moral issue." If you would look at books on marriage that have been written up until now, you could see how gracefully they sidestepped the whole issue of infidelity, so that they don't offend people.

Question: What are your perceptions on infidelity today? Is it a moral or a mental health issue?

Answer: Of course it is a moral issue, but it's increasingly seen as a mental health issue, because it sets forces into motion that drive people crazy. Unfortunately, rather than seeing it as a nasty habit or as a mean thing to do, mental health people have a tendency to try to relieve guilt, as if their responsibility is to assure people that whatever damn fool thing they do and whoever it hurts, it's not their fault, because they must be victims of something at some point—maybe from their childhood or a previous relationship. We have in mental health an aversion to slapping somebody's hand and saying, "don't do that, it will hurt people, you're hurting your children, etc." Psychotherapy is very largely about building character, but it's very hard to build character at the same time you're assuring people their behavior is not their fault. We can't do both at the same time. It's perfectly clear that the important thing is to help people understand how they made the decision to do something they know damn well they shouldn't have done. That is empowering.

Question: Is, then, the ultimate challenge, when seeing couples in therapy for infidelity, helping them build character, but also letting them know their actions were wrong and hurtful?

Answer: Yes, the ultimate challenge is to make them take responsibility for it, without getting them on the defensive. It's a matter of how hard you push. You've got to be able to be loving, understanding, compassionate, as you connect with people in your office, no matter what sort of terrible things they've done. What you're trying to do is to make them aware that they have choices and they're making choices. It's not that "my wife made me do it" or that "everyone in the neighborhood does it, and therefore, I should be able to." We've got to make people aware that they're not going to be rejected because they've misbehaved, as long as they acknowledge it and stop doing it and don't blame it on someone else. But they've got to know that they misbehaved in order to develop patterns that don't lead to this problem.

Question: I know that one point you emphasized in *Private Lies* and other writings is that once the "big secret" of infidelity gets out, the process of repair and healing begins, and the relationship can be salvaged. You've said that "when an affair is confessed and all secrets are known, there is a far higher salvage rate than in those relationships in which the truth is denied or stonewalled and remains a mystery rather than fading into an item of past history." At what point in your career did you learn that, or how did you learn that, and how did it change the way you then treated couples?

Answer: That's something I learned growing up. That's something I learned from my family history. Uncle Joe, my great uncle by marriage, got into an affair with his secretary, Kitty Collier, in 1904. He embezzled some money to cover some Christmas presents he'd given her.

He gambled and lost more money. Anyway, it led to the failure of the family cotton mill and Uncle Joe went to prison. It all came out in the open and Aunt Ora waited faithfully for him. Once the whole thing crashed down and the whole family fortune collapsed, the marriage was saved because the secrets were out. Getting the secrets out earlier might have saved the mills and the money, as well as the marriage. But when people are telling lies, when they're hiding something, they make that their priority and drive people around them nuts. They create much larger problems. This was the family mythology. This was the story that was told over and over again to make us aware that the things we do wrong bring certain consequences. But the lying brings bigger consequences, because the lying is more confusing, and perhaps more personal. An affair can be so unpremeditated it can almost be accidental, but a cover-up is always planned.

So this is something I've known all my life and brought into the field of therapy, particularly doing family therapy, trying to see things from many different directions, rather than seeing things only from the perspective of individual therapy, of the guilty person trying to relieve guilt by figuring out what his mama had done wrong when he was three. The principles, the value system that I had learned growing up, seemed to be rather different from the value system of the people making these grand messes in their lives. There are people who honestly have been raised to protect themselves; to guard themselves. I wonder, if Ken Lay had caught on earlier to the fact that when he throws a few million people out of work and tanks the economy in order to raise the value of his stock, God and the neighbors are going to get him. There are people who do not examine themselves to find out what they can do differently and what would change the pattern to change the outcome. Therapy, unfortunately, back 40 to 50 years ago when I got started in it, tried to be value neutral. From a value neutral posture, it's very, very difficult to help people use the crisis of the day or the crisis of the year, the crisis of the lifetime as instruction in character building.

Question: Explain your process in working with couples who are dealing with infidelity. More specifically, do you take the affair off center stage first, or do you deal with it initially, and then try to better understand the reason(s) or motive(s) the infidelity occurred in the first place?

Answer: The affairs, and the lies surrounding it, are the underlying problems. Rather than trying to find out what's wrong with this marriage—how did you make your husband do this—rather than trying to figure that out, you want to learn how that person got that in his or her repertoire. "What is it in your family that would lead you to believe that when your wife burns the toast, this gives you a free pass to engage in sexual relations with the neighbor? Where did you get such a ridiculous idea? How did it play out with people in previous generations of your family?" What we're trying to do is not distract from the fact that you did something wrong, but what we're trying to do is "Whoa, how could such a nice guy, a person who takes care of business so routinely, get this strange piece of behavior on your menu?"

Question: To better understand the behavior, do you see couples individually?

Answer: Yes. I prefer to see people the first time for a couple of hours. If they come from out of town, I might see them for several hours the first time, and then I make sure I see each one of them separately for at least one hour, where they can tell me whatever it is that they're uncomfortable discussing around their husband or wife. Now it's clear that I'm not promising to keep their secrets from their mate. Instead we are looking together at the things they're ashamed of—looking at the things they feel guilty about—the things they're scared of and run them through the filter in my brain about what's dangerous behavior and make a decision about whether to reveal it or not. But I expect them to reveal it, not me. I don't go around telling other people's secrets—at least not in my practice!

Question: Let's say you're seeing a couple who come to you for an issue not concerning infidelity. As you're seeing them individually, one comes out and admits to an affair. Do you encourage them to bring that out into the session?

Answer: I'd say, tell your spouse about it—you've got to make some decisions about what sort of marriage you're going to have—one filled with secrets and lies, or one in which you are known and intimacy is possible. It may be that I'll have to see them several more times before they get around to telling the truth. You see, they may think that if they can only find something to blame it on and get a divorce, then they can wreck everybody's lives without it being known that they were messing around with the babysitter or the neighbor. What happens at that point, if they don't reveal it, the chance of their marriage going to a divorce is far greater. We've got interesting statistics that come from Peggy Vaughn, whom you know of, because she's been working in the field of infidelity for as long as I have. She had to come at it the hard way, as she wrote in her first book, which is really about her husband's affair—how by telling the truth and having it all come out in the open, they salvaged that marriage for another 50 years. But her research on hundreds of thousands of cases, is that when (I believe these figures are accurate) the secret comes out and the person who's been messing around answers all questions and reveals everything and takes responsibility for the behavior, 88% of the marriages are salvaged and people live happily ever after. When the person who's been messing around clams up, either blames it on the marriage, blames it on the interloper, does not take responsibility and does not answer questions, there's only a 55% chance of salvaging the marriage. It's interesting that after the crisis of an affair, the marriages are salvaged. The ones that go for divorce are the ones that get to divorce before the secret comes out. Bringing things out in the open is the most important factor in saving the marriage. I don't have any data to prove that, just my own experience with however many thousands (maybe 10 or 12,000) of couples that if it comes out in the open, it stands a very high percentage that more often than not, the marriage can be salvaged. If the effort is made to keep it secret and not reveal anything to protect the identity of the spider woman who fell into bed with the guy, if his effort is to protect the affair partner, rather than to be concerned with the effect on the wife, husband, children, etc., then the marriage may well go to divorce. There are very few divorces without infidelity, but the infidelity does not determine that there will be a divorce. There are things that can be done to prevent divorce from happening. Most of them involve getting the truth out and the secrets out in the open.

Question: Let's say the perpetrator takes responsibility for his or her actions and states "I did it, but I don't know why I did it." Is the not knowing "why" that important of a component, or can the marriage still be salvaged?

Answer: Yes. You can reveal the secrets without knowing the answers. I think the point is—what I'm looking at are not "why questions"—"why questions" are notoriously difficult to answer, because there's always so many factors. What I'm looking at is "how" did you make the decision. You found the babysitter there in bed with you pulling your underpants off, how is that you decided not to call for help? How did you make the decision—"well, I didn't want to hurt her feelings, I did it out of sheer politeness," I'll buy that, I'll believe it. We're trying to get people to look at each step of the way. When did you first cross the boundaries? ("What" and "How" questions are far more important than "Why" questions, but they are not popular. You can't get into this field and please everybody.) Throughout the animal kingdom, among all monogamous species—wild dogs, rodents, birds—all nest-building species in which the father has some use, serves some useful purpose, the males are monogamous, but infidelities do still occur. However, they're generally initiated by the female—an aggressive female from a lower status in the flock, who takes after a male of higher status. This leads to a battle between the high-status males' long-standing mate and this new interloper. Generally, it's the female who does the pursuing. When men are flirting with women, it's generally for show. It's a way of showing off to the other guys, rather than with the hope of anything happening. Generally, the female is taking these things seriously. Part of what we end up doing when dealing with these infidelity cases, is what we would do with crows or rats—we try to find out why the male does not protect himself from the predatory female. It's his responsibility to protect himself, his marriage, his children, and his mate, from the predatory female. A guy may say "Well, she came on to me, what could I do?" "It was shiny, so I drove it home...duh." We've got an enormous number of men who let women make all their decisions for them. They're so accustomed to living their lives with women making all their decisions, that when some other woman comes along and starts making their decisions, it's perfectly natural to go along with it. We do have to retrain men who become prey. We need to teach them how to say no, "no thank you to the nice lady."

Women on the other hand are different. Males don't complain much about their marriages. They're happily married whether they like their wife or not. They reassure themselves that they're happily married, even as they allow themselves to be seduced by other women or seduce other women or get into affairs—they generally don't see much of a connection until all hell breaks loose, at which point, they try to figure out a way to blame it on their wives— "Honey, stop screaming. After all, you made me do it." Women, on the other hand, spend much of their time complaining to one another about their husbands. It's fascinating how much more frequently the female of the species will just trash her husband to any woman willing to listen.

Question: Why do you think that is?

Answer: Because I think women are socialized to be so aware of relationships and to feel such responsibility for relationships that they feel they've earned the right to complain, just as men complain about their jobs and their bosses. They feel entitled to more. They're almost apologizing for not having gotten their husbands or their children under better control. Men are not nearly as likely to do this, because men don't complain about their wives. They don't even complain very much about their children. The women who complain about their husbands all the time, they still don't betray their husbands nearly as much. And they're not likely to betray their marriage without first thinking through (inside their head) what the impact is going to be on their marriage if they go ahead and take up with the meter reader. They may make some sort of tentative conclusion that their husband doesn't deserve them—he's always reading the news, watching sports on TV (which I guess drives as many women to murder and infidelity as anything else). Maybe the guy doesn't make enough money; he doesn't have enough status or she expected him to turn out better. But for whatever reason, she evaluates whether the marriage is worth risking before she enters the affair, and she goes into the affair angry and self-justified. Men just don't do that. They don't think that there's anything at risk.

"He never considered that when he dropped his pants, he was turning the whole world over to a stranger—he promptly forgot. He never considered that possibility. It was as if he were invisible, or at least, no one was looking." (Look at Clinton, who grew up in Hot Springs, Arkansas, which is kind of the whorehouse of the Ozarks.) Women think that through—or they are much more likely. And yet, of course, when the crisis hits and all hell breaks loose, they are quite likely to reconsider what they had thought they had thought through previously. As I've often said, women have affairs because they're mad—they feel betrayed, because the guy has not been as loving, as romantic, as successful or whatever as she thought she deserved. Men have affairs because they're dumb—they haven't thought it through or considered the impact.

Here's another thing that's happened in the last 15 years. Every woman alive has read a book about how all men are sociopaths, narcissists, and how every one of them—even the guy who didn't smile at her in the elevator—has verbally abused her. Not smiling at her in the elevator is according to many people I know, verbal abuse. (It's kind of hard to figure that one out, but there's a book that says so.) Self-help books have been blight on the society—it's to American marriage what Boll weevils were to the cotton industry. You can find some self-help book that will assure you that whatever man you have in mind is defective and is not worth your loyalty. Go from there to watching *Desperate Housewives* or *Sex and the City* and you get a nice sense of what the options are or what the alternatives are. Compared to the fantasy on television, your husband has let you down. He has not lived up to your romantic female fantasy.

Question: It's obvious from our discussion that infidelity brings with it a range of different emotions from both parties. How are you able to work with the different feelings that come out in your session with couples?

Answer: First, this is familiar territory and it doesn't scare, appall, or surprise me. So I can hear whatever it is they have to say without feeling the need to leap out of my chair and go over and strangle them. I try to make the atmosphere friendly to marriage; when people complain about their marriages, I point out that marriage is not supposed to make you happy; it's supposed to make you married. The whole point of marriage is so you won't have to waste all of your time on the Internet with some fantasy lover. I keep pointing out to people that they don't know anything about happiness. That screwing up their family and running off with a stranger is not the secret of happiness. That if they can't make the marriage work with their real husband after this many years of trying, the chances are pretty slim that they're going to be able to do it with a stranger who is willing to mess up anybody's life for the sake of a small amount of pleasure. So I try to tell them they're misinformed. There are things about life, happiness, and marriage that they don't understand. It's about being a grown-up. My last book, about being grown up, points out that the happiest you can be is when you have some sense of honor and integrity about choices. It's a good-natured process, rather than my trying to shame people. As a matter of fact, I'm trying to relieve shame and get rid of the sense that you don't have it in you to do the right thing. I'm trying to relieve that shame and turn it into guilt. I want the perpetrator to be able to say, "I had the power to do the right thing, and I did the wrong thing. What adjustments do I need to make in my character, my world, my habits…what do I need to do in order to keep this from happening again?"

Question: How then, do you help the victim? What feelings do you try to help him/her overcome or change?

Answer: Well, the victim, it's very likely, is in a state of Post Traumatic Shock. You really have to take seriously what it's like to be the victim of infidelity—discovering that what you've based your life on is not quite the way you expected. And yet, if you're trying to reel an errant husband or wife back in, you're not going to do it while screaming at him or her—you can't do that. You have to suck him back in, seduce him back in.

The way in which you do it is by knowing your partner and reestablishing the intimacy and correcting the misinformation. The thing that makes marriages work is that we're with somebody who's been with us long enough to know us—better than anyone else does. So what you're trying to do with the victim is to help assure them that they didn't marry the wrong person, but that there's a defect in the human animal; that we lie to our partner when we are ashamed of ourselves, and thus, we no longer feel the same degree of intimacy with that partner. Rather than have the comfort of being with somebody who knows us, we might rather have the discomfort of being with somebody who idealizes us and doesn't really know us and all the things we are so ashamed of about ourselves. So we wreck the intimacy of our marriages by pretending to be better than what we really are.

When the truth starts coming out, that truth has to be accepted and heard compassionately. The victim of the affair has the unfair job of having to tolerate and accept realities that are not to his or her liking. (I saw a couple recently, where the wife had a couple dozen affairs about 20 years ago, I saw them and then saw them again recently, when they were having some problems making certain decisions. The wife had a sense of herself as a victim of an imperfect marriage that gave her the right to control everything. Somehow, the matter of the affairs 20 years ago came up, and she said "oh I thought you had forgotten about that, because they happened so long ago." He had to point out, "no I've never for a moment forgotten about it. Why do you think I've walked on tiptoes around you since?" It became apparent that what happened when I worked with them, is that I had him tiptoeing around her in the aftermath of the affair, but never gave him the opportunity to say "whoa, just because your mama was mean to you and your sister made faces at you does not mean I have to give up everything I want—I matter too." He finally got enfranchised again.

The person who has screwed around has kept it secret, has lived behind enemy lines for fear of discovery and has finally had to face his or her own loneliness. The one who has been screwing around shamefully has had less fun and more pain than the one who has been bopping around life as usual. You don't have to punish the person who's been having the affair—the affair is its own punishment. To get into a relationship with someone who followed you home is a terrible embarrassment and keeps you frightened most of the time. The fact that you're behind enemy lines with that person, means that you feel less intimacy with the real people in your life and more with the enemy, because that person who shares your secret knows something about you that no one would accept or tolerate. You have to see the person who has been working through this affair in secrecy, in silence, as having already been punished sufficiently. Toleration of imperfections and personal failures is one of the bases for intimacy. Even if I, as a therapist, go and kneel down by some guy's chair, hold his arm, and tell him "You've been a jerk, and you've been misinformed, and are the laughing stock of all the other guys who know better than to fall prey to predatory women," I point out to him that predatory women do not chase after the janitor—they chase after the guy who's getting paid what he's getting paid. "Don't take it personally—you're not the first married man that she's gone after, and you won't be the last." What we know about her, the spider woman, is that her mama was married five times and that marriage doesn't really count. "If you mess around with married men, what you're looking for is true love, and this guy just might be your soul mate, but you can't tell until you get him to toss aside his children and his wife, and if he lets you do that, you sure don't want him. Just think what he would do to you."

Question: So what then do you say to beginning therapists who have recently begun encountering this in their practice? How do you help them to not "mess up"?

Answer: All therapists mess up. It's okay. The world cuts you a fair amount of slack. People want you to care about them. The only way you can mess up is by declaring that certain things are too scary to talk about and keep them secret. If you indicate that that area is dangerous and scary, you're affirming their worst fears—that they've done the unforgivable and will have to live their lives in shame and darkness, never being known. They won't know that what they have done is forgivable. A therapist is not messing up by giving an honest reaction—that's not messing up. If you tell somebody "god that's disgusting what you did," but you're warm enough while you do it, it's perfectly okay to make value judgments. What's not okay is to reject people because they have misbehaved. You're no use to anybody if you're value neutral. You don't have to accept what they did, but you do have to accept them. Some things are troubling, and so at times, I've had to refer clients, like one who self-justified what he did to a degree that made me terribly uncomfortable. People who take no responsibility for their effect on other people, I feel I must hammer it into their heads, but of course I can't hammer it in at the same time that I'm rejecting them. But sometimes, I have to protect myself. There are some things, in my mind, that are beyond contempt. I can think of only two cases like that in my career. One involved multiple incests, and the other involved a man who had been married and divorced three times, leaving three children each time, and prided himself on escaping child support for any of them. But I hope the next time around, I can be able to find some way of accepting these people, but if I'm still appalled by their behavior, I must say so; I must let them know at the same time that I embrace them.

CHAPTER 15

Reflections on the Affair

An Experiential Perspective

AUGUSTUS NAPIER

She's beautiful I said almost imperceptibly to myself, and it was the last such detached observation I had the luxury to make. *And furious* sneaked in, and then they were off. I was in the final month of a post-doctoral fellowship in the Department of Psychiatry at the University of Wisconsin in Madison, and this couple was one of my last intakes as a trainee. Angela Ruth was tall and skinny, with a sharp face and huge, blazing dark eyes, with black eyebrows straight above them and a cascade of very black hair pouring around her face. I later learned that she was from South Boston, that her mother was Jewish and her father Irish—that was clearly where the war in her life started. Her parents had divorced when Angela was 15; her father had left with a neighbor, wounding all six kids, and of course their mother, in different ways. Though she never admitted it, Angela was as injured by his abandonment as if she had been his wife.

Angela, who was a secretary in a university department, paid the couple's bills, and she had discovered a charge on one of their credit cards for a motel room, one of those half-conscious slips that seemed intended to bring an affair to light. Ralph was a nice Southern boy, come to the Midwest on a graduate fellowship to study something like theoretical physics. From a cultured, financially ruined but plenty smart Southern family, he was no match for Angela's tough, pushy South Boston style. He was, she discovered when she confronted him, having an affair with another graduate student.

To say that Angela was furious is like saying that a tsunami is wet. Her anger was raw and anguished and poured out over the landscape of their lives: all the profanity of her street-raising roaring up in the service of punishing Ralph, who cowered on the far side of my small office. I tried to help Angela talk about the pain of betrayal, but she wasn't having it. She was all anger.

The second interview was a little calmer, but Ralph remained withdrawn. When Angela saw his encapsulated passivity, it made her more furious. By the third interview, I had responded to a sense of foreboding by bringing in a woman colleague who I hoped might reach Angela. My office was narrow, with just enough room for four people. My colleague and I were seated in the middle of the couple, Angela on the left near the door—which I later realized was strategic—Ralph on the far side against the one window.

"He's leaving. He's moving out!" Angela began the interview. "The fucker is leaving me!" More invective, a rising crescendo of anguish and anger, and then I saw rising as if it were an apparition a long silvery blade appearing out of Angela's large black purse and then it was raised in the air and seemed to hang suspended before me huge as a sword; and in a flash I had tackled her and felt her crumble surprisingly easily under my arms; then I was sitting beside her holding her arms down while she sobbed. My colleague had the knife. After a while I began to talk to Angela softly and said that this process had to stop and that she had to go in the hospital. She was acquiescent and quiet—with apparent relief.

As a psychologist I did not have admitting privileges at University Hospitals, but a resident friend admitted Angela into one of the two inpatient psychiatry floors next door. While a small team began to work with her, I began to receive phone calls from Ralph. He was understandably shaken and frightened; and he was depressed. After about the third call he revealed that he was feeling suicidal and had bought a gun to use on himself. I met with him individually and convinced him to let me arrange for him to be admitted to the other floor of the psychiatric hospital.

Over the next several weeks I lost most of my influence in the couple's treatment. At first Ralph and Angela tried to get access to each other, and both wards were locked. I achieved departmental notoriety as the psychologist who had involved both inpatient wards in a marital war. Eventually I participated in a meeting between Angela and Ralph in which Ralph announced that he was accelerating his leaving town for a job offer in Texas; and Angela agreed to continue meeting with me when she left the hospital.

My individual work with Angela was surprisingly easy and cordial. I did the things individual therapists do: helped her with insight into her childhood, helped her look at the shaky underpinnings of the marriage from the start—"I knew it was a mistake when I walked down the aisle, particularly when his mother, who was much more steel than magnolia, was so cold to me and he didn't stand up to her. Not a peep of opposition to the bitch." I was supportive and understanding. I allowed her to call me at home when she was especially depressed—a common failing for a young therapist.

Angela got a better job at the University with better pay; I leased a small office in the downtown area and began to try to face the terror of being in private practice. Angela followed me; she was my first patient, and for a while, my only patient. Her therapy progressed, and I imagined that Angela was actually fond of me. My empathy for her deepened: I learned about her mother's dedication to a lifetime of bitterness, and I discovered that her father had, in addition to leaving the family, beaten both Angela and her mother.

But why wasn't Angela paying her bill? And why couldn't I seem to talk to her about it? The anger was still there, masked, but brooding like a storm with potential energy. While I was trying valiantly not to depend on my mentor in the Psychiatry Department, I decided to get a consultation from Whitaker.

The consultation was very brief. After I talked a little about my work with Angela and the problem of her bill, Whitaker, who had obviously seen Angela's barely concealed anger, said rather nastily: "I don't think she has any intention of paying your bill." Whitaker had offered Angela a mug of coffee at the beginning of the interview, and with a single motion she threw the half-full cup at Whitaker's head, barely missing him. The heavy cup smashed against the wall, leaving a wash of coffee across the pastel green plaster.

"So that's why I couldn't raise the subject of the bill," I said later. "Thank you, I guess."

That night, I got a frantic call from the young man who lived in the rental unit above my office, and who also had a beige Volkswagen bug. "My tires have been slashed," he said, "and all the wires in my engine cut. I wonder if it could be one of your patients."

And of course it was highly likely that it was. I don't recall what arrangement I made with the young man, but I did not hear from Angela for 5 years. Over that time I learned to be more than a spectator in the lives of the couples and families I treated; I developed a busy private practice and began to teach family therapy. Then I received a call from a psychologist colleague in Madison. "I have just evaluated a woman for a job situation, and she said you were the only therapist she had ever had who cared about her. I wonder if I could refer her to you?"

"OK," I said warily.

I saw Angela for perhaps 10 sessions. They were polite, tentative, but fond encounters. I was still somewhat afraid of her, and never brought up the tire-slashing; nor did she mention the encounter with Whitaker. She had lost a number of jobs and been in and out of therapy maybe five times. She seemed more confident, however, and less angry. I suppose she came back to show me that she had survived and was doing better.

For the young therapist, dealing with an affair is a great teacher. Almost immediately, we learn that the metaphor of the tsunami is appropriate. In the beginning we see only the hugely disruptive outpouring of angry energy; only later will we get to know the geologic "faults" in the subterranean landscape of the marriage, where the "plates" of the two lives have abraded, often quietly, for many years. Conflicting family loyalties, differing communication styles, the accumulation of un-dealt-with daily angers, and the basic questions of love and respect have lain quiescently, accumulating energy. And then there is a shift in the "underground"; it may occur simply because the cumulative storage of tension in the marriage reaches a breaking point; and the affair occurs and is eventually revealed.

The therapist dealing with the affair has three fundamental jobs: (1) to assess, quickly, the risks to the individuals in the family, including the children if there are any; (2) to intervene forcefully in trying to keep the individuals as safe from further harm as possible; (3) to help the couple address the underlying issues that led to the affair, the latter being the major work of therapy; and (4) to help them make changes that will, one hopes, lead to their having a better marriage.

SOME BASIC ASSUMPTIONS ABOUT AFFAIRS

There are of course many kinds of affairs (a subject dealt with in Chapter 8), from the compulsive philandering of the sexual addict (or the character disorder) to the casual link-up at a convention or meeting, to the affair in which the betrayal of the partner announces a deeply made prior decision to leave the marriage; the other partner in the affair is not loved, only used as "leverage" to leave the relationship. There is of course the affair in which one partner falls in love with someone else, having never really been in love with his or her spouse. The abandoned partner may love the person who is rejecting him or her and be genuinely and perhaps forever broken-hearted.

As a young therapist I tended to project my own values, and my own marriage, onto my clients. I assumed that all couples fell deeply in love, as Margaret and I had, and that with an adjustment here and there, all would be well. Then I realized, of course, that people marry for all sorts of reasons, some of them self-sacrificial, some just plain dumb. Why, after all, should we expect partners who marry in their mid-twenties to have particularly good judgment, or to have had the luck to meet someone who is a true "soul mate," and where the attachment is deep enough to last a lifetime?

I do believe that there is usually an approximate *parity* between partners with regard to their choice of each other: that if the decision to marry was made out of anxiety about approaching 30 or because it seemed like a good idea and their friends were all getting married or because they were both good-looking and their families liked each other—that if there is a problem in their attachment to each other, it is a *shared* problem. One may be attachment-averse and the other hungrily anxious about sustaining an attachment, but they both have difficulty with attachment. But of course "expert" assumptions about any marriage should be made cautiously, especially in the early stages of marital therapy. There is much we don't know, and the interior realities in someone else's marriage may finally be unknowable. We should be attentive students to what this couple is going to teach us.

PRECURSORS TO THE AFFAIR: THEMES

Though far from exhaustive, here are some themes I found in my work with couples struggling with an affair. I am describing primarily the couple in which there is at least some commitment and some hope between them, the optimistic scenario (see Napier, 1991):

1. The marital impasse. Most affairs seem to be the product of the partners' failure to grow and change. Before the affair occurred, there was a pervasive feeling of deadness and stasis between the couple. They went over the same ground again and again; they felt flat and tired and bored. There was a sense of disconnection and drift. Conversations seemed to go nowhere; resolutions were not acted upon. One or both may have felt progressively more hopeless, as though they might literally die from the lack of emotional oxygen in the marriage.

The dilemmas in the impasse may be very complex and involve a series of binds or "traps" (Charney, 1992) in which any course of action leads to a dead end: "If I approach him, he backs away. If I don't, he complains that I don't care about him." The sense of defeat at the hands of the other is interlocking; and of course each tends to see the other as the source of his or her despair. Neither sees the collusive nature of their patterns, or the ways in which they both have failures of courage when they might instead push through to greater honesty or intimacy. And they do not know about the powerful weight of transference pushing down on them both, the sense that *of course* they can't speak up or ask for something or risk sharing a vulnerability—because they couldn't do so in their families of origin. And of course true intimacy, perhaps a lifelong stranger to them both, is frightening.

2. The emotional underground. Beneath the surface of the partners' lives, there are two people who want to live more fully, but who are trapped in a growing sense of despair and futility. Though only one partner may be intently conscious of discontent, I believe that this desperate realization grips them both: "What are we going to do? How can we ever get out of this agony?" She may approach him very tentatively about wanting a little more experimentation in their sexual lives, and then give up all too easily. He may want to stand up to her authoritative "I'm right" stance and be afraid to.

Before an affair begins, both partners have usually betrayed each other in other ways. As they begin to drift apart, she finds closeness with their daughter; he allows himself to be re-captured by his widowed mother's needs. He works late; she works out at the gym. Both partners move away from each other, hoping to be noticed and called back; they want, often poignantly, to be told that they are missed and desired. In the tumult and blaming of the affair, the bi-laterality of their "pre-affair" affairs is not noticed, and of course in the early stages of therapy the therapist doesn't point out the usually covert infidelity of the rejected partner.

It is my sense that most partners who initiate an affair have felt rejected (or bullied, or in some way mistreated) by the very partner they are rejecting, and that their internal justification for their actions represents a kind of destructive entitlement. But of course to point this out in the beginning of therapy, when the trauma of a more literal rejection is being absorbed by the "victim," would be not only counterproductive, but injurious.

3. The designated "patient." Out of the couple's desperation, they develop an unconscious "plan" to break the impasse. There may be almost-explicit conversations that signal the collusive decision to escalate their schism, but usually the "agreements" are half-conscious and largely inferential. In one couple, the tough-guy husband, who was a marathon runner and weight-lifter, risked asking his wife, as they turned to go to sleep one night, to hold him. Frightened by his sudden vulnerability, she replied, "You'll have to find somebody else to do that." Deeply hurt by the remark, he did find someone else to hold him. In another marriage, the wife said, only half-joking: "If you ever decide to have an affair, don't tell me about it," a remark that the husband took as implicit permission. In other instances the evidence that the betraying partner uses to justify the decision to have an affair is inferential: "If I'm gone this much and she doesn't complain, she must not love me."

4. The affair as an act of rebellion. Often, the person who enters an affair feels dominated and one-down in the marriage. He or she may have made tentative efforts to confront the partner, but these proved unsuccessful and were given up. The betraying spouse feels vulnerable, unappreciated, and unheard; and the affair is an angry attempt not only to hurt the other, but to gain more power in the relationship. Though an affair is carried out in stealth and deception, the eventual and anticipated revelation of the affair is effectively a fist in the face of the partner.

Though a highly respected and fiercely workaholic professional, Samuel was submissive and compliant at home. His wife, Alicia, appeared to be a forceful executive homemaker, running the household and assuming almost complete responsibility for their five children, one of whom was disabled; but she often felt overwhelmed and stressed. Samuel saw Alicia as bossy and critical, and over time he began to assume that her main interest in life was the control of their environment and that she did not love him. Alicia felt abandoned by Samuel, and though deeply hurt, she presented mostly anger toward him. By the time his long-standing affair with his secretary was revealed, they were both in their mid-60s; and in the early stages of the confrontations between the couple, Samuel assumed that the marriage was over.

Alicia was devastated by the revelation of the affair. She admitted how abandoned she had felt over the years, and she communicated in a variety of ways that she wanted to fight to save the marriage. She acknowledged that she had been dominating and controlling, and began to share with Samuel some of her childhood history of psychological abandonment by her parents. Surprised, and relieved to discover that Alicia loved him, Samuel agreed to be in therapy. The couple brought their adult children into the therapy process and made rapid progress in their marriage. Samuel also worked on his life-long struggle with his dominant mother, and he even involved his elderly parents in the therapy for several interviews.

In this kind of stereotypical dominant-submissive pattern, the one-down partner not only takes a stand to acquire more power, but is in some measure "fishing" to learn about the other partner's vulnerability. It is as if each could only see part of the other, and the affair allows both partners to reveal aspects of themselves that had been hidden. Through the affair both search for being more complete people, and try to see each other more clearly.

5. The affair as a search for personhood. A pervasive aspect of many marriages is a lack of courage in dealing with emotional issues. While the partners may be courageous in other aspects of their lives, they lose their nerve in close-in encounters, usually because of long-standing fears and anxieties that both have brought from childhood. An affair "calls the question" in the marriage; it forces both partners out into the open. If one partner has been too "selfless" in trying to please the other, this strategy of compliance and accommodation eventually produces first disrespect in the other partner, then anger. "Stand up and be somebody!" the rejecting partner cries out.

The challenge of whether the couple can break out of their compromised "identities" in the marriage is of course subject to the same fears and insecurities, and the same failures of nerve, that led them to their impasse. The decision by one partner to have an affair is an enormous gamble, and it may be a failure. One or both may lose their nerve in confronting their problems; they may break up unnecessarily, or they may paper over their anguish and decide to behave themselves. Periodic affairs may become the norm in the relationship. But it is also possible that both can take courage from having their difficulties squarely in their faces, and they may achieve greater levels of honesty and intimacy.

Even though the psychological injuries from the affair may be serious and lasting, their marriage may also be invigorated. One or both may make deeply held resolutions that they keep: "Never again will I be so naïve and trusting." "Never again will I be so patient and long-suffering." "Never again will I fail to speak up about what I want." "Never again will I settle for a non-sexual marriage."

The decision to try to live more fully, and to be more authentic selves, is of course dependent, as are all such issues in marriage, on both partners making changes. They may discover that only one partner is willing to grow; the other backs down or says, "I can't do this." There is then a truly agonizing choice between them: whether one partner's pursuit of growth necessitates their abandoning the marriage and the other partner.

The Affair as Psychotherapy

As Whitaker has said (Napier and Whitaker, 1978), it is possible to see the lover as a kind of psychotherapist: someone who, famously, listens and understands. The stereotype of the spouse who "doesn't understand me" is of course a convenient excuse for the affair, but it can also be true. The betraying partner may operate out of "destructive entitlement" (Boszormenyi-Nagy, 1987) and may justify the affair as a rightful response to rejection, abandonment, or abuse. As therapists we should not be too sympathetic with the rejecting partner, at least initially, as victim of his or her spouse; but it is wise to remember that underneath the decision to have an affair lies a considerable amount of pain and desperation.

What would have happened to the rejecting partner, who is involved in an affair, if he or she had not taken this path? Often, the underlying stakes for this "erring" individual are life and death; and far from being a lark or a simple self-indulgence, the affair is truly a desperate bid for help. That is, until the initiation of the affair, this individual may have felt truly hopeless about life, and about the chances for a better life in this marriage.

If we keep this possibility in mind, we will be less surprised when, if the affair is given up or collapses, the "rejecting" partner suddenly becomes suicidal, as Ralph did. If psychotherapy interferes with the progression of an affair, we should anticipate that we will need to be available to fill the gap left by the "amateur therapist." Our interposition in the life of this transgressing individual may offer possibilities for growth—that the affair did not—but we must be prepared to be available when the opening is created for our intervention. When the rejecting partner becomes more vulnerable, his or her covert resentments may then be more openly dealt with.

Professional psychotherapy has difficulty competing with the sexually charged atmosphere of the affair. Like the active drinker, the active participant in an affair is probably not available for psychotherapy. We must, therefore, attempt to negotiate some interruption of an affair. This suspension of the affair may be easier to achieve if the couple has children, but it is always a chancy and difficult negotiation. The affair-involved partner usually wonders: "If I give up my 'leverage' in our marriage, will you revert to your old self? Is it safe to assume that the changes you are promising will materialize?" Often the affair is not suspended until the betraying partner has some optimism about more lasting change in the other partner.

THE PHENOMENOLOGY OF THE AFFAIR

When an affair is revealed, the partners suddenly find themselves in alternative universes; our understanding of these extraordinarily different experiences is critical, and we must manage to have empathy for both partners. And we must provide them with some safety in encountering each other.

The Rejected Spouse

One partner has lived in an illusion of normalcy, trusting, at least consciously, in the surface that he or she can see. The couple has shared daily routines, had intimate conversations, managed child care together, even had sex. While the rejected partner can usually look back and see "signs" that he or she ignored or minimized, the trauma of a shattered sense of what is real and true is tremendous. It is as if the fabric of perceived reality is ripped asunder; what had seemed so is not. The experience is comparable to a death—in this instance, of trust. And for people who bring from childhood a formative experience of rejection and betrayal (and who doesn't?), the discovery of a partner's affair confirms deeply held fears and unconscious predictions: "What was I thinking? How could I ever have trusted you?" And perhaps covertly: "I knew it would happen, sometime." Just as a deeply bonded marriage can ameliorate childhood traumas in the individuals, betrayal in marriage exacerbates the earlier injuries: "I thought I could trust you; now I know I can't trust anybody, ever again."

When they learn the truth, betrayed partners can suddenly develop full-blown obsessional neuroses. In fact, the severity of the reaction may seem at the edge of psychosis. The need to know the identity of the co-conspirator is of course immediate, and important; but in an effort to re-construct a sense of reality, a great many details are brought up, often repeatedly: When did it begin? What did you do? Where did you go? The level of questioning can feel abusive to the rejecting partner, and this defensive response in the adulterer can add to the sense of outrage and injury in the rejected spouse. Against the replies, which may not be truthful, but which often reveal more and more as the rejected partner pursues each detail, the rejected partner measures himself or herself, feeling alternately inferior, wanting, ashamed, stupid, gullible; and, of course, angry.

Victims of affairs usually realize that they have participated, at least unconsciously, in the setup and enactment of the spouse's affair. They didn't *make* the decision to have the affair, but they may experience considerable shame as they look at the signs they ignored. It is later work in therapy for the rejected spouse to examine and to learn from the unconscious prediction of betrayal in the marriage; but it is important that this individual grapple with the childhood underpinnings of that predicted rejection.

Re-working the sense of reality, and of self-perception, is a profoundly important and difficult process for the rejected partner. In addition to increasing the self-blame and self-doubt in the "victim" of the affair, the adulterous partner's rejection may also cause the spouse to make a more accurate appraisal of his or her faults and weaknesses. While the rejected partner may be overtly blaming, he or she is also actively engaged with the question, "What did I do wrong?" This self-search, mixed as it is with rage and hurt, is an effort to attempt to make changes that may salvage the relationship. A partner who has been sexually "cool," may, for example, alternate being enraged with being sexually provocative; and the couple in the midst of tremendous emotional upheaval may have passionate sexual encounters, which may then degenerate into further rage and blaming. While the rejected partner's anger, if it is openly expressed, may be self-affirming, it may also be a way of concealing hurt, which may feel much too vulnerable an emotion to reveal to a partner whom he or she does not trust.

Particularly when the rejected partner is a woman, she may not feel safe enough to admit the depth of her anger. She may make an accurate appraisal that her husband has more power to leave her, has more control of their finances, and greater opportunity for re-marriage—and he already has a potential substitute. Her vulnerability is a serious impediment to her being confrontive and self-affirming; and in an effort to make her husband feel guilty—the only weapon she may feel she possesses—she may be tempted to attack herself openly. Of course the man whose wife is sleeping with someone else is profoundly threatened by this event; but in most relationships men have an inherent advantage of greater power if the marriage ends.

The Rejecting Spouse

While the rejected spouse has lived in a naïve, oversimplified version of marital reality, the individual involved in an affair has lived in a dichotomous, bifurcated world. As Pittman (1989) points out, some adulterous spouses may not be in much conflict about their two worlds, particularly those involved in the accidental encounter, or in habitual philandering, the latter being a version of sexual addiction. Pittman also describes the "marital arrangement" in which the partners at least on some level "agree" to participate in affairs to take the pressure off other areas of the marriage. But most adulterers feel torn and guilty as they move between the conventional world of the loyal marriage and the forbidden, stolen, guilty intensity of the affair. This split in the world of the adulterous partner is often the result of long-standing conflict within the self of this individual; it diagnoses intra-psychic difficulties with roots in childhood.

In discussing the divided self of the affairee, Kaslow (1993) calls upon the writings of object relations theorists Fairbairn and Klein, who present different aspects of "splitting" mental operations in the individual. Fairbairn (1955) posits that during the period of infantile dependence, the infant incorporates both the "good" (loving) and "bad" (rejecting) aspects of the "mothering one." These polarities must be dealt with by the child, and they result in a "splitting" within the child's self-system of "good" and "bad" perceptions. These dichotomies are not integrated in the child in a balanced perception of both the "good" and "bad" traits of the parent, but can remain separated in different systems of affect and attribution.

Klein (1948) treats a different kind of "splitting," one in which the infant's sensorimotor experiences are compartmentalized into those that make the infant feel good, versus those that make him or her feel bad. As they are too painful to deal with, the "bad" parts of the infant's self are split off internally and negated. These disavowed aspects of the self may then be projected onto another person, and attacked in that person, a process Klein labeled "projective identification."

From the clinician's perspective, we can assume that the affairee has almost invariably symbolized his or her spouse with negative attributions, and organized on the lover more positive connotations. The spouse is seen as dominating, or weak, or cold, or unloving, or inattentive, or unspontaneous, or some combination thereof. These perceptions are grounded both in the character traits of the spouse and in the affairee's symbolizing of these traits. My tendency is to put responsibility for these distortions mostly on the rejecting partner's transference of self and parental issues onto the spouse; but of course, addressing these issues in the rejected spouse is a therapeutic agenda.

Part of the therapist's job will be to help the rejecting partner examine these perceptions; yes, the spouse may be aloof and emotionally cool, but then the perception by the rejecting partner magnifies and overinterprets these issues through the lens of his or her childhood. The spouse can make some changes, and the adulterous partner can modify his or her perception of some of the symbolism brought from childhood: "Yes, your wife is bossy or critical; but she is not your mother, and you have more power in confronting her than you have realized."

Certainly the lover is in part a fantasy person. The secrecy, the compressed time frame of the encounters, the whispered nature of the conversations, the disconnection of the meetings from everyday routines, all conspire to give the lover a quality of dreamlike unreality: The lover is the idealized person who is adventurous, or sexually free, or loving and attentive, or friendly and companionate. The two meet, make passionate love, then separate to deal elsewhere with the mean-spirited and boring world. They don't stay to do the dishes and or take out the garbage.

And in most instances, the lover taps into deeply felt deficits from the rejecting partner's childhood. For a woman, the lover may be tender and attentive in the way that her father wasn't, and in the way that her husband isn't either. Men may find especially attractive the lover's ability to be both loving and freely, spontaneously sexual. We must remember, however, that while a married man or woman who seeks a lover may do so out of unsatisfied emotional needs, the respondent may be a more calculating individual. The "other side" of the affair may be a single woman who badly wants a husband, even if she has to steal him; and a man invading a marriage relationship may want to conquer another man's wife or simply have a dalliance.

While Dostoyevsky's portrait of the "compulsion to confess" lays guilt at the heart of this impulse to come clean, we can surmise that the adulterous lover may have a more growthful impulse: to connect the two separated and antagonistic parts of the self. How does one make oneself face up to having lived a duplicitous life? To having two split-off selves? Confess, or get discovered, in an affair. Here are the two realities, out in the open, compelling us to face who we are. And by the way, the person victimized by this process is really furious.

When the adulterous spouse is discovered or confesses, he or she often experiences some relief. While the affair has been mythologized in our culture as a romantic experience, in reality most affairs are rushed and guilty, and they have a quality of grimy, cheap desperation. Sneaking around and stealing pleasure isn't convenient or easy; and then there is the guilt. When the betrayed spouse finally knows the truth, his or her anger may be easier to deal with than the betraying partner's self-blame. The betraying spouse is also flooded with shame and embarrassment; and as the damage caused in the spouse becomes more visible, the adulterer must register the impact of his or her actions.

While the vulnerability of the rejected spouse is often palpable and poignant, the therapist must also deal with the vulnerability of the adulterous spouse, who is often a seriously unhappy, or seriously troubled, individual. The affair may have temporarily ameliorated this person's sense of self-doubt, or isolation, or underlying depression; but the progression of events may put this person at risk. If the affair ends, the marriage is usually unrepaired at that point; and the spouse is hardly ready to console the erring spouse around the sense of loss which he or she experiences. If the marriage ends and the affair becomes more "regularized," the idealization of the lover may then begin to crumble: "I have wrecked my marriage and my family, and now my lover is beginning to sound like my wife (or husband)."

TREATMENT ISSUES

The Therapist's Transference

In order to treat the affair-involved couple successfully, the therapist needs a sensible, calm, nonjudgmental stance, as free as possible of bias toward one spouse or the other. Because the couple's emotions are so raw and open, and the issue of the affair so charged with social meaning, this "neutral" stance is not easy to maintain. The therapist may have had an affair, or been the "victim" of an affair, or be from a family where a parent's affair was particularly destructive. These "transference" issues are not categorically different from other problems that therapists bring to their jobs, but the nature of the engagement with this type of presenting client couple is so emotionally demanding that special care must be taken by the therapist to maintain a professional stance. Training programs should help sensitize students to their vulnerabilities in treating affairs, and they should provide the trainee with some protective strategies.

My own difficulties with Alicia were complex, and undoubtedly related to issues that I brought to working with her. Not only was I inexperienced as a therapist, but I was afraid of Alicia—particularly her rage. My father was frightening to me as a child: His rages, particularly when he had been drinking, would have made any child wary. I also learned later in life that he had had several affairs. I was particularly unprepared to deal with these issues in a *woman*: My mother was co-dependent and soft, and this kind of rage in a woman was unfamiliar to me. So I was bewildered—here was a murderously jealous woman who clearly (in retrospect) reminded me of my jealous father.

The Use of Co-Therapy

The experiential approach advocates the use of co-therapy in treating couples and families (Napier, 1988). Because we consider the person of the therapist to be the primary vehicle of change in therapy, and because the therapist's being emotionally accessible to the couple or family puts the therapist at risk for over-involvement, co-therapy is seen as an important corollary to the approach itself. While the use of two therapists is expensive, and sometimes inconvenient to arrange, the turbulent nature of the affair-involved couple makes them the ideal candidate for co-therapy. And of course, having both male and female perspectives available to the client is especially valuable in these instances.

The availability of a co-therapy team to treat these couples does not obviate the need for careful monitoring of transference issues in the therapists; and the two therapists' different perspectives mandate discussion and negotiation between them. Time to discuss the case and to monitor the co-therapists' points of view is essential to effective work. At a minimum, the therapist should consider co-therapy as an option if his or her own transference issues become apparent. While therapists can obviously work alone if they must, the process of treating couples and families with a male-female team is not only more effective, but it allows the therapist(s) both to protect themselves emotionally, and to enjoy their work much more.

Dealing With Secrets and Lies

I once worked with a colleague who was comfortable working with couples when she knew that one partner was having an affair that he or she didn't want to disclose to the other partner. She would often become aware of the affair when she met separately with each spouse at the beginning of the therapy; she might then alternate separate and conjoint meetings with the partners. My colleague put no pressure on the adulterous spouse to confess the affair; she was dispassionate and rather cool emotionally, but very skilled and professional. She was comfortable with keeping, and working with, secrets.

My own stance, and that of my long-term professional and personal partner, Margaret Napier (Napier, 1988), has been quite different. Margaret and I found it both uncomfortable, and to some degree unethical, to keep such a secret while we worked conjointly with a couple. We feel that for the therapist to work conjointly with a couple while knowing something that has *serious import for the other spouse, and that we do not disclose to that spouse*, is highly problematic. The primary difficulty is that we are in an undisclosed coalition with the partner whose secret we "carry." That individual may be planning to leave his or her marriage, may meet with a lawyer, or may decide to continue the affair. Meanwhile, we are part of the deception; and to some degree we deceive the other partner as well.

We refused to work with couples for more than a few sessions when there was an undisclosed affair. Our communication with the adulterous spouse was clear: Disclose the affair, or find another therapist. Of course, life often defies simple prescriptions.

Margaret and I had worked with a family for about 6 months regarding their problems with their adolescent kids. Both partners had been married previously; they had a child from their present marriage, and each had a child from a prior marriage. When I fielded a telephone call from the husband, he blurted out that he was having an affair with a colleague; he wanted to come in and talk to me about it. Though we had only seen the family conjointly, I felt that to refuse to see Jim individually would probably mean that we would lose the involvement with the family, so I agreed; but I discussed the problem at some length with Margaret.

I learned that the affair had been going on for several months; and that while Jim was passionately involved with the other woman, he really did not intend to leave his wife. Over the next couple of sessions, we discussed possible courses of action (and his wife's likely reaction to learning the truth). Jim was fearful of breaking off the affair, and also afraid to tell his wife. While I was firm that we would not continue to see them unless he disclosed the affair, Jim kept procrastinating making any change.

Jim's wife, Barbara, sensed that something unusual was happening, and she called Margaret, who saw her individually and tried to be supportive without revealing what she knew. Margaret and I had several tense discussions about the case: "Gus, she knows something affecting her is going on. She is growing more and more frantic. Jim has got to tell her!" More than a month had elapsed since I learned about the affair.

I faced Jim with my own (and Margaret's) ultimatum: This was to be our last individual session. Tell Barbara, or find another therapist. He left the session looking grim.

Jim's reluctance to confess the affair, which he finally did, was at least partially grounded in an accurate anticipation of Barbara's reaction: She was as angry a "wronged" wife as we ever saw. Alternately profoundly depressed and enraged, she seemed mortally wounded. Worried about her suicide potential, we helped her get on an anti-depressant, and she was furious about that necessity. Jim dropped the affair, but the turbulence between him and Barbara continued unabated. They had tearful reconciliations, then intense love-making; then something would remind Barbara of Jim's infidelity and she would be enraged for days. The anger spilled out into their relationships with their kids; and we had several meetings with the whole family in which Jim confessed to them what had happened. One of the kids began to act out at school until we convinced him that he didn't need to distract his parents; we were there to help them.

Eventually Jim admitted to prior affairs, and it became apparent that he had a sexual addiction. He entered a 12-step program, and Barbara worked in the ancillary program for spouses. As our involvement with the couple deepened, their family of origin issues came to the forefront: Barbara had been rejected by her cool mother, who was preoccupied with Barbara's younger sister; when she was latency age and was being largely neglected by her parents, she had also been sexually abused by an older teenager.

Jim's mother had died of cancer when Jim was 6, and the father soon thereafter abandoned the five children to his wife's extended family. Jim was taken to live with his grandmother, whom he was admonished to "take care of." While his grandmother attempted to raise her angry and rebellious grandson, Jim began slipping out of the house as an early teen—first to meet friends, then to meet older girls who introduced him to sex. His unmet maternal needs were focused on these sexual contacts, establishing the basis of his later sexual addiction.

Jim did extensive work with his siblings, including some sessions with them, and their conjoint work helped them reconnect and form a supportive network; Barbara had to deal with still more jealousy as this process of reconnection in Jim's family unfolded.

Barbara's family was largely unavailable to her, but late in the therapy she did some individual work with Margaret and they had one meeting with Barbara's younger sister, where the mother's favoritism was addressed.

Eventually the couple moved to another city, and their marriage was, at our last contact, stable, and much more satisfying to both partners.

The Management of Chaos

While the pre-affair marriage is often clotted, shut down, and emotionally dead, the revelation of the affair often transforms the couple, as we have seen, into a cauldron of fury and despair. All the denied anger and pain of their muffled existence erupts into the open; and family of origin issues also break into the open, lending considerable force to the pent-up feeling between the partners.

In the midst of the couple's distress, it is important for the therapist to see the positive potential in this crisis. While their marriage has often been emotionally dead for some time, in dealing with the affair, it is at least now more alive. The pain, the open emotionality, have been "constructed" or scripted to force the partners to address their conflicts, and perhaps to make lasting change in their marriage. To some degree, the affair is a socially scripted alternative to the dead marriage—one that is treated with a dumbed-down naivety in popular media, but nevertheless a "play" that many couples enact.

Couples who do not seek therapy often seal over their injuries after the affair and reestablish their old problems; and some of our clients present with long-unresolved affairs in their histories. Other couples divorce unnecessarily, with injured pride and misunderstanding driving the outcome. When a couple does bring an affair to therapy, our job is twofold:

First, we must bring some measure of stability to the marriage so that the couple can "work" productively. Second, we must help them address deeper issues so that they do not reoccur. A common framing is, "Let's figure out what the affair is a symptom of, and address that set of problems."

In the early stage, therapy often consists of crisis intervention, and negotiation about the agenda. In the midst of the turbulence, is anyone's life at risk? In the case of Angela and Ralph (the first illustration), both lives were at risk, and the victory in the outcome is that both partners survived. Of course when the couple has children, the children's welfare is always an issue, and we should be prepared to work actively with the couple's children in the therapy process—if not in every session. How do we work supportively with the parents and children while protecting the children from the full brunt of their parents' distress? A complex combination of whole-family and couple's work is usually necessary.

And what is the *real* agenda in the therapy, as opposed to the stated one? While we probably owe every couple an effort at healing their marriage, sometimes one partner agrees to therapy in order to unload the distressed spouse on the therapist. The young therapist is particularly prone to seeing every marriage as salvageable, and he or she may try to impose this "burden" on a couple for whom it is not appropriate. One supervisee was working with a couple in which the husband had had a prior affair, and he had now reconnected with his lover. The therapist had unwisely pushed the couple into a truly fake "intimacy" in the session, re-traumatizing the already traumatized wife, who, when she learned the true agenda of the husband, was furious at the therapist for encouraging her to take unnecessary emotional risks. The therapist's being realistic about a couple's chances is important not only for the couple but also for the therapist's self-esteem and sense of optimism about the work of being a therapist. I often said to younger therapists: "Protect your clients, but also protect yourself from unnecessary disappointment."

Protecting clients during this tumultuous period is difficult work. The therapist must be "muscular" and active, intervening in an individual crisis, sometimes with medication or hospitalization, but more often with forceful management of the turbulence between the partners. Expression of anger is normal and expected; verbal abuse is not. The couple is riding a powerful wave of emotion, and it may swamp them both; our job is to teach them to surf, as it were. Sometimes we have to get on the wave as well.

The unproductive communication patterns that led the couple to this crisis are in operation, but in exacerbated form. The critical and controlling spouse may now be bitterly derisive; the withdrawing spouse may be "stonewalling" and refusing to interact (Gottman, 1999). The most decisive and helpful thing the therapist can do is to intervene in the process itself, attempting to turn these destructive stances toward connection rather than disconnection.

Many times, compromise agendas must be established first. Is the husband willing to suspend the affair so that they can work on the marriage? Is he serious about doing so? While Margaret and I have tended to work on these issues in conjoint sessions, our long-term colleagues Carl Johnson and Jeanne Montgomery (personal communication) evolved a process in which Carl met with the husband, Jeanne with the wife; they alternated these individual sessions with conjoint meetings. In the individual work, the partner involved in the affair could address the difficulty in giving up the affair, and could deal with grieving this loss outside the view of the injured spouse. And the rejected spouse could deal with some of his or her rage without risking the loss of the other spouse. With more stability between them, the couple could move toward conjoint work only.

Margaret and I felt that the danger in such an approach is that it could deepen an already pervasive sense of paranoia and mistrust in the marriage, and implicate the therapist in this system of suspicion and doubt. As difficult as it sometimes was, we chose to try to deal with these issues in conjoint sessions. Could the husband be honest about where he was in the relationship with the lover? Could the other spouse deal with this reality? Could the intense anger of the rejected spouse be verbalized safely, and could the affair-involved spouse hear it? In seeking the truth, the therapist must pay close attention to nonverbal cues; and we must carefully and supportively monitor the other spouse's reaction to every communication. The challenge is to turn anguish and suspicion toward connection and understanding; and presence of co-therapists working together makes a positive outcome much more likely.

One of the most difficult challenges of such conjoint work is that one is usually working both "individually" and "collectively" in the same session. In one moment the focus may be on helping the affairee admit the truth of his ambivalence about the marriage; in the next we may be helping the other spouse deal with this reality. Then we may turn to helping the partners talk to each other directly.

Brokering Hope

The operative question is: If there is hope for this marriage, where does it lie? In the experiential approach, we place strong emphasis on the importance of the therapist as a person (or persons, in the case of co-therapy) in determining the outcome of therapy (Napier, 1999a). We make the therapist's personal life, and personal involvement in the process of therapy, determinative. The therapist is intimately available to the clients: as relationship model; as teacher of skills; as, to some degree, "surrogate parent"; and as a source of support and morale. We minimize the application of technique in favor of creative involvement; and instead of the application of concepts, we stress the emotional level of the therapist's participation. Our late mentor, Carl Whitaker, sometimes said with regard to his approach to therapy: "I set a structure; then I say what I think." Some of us who came later have tried to construct a more accessible conceptual framework for the approach, while holding to some basic tenets.

We try to build a structure of protection around the therapist's personal approach to his or her job. We encourage co-therapy as allowing a more balanced and comfortable "outsider" status; we assume the therapist's own therapy as a given; and we recommend constant supervision and consultation for the therapist. The therapist is personally available to the clients, but "embedded" in a context of professional alliances which keep him or her, and the therapy process, safe.

So where does hope for a positive outcome for the therapy reside?

First, *we attempt to locate ultimate questions in the client*. We try not to decide whether a marriage should survive or come asunder. Such questions can only be answered by the clients, in the fullness of time and effort. We try to respond to client initiatives, including of course the exigencies of pain relief. We assume that the couple's underlying commitments to each other, historically and emotionally, deserve to prevail. Some of this stance is simply respectful, some of it self-protective and realistic. We also work at not supplying initiative for the work. The couple sets the agendas; we respond to their priorities and pressures. But we respond *actively*, supplying our own energy and involvement. It is not a passive approach; some of our interventions are forceful and confrontive; we set and maintain requirement for membership in the meetings, and we often share our own emotional reactions.

Second, *we are basically hopeful about marriage*. We tend to believe that partners choose each other with unconscious wisdom, and that investment in a relationship over time deserves a really good effort at making that relationship work. Sometimes we have been accused of being too pro-marriage, and not supportive of the decision to divorce. I believe that this accusation is mistaken; we try to respect the client's ultimate decision and to read accurately what it is. We believe that people often get themselves into difficult situations in order that they will have to change, or be pressured to change. One such situation is marriage; another is an affair. We don't recommend affairs, but once they have occurred, we often see them as having potential for positive change.

So our approach, while not naïve, is essentially optimistic: "Let's see what we can help you make of this agony. At least you aren't one of those dead couples you see at restaurants who aren't talking."

Third, *we search for empathy for the individuals, and try to teach it to the marriage*. Being a marriage and family therapist is one of the most privileged perspectives of any job. We are forced right into the middle of the human condition; and the drama of the betrayal of love and its possible redemption is a compelling, and highly "educational," story. We are continually stressed to develop more empathy for a wider range of the human character; and we are also challenged to interfere in things that are stupid or cruel. Mostly we work to get beneath surfaces. How can I understand a man who can have an affair while his wife is dealing with cancer? Can I help him come to grips with his treachery, and with himself; and can I work with his wife's excruciating reaction to his betrayal—in front of him—so that he takes in and is changed by her experience? If we can achieve empathy, we can usually teach it.

In developing a mature perspective on the protagonists in the drama of the affair, we will be required to struggle with our own prejudices, of course: not only our tendency either to identify vicariously with the affairee, or to judge him or her in the way the society does. There is so much blame and so much sense of injustice in the affair-involved relationship, that we have to work very hard to keep a balance in these tumultuous emotions. Of course the therapist needs to be aware of his or her own history regarding affairs, and to take it into account.

Fourth, *we encourage interpersonal risk-taking, and we take interpersonal risks ourselves*. The highest risk is to work in the here-and-now, which is where the highest emotional voltage is, and where the highest reward is. I have been very impressed by the work of the emotionally focused couples therapy practitioners, particularly Sue Johnson's work (Johnson, 2004). The focus is on helping couples expose vulnerability, and then to turn and acknowledge it to the partner in a way that invites connection, then to help the other party do the same. Experiential therapists also place strong emphasis on the encounter process between the partners, and we add our commitment to sharing our own experience. We may confront some behavior forcefully (abusive language, for example), and we attempt to model risk-taking by pushing ourselves to go into territory where we feel uncomfortable.

Early in my career, I was working with a couple where I developed a strong empathy for the wife, and a growing antipathy toward the rather obnoxious husband. One day I said to the husband, "You have to help me with something." I described my increasing sense of bias, and asked the husband to help me get a more balanced perspective on their marriage by helping me understand him, and identify with him more. The husband said, "I'm glad you spoke about this. I know I'm being obnoxious; I suppose I expect to be disliked—compared to my wife." Then she said, "And I play up to people. I guess I like to be the favorite, the way I was in my family." It was the turning point in the therapy. Such polarization in the therapy when there is an affair is common. We don't mean to, but we take sides; and then we become part of the couple's problems.

The highest risk for both partners is in risking being vulnerable, and in being open to engaging the other's vulnerability—in the present, in the consulting room; yet this territory is where the greatest rewards lie. Perhaps our greatest contribution to this risk is encouraging, as the emotionally focused

therapists do, the open disclosure between partners, with very careful monitoring as they are detoured into old evasions and defenses, mostly learned
from childhood, with encouragement to get back on track and to try again.
But an underpinning to the couple's risking is our own caring, and our own
expressed tenderness, toward the individuals, and toward their partnership.
The "they," which is their mutuality, is so tenuous and fractured; and our
caring for the *two* of them, together though separated, is vital. We see their
mutual agony, and we see their individual agonies, and we represent a possible bridge.

Fifth, *we focus intently on problematic communication sequences*. Like
many therapists, we see the ubiquitous criticism-defensiveness sequence.
Often we monitor such sequences very carefully, first pushing hard for the
critical partner to stop being judgmental and to be more revealing and vulnerable. We may block such critical comment entirely, in effect forcing into the
open more vulnerable material beneath the criticism. Then we monitor just as
carefully the defensive response, pushing the defensive partner to acknowledge the critical partner's vulnerability. Couples who are trying to change this
sequence often complain that we won't let them say *anything*. We reply that
they are trying to learn a foreign language; and of course it is difficult.

Of particular note is the alarm in the defensive (and usually less powerful) partner when the critical partner becomes more vulnerable. The defensive
partner often scrambles to get the other back into the critical stance, because
vulnerability in the critical partner is frightening. We are in fact trying to help
them change the very structure of power and vulnerability in the marriage,
and it is very difficult and ambitious work.

Working With Vulnerability

There are always issues of power at work in marriage: Does she have enough
courage, and enough support, to challenge her husband, who earns much
more of their money? Is a partner willing to risk losing the relationship in
order to demand more of it? These are existential issues, grounded in character, and in life-situation.

But power is not the primary arena for establishing new levels of intimacy
in a split and damaged partnership. The way the spouses deal with their vulnerabilities often determines the outcome of the therapy; and we can try to
help them make the sharing of vulnerability safer and more productive.

The vulnerability of the rejected spouse is usually palpable and intense,
though not always highly visible. Nor is he or she the only one at risk. Mostly
we begin with the rejected partner, trying to offer support. Anger is understandable and healthy, and we shouldn't cut its expression short; nor should
we fail to offer support and validation. We should also put pressure on the
rejecting partner to look at the pain they are causing, to try to take it in and
acknowledge to the rejected spouse that they take responsibility for the decision to have an affair, emphasizing that it was in fact a decision. Often there

is a debt of guilt that can be called upon in the rejecting spouse, who "owes" the spouse an accounting.

If the rejected spouse has been critical in the past, he or she is likely to be acutely blaming when the affair comes to light, which is understandable. Can we help the angry, rejected spouse shift to a more vulnerable stance, and talk about hurt, shame, self-deprecation, disappointment, feeling unloved and unlovable? This is risky territory, but necessary to get to. And can the affair-involved partner not be defensive, not make excuses? Just to look squarely at the damage caused? No rationalizations: I did this thing. Is an apology appropriate? Truthful? Or would it be at this point forced and fake?

Vulnerability shifts when the rejected partner gets some support and validation, particularly when it comes from the offending spouse. Does he or she then have the courage to ask the obvious question: Why do you think you did it? What was, is, wrong with our marriage, with me? Whoever asks it, this question opens the groundwork for examining the underlying problems in the marriage, the stage after the crisis of raw injury. We don't encourage the rejected partner to ask this question when he or she is still bleeding profusely. But it must be asked, and is valid territory even if the marriage is headed for dissolution.

Vulnerability in marriage rarely surfaces simultaneously in both partners; it alternates between them. The "woundedness" of the rejecting partner usually emerges if he or she relinquishes the affair. Power also shifts when the lover is given up; suddenly the rejecting partner may feel rejected and lost.

Jennifer and Gerald came into therapy when Jennifer discovered that Gerald, an advanced graduate student in accounting, was having an affair with a junior faculty member in his department. Married for 10 years, the couple had two children in early grade school. Jennifer, a petite, controlled (and, I later learned, controlling) blonde, was very pretty and looked frightened; she also seemed fiercely determined to try to save the marriage. Gerald was a large, rather awkward-looking but handsome man, friendly but very anxious. He didn't look like one's stereotype of the accountant; and in fact he later revealed that he was unhappy with his choice of field.

Jennifer talked about her hurt and the fright of losing Gerald: "And I'm very worried about what will happen to our kids if we divorce." She was not visibly angry.

I offered Jennifer some support, and tried to help them negotiate Gerald's taking a "vacation" from the affair. He didn't refuse to stop the affair; he just continued it. When the subject of his not seeing his lover came up, he had a wild, panicky look. He apologized for the fact that he couldn't seem to stop seeing Anise. The tension between the couple escalated, and within a short time they had separated. Gerald rented an apartment near Jennifer and their children and saw the kids regularly, mostly on weekends.

I began to reconcile myself to the likelihood that the couple, who seemed so earnest and hard-working, and so were intensely dedicated to their kids, would divorce. Shifting my stance, I proposed that since the three adults were likely to be in each other's lives for a long time, I meet with the three of them to help them discuss the future and what it held. Ever earnest and cooperative, Gerald agreed, and said he would talk to the lover, Anise, who also, after a few days' hesitation, said she would come.

On the day of the meeting, Jennifer brought the two children. When Anise walked into our waiting room, there was Jennifer and the kids; and sitting beside one of the kids catching up on the school day, was Gerald, who had arrived moments before Anise. The kids stayed in the waiting room, and I attempted to run a rational meeting. Anise seemed attractive, but plain and rather severe. She was tall and had short, cropped brown hair; and she had a sense of authority. She was two years older than Gerald.

"So, what do you think will happen as things move forward?" I asked.

"I want this marriage to survive," Jennifer said with determination and a steely undertone of anger.

"I don't know what I want," Gerald said, glancing anxiously between the two women, looking like he desperately wanted to flee.

I myself wanted to escape. I can't recall ever being so uncomfortable in a therapy hour. I wondered where I had gotten the idea of proposing such a meeting. I can't remember much of the conversation, but there were long pauses, and there was tremendous tension. If the affair had existed in the realm of fantasy, it was now a fantasy contaminated by grim reality.

Finally Anise, who looked absolutely furious, said, "I feel set up"; and she left the meeting early. I felt like the experiment was a total flop. With some embarrassment, I scheduled a meeting the following week with the couple.

The next day Gerald called me, and I returned his call between sessions. He and Anise had had a furious row on the phone and she had broken their relationship off. In addition to being angry at me, and at Gerald, and at Jennifer for bringing the kids, she had gotten worried about losing her job. Gerald sounded devastated; and I began to worry about him. That evening he called again: "I saw Anise on the street, and she wouldn't speak to me; she looked at me like she wanted me dead." His voice was flat and lifeless; I asked him if he was OK, and he said he guessed so.

I didn't hear from Gerald the next day, but that evening I got a call from my answering service saying that he was trying to reach me. He had left a phone number, which I called. His voice was emptier than ever. I tried to give him some support, and we talked about the meeting we had scheduled in a couple of days. When he said goodbye at the end of the conversation, it sounded like a final kind of leave-taking, trailing off into despair. I hesitated, talked to Margaret about my worry about him (at that time we were not working together), and she said, "You should call him back."

When I called Gerald, he burst into tears. After some long pauses, he finally admitted, "I was about to turn on the gas in my apartment."

"Tell me where you live," I said. "I'm coming over." He lived near our home, as it turned out, and when I walked up the short flight of stairs to his bare, second-floor apartment, it had the distinct smell of natural gas. He had opened the windows after I called him.

We sat and talked for about an hour. He cried some, and said that he had ruined everything, messed up his relationship with Jennifer and now lost Anise. He didn't like being an accountant. What was there to live for? But the crisis seemed to have passed. He seemed tremendously relieved that I had reached out to him.

I met with the couple the next day, and for several days after that. Jennifer mostly sat and observed as I worked with Gerald; but she did say that she still loved him and wanted their marriage to work. Their separation continued, however; there was still tremendous tension between them, and reluctance on Gerald's part to return to Jennifer. They had still not had a really angry exchange, a fact that I remarked upon a couple of times: "My wife and I fight, but you can't seem to. Even after one of you has had an affair. You're so nice."

A few days after that interview, I had a call from Jennifer, who sounded elated. They wanted to come in and would tell me what had happened when they did. When they came in my office, they were animated and looked energized and, could it be, happy? Gerald began: "We had our daily phone call about the kids or whatever, and Jennifer started in on her critique of me, and I just boiled over. I don't know where it came from, but I was screaming at her on the phone. Then she started screaming at me. We must have yelled at each other for a half hour, or more." Jennifer then confirmed his story, and said that they had spent the night together and that Gerald was going to give up his apartment and come home. She was beaming, and so was he.

It was of course not the end of the therapy, but it was the end of the crisis phase.

The experiential therapist tracks the vulnerability of the spouses, dealing with the feelings that surface, and attempting to help the partners join around shared vulnerability, meeting in the middle, as it were. Attempts to help the couple transcend their usual evasions and defenses can be pushed through, as the emotionally focused therapists do, but often the long shadow of childhood intervenes. The partners retreat from, and spoil, their experiments at intimacy. I don't know how many sessions I presided over when an hour of hard and good work was ruined by the couple as they got up to leave.

Of course most therapists attempt to address family of origin issues through raising the couple's awareness of their histories and the way these histories intersect in the marriage; and such insight is usually helpful. It may have to suffice, in fact. But in the experiential approach, not only do we work with the couple and their kids (though not in every session), but we often attempt to involve the extended family in the treatment. Often we are successful in getting the families to come; and these sessions can be pivotal.

Working With History in the Present

Because we believe the involvement of the extended family can be so useful, we begin orienting the couple to these sessions early in the process—as soon as the historical issues are identified. The fact that we work in teams makes these sessions much less anxious for us than they would be for the therapist working alone; and we push, sometimes hard, for the meetings to occur. Because of the anxiety level of dealing with their families, most clients resist for some time; and it is likely to be in the mid-phase of therapy before the parents and siblings finally show up.

We try to allow for at least three meetings. If the extended family is coming from a considerable distance, we will often work weekends. A typical sequence would be two meetings on a Saturday, and the third on Sunday morning. The meetings may last two or more hours each, and are generally open-ended. This may be our only shot at the extended family, and we work very hard. The client couple generally come to see these sessions as an unusual opportunity. By then they see the influence of these early issues in their lives; and there are likely to be current struggles as well, some of them highly charged. If the extended family lives nearby, there is of course more opportunity for meetings spread over time, which is an advantage. If the families are nearby, there are also likely to be real-time complexities to deal with.

While we try to help the client prepare for the extended family encounters by verbalizing to us what they want to try to accomplish, we know that the agenda may shift when the family arrives. We discourage a focus on in-law relationships, which can be an easy detour into unproductive territory, though sometimes these issues are so thorny that they must be addressed first. But the focus is on the original family and its dilemmas.

Early in the meetings there is of course some testing by the extended family. Are we therapists in charge, and are we willing to treat them fairly and not blame them? We try to join with the anxious parents first, and we alert our primary client for the fact that we will do so. But we have learned that once they begin to trust the therapists, the family has plenty to work on; and they usually guide the agenda and raise the affect level as they proceed. The most loaded issues may occur at the last meeting, and we are prepared for that likelihood. If there is too much raw pain at the scheduled ending, we may extend the time or try to schedule more meetings. We are especially careful to avoid leaving older parents "opened up" with nowhere to go. Often we recommend therapists in their area for continuing work.

Meeting with the extended family can be a volatile and unpredictable process. Sometimes we uncover a history of abuse, for example, that if not dealt with very carefully can re-traumatize someone in the family. Often issues that are peripheral to our client are raised and must be addressed. In one family, the husband was having an affair and agreed to an extended family meeting to explore his childhood issues. In the second of three meetings, our client's younger sister made a vague reference to "feeling different" in the family, and the inference was that she was gay. When our client's older brother responded to her remark, it was a hostile reply, indicating that the younger woman was indeed different. Ex-military and very angry looking, the brother seemed prepared to attack his sister. Anxious but gathering my courage, I addressed him: "Do you think your sister is gay?"

"Yes, I think she is."

"And how do you feel about that?" He looked flustered and confused, as if the tables were turned against him. There was a murmured hubbub in the family, and finally the sister spoke, her voice shaking:

"Well, I am gay. So there. I wish we could talk about it." Of course the family knew, but everyone except the ex-military brother seemed relieved to be able to discuss the sister's sexual orientation. While our client couple proceeded to divorce, I encountered the lesbian sister years later, by accident, in a vacation setting.

"I want to thank you for that session," she said. "It changed my relationship with my family. Everyone but my brother accepted my choice, and my partner is now close to my family." I had not realized how significant the incident had been, but I did remember my anxiety in confronting the brother.

There were several meetings with Gerald's family. Jennifer's family lived in Hawaii and were not available; and she did not seem to have pressing conflicts with them. Gerald's parents had divorced when he was 12, and Gerald seemed quite tenuously connected with his father. Gerald's mother came to a session first. An attractive woman in her late 50s, she was a school administrator with an aura of authority. Gerald was the eldest of two boys, and his mother was deeply, if somewhat playfully, involved with him. She was flirtatious in an ironic way, just the opposite of Jennifer's earnest demeanor. In her presence, Gerald seemed quiet and wary. His mother also had a distinctly manipulative quality, giving him advice a number of times; and she barely looked at Jennifer. When Gerald's mother spoke playfully about his affair, I challenged her:

"You don't seem to take very seriously the fact that these two nearly divorced."

"I take it seriously."

"But you smiled and sort of teased him about it. Do you think you would have been pleased if they had divorced?" The mother was offended by my challenge, of course, and asserted that she only had charitable feelings for the young family.

"I have never felt you supported our marriage," Jennifer said cautiously.

"Nonsense," the mother replied. "I love you, Jennifer." But it was said angrily and defensively.

Even after a second meeting, Gerald made little progress in getting his mother to speak honestly. He emerged from the meetings realizing why he had been attracted to a rather angry and manipulative, and slightly older, woman. "I see now that I was sort of hypnotized by Anise." He also became aware that he had never felt safe, or particularly loved, by his mother, and that he was very hungry for something he thought that Anise offered, but that in fact Jennifer had for him: genuine caring.

There were a couple of meetings with his father, who was distant, formal, and uninvolved, a middle-level manager in a large company. Gerald's mother had made it hard for him to see Gerald and his brother; and at some point he had given up trying. He had remarried and was much more involved with his two children from that marriage. The meetings did produce more contact between Gerald and his father; and I realized why my reaching out to him had been so important to Gerald.

A couple of years after the couple terminated, I received a card from Jennifer inviting me to a showing of her art at a local gallery. The kids were doing fine, as were she and Gerald. Gerald had left the accounting program and was teaching economics at a local high school.

Gerald had talked briefly about perhaps becoming a therapist, but decided that he wanted a more normal kind of job.

My later work with extended families was usually with Margaret, and it was the most enjoyable aspect of my career. Even if we were working separately with families, we often enlisted each other's support in meeting with the extended family.

CONCLUSION

What distinguishes the experiential approach to working with couples where one partner is having an affair? I think it is primarily the level of the therapist's involvement. We are referees, teachers, disciplinarians, quasi-parents, analysts, coaches, and to some degree, lovers as well. It is our conviction that many clients have not been really cared about with much generosity; and we try to offer at least a sliver of that kind of emotional involvement. We believe that most people marry with unconscious wisdom, and that we should help them examine and fight for their investments. We believe that most of the messes couples get themselves into, including marrying, are efforts to grow; that the drive to improve oneself is present throughout life. We experiential therapists push ourselves to be open and honest with our clients about what we think and feel. We tend to work in teams because dealing with families alone is scary and discouraging. And we believe that families hunger for honesty and for the resolution of long-standing grievances. We believe in assembling people in these critical groups and in helping them talk to each other.

The stories crowd in upon me; but one must stop somewhere.

REFERENCES

Boszormenyi-Nagy, I. (1987). *Foundations of contextual therapy*. New York: Brunner/ Mazel.

Boszormenyi-Nagy, I., & Spark, G. M. (1973). *Invisible loyalties*. New York: Harper and Row.

Charney, I. (1992). *Existential-dialectical marital therapy*. New York: Brunner/Mazel.

Fairbairn, W. R. D. (1955). Observations in defence of the object relations theory of personality. *British Journal of Medical Psychology, 28*, 144–156.

Gottman, J. M. (1999). *The seven principles for making marriage work*. New York: Crown.

Johnson, S. M. (2004). *The practice of emotionally focused couple therapy*. New York: Brunner-Routledge.

Kaslow, F. W. (1993). Attractions and affairs: Fabulous and fatal. *Journal of Family Psychotherapy, 4*(4), 1–34.

Klein, M. (1948). *The psychoanalysis of children*. London: Hogarth Press.

Napier, A. Y. (1988). *The fragile bond*. New York: HarperCollins.

Napier, A. Y. (1991). An approach to treating the affair. *The Family Psychologist*, pp. 22–23.

Napier, A. Y. (1999a). Experiential approaches to creating the intimate marriage. In J. Carlson & L. Sperry (Eds.), *The intimate couple* (pp. 298–327). Philadelphia: Brunner/Mazel.

Napier, A. Y. (1999b). Experiential therapy with Dr. Gus Napier. In J. Carlson & D. Kjos (Eds.), *Family therapy with the experts* (videotape series). Needham Heights, MA: Allyn and Bacon.

Napier, A., & Whitaker, C. (1978). *The family crucible*. New York: HarperCollins.

Nichols, W., Pace-Nichols, M. A., Becvar, D., & Napier, A. Y. (2000). *Handbook of family development and intervention*. New York: Wiley.

Pittman, F. (1989). *Private lies*. New York: Norton.

CHAPTER 16

Summarizing *Infidelity*
Lessons Learned Along the Way

PAUL R. PELUSO

This book began with a very personal reflection. In the preface, I confessed my lack of preparedness for dealing with the complexities of infidelity in couples therapy early in my career. As I went through the process of writing and editing this book, I found myself thinking of the couples that I had worked with for whom I was not very successful. In reading the chapters of this text, I discovered insights and answers that I wish that I had had years ago. I thought about myself as a young therapist, and the deficits that I had in my knowledge and abilities to work with these couples. I categorized these deficits as one of two fallacies that I believe affects most beginning therapists dealing with infidelity. One was the "*fallacy of remaining too shallow.*" In these instances, I was unable or unwilling to deepen the discussion with the couple and delve into the strong emotions that were present. As a result, the couple never had a chance to genuinely experience the deeper affective consequences of the infidelity, along with the underlying attachment needs, which may have allowed for real connection and intimacy. The second fallacy is the "*fallacy of missing the obvious.*" In these instances, I was either too quick to buy into either client's explanation of the infidelity and relationship status, or too quick to buy into my own beliefs and (limited) conceptualization of the couple's issue. As a result, I attempted to work with couples as they appeared (or presented

319

themselves), and not as they really were. Many of these couples were content to make pseudo-progress (e.g., complete "homework" assignments, etc.), but not be honest enough with themselves to acknowledge the dire state of their relationship and make the critical changes necessary for survival. When real progress was not made, and deeper dynamics of the relationship were not explored or brought to light, eventually one or both members of the couple would simply give up.

In the end, it is impossible to say whether any of these insights or approaches would have changed the outcomes for any of the clients, but I would like to think that it would have. At the very least, I would have had greater confidence in my approach, and my interventions would have been better informed. In this chapter, I hope to demonstrate each of these fallacies in action by sharing two case studies* and reflecting on how information from this text may have helped to dispel these fallacies, and shaped the interventions or understanding for the cases.

CASE #1: THE FALLACY OF REMAINING TOO SHALLOW

Kurt (aged 40) and Janet (aged 39) had been married for 17 years. They met in their freshman year of college, and married while Janet was still in college. They struggled through the "lean years" but decided that when they started having children that Janet would stay at home to raise them. They both shared a deep commitment to their faith, and were active in their church, eventually taking leadership positions in their congregation. Kurt became very successful managing several manufacturing factories for a large corporation, and rose in the ranks of his firm quickly. As a result, he was given more responsibility for managing overseas factories, as well as domestic factories. He disliked the amount of time that he spent away from home, but justified it because it afforded the family a very comfortable existence.

During this time, Janet turned a lot of her attention to her growing family. They had four children in the span of 6 years. As often happens in these cases, Kurt began to feel more and more marginalized at home, and more lonely on the road. He began to drink more frequently, which upset Janet (her father was an alcoholic, and it was contrary to her religious beliefs). This created tension between the two of them, and each began to feel that the other was deliberately hurting them. After a skiing accident left him with knee problems, Kurt began to abuse prescription painkillers as well. He used his pain to justify the need for these medications, although Janet thought that he was abusing them.

While on the road, Kurt began to have a series of "one-night stands." Although Janet had begun to suspect this for some time, she did not want to

---

* These represent amalgamations of several couple profiles in order to protect client confidentiality.

bring it up for fear of learning the truth, dealing with the dysfunction, and shattering her image of her family. Approximately 18 months ago, Kurt began to have a persistent low-grade fever that would spike in the evening and subside during the morning. He would frequently feel achy and sore all over his body, and would take pain medication to alleviate the symptoms. Inevitably, he went to his doctor and through a series of blood tests, confirmed that he was HIV-positive. It took him about three months to work up the courage to tell Janet.

Initially, Janet reacted with fear. First, she was fearful of her and her children's health. She became hypervigilant about Kurt's toothbrush, silverware, plates, and glasses, putting them in a separate cupboard, and admonishing the children never to use them. She refused to tell anyone in her family, and became terrified that someone in her church community would find out and they would be ostracized. She felt that her position in the church, and the image that everyone had of their "normal" family, was all that she had left, and to lose that would be devastating. Then, after getting tested and finding out that everyone was HIV-negative, she began to react with fear and anger.

Toward Kurt, Janet presented a cold rage. She initially refused to sleep in the same room with him (often sleeping with the children), but she feared that this would "raise questions." She started to sleep in the same bed with Kurt, but refused any and all intimacy with him. As a result, Kurt felt even more alone and isolated in the family. In addition, he was racked with guilt for his actions. He became depressed and contemplated suicide. He was desperate to get any affection from Janet, but was often brushed aside. She would often express her fear of having to raise the children alone, even though Kurt was perfectly healthy and on medication. Work no longer had any meaning for him, but he continued to "put up a front" in order to maintain their comfortable existence.

Treatment started with Kurt alone. He presented with depression, though the marital issues very quickly took a central role in his therapy. As a result, Janet was invited to join the counseling. She was hesitant, but agreed. From the beginning, the depth of their emotional despair was so vast that I felt overwhelmed. In addition, Janet's lack of willingness to talk about the marital issues (lack of connection, etc.) effectively stalled the therapy. Kurt would ask for ways to be close, but Janet would become too fearful whenever they got close. She would immediately convert the fear into anger, which she would redirect to Kurt's past misdeeds and failings (drinking, drug abuse), ultimately bringing her back to the "unpardonable" sins (for her) of adultery and HIV. In fact, at one point, she even went so far as to say "I wish that he had told me that he had gotten the HIV as a result of doing drugs (i.e., shooting up heroin), rather than through sex with some whore."

Janet and Kurt came for approximately four sessions, but never got past the hurt and anger. Therapy abruptly stopped with no follow-up. In retrospect, I wish that I had deepened the discussion with Janet and Kurt, and probed into the strong emotions that each felt. Kurt acted out his need for affection and attention from his wife, but accomplished the opposite. He became more isolated and alone. I think that if I had been able to present that theme in a way that Janet could have heard, she might have softened her stance toward Kurt. However, I would have had to have simultaneously presented Janet's deep attachment injury due to the infidelity, which was preventing her from seeing beyond her own pain. This is reflected by her statement that implied that the HIV wasn't as bad as the infidelity itself. I think that many of the chapters in section 2 would have been helpful. In particular, Macintosh et al.'s chapter on Emotion-Focused Therapy and forgiveness in infidelity would have served as a guide for dealing with the emotions and attachment injury. In addition, Snyder et al.'s integrative model would have been useful in planning out a logical sequence of treatment steps that could have helped resolve some of the impasses that were encountered. Likewise, consulting the section in Henriksen's chapter on the multicultural impact of infidelity on religious couples would have also helped to get to the more primary needs and hurts in this couple. Lastly, consulting Brown's typology of affairs would have revealed this affair as being either a "split-self affair" or a "conflict avoidance affair" where the unspoken idea that they were the ideal couple who never had problems is forced out into the open. All of these contributions would have been ways to address the fallacy of remaining too shallow.

CASE #2: THE FALLACY OF MISSING THE OBVIOUS

Analeese (aged 42) and Derek (aged 45) had been married for 21 years. They had two children, a 15-year-old daughter named Jill and a 10-year-old son named Alex. They came in for couples counseling after it was revealed that Analeese had an affair with a co-worker. An additional complicating factor was that Analeese and Derek both work at the same law firm (she as a paralegal, he as an attorney), and that Analeese's lover, Phil, also worked at the same firm.

Analeese and Derek reported that the quality of their relationship had been suffering over the last few years. Derek stated that he felt that this was due to their increased involvement with the children's lives (coaching teams, etc.), and admitted that he had become over-committed at work, but justified it by saying that his success had provided a very comfortable lifestyle for his family. Analeese angrily stated that she spent almost two decades sacrificing her ambitions (to go back to law school, etc.) in order to support Derek's career, and that in return, he was often cold and uncommunicative. She reflected that she married Derek because she saw herself as a "good girl" and that "it was the thing you were supposed to do." However, she recently had begun to wonder if she really ever loved Derek at all. On the other hand, being with Phil made her feel "alive."

In the midst of the marital chaos, there were problems with the children. Jill was acting out primarily against her mother by arguing, running away for several days at a time, experimenting with drugs, and eventually becoming pregnant. The younger son, Alex, began to flunk classes in school and dropped his sports activities, when previously he was an "A" student and enjoyed playing several sports.

The course of therapy seemed normal, at first. Analeese and Derek stated that they wanted to work on their marriage and stay together. Their work schedules were complicated so they came every 2 weeks for approximately 4 months. After the third session, Analeese began expressing some ambivalence about the relationship, and communicating a lot of anger toward Derek. Derek was confused and felt that he was making every effort at saving the marriage, but was being pushed away by Analeese at every turn. Sessions began to also get erratic as Analeese and Derek would often come to session needing to talk about a recent crisis regarding the children, and strategize how to best deal with it. Gradually the focus on the infidelity and working through it subsided, and eventually Analeese and Derek began to cancel sessions, and finally decided not to re-schedule.

Approximately 1 year later, Derek contacted me and gave me an update on the family. First he stated that he and Analeese filed for divorce soon after stopping therapy, and that she was living with Phil (who had also divorced his wife). That didn't surprise me. What stunned me was that she had not stopped seeing Phil during the time that she was in couples counseling with Derek. The thing that was most stunning was now, in retrospect, it was so obvious! I was shocked that I hadn't seen it coming, or perhaps I just didn't want to see it. Looking back, I was aware of my own frustration at the lack of progress and erratic-ness of the therapy, but I never took any action to address it. Often I have wondered what would have happened if I had voiced my feelings aloud and pursued the idea that Analeese might not have wanted the marriage to *really* continue. Maybe she felt that to commit to Derek would have meant abandoning the "alive" feeling that she got with Phil. Would she have admitted it, and would it have changed the course of treatment? It is impossible to say, but regardless, it sabotaged the treatment, and doomed the couple to failure from the beginning.

The second bit of news, which surprised me, was when Derek shared with me that his daughter (who had "lost" the baby, though it was unclear if it was a miscarriage or abortion) knew all along that Analeese was continuing the relationship with Phil. She was *very* angry with Analeese and blamed her for the divorce. Derek stated that after the divorce, when he learned that Jill knew about the relationship, he asked her why she didn't say something. Jill responded that she didn't feel comfortable saying anything because she was afraid that if she did speak the truth, it would break up the marriage. She hoped that Analeese would come to her senses, or "wake up" and end the relationship with Phil. As Analeese continued her relationship with Phil, and Jill saw that Derek was in the dark about it (during therapy when he was making a real effort to be with the family, etc.), she became increasingly angry and bitter toward her mother for continuing and her father for not seeing it. She became discouraged and "gave up" on the family.

In reflecting on the chapters of this book, and how the information in them could be applied to this case, a few key points come to mind. First, the underlying purpose of Analeese's affair, according to Brown's typology, is clearly an exit affair. Analeese was looking for a way out of the box that she perceived herself to be in, and the affair provided a way out. When confronted with the prospect of going back in the box (by staying married to Derek), she refused, even though there was the promise of change. I believe that this couple never got past the tasks of Phase 1 of the intersystems model advocated by Fife et al., due in part to the therapist's unawareness of the ongoing infidelity and overall lack of trust between Derek and Analeese. In working with the children, I think that many of the behaviors that were exhibited were easily explained in Sori's chapter, and, in hindsight, having them come for counseling of their own would have been useful. For this couple, and these types of fallacies, I think that re-reading Pittman and Napier's chapters would help younger therapists to push through the shallow explanations and probe beneath the surface to honestly address the problems in the relationship. Short of doing that, therapists run the risk of buying into the fantasy that real progress is being made when it is not, and giving one or both members of the couple false hope when there should be real alarm. To do this requires a willingness to upset the status quo, but to avoid doing this runs the risk of missing what is too readily obvious and too important to overlook.

CONCLUSION

Overall, the aim of this book was to present the best synthesis, to date, of the various treatment approaches, treatment issues, and scholarly work that has been done in the area of infidelity and couples therapy. The purpose behind it was twofold. First, it was designed to help practitioners already out in the field struggling with their clients to deal with the dizzying nature of infidelity and all of its challenges. For them, perhaps, this book can help provide some useful guidelines toward helping and encouraging couples. The second purpose was to provide trainees with the best information about the treatment of infidelity while in training in the hopes of avoiding many of the fallacies presented in this chapter that many beginning counselors face when dealing with infidelity. It is my sincere belief that this text has met those objectives, and provided a substantive and substantial contribution to the study of infidelity in the practice of couples counseling.

Index